Main Problems in
American
History

Advisory Editor
in
History

R. Jackson Wilson
Smith College

VOLUME ONE

Main Problems in American History

Edited by

Howard H. Quint
Late of the University of Massachusetts, Amherst

Milton Cantor
University of Massachusetts, Amherst

Dean Albertson
University of Massachusetts, Amherst

1987 FIFTH EDITION

The Dorsey Press
Chicago, Illinois 60604

Acquisitions editor: David Follmer
Project editor: Mary Lou Murphy
Production manager: Charles J. Hess
Designer: Paula Lang
Compositor: Arcata Graphics/Kingsport
Typeface: 10/12 Times Roman
Printer: Arcata Graphics/Kingsport

ISBN 0-256-06021-5

Library of Congress Catalog Card No. 87–71668

Printed in the United States of America

1 2 3 4 5 6 7 8 9 0 K 5 4 3 2 1 0 9 8

To the memory of our friend and colleague
Howard H. Quint

Preface

We have designed this two-volume work, the collaborative effort of thirty-seven scholars, primarily for college survey courses in American history. It does not replace textbooks customarily used to impart basic information to the student. Nor does it serve as a substitute for the reading of historical literature. Its function is to acquaint students with historical problems that are directly related to the general context of a survey course—yet highly significant in themselves.

These problems, we believe, are particularly well adapted for use in small discussion sections of large lecture courses, inasmuch as they offer both a focus and a direction to such class meetings. As instructors and students know, such sessions are frequently a chore for the former and a bore to the latter. The reasons are not hard to discover: either the law of diminishing returns is defied by a review of the week's work, or a brave but futile effort is made to discuss documentary readings—assigned with little or no relationship to an understood frame of reference. In recent years, efforts have been made for students to read articles giving conflicting interpretations of historical events in the hope that they will see the exciting clashes of issues that make history the fascinating discipline that it is. But often such articles, appearing in scholarly journals and written for specialists, have a strong historiographical emphasis. They may confuse—more than enlighten—freshmen and sophomores.

We have attempted to write each in his own way, an interpretive essay that will serve as a point of departure for a challenging class discussion. We do not claim the final word on any subject; we have sought only to open up problems for further probing. Many instructors and students will take issue with our analyses or interpretations; their independent reactions should generate the intellectual interplay that must be at the heart of any satisfactory class discussion. We have made no effort to shape the essays to any particular pattern, to prevent the various writers from stepping on each other's scholarly toes, or at times from traversing the same historical ground, although we have sought to avoid repetition of the same factual details as much as possible.

Appended to each essay is a small number of documents that have a direct relationship to points raised in the essays. In this way, documents that alone might be dull and insignificant become alive and meaningful. This method of presentation helps students understand how historians use primary source materials in arriving at conclusions and in writing history. Whenever possible, the contributors have selected documents that have not been overworked in source books; consequently, they are reasonably fresh for students and instructors alike.

In this fifth edition of *Main Problems in American History* we have totally eliminated seven of the problems appearing in the last edition, replaced ten existing ones, markedly revised others, and added new contributions on the women's movement and recent social and political history. Nearly all remaining problems have been revised in response to suggestions by individuals who previously have taught from these volumes.

February 1987

Howard H. Quint
Milton Cantor
Dean Albertson

Contents

Indians, Europeans, and the Colonizing of North America

Neal Salisbury
Smith College

American history, we like to think, began with the arrival of Europeans in a virgin land; their spread over the continent was impeded only by a shortage of labor and, perhaps, some vestiges of a feudal mentality. But this well-entrenched view overlooks the fact that Europeans invaded and eventually displaced somewhere between seven and ten million native inhabitants. The importance of these "Indians," as they were called by Christopher Columbus and those who came after him, is not due simply to the fact that they were here first. In a literal way, their presence gave shape to the patterns of European settlement, stifling it for a full century and thereafter making some lands available and keeping others closed. As partners or rivals in trade, as enemies or allies in war, as willing or unwilling listeners in religious schools and missions, as neighbors and even as spouses and kin, Indians everywhere interacted with Europeans. They brought to the colonial scene cultural traditions and historical backgrounds that antedated the colonists' arrival. And they participated, along with whites and blacks, in the large-scale social, economic, and cultural transformations that overtook North America from the sixteenth through the eighteenth centuries. Despite the

fact that, in conventional terms, they lost and the English won, Indians fully participated in making colonial American history.

That they did so prompts a number of questions. How did Indians influence the patterns of settlement by Europeans? How did they interact with these white settlers? What were their contributions to colonial trade and society? How did they react to the Europeans' desire for land and trade? How did the colonists treat Indian groups and respond to their needs? In what ways did Indians help shape colonial culture?

North America in 1492 represented the cumulative developments of more than 10,000 years of human occupation. Over the course of about 8,000 years before the birth of Christ, small bands of a few dozen individuals each moved into every ecological niche—from the arid deserts of the West to the lush forests of the East. They prospered in these areas as they gradually learned to exploit the many flora, fauna, and mineral resources available for food and other survival needs. At the same time, Indians all over the continent exchanged resources, goods, and ideas. Archaeologists have found obsidian from the Yellowstone Park area, copper from the Great Lakes, and marine shells

1

from the Atlantic coast at sites widely scattered over the continent. From these materials and other evidence, such as artistic motifs and burial mounds, we glimpse aspects of a common culture that transcended the boundaries of tribe and language. Later, between the fifth and tenth centuries, A.D., these exchange networks introduced Indian groups (where climate permitted) to crops and agricultural techniques that originated in Mexico, and to the bow and arrow, which came from Asia via the Bering Strait.

In much of the Midwest and Southeast, the networks through which goods and ideas were exchanged became formalized. Monumental temple plazas and burial mounds were the setting for elaborate rituals that accompanied these exchanges and honored the chiefs, living and dead, who oversaw them. Yet, despite the chiefs' prestige and vast material wealth they gained for themselves and their communities, the village bands that constituted their outlying subjects remained self-sufficient in food and other subsistence needs. As a result, the authority chiefs could extend over their tributaries was sharply limited. These limits were most apparent in Cahokia, a full-scale urban marketing center near modern St. Louis—where the movement of goods throughout much of mid-America from the tenth century to the thirteenth century was coordinated. Recent archaeological evidence indicates that Cahokia's decline in the thirteenth century was accompanied by warfare on its periphery, presumably rebellion by groups of satellite tribes. Europeans witnessed the legacy of this strife when they encountered newly formed confederations of Hurons, Iroquois, and other groups as well as the widespread antagonism among Indians toward centralized authority imposed by outsiders.

While Cahokia was in upheaval, a different series of developments was transforming the social landscape in the Southwest. A long drought and attendant arroyo cutting in the late thirteenth century destroyed much of the fertile cropland. As a result, the many small communi-

ties were consolidated into fewer and larger pueblos that operated large irrigation projects. The Pueblo Indians also responded to the arrival of Apaches and Navajos from the North by shifting their trade focus from tribes in Mexico to these nomadic newcomers and others on the southern Plains. These social and economic changes contributed to the intensified religious life that the Spanish would later encounter among the Pueblo Indians.

Europeans succeeded in establishing permanent settlements in North America only after a century of experience with the continent and its peoples. Though thousands of fishermen, sailors, explorers, and would-be colonists visited North America before 1600, most of the newcomers—except a few exploring parties—never traveled beyond the coasts and lower river valleys. But because of the myriad exchange routes linking Indian groups throughout the continent, the material goods of Europeans traveled far ahead of them, often reaching native communities a hundred years or more before the arrival of permanent settlers. During the sixteenth century, brass and glass beads, mirrors, iron nails, awls, knives, axes, copper pots, cloth, and countless other European products were spread over eastern North America as natives came to appreciate their utilitarian value or spiritual power. By the last quarter of the century, the casual trading of fishermen and explorers gave way to a commercial fur trade in the Northeast. Though the trade fostered new alliances among some Indian groups, it led to deadly rivalries among other groups that sought to expand their hunting territories at one another's expense in the quest for furs. When the French reentered the St. Lawrence valley forty years after their initial explorations of 1534–41, they found a war-torn region from which their former hosts had disappeared. Before any colonies had been established, then, the trade in European goods fused with and modified earlier patterns of alliance and hostility.

The Europeans' diseases also traveled ahead

of them—with even more destructive effects. The long separation of the earth's two hemispheres isolated the Americas from Eurasia and Africa; so that Indians lacked immunities to diseases such as smallpox and measles which were confined to children or small-scale epidemics in Europe by the sixteenth century. The most readily apparent result of this discrepancy was in the Southeast; explorers, missionaries, and other newcomers repeatedly spread epidemics that drastically depopulated the region and undermined existing temple-building and mound-building societies. By the time sustained Indian-European relations began in the southeastern interior late in the seventeenth century, the survivors of the catastrophe had regrouped to form the Creeks, Choctaws, Chickasaws, and other new tribes. But these successor tribes were smaller than their predecessors and, except for the Natchez on the lower Mississippi, much of the pre-Columbian ideological content was gone.

The colonies founded in the early seventeenth century, then, inherited a history of Indian-European relations that determined their locations and their subsequent histories. On Chesapeake Bay, more than three generations preceding Jamestown's founding in 1607, the Powhatan confederacy arose in response to rivalries generated by trade, Spanish and English efforts to establish bases in the region, and depopulation by disease. English efforts to penetrate Dutch and French trade networks in the future New England succeeded only after two massive epidemics, in the late 1610s and early 1630s, depopulated portions of the region by as much as 90 percent. In 1609 and 1610, New France introduced guns to the war-torn St. Lawrence valley to help the Hurons and other Indians exclude Iroquois from the region. The Iroquois turned to the newly arrived Dutch on the Hudson as a source of guns and other trade goods. They began a relationship that provided the foundation of New Netherland's economy until its demise in 1664.

What differentiates the seventeenth century from the sixteenth is the rise of England and a new approach to colonization. Spain, France, and the Netherlands sent small numbers of countrymen who related with large numbers of Indians as laborers, potential religious converts, and trading partners. While the English also expected to subordinate Indians within grander economic, political, and religious schemes, they sought above all to plant new communities of their countrymen to solve the problems generated by social and economic upheaval at home—overpopulation, underemployment, a shortage of land, social and religious disorder—and gain access to raw materials and markets for expanding industries. These upheavals sundered older feudal relationships more decisively in England than elsewhere in Europe; land became a commodity that could be bought and sold easily. Social disorder also prompted the expectation that most English males who migrated to North America would own personal property in land—either immediately or after serving as indentured servants.

These goals were noteworthy for their utopian quality: Englishmen in both the tobacco plantations of Virginia and the Puritan villages of New England envisioned working the land and becoming independent if not rich; Indians would go along or suffer the consequences. Since Indians could only be a hindrance to the spread of English farming, the colonies pursued various practices that expropriated Indian land for their settlers—warfare, purchase, religious missions, and occupation of areas left vacant by epidemics—always justifying their actions in the name of "civilization" and Christianity. But, however much they eschewed dependence on Indians, the early colonists relied heavily on them—first for food, legitimacy, and support against hostile natives—later for trade that bolstered their economies and for political-military alliances against colonial rivals.

Meanwhile, behind the settlement frontier, the League of the Iroquois, or Five Nations, was the linchpin of New Netherland's economy and a perennial threat to New France's economy. With their hunting territories largely depleted of beaver, the Iroquois used Dutch-supplied guns to raid enemies carrying pelts to the French in Canada. Above all, they sought furs that they could then sell to the Dutch for more guns and other goods, and captives for adoption to replace the heavy attrition within their ranks due to disease and constant warfare. With these goals, they undertook the successful "Beaver Wars" of the 1640s and 1650s (upon which their military reputation rests); they dispersed the formidable Hurons, Eries, and Neutrals of the eastern Great Lakes. But these were not simply wars of expansion waged to acquire wealth or power as Europeans understood such goals. The Iroquois saw their Five Nations as embodying an ideal of peace that might ultimately embrace all Native Americans of the Northeast. They also saw themselves as a people besieged and depleted, for whom war was necessary for their very survival.

After 1660, the situation of the Iroquois and their Indian neighbors shifted quickly and dramatically. The accessions of Charles II in England and Louis XIV in France marked the beginning of more concerted and centralized colonial efforts by the two empires. In North America, these efforts began with the English conquest of New Netherland and with moves by both powers to subordinate and use the Iroquois against other Indians. In 1675–76, settler pressures on Indian land led to open warfare in both New England, with King Philip's War, and in Virginia, with Bacon's Rebellion. Out of these conflicts, the Iroquois emerged as English allies with their own goals. With the backing of New York's Governor Edmund Andros, they helped defeat the coalition of New England Indians led by Metacom, or King Philip. Then they joined New York in establishing and overseeing a Covenant Chain system of alliances linking Indians and colonies from Virginia to Massachusetts. In the meantime, French Jesuit missionaries were making inroads among the

Iroquois, which created religious and political divisions that widened during the 1680s as Iroquois warriors fought Indian allies of the French along a front extending from Maine to Minnesota. The Iroquois turned their factionalism to diplomatic advantage by signing a treaty of neutrality with France in 1701 to augment their special relationship with England. Having made peace with both major powers, they continued to hunt, trade, and generally limit the impact of colonization upon everyday life in their society.

Considerations of European imperial rivalry and Indian diplomacy, then, show how seemingly localized conflicts such as Bacon's Rebellion and King Philip's War were part of a larger, regional upheaval that was tied, in turn, to developments in Europe. The same is true for events in the Southeast and Southwest during this period. The 1670 founding of Charleston, Carolina, marked a major intrusion between Virginia fur traders and the Spanish in Florida by an even more ruthless group of Englishmen. These "Goose Creek men," as the Carolina traders were known, rose to commercial supremacy by supplying guns to favored tribes in exchange for deerskins and Indian captives—selling the latter as slaves in England's West Indian colonies. Though both the Spanish and the Virginians enslaved Indians, the Carolina newcomers transformed this mode of subjugation into a flourishing overseas enterprise; one that coincided with the expansion of black slavery in the British colonies via the chartering of the Royal African Company. After the Carolinians' Shawnee and Yamasee allies captured, killed, and drove tens of thousands of Indians from the region, they recognized that a similar fate awaited them and waged the largest nativist rebellion to date in the British colonies. Though the uprising helped end the overseas sale of Indian slaves, this form of Indian-European exchange played a critical role in developing South Carolina and its economy.

In the lower Mississippi River valley, the

French established a base in 1699 where they hoped to link up with Canada through a string of Indian alliances and thereby contain the westward expansion of the English. The same enslavement fears that drove Indians in Carolina to revolt led Indians further west, such as the Choctaws, Chickasaws, and Natchez, to shift their trade relations to the less-threatening newcomers. Many Yamasees, having fled to Creek country after the uprising, also established ties with the French.

In the Southwest, Spanish efforts to root out native religious beliefs and structures of authority also provoked a major rebellion. The Pueblo Revolt of 1680 involved most of the normally autonomous and peaceful Pueblos as well as some Apaches and Navahos. Though the Spanish ultimately regained control of the region, they wisely refrained from trying to reimpose the total transformation of native life that was attempted initially. Indians attended Catholic services if they chose, but they simultaneously were permitted to continue their traditional religious practices undisturbed. From the St. Lawrence to the Rio Grande, then, the closing years of the seventeenth century were marked by conflicts arising from European expansion. Yet, while many native bands and tribes were vanquished, other groups—frequently augmented by refugees from the vanquished bands—accommodated to new realities, if not new opportunities.

Through the first half of the eighteenth century, a number of tribes that were beyond the range of colonial settlement maintained economic and political relationships with Europeans in traditional terms. They exchanged furs for European goods, after agreeing to prices that reflected both sides' notions of what was fair, with all European powers in the vicinity. In the South, such exchanges reinforced redistribution on the pre-Columbian pattern among the Creeks, Choctaws, and Chickasaws. In the North, it reinforced an expanded Iroquois-English Covenant Chain. In both regions, the stronger, more favorably located groups played British and French traders and diplomats against each other.

As the century wore on, however, the meaning of these relationships shifted with the historical setting. The pressure of a growing, land-hungry colonial population was increasingly felt. Between 1700 and 1775, the number of whites and blacks in the British colonies increased tenfold—from a quarter million to two and a half million. Nine out of ten colonists worked the land, voluntarily or involuntarily, with an increasing proportion of their production sent to urban and overseas markets. The effects of this pressure were most apparent in Pennsylvania, where Iroquois acquiescence to a series of fraudulent seizures of Delaware lands between 1737 and 1741 marked the beginning of the end of the Covenant Chain. The opening of Delaware lands to settlers allowed Pennsylvania to become the most productive and wealthiest colony in North America by the eve of the American Revolution. Closely related to the expansionist pressures of the colonies was the imperial rivalry between Britian and France. Though the two nations were formally at peace for thirty years after the Treaty of Utrecht (1713), their rivalry continued unabated in North America. After midcentury, as the fur trade's commercial potential declined in the East, the English followed the French lead in using the trade to distribute gifts and thereby secure Native American allies. Though the form of these exchanges was consistent with native tradition, the Indians' value to Europeans was no longer in their productivity but in their ability to aid one power in making territorial gains at the other's expense.

Only after the French were eliminated in 1763 did most inland groups recognize how vulnerable they had become. Groups nearer the eastern seaboard developed accommodation strategies that enabled them to survive as communities and to retain their distinctive identities and traditions—even as they were enveloped by the agrarian-commercial society of the new-comers. Throughout the colonies, they suffered from continued depopulation due to disease, the ravages of alcohol, the loss of resources and skills, pressure to sell additional land and to convert to Christianity. In Rhode Island, the Narragansetts held on to a shrinking portion of the land that they had occupied long before the arrival of Europeans. After resisting Puritan missionary efforts for more than a century, they found meaning in the enthusiastic revivalism of the Great Awakening—but on their own terms. The Delawares' first major land losses coincided with the outbreak of Awakening Religion among whites. Thereafter, both Christian missionaries and antiwhite natives, most notably the Delaware Prophet, struck responsive chords among Delawares seeking to reconstitute their shattered communities and lifestyles as war and settler rapacity hounded them from their homeland. The Catawbas in North and South Carolina reacted differently. Like the Narragansetts, but unlike the Delawares, they retained a portion of their old homeland as a reservation and continued as a distinctive community at the margin of colonial society. But, unlike the others, they steadfastly resisted missionaries and continued many of the rituals and oral traditions that they had known for centuries. Thus, Indian responses to the realities of colonization varied widely—depending on the traditions and expectations of both natives and colonists. What emerges in all cases, however, is the quest for communal integrity even in the most hostile of circumstances; an integrity that attracted many blacks and whites to life in Indian communities even as these communities were, in political and economic terms, declining.

The effects of colonization spread far west of the narrow strip of territory actually settled by Europeans. Maps of Indian North America are generally blank in the Ohio River Valley, not because it was unoccupied at the beginning of the colonial era, but because the Iroquois drove out the occupants before Europeans ar-

rived to assign them names. Though the Iroquois exercised a loose sovereignty in the eighteenth century, refugee Indians from the North, the South, and the East converged on the region to form what one French official termed "a sort of republic" in which they organized trade and diplomatic relations. In the upper Great Lakes and in the Illinois area, Iroquois raids in the seventeenth century and subsequent French trade and diplomatic activity both uprooted native communities, driving them southward and westward. The spread of tobacco plantations in Louisiana led the French to attack and disperse the Natchez, the last of the bona fide pre-Columbian chiefdoms, between 1729 and 1731. On the Great Plains, Indian groups (many displaced by the fur trade) adopted the horse—introduced by the Spanish, from the South—and the gun—introduced by the French, from the North—to develop a new way of life based on the pursuit of buffalo herds. Although using European materials and participating in trade with Europeans, they lived largely free of European coercion. In all these areas, the Indian population's mobility and cultural adaptation matched that of the more familiar British colonies during the same period.

Besides Europeans and Africans, the broad social landscape of colonial America included a diverse population of Native Americans, most of whom rejected private property, capital accumulation, and the territorial nation-state. By the end of the colonial period, Indians had confronted and were pulled into an expanding European world economy. To be sure, many groups still possessed rich stores of cultural resources that they drew upon as whites pressed for their lands in the century following the American Revolution. But, except in a few isolated mountain areas of the far West, Indians that encountered the expanding United States already had extensive experience with whites, their material goods, and their ideas. The Shawnee Prophet, who inspired the massive pan-Indian resistance movement in the War of 1812 led by his brother, Tecumseh, was influenced by the messages of Christian revivalists as well as Native American prophets in urging Indians to discard the corrupt and demeaning ways of whites. On the other hand, the Cherokees, who resisted removal by Andrew Jackson's administration in the 1830s, were led by the educated, mixed-blood sons of British traders, soldiers, and Loyalists who had joined the tribe in the eighteenth century and married prominent Cherokee women. They sought a place within the legal and governmental framework of the United States for the Cherokee Nation, a remarkable political entity that blended white and Native American values and institutions. Later in the century and further west, many Plains Indians turned their horses and guns—first obtained from Europeans—against the whites who sought to end Indian buffalo hunting and confine them to reservations. All these resistance movements failed. More successful was the formula of Handsome Lake, the Seneca Iroquois prophet of the early nineteenth century. His visions and preachings laid the basis for a revived Iroquois nationalism that enabled his followers to resist Christianity and retain their lands while incorporating some of the farming methods and domestic morality of the now-dominant whites. Regardless of their outcomes, however, all of these movements demonstrate the persistance and variety of indigenous cultural expressions during the colonial phase of America's history.[*]

SUGGESTED READINGS

Axtell, James. *The Invasion Within: The Contest of Cultures in Colonial North America.* New York: Oxford University Press, 1985.

Berkhofer, Robert F., Jr. *The White Man's Indian: Images of the American Indian from Columbus to the Present.* New York: Alfred A. Knopf, 1978.

Cronon, William. *Changes in the Land: Indians, Colonists, and the Ecology of New England.* New York: Hill and Wang, 1983.

Edmunds, R. David. *The Shawnee Prophet.* Lincoln: University of Nebraska Press, 1983.

Jennings, Francis. *The Invasion of America: Indians, Colonialism, and the Cant of Conquest.* Chapel Hill: University of North Carolina Press, 1975.

————. *The Ambiguous Iroquois Empire: The Covenant Chain Confederation of Indian Tribes with English Colonies from Its Beginnings to the Lancaster Treaty of 1744.* New York: W. W. Norton, 1984.

Martin, Calvin, ed. *The American Indian and the Problem of History.* New York: Oxford University Press, 1987.

McLoughlin, William G. *Cherokees and Missionaries, 1789–1839.* New Haven: Yale University Press, 1984.

Ray, Arthur J. *Indians in the Fur Trade: Their Role as Hunters, Trappers, and Middlemen in the Lands Southwest of Hudson Bay, 1660–1870.* Toronto: University of Toronto Press, 1974.

Salisbury, Neal. *Manitou and Providence: Indians, Europeans, and the Making of New England, 1500–1643.* New York: Oxford University Press, 1982.

Spicer, Edward. *Cycles of Conquest: The Impact of Spain, Mexico, and the United States on the Indians of the Southwest, 1533–1960.* Tucson: University of Arizona Press, 1962.

Trigger, Bruce G. *Natives and Newcomers: Canada's "Heroic Age" Reconsidered.* Kingston, Ont.: McGill-Queen's University Press, 1985.

Wallace, Anthony F. C. *The Death and Rebirth of the Seneca.* New York: Random House, 1969.

White, Richard. *The Roots of Dependency: Subsistence, Environment, and Social Change among the Choctaws, Pawnees, and Navajos.* Lincoln: University of Nebraska Press, 1983.

Wright, J. Leitch, Jr. *The Only Land They Knew: The Tragic Story of the American Indians in the Old South.* New York: The Free Press, 1981.

---

[*] "Indians in Colonial History," in *The Impact of Indian History on the Teaching of United States History,* D'Arcy McNickle Center for the History of the American Indian Occasional Papers in Curriculum Series 4 (Chicago: The Newberry Library, 1986), pp. 1–26.

DOCUMENT 1.1
The Founding of the League of the Iroquois

This excerpt is drawn from a version of the Iroquois oral tradition that was recorded in the nineteenth century. Though mythic in proportion and reflecting some Christian influences, the legend makes clear the violent conditions that attended the League's founding some four hundred years earlier and against which it sought to impose its ideal of peace. The remarkable unity achieved by the Iroquois, without any of the trappings of the European nation-state, made them the most powerful and feared of all Native Americans during the colonial period.

DEKANAWIDA'S BIRTH

North of the beautiful lake [Ontario] in the land of the Crooked Tongues, was a long winding bay and at a certain spot was the Huron town, Ka-ha-nah-yenh. Near by was the great hill, Ti-ro-nat-ha-ra-da-donh. In the village lived a good woman who had a virgin daughter. Now strangely this virgin conceived and her mother knew that she was about to bear a child. The daughter about this time went into a long sleep and dreamed that her child should be a son whom she should name Dekanawida. The messenger in the dream told her that he should become a great man and that he should go among the Flint people to live and that he should also go to the Many Hill Nation and there raise up the Great Tree of Peace. . . .

THE TROUBLED NATIONS

The Ongwe-oweh had fought long and bravely. So long had they fought that they became lustful

Source: Arthur C. Parker, ''The Constitution of the Five Nations,'' *New York State Museum Bulletin*, vol. 184 (1916), pp. 14, 16–17, 26, 27, 28–29.

for war and many times Endeka-Gakwa, the Sun, came out of the east to find them fighting. It was thus because the Ongwe-oweh were so successful that they said the Sun loved war and gave them power.

All the Ongwe-oweh fought other nations sometimes together and sometimes singly and, ah-gi! ofttimes they fought among themselves. The nation of the Flint had little sympathy for the Nation of the Great Hill, and sometimes they raided one another's settlements. Thus did brothers and Ongwe-oweh fight. The nation of the Sunken Pole fought the Nation of the Flint and hated them, and the Nation of the Sunken Pole was Ongwe.

Because of bitter jealousy and love of bloodshed sometimes towns would send their young men against the young men of another town to practise them in fighting.

Even in his own town a warrior's own neighbor might be his enemy and it was not safe to roam about at night when Soi-ka-Gakwa, our Grandmother, the Moon, was hidden.

Everywhere there was peril and everywhere mourning. Men were ragged with sacrifice and the women scarred with the flints, so everywhere there was misery. Feuds with outer nations, feuds with brother nations, feuds of sister towns and feuds of families and of clans made every warrior a stealthy man who liked to kill.

Then in those days there was no great law. Our founder had not yet come to create peace and give united strength to the Real Men, the Ongwe-oweh.

In those same days the Onondagas had no peace. A man's life was valued as nothing. For any slight offence a man or woman was killed by his enemy and in this manner feuds started between families and clans. At night none dared leave their doorways lest they be struck down by an enemy's war club. Such was the condition when there was no Great Law.

South of the Onondaga town lived an evil-minded man. His lodge was in a swale and his nest was made of bulrushes. His body was distorted by seven crooks and his long tangled locks were adorned by writhing living serpents. Moreover, this monster was a devourer of raw meat, even of human flesh. He was also a master of wizardry and by his magic he destroyed men but he could not be destroyed. Adodarhoh was the name of the evil man.

Notwithstanding the evil character of Adodarhoh the people of Onondaga, the Nation of Many Hills, obeyed his commands and though it cost many lives they satisfied his insane whims, so much did they fear him for his sorcery. . . .

THE ESTABLISHMENT OF THE GREAT PEACE

Dekanawida requested some of the Mohawk chiefs to call a council, so messengers were sent out among the people and the council was convened.

Dekanawida said, "I, with my co-worker, have a desire to now report what we have done on five successive midsummer days, of five successive years. We have obtained the consent of five nations. These are the Mohawks, the Oneidas, the Onondagas, the Cayugas and the Senecas. Our desire is to form a compact for a union of our nations. Our next step is to seek out Adodarhoh. It is he who has always set at naught all plans for the establishment of the Great Peace. We must seek his fire and look for his smoke."

The chief speaker of the council then said, "We do agree and confirm all you have said and we wish to appoint two spies who shall volunteer to seek out the smoke of Adodarhoh. . . ."

* * * * *

When the spies returned the speaker of the council said, "Ska-non-donh, our ears are erected." Then the spies spoke and they said, "At great danger to ourselves we have seen Adodarhoh. We have returned and tell you that the body of Adodarhoh has seven crooked parts, his hair is infested with snakes and he is a cannibal."

The council heard the message and decided to go to Onondaga at midsummer.

Then Dekanawida taught the people the Hymn of Peace and the other songs. He stood before the door of the longhouse and walked before it singing the new songs. Many came and learned them so that many were strong by the magic of them when it was time to carry the Great Peace to Onondaga.

When the time had come, Dekanawida summoned the chiefs and people together and chose one man to sing the songs before Adodarhoh. Soon then this singer led the company through the forest and he preceded all, singing the Peace songs as he walked. Many old villages and camping places were passed as they went and the names were lifted to give the clan name holders. . . .

* * * * *

The frontier of the Onondaga country was reached and the expedition halted to kindle a fire, as was customary. Then the chiefs of the Onondagas with their head men welcomed them and a great throng marched to the fireside of Adodarhoh, the singer of the Peace Hymn leading the multitude.

The lodge of Adodarhoh was reached and a new singer was appointed to sing the Peace Hymn. So he walked before the door of the house singing to cure the mind of Adodarhoh. He knew that if he made a single error or hesitated his power would be weakened and the crooked body of Adodarhoh remain misshapen. Then he hesitated and made an error. So another singer was appointed and he too made an error by hesitating.

Then Dekanawida himself sang and walked before the door of Adodarhoh's house. When he finished his song he walked toward Adodarhoh and held out his hand to rub it on his body and to know its inherent strength and life. Then Adodarhoh was made straight and his mind became healthy.

When Adodarhoh was made strong in rightful powers and his body had been healed, Dekanawida addressed the three nations. He said, "We have now overcome a great obstacle. It has long stood in the way of peace. The mind of Adodarhoh is now made right and his crooked parts are made straight. Now indeed may we establish the Great Peace.

"Before we do firmly establish our union each nation must appoint a certain number of its wisest and purest men who shall be rulers, Rodiyaner. They shall be the advisers of the people and make the new rules that may be needful. These men shall be selected and confirmed by their female relations in whose lines the titles shall be hereditary. When these are named they shall be crowned, emblematically, with deer antlers."

So then the women of the Mohawks brought forward nine chiefs who should become Rodiyaner and one man, Ayenwaehs, as war chief.

So then the women of the Oneidas brought forward nine chiefs who should become Rodiyaner, and one man, Kahonwadironh, who should be war chief.

So then the Onondaga women brought forward fourteen chiefs who should become Rodiyaner, and one man, Ayendes, who should be war chief.

Each chief then delivered to Dekanawida a string of lake shell wampum a span in length as a pledge of truth.

Dekanawida then said: "Now, today in the presence of this great multitude I disrobe you and you are not now covered by your old names. I now give you names much greater." Then calling each chief to him he said: "I now place antlers on your head as an emblem of your power. Your old garments are torn off and better robes are given you. Now you are Royaner, each of you. You will receive many

scratches and the thickness of your skins shall be seven spans. You must be patient and henceforth work in unity. Never consider your own interests but work to benefit the people and for the generations not yet born. You have pledged yourselves to govern yourselves by the laws of the Great Peace. All your authority shall come from it.

"I do now order that Skanawateh shall in one-half of his being be a Royaneh of the Great Peace, and in his other half a war chief, for the Rodiyaner must have an ear to hear and a hand to feel the coming of wars."

Then did Dekanawida repeat all the rules which he with Ayonhwatha had devised for the establishment of the Great Peace.

Then in the councils of all the Five Nations he repeated them and the Confederacy was established.

DOCUMENT 1.2
Indians versus English: An English View

In this account of the Pequot War (1637), William Bradford, Governor of the Plymouth colony, makes clear the Puritan attitude toward Indians who resisted colonization. Here is his version of the war's origins plus the account of a surprise attack on a village of sleeping Pequot families—an attack that most of us would consider an atrocity.

Anno Dom: 1637

In the fore part of this year, the Pequots fell openly upon the English at Connecticut, in the lower parts of the river, and slew sundry of them as they were at work in the fields, both men and women, to the great terrour of the

Source: William Bradford, *Of Plymouth Plantation, 1620–1647*, ed. Samuel Eliot Morison (New York: Modern Library, 1952), pp. 294–96.

rest, and went away in great pride and triumph, with many high threats. They also assaulted a fort at the river's mouth, though strong and well defended; and though they did not there prevail, yet it struck them [the English] with much fear and astonishment to see their bold attempts in the face of danger. Which made them [the English] in all places to stand upon their guard and to prepare for resistance, and earnestly to solicit their friends and confederates in the Bay of Massachusetts to send them speedy aid, for they looked for more forcible assaults. . . .

In the meantime, the Pequots, especially in the winter before, sought to make peace with the Narragansetts, and used very pernicious arguments to move them thereunto: as that the English were strangers and began to overspread their country, and would deprive them thereof in time, if they were suffered to grow and increase. And if the Narragansetts did assist the English to subdue them, they did but make way for their own overthrow, for if they were rooted out, the English would soon take occasion to subjugate them. And if they would hearken to them they should not need to fear the strength of the English, for they would not come to open battle with them but fire their houses, kill their cattle, and lie in ambush for them as they went abroad upon their occasions; and all this they might easily do without any or little danger to themselves. The which course being held, they well saw the English could not long subsist but they would either be starved with hunger or be forced to forsake the country. With many the like things; insomuch that the Narragansetts were once wavering and were half minded to have made peace with them, and joined against the English. But again, when they considered how much wrong they had received from the Pequots, and what an opportunity they now had by the help of the English to right themselves; revenge was so sweet unto them as it prevailed

above all the rest, so as they resolved to join with the English against them, and did. . . .

* * * * *

. . . From Connecticut, who were most sensible of the hurt sustained and the present danger, they set out a party of men, and another party met them from the Bay, at Narragansetts', who were to join with them. The Narragansetts were earnest to be gone before the English were well rested and refreshed, especially some of them which came last. It should seem their desire was to come upon the enemy suddenly and undiscovered. There was a bark of this place, newly put in there, which was come from Connecticut, who did encourage them to lay hold of the Indians' forwardness, and to show as great forwardness as they, for it would encourage them, and expedition might prove to their great advantage. So they went on, and so ordered their march as the Indians brought them to a fort of the enemy's (in which most of their chief men were) before day. They approached the same with great silence and surrounded it both with English and Indians, that they might not break out; and so assaulted them with great courage, shooting amongst them, and entered the fort with all speed. And those that first entered found sharp resistance from the enemy who both shot at and grappled with them; others ran into their houses and brought out fire and set them on fire, which soon took in their mat; and standing close together, with the wind all was quickly on a flame, and thereby more were burnt to death than was otherwise slain; It burnt their bowstrings and made them unserviceable; those that scaped the fire were slain with the sword, some hewed to pieces, others run through with their rapiers, so as they were quickly dispatched and very few escaped. It was conceived they thus destroyed about 400 at this time. It was a fearful sight to see them thus frying in the fire and the streams of blood quenching the same, and horrible was the stink and scent thereof; but the victory seemed a sweet sacrifice, and they gave the praise thereof to God, who had wrought so wonderfully for them, thus to enclose their enemies in their hands and give them so speedy a victory over so proud and insulting an enemy.

DOCUMENT 1.3
Indians versus English: An Indian View

Four decades later, war again erupted in New England. This time a coalition of tribes sought to arrest the astonishingly swift growth of the Puritan colonies before their communities and cultures disappeared altogether. After the initial outbreak of hostilities in June 1675, a delegation of Rhode Island Quakers sought to bring the two sides together to prevent further violence. In the delegation's interview with Metacom (King Philip), leader of the uprising, as recorded by John Easton, we can sense the Indians' desperation.

We said we knew the English said the Indians wronged them and the Indians said the English wronged them, but our desire was the quarrel might rightly be decided in the best way, and not as dogs decide their quarrels. The Indians owned that fighting was the worst way, then they propounded how right might take place, we said by arbitration. They said all English agreed against them, and so by arbitration they had had much wrong, many miles square of land so taken from them, for English would have English arbitrators, and once they were persuaded to give in their arms, that thereby jealousy might be removed, [then] the English having their arms would not deliver them as

they had promised, until they consented to pay 100 pounds, and now they had not so much land or money, that they were as good be killed as leave all their livelihood. We said they might choose an Indian king, and the English might choose the Governor of New York, that neither had cause to say either were parties in the difference. They said they had not heard of that way and said we honestly spoke, so we were persuaded if that way had been tendered they would have accepted. We did endeavor not to hear their complaints, said it was not convenient for us now to consider of, but to endeavor to prevent war, said to them when in war against English, blood was spilt that engaged all Englishmen, for we were to be all under one king. We knew what their complaints would be, and in our colony had removed some of them in sending for Indian rulers in so far as the crime concerned Indians' lives, which they very lovingly accepted and agreed with us to their execution and said so they were able to satisfy their subjects when they knew an Indian suffered duly, but said what was only between their Indians and not in townships that we had purchased, they would not have us prosecute and that they had a great fear lest any of their Indians should be called or forced to be Christian Indians. They said that such were in everything more mischievous, only dissemblers, and then the English made them not subject to their kings, and by their lying to wrong their kings. We knew it to be true, and we promising them that however in government to Indians all should be alike and that we knew it was our King's will it should be so, that although we were weaker than other colonies, they having submitted to our King to protect them, others dared not otherwise to molest them, so they expressed they took that to be well, that we had little cause to doubt but that to us, under the King, they would have yielded to our determinations in what any should have complained to us against them, but Philip charged it to be dishonesty in us to put off the hearing the

Source: Charles M. Segal and David C. Stineback, eds., *Puritans, Indians, and Manifest Destiny* (New York: G. P. Putnam's Sons, 1977), pp. 191–93.

complaints. Therefore we consented to hear them. They said they had been the first in doing good to the English, and the English the first in doing wrong, said when the English first came their king's father was as a great man and the English as a little child, he constrained other Indians from wronging the English and gave them corn and showed them how to plant and was free to do them any good and had let them have a 100 times more land than now the king had for his own people, but their king's brother when he was king came miserably to die by being forced to court, as they judged poisoned, and another grievance was if 20 of their own Indians testified that an Englishman had done them wrong, it was as nothing, and if but one of their worst Indians testified against any Indian or their king, when it pleased the English that was sufficient. Another grievance was when their kings sold land, the English would say it was more than they agreed to and a writing must be proof against all them, and some of their kings had done wrong to sell so much. He left his people none, and some being given to drunkenness the English made them drunk and then cheated them in bargains, but now their kings were forewarned not to part with land for nothing in comparison to the value thereof. Now whom the English had owned for king or queen they [the English] would disinherit, and make another king that would give or sell them their land, that now they had no hopes left to keep any land. Another grievance the English cattle and horses still increased, that when they removed 30 miles from where English had anything to do, they could not keep their corn from being spoiled, they never being used to fence, and thought when the English bought land of them that they [the English] would have kept their cattle upon their own land. Another grievance, the English were so eager to sell the Indians liquor that most of the Indians spent all in drunkenness and then ravened upon the sober Indians and, they did believe, often did hurt the English

cattle, and their kings could not prevent it. We knew before [that] these were their grand complaints, but then we only endeavored to persuade that all complaints might be righted without war, but could have no other answer but that they had not heard of that way for the Governor of [New] York and an Indian king to have the hearing of it. We had cause to think if that had been tendered it would have been accepted. We endeavored that, however, they should lay down their arms, for the English were too strong for them. They said then the English should do to them as they did when they were too strong for the English. . . .

DOCUMENT 1.4
Indian-English Treaty Making: The Covenant Chain

Maryland's proposal of peace to the five Iroquois Nations, as dictated by Governor General Andros in 1677, is followed by the reply of one of them, the Mohawks. Note how the conference incorporates Indian and English diplomatic protocol, especially in the speeches, songs, and presentations of gifts.

Propositions of Col. Henry Coursey, Esq.; Authorized by Charles, Lord Baron of Baltimore, Lord Proprietor of Maryland, to the Mohawks and Other Indians Westward as Far as the Senecas, New York the 30th of June 1677

Being informed that the Mohawks, Senecas, et al., are of this government, and faithful and constant friends to the English under our great king, I am come from the Lord Baltimore, Lord Proprietor of Maryland and all His

Source: Lawrence Leder, ed., *The Livingston Indian Records, 1666–1723* (Gettysburg: Pennsylvania Historical Association, 1956), pp. 42–43, 45–47.

Majesty's Subjects of Virginia and Maryland to see and speak with you here.

Though through mistakes, some discontents or injuries may have happened between us heretofore, now upon the good report of you which I find, we are willing that all what is past be buried and forgotten, you taking care (as we shall on our parts) that your Indians, nor none living among you or coming through your country, do for the future [not] injure any of our persons (Piscataway or other . . . Indians living with us) or goods, and if any ill person should do any harm, that there be present full satisfaction given for all injuries or damages.

The above being observed so that no injury or damage be done, or satisfaction given for the same, we shall always esteem and treat you our good neighbors and friends.

To each nation a hundred and fifty guilders [worth of] white strung wampum, in three parts, fifty each.

*   *   *   *   *

The Mohawk's answer to the Proposition made to them the 4th of this Instant by the Honored Col. Henry Coursey, authorized by Charles, Lord Baron of Baltimore, Lord Proprietor of Maryland in the Court House of Albany, 6 August 1677

Interpreted by Akus Cornelise, Who was Assisted by Arnout Cornelise Viele

The names of the Sachems are:

1st Castle:	Canneachko
	Aihagari
	Roote
2nd Castle:	Cassenossacha
3rd Castle:	Cannodacgoo, who was Speaker
	Odiana
	Tagansarigoo
	Semachegi

1. They say with a present we are glad that the King's Governors of Maryland and Virginia have sent you hither to speak with the Mohawks as also that the Governor General hath been pleased to destinate and appoint this place to speak with all nations in peace . . . for which we do return his honor hearty thanks, especially that his honor hath been pleased to grant you the privilege for to speak with us here. Seeing that the Governor General and we are one, and one heart and one head, for the Covenant that is betwixt the Governor General and us is inviolable, yea so strong that if the very thunder should break upon the Covenant Chain it would not break it in sunder, we are likewise glad that we have heard you speak and now we shall answer. That in case that any of our Indians should injur any Christians or Indians in your parts, or your Christians or Indians do any damage to our Indians, we desire that on both sides the matter be composed, and that which is past to be buried in oblivion. They . . . do give thereupon one dressed elk skin and one beaver.

21y. We have heard you speak and now we shall answer unto your propositions. You have said that all which is past formerly shall be buried and forgot which we do likewise, holding ourselves innocent of any injury done to any of the nations of Maryland or Virginia. [We] have always spoke with one another in friendship and have likewise received many favors—bread and other provisions—for which we humbly thank you. And if any do accuse us of having done any injury or damage there, they do belie us, we having been there but twice, and do give thereupon two beavers.

31y. If any difference should arise betwixt your Indians and our Indians we desire that there may not immediately a war arise upon the same but that the matter may be moderate and composed betwixt us. And we do engage for our parts to give satisfaction to you for any evil that our Indians might happen to do and do give thereupon two beavers.

41y. They sing a song after their manner, being their method of a new Covenant made, which they do undertake to hold firm, being the first time they have seen any[one] authorized from Maryland and Virginia. And say further we are glad and do welcome His Honor the Colonel with a beaver and one dressed elk skin for his trouble in coming [on] so far a journey.

51y. They do sing another song, the meaning thereof is that their people might not forget what is past betwixt them and the Colonel but might be always mindful of what is done in the house ordained to that end by the Governor General. . . . And all that was proposed by you the 4th Instant, we desire that it may be punctually observed upon your side (as we shall upon ours). And if you have a mind hereafter to speak with us, we desire that it may be here and nowhere else, [and] do give thereupon one dressed elk skin.

61y. They say we do return you hearty thanks for the releasing of the two sons of Canondondarwe, the chief sachem of the Mohawks, and likewise that you beheaded the sachem of the Susquehannas named Acknaetsachawey, who was the cause of their being taken prisoners, and do present 5 beavers.

DOCUMENT 1.5
European Goods and Indian Culture

Scottish fur trader James Adair sought to demonstrate that Native Americans were descended from the Ten Lost Tribes of Israel. To prove his theory, Adair described in detail the customs of the Cherokees and other southeastern tribes among whom he lived. In this excerpt, on native burial practices, he also shows the impact of European material goods on native customs and beliefs.

Source: *Adair's History of the American Indians,* ed. Samuel Cole Williams (Johnson City; Tennessee: Watauga Press, 1930), pp. 186–87.

The Hebrews have at all times been very careful in the burial of their dead—to be deprived of it was considered as one of the greatest of evils. They made it a point of duty to perform the funeral obsequies of their friends—often embalmed the dead bodies of those who were rich, and even buried treasure in the tombs with their dead. . . . Thus it was an universal custom with the ancient Peruvians, when the owner died to bury his effects with him, which the avaricious Spaniards perceiving, they robbed these store-houses of the dead of an immense quantity of treasures. The modern Indians bury all their moveable riches, according to the custom of the ancient Peruvians and Mexicans, insomuch, that the grave is heir of all.

Except the Cheerake, only one instance of deviation, from this ancient and general Indian custom occurs to me: which was that of *Malahche,* the late famous chieftain of the *Kowwetah* head war-town of the lower part of the Muskohge country, who bequeathed all he possessed to his real, and adopted relations,—being sensible they would be much more useful to his living friends, than to himself during his long sleep: he displayed a genius far superior to the crowd.

The Cheerake of late years, by the reiterated persuasion of the traders, have entirely left off the custom of burying effects with the dead body; the nearest of blood inherits them. They, and several other of our Indian nations, used formerly to shoot all the live stock that belonged to the deceased, soon after the interment of the corpse; not according to the Pagan custom of the funeral piles, on which they burned several of the living, that they might accompany and wait on the dead, but from a narrow-hearted avaricious principle, derived from their Hebrew progenitors.

Notwithstanding the North-American Indians, like the South-Americans, inter the whole riches of the deceased with him, and so make his corpse and the grave heirs of all, they never give them the least disturbance; even a blood-thirsty enemy will not despoil nor disturb the dead. The grave proves an asylum, and a sure place of rest to the sleeping person, till at some certain time, according to their opinion, he rises again to inherit his favourite place,—unless the covetous, or curious hand of some foreigner, should break through his sacred bounds. This custom of burying the dead person's treasures with him, has entirely swallowed up their medals, and other monuments of antiquity, without any probability of recovering them.

DOCUMENT 1.6
The Delaware Prophet: An Indian Resistance Leader

The kinds of cultural changes noted by Adair eventually brought a reaction among many Indians, especially after they saw that the result was loss of autonomy and resources plus greater dependence on the newcomers. That reaction was often expressed in religious terms, and its most forceful spokesman in the colonial period was Neolin, better known as the Delaware Prophet. What is noteworthy about his message, as recorded by an unsympathetic Moravian missionary, is the obvious influence of both Christianity and Native American traditions.

In the year 1762, there was a famous preacher of the Delaware nation, who resided at *Cay-ahaga*, near Lake Erie, and travelled about the country, among the Indians, endeavouring to persuade them that he had been appointed by the great Spirit to instruct them in those things that were agreeable to him and to point

Source: John Heckewelder, *History, Manners, and Customs of the Indian Nations Who Once Inhabited Pennsylvania and the Neighbouring States*, ed. William C. Reichel (Philadelphia: Historical Society of Pennsylvania, 1876), pp. 291–93.

out to them the offences by which they had drawn his displeasure on themselves, and the means by which they might recover his favour for the future. He had drawn, as he pretended, by the direction of the great Spirit, a kind of map on a piece of deer skin, somewhat dressed like parchment, which he called "the great Book or Writing." This, he said, he had been ordered to shew to the Indians, that they might see the situation in which the Mannitto had originally placed them, the misery which they had brought upon themselves by neglecting their duty, and the only way that was now left them to regain what they had lost. This map he held before him while preaching, frequently pointing to particular marks and spots upon it, and giving explanations as he went along.

The size of this map was about fifteen inches square, or, perhaps, something more. An inside square was formed by lines drawn within it, of about eight inches each way, two of those lines, however, were not closed by about half an inch at the corners. Across these inside lines, others of about an inch in length were drawn with sundry other lines and marks, all which was intended to represent a strong inaccessible barrier, to prevent those without from entering the space within, otherwise than at the place appointed for that purpose. When the map was held as he directed, the corners which were not closed lay at the left hand side, directly opposite to each other, the one being at the south east by south, and the nearest at the northeast by north. In explaining or describing the particular points on this map, with his fingers always pointing to the place he was describing, he called the space within the inside lines "the heavenly regions," or the place destined by the great Spirit for the habitation of the Indians in future life; the space left open at the southeast corner, he called the "avenue," which had been intended for the Indians to enter into this heaven, but which was now in the possession of the white people, wherefore the great

Spirit had since caused another "avenue" to be made on the opposite side, at which, however, it was both difficult and dangerous for them to enter, there being many impediments in their way, besides a large ditch leading to a gulf below, over which they had to leap; but the evil spirit kept at this very spot a continual watch for Indians, and whoever he laid hold of, never could get away from him again, but was carried to his regions, where there was nothing but extreme poverty; where the ground was parched up by the heat for want of rain, no fruit came to perfection, the game was almost starved for want of pasture, and where the evil spirit, at his pleasure, transformed men into horses and dogs, to be ridden by him and follow him in his hunts and wherever he went.

The space on the outside of this interior square, was intended to represent the country given to the Indians to hunt, fish, and dwell in while in this world; the east side of it was called the ocean or "great salt water Lake." Then the preacher drawing the attention of his hearers particularly to the south-east avenue, would say to them: "Look here! See what we have lost by neglect and disobedience; by being remiss in the expression of our gratitude to the great Spirit, for what he has bestowed upon us; by neglecting to make to him sufficient sacrifices; by looking upon a people of a different colour from our own, who had come across a great lake, as if they were a part of ourselves; by suffering them to sit down by our side, and looking at them with indifference, while they were not only taking our country from us, but this (pointing to the spot), this, our own avenue, leading into those beautiful regions which were destined for us. Such is the sad condition to which we are reduced. What is now to be done, and what remedy is to be applied? I will tell you, my friends. Hear what the great Spirit has ordered me to tell you! You are to make sacrifices, in the manner that I shall direct; to put off entirely from yourselves

the customs which you have adopted since the white people came among us; you are to return to that former happy state, in which we lived in peace and plenty, before these strangers came to disturb us, and above all, you must abstain from drinking their deadly *beson,* which they have forced upon us, for the sake of increasing their gains and diminishing our numbers. Then will the great Spirit give success to our arms; then he will give us strength to conquer our enemies, to drive them from hence, and recover the passage to the heavenly regions which they have taken from us."

Such was in general the substance of his discourses. After having dilated more or less on the various topics which I have mentioned, he commonly concluded in this manner: "And now, my friends, in order that what I have told you may remain firmly impressed on your minds, and to refresh your memories from time to time, I advise you to preserve, in every family, at least, such a book or writing as this, which I will finish off for you, provided you bring me the price, which is only one buckskin or two doe-skins a piece." The price was of course bought, and the book purchased. In some of those maps, the figure of a deer or turkey, or both, was placed in the heavenly regions, and also in the dreary region of the evil spirit; the former, however, appeared fat and plump, while the latter seemed to have nothing but skin and bones.

DOCUMENT 1.7
Andrew Jackson on Indians as a Vanishing Race

Although Indians' cultures and their relations with the United States varied widely in the early nineteenth century, many whites viewed

Source: *A Compilation of the Messages and Papers of the Presidents, 1797–1897,* James D. Richardson ed. (Washington, 1896) II, 520–23.

Indians as a single race of savages doomed to extinction. In his presidential address to Congress in 1830, Andrew Jackson argues that removal of Indians east of the Mississippi will benefit both peoples and fulfill their destinies. At the same time, he shows the benefits that the removal of Indians will bring to whites.

Toward the aborigines of the country no one can indulge a more friendly feeling than myself, or would go further in attempting to reclaim them from their wandering habits and make them a happy, prosperous people. I have endeavored to impress upon them my own solemn convictions of the duties and powers of the General Government in relation to the State authorities. For the justice of the laws passed by the States within the scope of their reserved powers they are not responsible to this Government. As individuals we may entertain and express our opinions of their acts, but as a Government we have as little right to control them as we have to prescribe laws for other nations.

*   *   *   *   *

Humanity has often wept over the fate of the aborigines of this country, and Philanthropy has been long busily employed in devising means to avert it, but its progress has never for a moment been arrested, and one by one have many powerful tribes disappeared from the earth. To follow to the tomb the last of his race and to tread on the graves of extinct nations excite melancholy reflections. But true philanthropy reconciles the mind to these vicissitudes as it does to the extinction of one generation to make room for another. In the monuments and fortresses of an unknown people, spread over the extensive regions of the West, we behold the memorials of a once powerful race, which was exterminated or has disappeared to make room for the existing savage tribes. Nor is there anything in this which, upon a comprehensive view of the general inter-

ests of the human race, is to be regretted. Philanthropy could not wish to see this continent restored to the condition in which it was found by our forefathers. What good man would prefer a country covered with forests and ranged by a few thousand savages to our extensive Republic, studded with cities, towns, and prosperous farms, embellished with all the improvements which art can devise or industry execute, occupied by more than 12,000,000 happy people, and filled with all the blessings of liberty, civilization, and religion?

The present policy of the Government is but a continuation of the same progressive change by a milder process. The tribes which occupied the countries now constituting the Eastern States were annihilated or have melted away to make room for the whites. The waves of population and civilization are rolling to the westward, and we now propose to acquire the countries occupied by the red men of the South and West by a fair exchange, and, at the expense of the United States, to send them to a land where their existence may be prolonged and perhaps made perpetual. Doubtless it will be painful to leave the graves of their fathers; but what do they more than our ancestors did or than our children are now doing? To better their condition in an unknown land our forefathers left all that was dear in earthly objects. Our children by thousands yearly leave the land of their birth to seek new homes in distant regions. Does Humanity weep at these painful separations from everything, animate and inanimate, with which the young heart has become entwined? Far from it. It is rather a source of joy that our country affords scope where our young population may range unconstrained in body or in mind, developing the power and faculties of man in their highest perfection. These remove hundreds and almost thousands of miles at their own expense, purchase the lands they occupy, and support themselves at their new homes from the moment of their arrival. Can it be cruel in this Government when, by events which it can not control, the Indian is made discontented in his ancient home to purchase his lands, to give him a new and extensive territory, to pay the expense of his removal, and support him a year in his new abode? How many thousands of our own people would gladly embrace the opportunity of removing to the West on such conditions! If the offers made to the Indians were extended to them, they would be hailed with gratitude and joy.

And is it supposed that the wandering savage has a stronger attachment to his home than the settled, civilized Christian? Is it more afflicting to him to leave the graves of his fathers than it is to our brothers and children? Rightly considered, the policy of the General Govern-

ment toward the red man is not only liberal, but generous. He is unwilling to submit to the laws of the States and mingle with their population. To save him from this alternative, or perhaps utter annihilation, the General Government kindly offers him a new home, and proposes to pay the whole expense of his removal and settlement.

May we not hope, therefore, that all good citizens, and none more zealously than those who think the Indians oppressed by subjection to the laws of the States, will unite in attempting to open the eyes of those children of the forest to their true condition, and by a speedy removal to relieve them from all the evils, real or imaginary, present or prospective, with which they may be supposed to be threatened.

Character and the Social Order in Puritan New England

John Demos
Brandeis University

F ew aspects of American history have been as widely canvassed as New England Puritanism. Imbued from the start with a sense of divine mission, the Puritan settlers were continually evaluating themselves; and generation after generation of their descendants have returned to the task with monotonous regularity. These investigations have produced some important insights into early American society—and later American character—but they have also fostered serious misconceptions. The subject has evoked the interest of the best of professional scholars and the worst of nonprofessional mythmakers; the result is a maze of history, apologetics, prejudice, legend, and plain bewilderment.

According to one viewpoint, perhaps the most common, Puritanism was a personal style, a character type, based on intense and unswerving moral commitment. This portrayal has been shaded in vastly different ways, depending on the bias of its supporters. In the nineteenth century, the Puritans were hailed as determined exemplars of the nation's destiny. In the early twentieth century a reaction set in, and they were increasingly written off as repressed, pleasure-hating bigots. Moral or moralistic, singleminded or narrowminded, upright or uptight—

these impressions of Puritans die hard, and there is certainly some truth in them. The Puritans *were* remarkably tenacious in holding to their own view of human and superhuman activity. They were not, however, so rigidly opposed to pleasure as is sometimes claimed. More particularly, they were not opposed to sexual pleasure. In this regard our own usage of the term *puritanical* is misleading and reflects a larger tendency to confuse Puritans with Victorians. By almost any standard imaginable, sex was more problematic in the nineteenth century than in the seventeenth century.

Puritanism was also, according to a variant interpretation, an ethic, a pervasive cult of hard work, thrift, and prudent calculation. As such it laid the psychological foundations for the rise of capitalism. Moreover, it long outlived its specifically doctrinal trappings, and it remains with us, perhaps *in* us, today. This view contains a mix of defects and virtues. On the one hand, it explains too much: Members of the bourgeoisie have come from a variety of backgrounds, while some men who most epitomized orthodox Puritanism have looked askance at business pursuits. On the other hand, there is an overlap between Puritan and bourgeois virtues, as well as a rough geographical correlation between capitalist development and exposure to the more extreme forms of Protestantism.

The most subtle and penetrating studies of the subject belong to another scholarly chain. Beginning from about 1925, they have all been designed to meet Puritanism, especially New England Puritanism, on its own terms as a *religious* movement. Nonseparating Congregationalism, Federal Theology, the Half-Way Covenant, scriptural typologies, the morphology of salvation: these are only a few of the knotty questions that are now unraveled. The pioneers in the field were Kenneth Murdock, Samuel Eliot Morison, and, above all, Perry Miller, but many other hands have contributed, and the work continues. Altogether, such scholarship justifies the claim that ''the historiography of early New England has reached . . . a level of sophistication unmatched in the study of any other part of American history.'' [1] Yet, the feeling is growing in certain quarters that these studies have been ''too exclusively intellectual,'' that they have told us ''too much about the Puritan mind and too little about the Puritan's feelings.'' [2]

It is, indeed, the individual Puritan who has been most neglected under all of the foregoing historiographic traditions. He is presented regularly as a kind of vessel; he must always be ''filled'' with something else—whether moral zeal, or bourgeois virtue, or weighty religious doctrine. In each case, he is both larger and smaller than life, and he loses his roots in concrete historical circumstance. He appears in the end as one part abstraction and one part caricature. Thus, it seems important to try to relocate the human element in all this—to study Puritan man rather than Puritan ''ism'' and

to evoke the particular drama of time and place in which his life was acted out. This may well be the task of the next generation of Puritan scholarship.

It is easy enough to make a start, for individual Puritans can be identified, classified, and traced to their various origins. In many ways they were average men of their time—yeomen, tradesmen, a few ''gentlemen,'' but scarcely any representatives of either the highest or the lowest ranks of their society. They emerged from all over the map of England, though with distinct concentrations in East Anglia and the West country and a sizable group in London. It is not immediately apparent what they shared, except their allegiance to a powerful movement of religious reform. The Anglican church, they believed, was still infested with papist corruptions; the Elizabethan settlement had not gone far enough. Their concerns embraced doctrine, worship, and church governance. A more direct and *personal* relation to God, a deepened sense of human sinfulness, a simplified ritual, and a decentralized system of administration: such were their goals. They supported their own preaching ministry and followed a leadership of exceptionally learned men. Perkins, Ames, Baxter, Preston, Sibbes, Cotton, and Hooker were names to be reckoned with among Puritans on both sides of the Atlantic. They were deeply influenced by the Protestant movement in Europe, and the starting point for much of their thinking was the work of John Calvin. Yet, too, they were divided on specifics. Presbyterians, Independents, Separatists, Quakers, and a host of smaller, more exotic sects all clamored for recognition. Allies in the larger struggle, they were often competitors as well.

The details of this situation need not detain us here. But we should ask what it was that induced people to become and remain Puritans of any stripe. It is not sufficient to record the factors they would themselves have pointed out—the need to reform the Church and the quest for personal holiness. History cannot be

---

[1] Edmund Morgan, ''The Historians of Early New England,'' in *The Reinterpretation of Early American History,* ed. Ray Allen Billington (New York, 1968), p. 41.

[2] Alan Simpson, *Puritanism in Old and New England* (Chicago, 1955), p. 21.

read entirely on its face; motivation is always complex and ''over-determined''; and social movements respond to an enormous range of environmental circumstance. This point has been brilliantly demonstrated, with specific reference to Puritanism, in the recent work of Michael Walzer.

Central to Walzer's analysis are the concepts of ''anxiety'' and ''discipline.'' The Puritans were living through a time of unprecedented social change. The enclosure movement, runaway inflation, a new world of commerce, population growth, the swollen sprawl of the city of London, the disruption of the manorial and parochial systems, a decline in the vitality of local churches: these trends converged to undermine the traditional structure of English life. The social costs seemed enormous. Vagabonds roamed the countryside, beggars infested the cities, and plague, fire, and crime seemed more devastating than ever before. The response of individual persons to all this was extremely varied, but for many persons there was a profound sense of dislocation, a loss of inner bearings. The men and women who became Puritans seem to have been especially unsettled. Their writings form a litany of warning against the evils of the time. Anxious, alienated, in some cases personally uprooted, they lived, as Walzer puts it, ''on the brink of chaos.'' A fear of disorder pervaded all their thoughts and organized many of their activities. Yet, they found in their religious faith a vital measure of reassurance—strength, hope, the promise of ''a new life.'' For Puritanism enshrined precisely those values that history was destroying. It was rooted, above all, in the principle of *control,* both inner control of the individual man and outer control among the community of saints. Intense and unrelenting discipline was the appropriate answer to disorder.

This is a brief picture of Walzer's view of English Puritans. It is intended to embrace the entire movement, although the documentation comes chiefly from a small circle of leaders. It is an excellent introduction to the particular

groups and individuals who left the mother country and made their way to a New World, indeed a New England. They were manifestly disturbed by the social trends previously mentioned; their leaving was, in large part, a protest against such trends. John Winthrop expressed their shared concern when he asked: ''What means then the bleating of so many oppressed with wrong, that drink wormwood for righteousness? Why do so many seely sheep that seek shelter at the judgement seats return without their fleeces? Why meet we so many wandering ghosts in shape of men, so many spectacles of misery in all our streets, our houses full of victuals, and our entries of hunger-starved Christians? Our shops full of rich wares, and under our stalls lie our own flesh in nakedness?''

The answers that Puritans gave to these questions were of two sorts. There was, most obviously, the corrosive force of human selfishness. Proud, acquisitive, contentious—such was the inherent tendency of human nature. Without some system of external constraints, the invariable choice would be a self-serving course. Yet, in scanning the world around them, the Puritans saw few constraints. They saw a host of contrary impulses that collectively served only to encourage wickedness. They shared the widely current belief that England had become overpopulated. ''This land becomes weary of her inhabitants,'' declared Winthrop, ''so as man, which is the most precious of all creatures, is here more vile and base than the earth they tread upon.'' In such unnatural circumstances, as Robert Cushman noted, ''even the most wise, sober, and discreet men go often to the wall.'' By their lights, this alone was diagnostic of a sickness in the vitals of society.

It was no wonder that they chose withdrawal as the best, perhaps the only, solution to their predicament. They were not, however, fully in agreement about the meaning of this decision. Some Puritans envisioned a permanent departure; they would leave England and its church to a fate that was long beyond their power to reverse. This group, usually known as Separatists, included the little band of Pilgrims who went first to Holland and then across the Atlantic to the spot they named "Plimoth Plantation." John Winthrop and his colleagues in the Massachusetts Bay Company professed a different motive. Their affection for the mother church remained strong—so they declared—and they could see much good in her. Their departure for the New World was a strategic retreat, a flanking movement in the struggle for final reform. Theirs would be a pilot venture that might eventually show the way to a far more perfect society. For this they deserve recognition as the first in a long line of American "Utopians."

But the differences between the settlers at Plymouth and those at Massachusetts Bay were far less important than what they shared. Both groups seized the unique opportunity to begin anew, to found communities where the law of God and the law of man would become identical. That they expressed such goals in theological terms should not mislead us; there were, after all, no other terms available to them. Their concerns reached far beyond religion proper (in our sense) to fundamental issues of social organization. In contrast to the individualism characteristic of seventeenth-century England, they would try to recreate an organic connection among men. In contrast to disorder, they would establish harmony, peacefulness, and the subordination of self to "commonwealth" at the center of life. Countless New England sermons bear witness to the preeminence of these values; here was the real meaning of Christian love. Occasionally, in dealing with historical materials, one encounters a word or phrase that epitomizes an entire subject; for the Puritans, the phrase "knit together" would best qualify. Repeated in the literature, it precisely captures the spirit of their innermost commitments.

The full scope of these commitments cannot be appreciated apart from the practical arrangement they inspired. From their arrival in the New World, the settlers strove to render their system operational. There were countless decisions to make affecting land and other property, local and provincial government, courts of law, agriculture, trade, and Indians. Initially, all decisions involved collective interests and were worked out with painstaking care. Even minor issues were measured against assumed first principles. Piece by piece, leaders and followers worked to stitch together the fabric of a distinctive "New England way."

Yet, almost from the beginning, there were difficulties—special conditions that frustrated the vision that Puritans held. Time passed, circumstances changed; the obstacles became more numerous, and the vision more distant. Still, each new generation produced fresh recruits to carry on the struggle. In fact, the entire history of early New England can be read as a kind of dialectical process encompassing the forces of order, harmony, and permanence on one side, and fluidity, pluralism, and change on the other side. Eventually, it was plain that final success would never come, and some settlers yielded to despair. To them, New England was set on a path of decline. To one recent historian of the period, "the story is cast in the form of a tragedy." To another, it has the shape of an "ironic paradigm."

But, in truth, this story is full of unresolved questions. Scholars are themselves divided on the details—and even on some of the essentials. What exactly was the sequence and pace of change? Which side of the "dialectic" was dominant, in which places, and at which times? How deep was the commitment to "order" in the first place? What was the role of the many non-Puritans in the settler group? What was the impact of an "empty" "wilderness" environment of Indians; of other colonies? The range of possibilities is large; the issue is really one of emphasis. In a complex and ever-shifting course of historical development, which themes were *most* central and what factors supplied the *greatest* amount of energy to the system?

The most lively current work bearing on these questions has fixed on the individual town as the prime unit of study. Efforts continue to uncover the structure of local communities, to identify their inhabitants, to probe the routines of their day-by-day existence. The data for such investigations are extremely varied. Genealogical and vital records permit demographic reconstruction; town meeting reports and church records depict important aspects of collective behavior; court dockets reveal much about interpersonal relations; letters, diaries, and family papers (to the extent they can be located) add valuable human detail. By utilizing all these materials, scholars have sought to convey the wholeness of life in a typical New England community. But the word *typical* suggests the weakness, at least the obvious limitations, of the work. How similar in actual fact were these towns anyway? Are the recent local studies simply that and no more? Has the gain in depth been purchased at too great a cost in breadth? Doubts on this score are sharpened by the substantial discrepancies in the results already obtained for various communities.

There has been, for example, considerable interest in the spatial dimensions of settlement. The hopes and plans of the Puritan leadership seem clear enough. Plantations would develop according to a careful plan and would, above all, be compact. At first, there would be just one settlement with inhabitants who would live and work in close proximity. This would benefit everyone, given the special difficulties of subduing a wilderness and the need for defense against Indians. More importantly, it would reflect the fundamental Puritan commitment to harmony and mutual striving toward holiness. Thus, John Winthrop envisioned Massachusetts as "a city upon a hill"—one city, in which "we must be knit together . . . as one man . . . and . . . must delight in each other, make others' condition our own, rejoice together, mourn together, labor and suffer together, al-

ways having before our eyes our commission and community in the work." A certain density of human contact was central to Puritan conceptions of the good society.

The prospect of growth beyond a single settlement was little anticipated. Yet, such growth was inevitable as the population increased and succumbed to the lure of fresh lands. The process appears prominently in William Bradford's famous chronicle *Of Plymouth Plantation,* for Bradford (in his role as governor) was deeply perplexed and disturbed by it. Begun in 1620, the original Pilgrim community soon split apart, and a sizable group moved off to found the town of Duxbury. This, in turn, was merely the prototype for a long chain of similar fissions. By 1640, there were seven incorporated towns in the colony, by 1670 there were fourteen, and by 1691, when Plymouth was merged with Massachusetts Bay, the number had risen to twenty-one.

The same trend was evident—and far more quickly—in Massachusetts. The Winthrop company landed at Charlestown in the summer of 1630, but this site proved untenable for various reasons. It was relatively infertile, it was low and marshy (hence, conducive to disease), and it was vulnerable to attack from the sea. In the months that followed, the settlers scattered to several different points around the bay. They expected to regroup in a new area a year or so later, but when the time came, few were willing to move again. Thus, Winthrop's model city became six or seven. In another few years, men from these communities began to consider a far more ambitious migration. Complaining of the "straitness" of their lands and the "fundamental error, that towns were set so near to each other," they proposed a new settlement, far to the west, in the Connecticut River valley. The leaders of the Bay Colony were against it, but to no avail. The project went forward under the leadership of the Rev. Thomas Hooker, culminating in what Alan Heimert has called "the earliest of the great American land-manias.'' The result was the founding of an entirely new colony. Meanwhile, other men began to push northward, establishing the first towns in what later became New Hampshire. And in the 1640s, a settlement was started on Narragansett Bay, the nucleus for the colony of Rhode Island.

This expansion did not destroy the Puritan social order. Its scope could be narrowed and its effects limited by regulatory legislation, and the Puritan leadership, especially in the Bay Colony, was equal to the task. By the middle of the seventeenth century, there were systematic procedures for founding new towns. The General Court had to first grant permission. The proposed site had to be carefully "bounded." A group of reputable men, usually designated as "proprietors," had to supervise the framing of town government and the distribution of lands. Inhabitants had to be people of Christian character and "peaceable conversation;" all who failed to meet this standard were liable to be "warned out." Deputies had to be sent to the General Court, from which orders were received and enforced at the local level.

Much more serious was the prospect of growth and fragmentation within the individual communities. In time, the original center was seen as too confining, and some persons considered moving away. They either left the area altogether or tried to establish a new settlement in some other corner of the town lands. In either case, there was a loss of cohesiveness. The overall extent of movement among individuals in seventeenth century New England is not known. Some scholars believe it was substantial, others hold a contrary opinion—and we have as yet no hard figures that would resolve the issue. But it does seem that settlement became increasingly disorganized in a spatial sense, with towns and villages of varying sizes, and even some isolated homesteads, strung out willy-nilly across the countryside. Moreover, the existence of two or more villages within

a single township was bound to raise some troublesome questions. Would each unit have administrative autonomy? Where should school be held? If a new meetinghouse is needed, what should be its location? The center would wish to preserve its position of dominance, but the people in newer villages, the "out-livers" as they were sometimes called, wanted some recognition.

The potential for conflict inherent in these situations is quite apparent—but how much conflict was actually realized? Again, scholars disagree. In fact, recent investigation of these questions has produced two contrasting models. There is, on the one side, the "Utopian, Closed, Corporate Community," or "peaceable kingdom," as it has been called. Towns that conform to this type appear immobile and unchanging, successful at stifling conflict, unswervingly committed to the Puritan ideal of harmony.[3] But there are, on the opposite side, the dynamic, unstable, and above all contentious communities that emerge from a different group of studies.[4] The student of early New England cannot help but be troubled by these divergent pictures. Here the progress of scholarship has yielded only a contradiction, a pair of alternatives that cancel each other out; or so it appears.

To some degree, the contradiction is rooted in differing research priorities. The studies that emphasize harmony have concentrated on the collective ideals and structural forms of New England society—in short, on the *normative* aspects of Puritan life. The evidence from this quarter is indeed impressive. A few specific procedures are worth considering here, if only by way of illustration. "Contrary-minded" individuals could be excluded in the beginning

---

[3] Kenneth Lockridge's picture of Dedham, Mass., provides an obvious case in point—also, Philip Greven's Andover and Michael Zuckerman's Massachusetts towns in the eighteenth century.

[4] Darrett Rutman's Boston, Sumner Powell's Sudbury, and, for a later period, Richard Bushman's Connecticut.

or at any time thereafter. Arbitration was the characteristic response to conflict—neutral parties sat down with adversaries in a given situation and negotiated a compromise agreeable to all. (Arbitration was always preferable to a legal action, for in court the issue would become more open and the lines of division much sharper.) The same spirit infused all forms of political activity, especially in regard to the town meeting. Puritan leaders were remarkably adept at creating compromise and the adjustment of different interests. Their purpose was to always obtain a *total* consensus, not the victory of the greater over the lesser part. Time and again the records inform us that matters were settled by unanimous votes.

But nothing so clearly epitomized Puritan ideals as the theory and practice of the covenant. This was not just a theological concept, a doctrine; it was also something that Puritans *did*. All over New England, men and women were occupied with making, reaffirming, and modifying covenants. Here, quite literally, was the foundation of their church and state—a pledge against the disorder otherwise inherent in the human condition.

So much for one side of the argument; the other also deserves its due. Here the evidence turns more *behavioral,* stressing the actions of individual persons; process, not structure, becomes the focus of investigation. Court records assume a special importance for the views they offer of ordinary citizens caught up in a round of everyday circumstance. The range of issues is considerable: boundaries, cattle, fences, debt, theft, and slander to mention a few. And the total quantity seems truly enormous. In spite of all the pressures to avoid conflict, in spite of the commitment to arbitration, New Englanders went to court with remarkable frequency. To read their court records in any amount is to form the impression of an extremely contentious people.

The bulk of these actions involved only a few individuals at a time, responding to clearly personal grievances. But sometimes they reflected wider divisions as well. Careful investigation of New England towns suggests the presence of a kind of factionalism—blocs of people united around some common purpose or viewpoint struggling for positions of dominance. Usually covert, always deplored, these patterns nonetheless seem to have figured prominently in the experience of most of the settlers and their immediate descendants. Occasionally, they came right into the open. Such was the case, for example, at Sudbury during the early 1650s, when issues of land, pasturing rights, and the location of a new meetinghouse converged to rend the town apart. The bitterness that infused the whole affair is still evident in the records. The leader of one faction declared bluntly: "be it right or wrong, we will have [our way] . . . if we can have it no other way, we will have it by club law." The other side retorted with a threat of secession: "If you oppress the poor, they will cry out; and if you persecute us in one city, we must fly to another."

Another type of conflict—extremely common, and particularly distressing to all concerned—set ministers against their local congregations. Both sides squabbled over practical matters like the payment of salary, the delivery of firewood, and the repair and remodeling of the meetinghouse. Sometimes there was wrangling over doctrine, or simply the clash of discordant personalities. In all cases, arbitration seemed especially appropriate, but it could not assure an amicable outcome. Some disputes, apparently settled by this method, simmered for years and eventually required further intervention. When the strain became too great, the minister might have to look for a new calling in another town. It is astonishing, given the official code of peacefulness, how many New England ministers were sent packing.

Here is the nub of the interpretive puzzle, the seeming contradiction. Careful effort has gone into the study of Puritan society, and we should not dismiss it as one more inconclusive argument among scholars. In fact, there are several ways of trying to reconcile the two major viewpoints. One should, for example, appreciate the possibilities of real difference among the various New England communities in terms of mobility, dispersion, population growth, and internal conflict. Such possibilities can be credited—up to a point. One may also attempt to sort these patterns over time. Perhaps orderliness and stability were dominant themes in the early history of New England, but they lessened as the years passed. This viewpoint, too, can be accepted up to a point.

But, a problem remains. There was only a *limited* range of difference among the communities in question, and a lmited rate of change over time. It is the final, inescapable task to face head on the issue of social stability and social change. One point bears immediate emphasis: our two alternatives are perfect opposites (or as nearly perfect as history allows). This suggests that they do at least occupy common ground; it may even imply some inner mutuality. But we can more easily pursue such questions by refocusing our attention on the individual person—the typical Puritan, if such a creature ever existed. The community had no existence apart from the likes of this person.

This perspective seems a valuable one, because contradiction is more readily understood in individuals than in group behavior. We have indeed a sharper, more evocative term for it— the clinical term *ambivalence*. There are for all people certain special issues that evoke a strong emotional charge composed of fear, fascination, pleasure, yearning, and avoidance. Rooted in personality during the first years of life, they hold their power through adulthood. But official taboos also exist. So here is the familiar rhythm: feeling is engaged, impulse is aroused, and conscience interferes. Childhood—and, more specifically, *childrearing*— becomes the critical variable, transmitting such

patterns throughout a whole culture and across the generations. A people, or an era, may come in this way to share common goals, common preoccupations, and common problems.

Consider the particular case of the Puritans. Recall, first, their beginnings in a time of pervasive flux and change. To them, this period was simply a slide into chaos, a retreat from the reliable structures of traditional life. Increasingly, they lived with anxiety, with a sense of alienation, and with the fear of disorder. They fought back with *discipline* of self and others. Human willfulness was at the root of the problem, as they saw it, and it was in this direction that they exercised their most vigorous repressions. Naturally, they concentrated hard on the young. Cotton Mather remarked, in connection with the rearing of his own children: ''I make them sensible, 'tis a folly for them to pretend unto any wit or will of their own; they must resign all to me, who will be sure to do what is best.'' Years before, John Robinson had put the case more bluntly: ''And surely there is in all children . . . a stubborness and stoutness of mind . . . which must, in the first place, be broken and beaten down. . . . Children's wills and wilfulness [must] be restrained and repressed, and that in time.'' From such a breaking process, much good might come. If evil were stifled at the beginning of life, Puritans might one day be ''knit together'' in perfect harmony. History, moreover, had provided a unique opening for their plans and projects. At the time when their movement was most sharply persecuted in England, an empty continent beckoned from across the sea. Puritans were quick to grasp the opportunity to build a new society, with new people, in a New World.

And yet, as we have seen, they did not find the life they looked for. They had hoped, as one of them put it, to ''be more free here than there from temptation; but I find here a devil to tempt, and a corrupt heart to deceive.'' Steadily, as the years passed, settlement became dispersed, communities divided and sub-divided, men struggled for personal advantage, and "heart-burning" contentions appeared on all sides. Cohesion and harmony remained the preeminent values, but in trying to practice such values the Puritans constantly disappointed themselves. They were not the first people to whom this has happened, nor have they been the last. But, more than many, they knew the agonies of the divided self. We can now take a longer view of the contradictions that seem to have muddled their history. To a considerable degree, the inner life of Puritanism turned on a kind of axis between the opposite poles of order and chaos, conflict and conciliation, willfulness and submission. Perhaps tragic, certainly ironic—their legacy is still with us.

SUGGESTED READINGS

Bailyn, Bernard. *The New England Merchants in the Seventeenth Century*. Cambridge, Mass.: Harvard University Press, 1955.

Battis, Emery. *Saints and Sectaries: Anne Hutchinson and the Antinomian Controversy in the Massachusetts Bay Colony*. Chapel Hill, N.C.: The University of North Carolina Press, 1962.

Bushman, Richard L. *From Puritan to Yankee: Character and the Social Order in Connecticut, 1690–1765*. Cambridge, Mass.: Harvard University Press, 1967.

Demos, John. *A Little Commonwealth: Family Life in Plymouth Colony*. New York: Oxford University Press, 1970.

Dunn, Richard S. *Puritans and Yankees: The Winthrop Dynasty of New England, 1630–1717*. Princeton, N.J.: Princeton University Press, 1962.

Erikson, Kai T. *Wayward Puritans: A Study in the Sociology of Deviance*. New York: John Wiley & Sons, 1966.

Greven, Philip J. *Four Generations: Population, Land, and Family in Colonial Andover, Massachusetts*. Ithaca, N.Y.: Cornell University Press, 1970.

Haskins, George Lee. *Law and Authority in Early Massachusetts: A Study in Tradition and Design*. New York: Macmillan, 1960.

Lockridge, Kenneth A. *A New England Town: The First Hundred Years*. New York: W. W. Norton, 1970.

Miller, Perry. *Errand into the Wilderness*. Cambridge, Mass.: Harvard University Press, 1956.

———. *The New England Mind: From Colony to Province*. Cambridge, Mass.: Harvard University Press, 1953.

———. *The New England Mind: The Seventeenth Century*. New York: Macmillan, 1939.

Morgan, Edmund S. *The Puritan Family*. 2d ed. Boston: Boston Public Library, 1956.

———. *Visible Saints: The History of a Puritan Idea*. New York: New York University Press, 1963.

Pope, Robert G. *The Half-Way Covenant: Church Membership in Puritan New England*. Princeton, N.J.: Princeton University Press, 1969.

Powell, Sumner Chilton. *Puritan Village: The Formation of a New England Town*. Middletown, Conn.: Wesleyan University Press, 1963.

Rutman, Darrett B. *Winthrop's Boston: Portrait of a Puritan Town, 1630–1649*. Chapel Hill, N.C.: University of North Carolina Press, 1965.

Simpson, Alan. *Puritanism in Old and New England*. Chicago: University of Chicago Press, 1955.

Walzer, Michael. *The Revolution of the Saints*. Cambridge, Mass.: Harvard University Press, 1965.

Winslow, Ola Elizabeth. *Meetinghouse Hill, 1630–1783*. New York: Macmillan, 1952.

Zuckerman, Michael. *Peaceable Kingdoms*. New York: Alfred A. Knopf, 1970.

DOCUMENT 2.1
Reasons to Migrate

Puritans, like other migrants, were anxious to square their settlement of the New World

Source: *Collections of the Massachusetts Historical Society*, 2d ser., 9 (Boston, 1832), pp. 67–71.

To make this and other documents in the problem easier for students to read and understand, the language of the seventeenth century has been put into modern prose.

with law and conscience. The following selection is from a treatise entitled "Reasons and Considerations Touching the Lawfulness of Removing out of England into the Parts of America," published in England in 1622. It was signed "R. C."—almost certainly Robert Cushman, a member of the Mayflower group that had founded Plymouth two years before.

. . . And first, seeing we daily pray for the conversion of the heathens, we must consider whether there be not some ordinary means and course for us to take to convert them, or whether prayer for them be only referred to God's extraordinary work from Heaven. Now it seemeth unto me that we ought also to endeavor and use the means to convert them, or they come to us. To us they cannot come, our land is full; to them we may go, their land is empty.

This, then, is a sufficient reason to prove our going thither to live lawful. Their land is spacious and void, and they are few, and do but run over the grass, as do also the foxes and wild beasts. They are not industrious, neither have art, science, skill, or faculty to use either the land or the commodities of it, but all spoils, rots, and is marred for want of manuring, gathering, ordering, etc. . . . So is it lawful now to take a land which none useth and make use of it.

And as it is common land or unused and undressed country, so we have it by common consent, composition, and agreement, which agreement is double. First, the imperial governor, Massasoit, whose circuits in likelihood are larger than England and Scotland, hath acknowledged the King, Majesty of England, to be his master and commander; and that once in my hearing, yea, and in writing under his hand to Captain Standish. . . . Neither hath this been accomplished by threats and blows, or shaking of sword, or sound of trumpet. For as our faculty that way is small and our strength less, so our warring with them is after another manner, namely by friendly usage, love, peace, honest and just carriages, good counsel, etc.,

that so we and they may not only live in peace in that land, and they yield subjection to an earthly prince, but that as voluntaries they may be persuaded at length to embrace the Prince of Peace, Christ Jesus, and rest in peace with him forever.

Secondly, this composition is also more particular and applicatory, as touching ourselves there inhabiting. The emperor, by a joint consent, hath promised and appointed us to live at peace, where we will in all his dominions, taking what place we will, and as much land as we will, and bringing as many people as we will. . . .

It being, then, first a vast and empty chaos, secondly, acknowledged the right of our sovereign king, thirdly, by a peaceable composition in part possessed of diverse of his loving subjects, I see not who can doubt or call in question the lawfulness of inhabiting or dwelling there. But [I believe] that it may be as lawful for such as are not tied upon some special occasion here to live there as well as here. Yea, and as the enterprise is weighty and difficult, so the honor is more worthy, to plant a rude wilderness, to enlarge the honor and fame of our dread sovereign, but chiefly to display the efficacy of power of the gospel, both in zealous preaching, professing, and wise walking under it, before the faces of these poor blind infidels.

As for such as object the tediousness of the voyage thither, the danger of pirates' robbery, of the savages' treachery, etc., these are but lions in the way, and it were well for such men if they were in Heaven. For who can show them a place in this world where iniquity shall not compass them at the heels, and where they shall have a day without grief, or a lease of life for a moment? And who can tell but God what dangers may lie at our doors, even in our native country, or what plots may be abroad, or when God will cause our sun to go down at noondays, and in the midst of our peace and security lay upon us some lasting scourge for our so long neglect and contempt of His most glorious gospel?

Objection: But we have here great peace, plenty of the gospel, and many sweet delights and variety of comforts.

Answer: True indeed; and far be it from us to deny and diminish the least of these mercies. But have we rendered unto God thankful obedience for His long peace, whilst other peoples have been at wars? Have we not rather murmured, repined, and fallen at ears amongst ourselves, whilst our peace hath lasted with foreign power? Was there ever more suits in law, more envy, contempt, and reproach than nowadays? Abraham and Lot departed asunder when there fell a breach betwixt them which was occasioned by the straitness of the land. And surely I am persuaded that, howsoever the frailties of men are principal in all contentions, yet the straitness of the place is such as each man is fain to pluck his means, as it were, out of his neighbor's throat. There is such pressing and oppressing in town and country about farms, trade, traffic, etc., so as a man can hardly anywhere set up a trade but he shall pull down two of his neighbors.

The towns abound with young tradesmen, and the hospitals are full of the ancient. The country is replenished with new farmers, and the alms-houses are filled with old laborers. Many there are who get their living with bearing burdens, but more are fain to burden the land with their whole bodies. Multitudes get their means of life by prating, and so do numbers more by begging. Neither come these straits upon men always through intemperance, ill husbandry, indiscretion, etc., as some think; but even the most wise, sober, and discreet men go often to the wall, when they have done their best. Wherein, as God's providence swayeth all, so it is easy to see that the straitness of the place, having in it so many strait hearts, cannot but produce such effects more and more; so as every indifferent-minded man should be ready to say with father Abraham, "Take thou the right hand, and I will take the left." Let us not thus oppress, straiten, and afflict one another; but seeing there is a spacious land, the way to which is through the sea, we will end this difference in a day. . . .

DOCUMENT 2.2
Founding a Puritan Community

The first published history of the Puritan plantations in the New World was Edward Johnson's The Wonder-Working Providence of Sion's Saviour in New England *(1654). Johnson was for many years a leading citizen of Woburn, in Massachusetts Bay, and the following selection is his account of the founding of that community.*

There was a town and church erected called Woburn this present year; but because all the action of this wandering people meet with great variety of censures, the author will in this town and church set down the manner how this people have populated their towns and gathered their churches, that . . . other that are experienced in the holy Scriptures, may lay the actions of N. E. [New England] to the rule, and try them by the balance of the sanctuary. For assuredly they greatly desire they may be brought to the light, for great is the truth and will prevail, yet have they their errings as well as others; but yet their imperfections may not blemish the truths of Christ. Let them be glorified, and these, His people, will willingly take shame to themselves, wherein they have miscarried.

But to begin: this town, as all others, had its bounds fixed by the General Court, to the contents of four miles square (beginning at the end of Charlestown bounds). The grant is to seven men of good and honest report, upon condition that within two years they erect houses for habitation thereon, and so go on to make a town thereof, upon the act of Court.

Source: J. Franklin Jameson, ed., *Johnson's Wonder-Working Providence* (New York: C. Scribner's Sons, 1910), pp. 212–18.

These seven men have power to give and grant out lands unto any persons who are willing to take up their dwellings within the said precinct and to be admitted to all common privileges of the said town, giving them such an ample portion, both of meadow and upland, as their present and future stock of cattle and hands were like to improve, with eye had to others that might after come to populate the said town. This they did without any respect of persons, yet such as were exorbitant and of a turbulent spirit, unfit for a civil society, they would reject till they come to mend their manners. Such came not to enjoy and freehold. These seven men ordered and disposed of the streets of the town as might be best for improvement of the land, and yet civil and religious society maintained—to which end those that had land nearest the place for Sabbath assembly had a lesser quantity at home, and more farther off to improve for corn of all kinds. They refused not men for their poverty, but according to their ability were helpful to the poorest sort in building their houses, and distributed to them land accordingly. The poorest had six or seven acres of meadow and twenty-five acres of upland, or thereabouts. Thus was this town populated, to the number of sixty families or thereabouts, and after this manner are the towns of New England peopled. . . .

Now, to declare how this people proceeded in religious matters, and so consequently all the churches of Christ planted in New England: when they came once to hopes of being such a competent number of people as might be able to maintain a minister, they then surely seated themselves (and not before)—it being as unnatural for a right N. E. man to live without an able ministry as for a smith to work his iron without a fire. Therefore this people that went about placing down a town, began the foundation-stone, with earnest seeking of the Lord's assistance, by humbling of their souls before Him in days of prayer and imploring His aid in so weighty a work. Then they address

themselves to attend counsel of the most orthodox and ablest Christians, and more especially of such as the Lord had already placed in the ministry, not rashly running together themselves into a church before they had hopes of attaining an officer to preach the Word and administer the Seals unto them, choosing rather to continue in fellowship with some other church for their Christian watch over them till the Lord would be pleased to provide. They after some search met with a young man named Mr. Thomas Carter, then belonging to the church of Christ at Watertown, a reverend, godly man, apt to teach the sound and wholesome truths of Christ. Having attained their desires, in hopes of his coming unto them, were they once joined in church-estate—he exercising his gifts of preaching and prayer among them in the meantime, and more especially in a day of fasting and prayer. Thus these godly people interest their affections one with the other, both minister and people. After this they make ready for the work, and the 24th of the sixth month, 1642 they assemble together in the morning about eight of the clock. After the reverend Mr. Symmes had continued in preaching and prayer about the space of four or five hours, the persons that were to join in covenant, openly and professedly before the congregation and messengers of diverse neighbor churches . . . stood forth and first confessed what the Lord had done for their poor souls, by the work of His Spirit in the preaching of His Word and providences, one by one. And that all might know their faith in Christ was bottomed upon Him, as He is revealed in His Word—and that from their own knowledge—they also declare the same, according to that measure of understanding the Lord had given them. The elders, or any other messengers there present, question with them, for the better understanding of them in any points they doubt of; which being done, and all satisfied, they in the name of the churches to which they do belong, hold out the right hand of fellowship unto them, they declaring their covenant. . . .

The 22nd of the ninth month following, Mr. Thomas Carter was ordained pastor in presence of the like assembly. After he had exercised in preaching and prayer the greater part of the day, two persons in the name of the church laid their hands upon his head and said, "We ordain thee, Thomas Carter, to be pastor unto this church of Christ." . . . After this there were diverse added to the church daily, after this manner. The person desirous to join with the church cometh to the pastor and makes him acquainted therewith, declaring how the Lord hath been pleased to work his conversion—who discerning hopes of the person's faith in Christ, although weak, yet if any appear, he is propounded to the church in general for their approbation, touching his godly life and conversation, and then by the pastor and some brethren heard again, who make report to the church of their charitable approving of the person. But before they come to join with the church, all persons within the town have public notice of it. Then publicly he declares the manner of his conversion, and how the Lord hath been pleased, by the hearing of His Word preached and the work of His spirit in the inward parts of his soul, to bring him out of that natural darkness which all men are by nature in and under, as also the measure of knowledge the Lord hath been pleased to endow him withal. . . .

After this manner were many added to this church of Christ, and those seven that joined in church fellowship at first are now increased to 74 persons or thereabouts; of which, according to their own confession, as is supposed, the greater part having been converted by the preaching of the Word in N. E., by which may appear the powerful efficacy of the Word of Christ in the mouth of his ministers, and that this way of Christ in joining together in church covenant is not only for building up of souls in Christ, but also for converting of sinners and bringing them out of the natural

condition to be ingrafted into Christ. For if this one church have so many, then assuredly there must be a great number comparatively throughout all the churches in the country. After this manner have the churches of Christ had their beginning and progress hitherto; the Lord continue and increase them the world throughout. . . .

DOCUMENT 2.3
A Town Covenant

In the summer of 1636, the General Court of Massachusetts Bay granted the petition of some thirty families to found the town of Dedham. They began, as so many Puritans did, with a covenant embodying the general principles that would govern their lives together. The 124 names appended to this document (some added after the founding) have been omitted here.

One: We whose names are hereunto subscribed do, in the fear and reverence of our Almighty God, mutually and severally promise amongst ourselves and to each other to profess and practice one truth according to that most perfect rule, the foundation whereof is everlasting love.

Two: That we shall by all means labor to keep off from us all such as are contrary minded, and receive only such unto us as may be probably of one heart with us, as that we either know or may well and truly be informed to walk in a peaceable conversation with all meekness of spirit, for the edification of each other in the knowledge and faith of the Lord Jesus, and the mutual encouragement unto all temporal comforts in all things, seeking the good of each other, out of which may be derived true peace.

Three: That if at any time differences shall rise between parties of our said town, that then such party or parties shall presently refer all

Source: *Early Records of the Town of Dedham*, ed. Don Gleason Hill (Dedham, Mass., 1896), vol. 3, pp. 2–3.

such differences unto some one, two, or three others of our said society, to be fully accorded and determined without any further delay, if it possibly may be.

Four: That every man that now, or at any time hereafter, shall have lots in our said town shall pay his share in all such rates of money and charges as shall be imposed on him rateably in proportion with other men, as also become freely subject unto all such orders and constitutions as shall be necessarily had or made, now or at any time hereafter from this day forward, as well for loving and comfortable society in our said town as also for the prosperous and thriving condition of our said fellowship, especially respecting the fear of God, in which we desire to begin and continue whatsoever we shall by His loving favor take into hand.

Five: And for the better manifestation of our true resolution herein, every man so received to subscribe hereunto his name, thereby obliging both himself and his successors after him forever, as we have done.

DOCUMENT 2.4
Dispersion

Governor of Plymouth Colony for most of the period between 1621 and 1656, William Bradford (1590–1657) was easily the dominant figure among the ''Pilgrim Fathers.'' He was also their historian; his account Of Plymouth Plantation, *written between 1630 and 1651 and often called an American classic, is the source of the following selection. Like Puritan leaders elsewhere, Bradford was deeply troubled by the tendency of New World settlements to split and scatter across an everwidening landscape.*

Also the people of the Plantation began to grow in their outward estates, by reason of the flowing of many people into the country, especially

Source: William Bradford, *History of Plymouth Plantation* (Boston, 1856), pp. 302–4.

into the Bay of the Massachusetts. By which means corn and cattle rose to a great price, by which many were much enriched and commodities grew plentiful. And yet in other regards this benefit turned to their hurt, and this accession of strength to their weakness. For now as their stocks increased and the increase vendible, there was no longer any holding them together, but now they must of necessity go to their great lots. They could not otherwise keep their cattle, and having oxen grown they must have land for plowing and tillage. And no man now thought he could live except he had cattle and a great deal of ground to keep them, all striving to increase their stocks. By which means they were scattered all over the Bay quickly and the town in which they lived compactly till now was left very thin and in a short time almost desolate.

And if this had been all, it had been less, though too much; but the church must also be divided, and those that had lived so long together in Christian and comfortable fellowship must now part and suffer many divisions. First, those that lived on their lots on the other side of the Bay, called Duxbury, they could not long bring their wives and children to the public worship and church meetings here, but with such burden as, growing to some competent number, they sued to be dismissed and become a body of themselves. And so they were dismissed about this time, though very unwillingly. But to touch this sad matter, and handle things together that fell out afterward: to prevent any further scattering from this place and weakening of the same, it was thought best to give out some good farms to special persons that would promise to live at Plymouth, and likely to be helpful to the church or commonwealth, and so tie the lands to Plymouth as farms for the same; and there they might keep their cattle and tillage by some servants and retain their dwellings here. And so some special lands were granted at a place generally called Green's Harbor, where no allotments had been in the former division, a place very well meadowed and fit to keep and rear cattle good store. But alas, this remedy proved worse than the disease; for within a few years those that had thus got footing there rent themselves away, partly by force and partly wearing the rest with importunity and pleas of necessity, so as they must either suffer them to go or live in continual opposition and contention. And others still, as they conceived themselves straitened or to want accomodation, broke away under one pretence or other, thinking their own conceived necessity and the example of others a warrant sufficient for them. And this I fear will be the ruin of New England, at least of the churches of God there, and will provoke the Lord's displeasure against them.

DOCUMENT 2.5
Remarkable Providences

Among the thousands of immigrants who came to Massachusetts Bay during the 1630s was a young tailor named John Dane. After living some forty years in the colony, Dane wrote a short autobiography, ''A Declaration of Remarkable Providences in the Course of My Life.'' This document is an excerpt from the American part of his story; it shows the assumptions with which average Puritans sought to find meaning in their personal experiences.

. . . When these storms were a little over, there was a great coming to New England; and I thought that the temptations there were too great for me. I then bent myself to come to New England, thinking that I should be more free here than there from temptations; but I find here a devil to tempt, and a corrupt heart to deceive. But to return to the way and manner of my coming: when I was much bent to come I went to Stortford to my father to tell him.

Source: *The New England Historical and Genealogical Register* (1854), vol. 8, pp. 154–56.

My brother How was there then. My father and mother showed themselves unwilling. I sat close by a table where there lay a Bible. I hastily took up the Bible, and told my father, if, where I opened the Bible, there I met with anything either to encourage or discourage, that should settle me. I opening of it, not knowing no more than the child in the womb, the first I cast my eyes on was: ''Come out from among them, touch no unclean thing, and I will be your God and you shall be my people.'' My father and mother never more opposed me, but furthered me in the thing, and hastened after me as soon as they could.

My first coming was to Roxbury. There I took a piece of ground to plant of a friend. And I went to plant; and having kept long in the ship, the weather being hot, I spent myself and was very weary and thirsty. I came by a spring in Roxbury street, and went to it, and drank, and drank again and again many times; and I never drank wine in my life that more refreshed me, nor was more pleasant to me in my life as then I absolutely thought. But Mr. Norton being at Ipswich, I had a mind to live under him. And one time I came to Ipswich alone when there was no path but what the Indians had made; sometimes I was in it, sometimes out of it, but God directed my way. By the way I met in one place with forty or fifty Indians, all of a row. The foremost of them had a long staff that he held on his forehead like a unicorn's horn. Many of them were powwows; and as I passed by them I said, ''what cheer.'' They all, with a loud voice, laughing, cried out, ''what cheer, what cheer,'' that they made the woods ring with the noise. After I parted with them about a mile, I met with two Indians, one of them a very lusty sannup. I had a packet under my arm, and he took hold of it and peeked into it. I snatched it away, with an angry countenance, and he made no more of it. So I came to Ipswich, and agreed with Goodman Metcalf's vessel to bring me from Boston, where I had brought my goods. I brought a year's provision with me, but I soon parted with it. My meal I parted with for Indian [corn] the next year. I thought if one had it, another should not want. There came a neighbor to me and said he had no corn. He made great complaints. I told him I had one bushel and I had no more, but he should have half of it. And he had; and after, I heard of certain [people] that at the same time he had a bushel in his house. It troubled me to see his dealings and the dealings of other men.

Many troubles I passed through, and I found in my heart that I could not serve God as I should. What they were, were too tedious to mention. But upon a time, walking, with my gun on my shoulder charged, in the mile brook path beyond Deacon Goodhewe's, I had several thoughts came flocking into my mind that I had better make away myself than to live longer. I walked discoursing with such thoughts the best part of an hour, as I judged it. At length I thought I ought of two evils to choose the least, and that it was a greater evil to live and to sin against God than to kill myself— with many other satanical thoughts. I cocked my gun, and set it on the ground, and put the muzzle under my throat, and took up my foot to let it off. And then there came many things into my head; one [was] that I should not do evil that good might come of it. And at that time I no more scrupled to kill myself than to go home to my own house. Though this place is now a road, then it was a place that was not much walked in. I was then much lost in my spirit; and, as I remember, the next day Mr. Rogers preached, expressing himself that those were blessed that feared God and hoped in His mercy. Then I thought that that blessedness might belong to me, and it much supported my spirit.

Upon a time we were in some present want in the family, and my wife told me she had nothing for the children. She desired me to take my gun and see if I could get nothing. And I did go; and I had one pig then that was highly esteemed on, and that followed me a great way into the marshes. I thought the providence of God seemed to tell me that I should not go out today. So I returned back again with my pig; and when I came within less than forty rods of my house a company of great gray geese came over me, and I shot and brought down a gallant goose in the very nick of time.

In [sixteen] sixty-one, my house was burnt, as near as I can remember; and it was a most violent fire. At that time I could not but take notice of several providences concurring with [it]. I do not know that I did murmur at it, but was silent—looking up to God to sanctify it to me. It pleased God to stir up the hearts of my loving friends to help me to the carrying on of another. I had been ill before, and not well-fitting to go abroad, and could not endure wet on my feet. When the carts went into the woods I went with them, and many times in the swamps broke in up to the knees in cold water, in the winter. And it pleased God I grew better than before, which I looked on as a special hand of God. A second providence was this: that, though my provisions were all burnt, I had a stock of fine swine; and the corn that was burnt—when the flowers fell down and the fire out—these swine fell to eating the burned corn, and fattened to admiration, and that in a small time; so that I had good pork for the workmen to carry on the work.

Thus God hath all along preserved and kept me all my days. Although I have many times lost His special presence, yet He hath returned to me in mercy again. . . .

DOCUMENT 2.6
The Care and Training of Children

Cotton Mather, perhaps the best-known Puritan clergyman, is the author of the

Source: Worthington C. Ford, ed., *The Diary of Cotton Mather*, in Massachusetts *Historical Society Collections*, 7th ser., (1911), vol. 7, pp. 534–37.

*following selection entitled "Some Special
Points Relating to the Education of My
Children." It seems in most respects
representative of what is known of Puritan
childhood generally.*

I. I pour out continual prayers and cries to
the God of all grace for them, that He will
be a Father to my children, and bestow His
Christ and His Grace upon them, and guide
them with His councils, and bring them to His
glory. And in this action I mention them distinctly, every one by name, unto the Lord.

II. I begin betimes to entertain them with
delightful stories, especially scriptural ones,
and still conclude with some lesson of piety,
bidding them to learn that lesson from the story.
And thus every day at the table I have used
myself to tell a story before I rise, and make
the story useful to the olive plants about the
table.

III. When the children at any time acciden-
tally come in my way, it is my custom to let
fall some sentence or other that may be moni-
tory and profitable to them. This matter proves
to me a matter of some study and labor and
contrivance. But who can tell what may be
the effect of a continual dropping?

IV. I essay betimes to engage the children
in exercises of piety, and especially secret
prayer, for which I give them very plain and
brief directions, and suggest unto them the petitions which I would have them to make before
the Lord and which I therefore explain to their
apprehension and capacity. And I often call
upon them, "Child, don't you forget every
day to go alone and pray as I have directed
you!"

V. Betimes I try to form in the children a
temper of benignity. I put them upon doing
of services and kindnesses for one another and
for other children. I applaud them when I see
them delight in it. I upbraid all aversion to
it. I caution them exquisitely against all re-
venges of injuries. I instruct them to return

good offices for evil ones. I show them how
they will by this goodness become like to the
good God and His glorious Christ. I let them
discern that I am not satisfied except when
they have a sweetness of temper shining in
them.

VI. As soon as 'tis possible, I make the
children learn to write. And when they can
write, I employ them in writing out the most
agreeable and profitable things that I can invent
for them. In this way I propose to freight their
minds with excellent things, and have a deep
impression made upon their minds by such
things.

VII. I mightily endeavor it that the children
may betimes be acted by principles of reason
and honor. I first beget in them an high opinion
of their father's love to them, and of his being
best able to judge what shall be good for them.
Then I make them sensible, 'tis a folly for
them to pretend unto any wit and will of their
own; they must resign all to me, who will be
sure to do what is best; my word must be their
law. I cause them to understand that it is an
hurtful and a shameful thing to do amiss. I
aggravate this on all occasions, and let them
see how amiable they will render themselves
by well doing.

The first chastisement which I inflict for
an ordinary fault is to let the child see and
hear me in an atonishment, and hardly able
to believe that the child could do so base a
thing, but believing that they will never do it
again. I would never come to give a child a
blow, except in case of obstinacy or some gross
enormity. To be chased for a while out of my
presence I would make to be looked upon as
the sorest punishment in the family.

I would by all possible insinuations gain
this point upon them, that for them to learn
all the brave things in the world is the bravest
thing in the world. I am not fond of proposing
play to them, as a reward of any diligent application to learn what is good, lest they should
think diversion to be a better and a nobler thing

than diligence. I would have them come to propound and expect at this rate: "I have done well, and now I will go to my father; he will teach me some curious thing for it." I must have them count it a privilege to be taught; and I sometimes manage the matter so that my refusing to teach them something is their punishment. The slavish way of education, carried on with raving and kicking and scourging (in schools as well as families), 'tis abominable, and a dreadful judgment of God upon the world.

VIII. Though I find it a marvellous advantage to have the children strongly biassed by principles of reason and honor (which, I find, children will feel sooner than is commonly thought for), yet I would neglect no endeavors to have higher principles infused into them. I therefore betimes awe them with the eye of God upon them. I show them how they must love Jesus Christ, and show it by doing what their parents require of them. I often tell them of the good angels who love them and help them and guard them, and who take notice of them, and therefore must not be disobliged. Heaven and Hell I set before them as the consequences of their behavior here.

IX. When the children are capable of it, I take them alone, one by one; and after my charges unto them to fear God and serve Christ and shun sin, I pray with them in my study and make them the witnesses of the agonies, with which I address the throne of grace on their behalf.

X. I find much benefit, by a particular method, as of catechising the children, so of carrying the repetition of the public sermons unto them. The answers of the catechism I still explain with abundance of brief questions, which make them to take in the meaning of it; and I see that they do so. And when the sermons are to be repeated, I choose to put every truth into a question, to be answered still with "yes" or "no." In this way I awaken their attention as well as enlighten their understanding. And in this way I have an opportunity

to ask, "Do you desire such or such a grace of God?" and the like. Yea, I have an opportunity to demand, and perhaps to obtain, their consent unto the glorious articles of the new covenant. The spirit of grace may fall upon them in this action; and they may be seized by Him, and held as His temples through eternal ages.

DOCUMENT 2.7
A Confession of Wrong

Public confession was an extremely important part of the Puritan way, both in doctrine and in the social order. Town and church records from seventeenth-century New England are filled with avowals of personal blame and repentance. The following selection is a typical example. Its source, Mary Hoomeyhoo of Portsmouth, Rhode Island, belongs to the legions of anonymous people who have literally made history.

These may manifest unto all whom it may concern that whereas upon the complaint of William Brownell of this town of Portsmouth, made unto the magistrates, against Mary, the wife of John Hoomeyhoo, dwelling in the same town: raised and reported by the said Mary against the said William Brownell, much tending to the disgrace, disparagement, and great reproach of the said William Brownell, in saying that if the mare of John Tripp, Junior were dead, William Brownell had buggered her to death. Whereupon the said Mary Hoomeyhoo, being by warrant brought before the magistrates for examination of the truth thereof, it being a charge of a high nature if true, and accordingly being examined, she at first positively, with confidence denied that ever she had spoken any such words of the said William Brownell. But at length, it being by two evidences (viz.

Source: *The Early Records of the Town of Portsmouth* (Portsmouth, R.I., 1901), pp. 427–28.

John Tripp, Junior and Thomas Page) attested that she had so reported, she then owned it and confessed she had so said. And whereas she had said to one of the testimonies that her husband told her what she had reported, she owned she had so done. But in that also she had spoken that [which] was false, for neither her husband nor anyone else had so told her, but it was a matter made by herself. And [she] declared she knew no such evil by the said William Brownell, whereby she should raise any such false reports of him, and there-fore confessed she had done the said William Brownell great wrong, and desired that she being a poor woman the matter might upon her confession be passed by without further trouble. And this was done and confessed at the dwelling house of John Tripp, Senior on the 28th day of December, 1674. Witness our hands.

Joshua Coggeshall, *Assistant*

John Tripp, *Assistant*

A true copy entered and recorded per me, John Sanford, town clerk.

chapter 3

The Virginia Gentry and the Democratic Myth

D. Alan Williams
University of Virginia

Colonial Virginia invariably provides the model for the typical southern colony—an aristocratic, staple-producing, agrarian society divided geographically, economically, and socially into a coastal tidewater and an upcountry piedmont and valley. Originally conceived as a home for free laborers, craftsmen, and small farmers, Virginia exploited slave labor, nearly destroyed its yeoman farmer class, and turned over its government to a planter gentry by the eighteenth century. Land ownership was a prerequisite for voting and essential for political advancement and social prestige, and although there were many landowners, government remained a monopoly of the wealthy. The Anglican church was more firmly established in law than New England Congregationalism. All political officials were appointed, except members of the House of Burgesses. In sum, Virginia possessed most of the classic ingredients for social and political conflict.

Yet, in fact, sectional and social controversy were at a minimum in eighteenth-century Virginia. Some historians have even proclaimed the colony a democratic society with power in the hands of the people rather than the gentry. They have duly noted the presence of such Virginia revolutionaries, republicans, and lib-

ertarians as George Washington, Patrick Henry, George Mason, Thomas Jefferson, and James Madison. They have seen in Virginia's golden age (1720–70) the symbol of the ideal agrarian society whose monuments have been preserved in Williamsburg, Mount Vernon, Monticello, and the great James River plantations.

Clearly, Virginia presents us with contradictions. How do we explain them? Are historical appearances deceiving? Or is it a matter of semantics? Does government led by the wealthy necessarily mean aristocracy? Does democracy exist just because a majority of the populace has the right to vote?

Essentially, seventeenth-century Virginia society was a small-farmer society. Although some large landholders existed, most settlers cultivated the fields with the aid of an occasional indentured servant. Even the large farmers were self-made men who had attained their positions by hard work. Small farmer and large planter sat together on the county courts, the vestries, and in the assembly. Class distinctions were blurred in a society made up entirely of struggling farmers, most of whom found life crude and precarious.

Three major developments between 1660

39

and 1720 changed the kind of society and government Virginia would have: (1) establishment of the English imperial system, (2) Bacon's Rebellion, and (3) introduction of slavery and the large plantation.

The great test of whether Virginia would manage its own affairs came between 1660 and 1720. From the collapse of the London Company until the restoration of Charles II in 1660, Virginia, an isolated and insignificant royal colony, had been virtually free from English control. After 1660, the English formulated a uniform policy for their expanding empire. Political economists, royal officials, merchants, and parliamentary leaders were confident that they could construct a thoroughly planned and integrated economy by fitting all parts into the whole and enforcing mercantilistic principles through the navigation acts. The Crown would manage the operation. Charles II and James II appointed governors loyal to them and issued orders making the royal colonies responsive to their wishes. No longer could Virginia act without recourse to the motherland; the colony must fit the pattern.

In Virginia, it fell to popular Governor William Berkeley (1642–52; 1660–77) to reconstitute royal government after the English civil war and to enforce imperial policies with which he frequently disagreed. These were years of poverty, turmoil, and upheaval. By vigorous enforcement of the navigation acts and after fighting a series of naval wars with the Dutch, the English drove the Dutch from the Virginia tobacco market, but they were unable to replace the Dutch effectively as processors and distributors of tobacco in Europe until late in the seventeenth century. Consequently, the tobacco trade was seriously disrupted and Virginia was plunged into a prolonged depression in the 1670s and 1680s. Moreover, King Charles not only granted the Carolinas, the Jerseys, and Pennsylvania to his favorites, but he also gave away valuable Virginia lands. All colonists suffered, but none more than the small farmers

and the older colonial leaders. Bacon's Rebellion of 1676 was the result.

Bacon's Rebellion has been called the forerunner of the American Revolution, a class war between small farmers and planter aristocrats, a struggle for selfgovernment against a despotic governor, and a typical encounter between irresponsible frontiersmen and ill-treated Indians. Some have contended that the revolutionary generation, eager to find precedents for its own rebellion, created a myth out of a minor incident little different from numerous rural disturbances in North Carolina, New Jersey, Maryland, and in England itself.

An Indian war was the immediate cause of the rebellion. The obvious sources of upheaval were economic—depression, high taxes, war, and the destruction of the Dutch tobacco trade by the navigation acts. The underlying source was social—the old leaders' loss of status to new migrants coming into the colony after 1650.

For several years, both large landholders and small farmers had been gradually moving westward in search of rich tobacco land. They paid scant attention to Indian treaty rights or possible reprisals. Although settlement had reached only fifty miles beyond Jamestown and had barely penetrated inland from the rivers, incidents along the frontier mounted with both whites and Indians committing raids and atrocities. The frontiersmen were no more restrained than the Indians. Though undeclared war raged by early 1676, Governor Berkeley vacillated. He feared starting a general Indian war, which would bring needless bloodshed, as in King Philip's War in New England, and would upset the Indian trade that several of his friends engaged in. The harassed settlers, some large landholders among them, rallied behind Nathaniel Bacon, a financially embarrassed young councillor whose overseer had been killed by roving Indians. Against Berkeley's express orders, Bacon attacked and slaughtered two tribes allied with Virginia. He contended that they were hostile Indians, but some cynics noted that these Indians also held choice lands and large caches of furs. The governor promptly proclaimed the attackers in rebellion.

Bacon's forces, fully aroused and armed, turned from Indian problems to redress their political grievances, thereby revealing the social facet of the conflict. During the English Civil War, Virginians had had a taste of the independent local government they long savored. In the early part of the war, Berkeley set up efficient county and parish governments. After his triumph in England, Cromwell abolished royal government in the colony and replaced Berkeley with powerless governors elected by the assembly. In the absence of effective central leadership, county justices of the peace, parish vestrymen, and local burgesses became Virginia's political leaders.

However, when the Restoration came in 1660, Berkeley regained his office and attempted to reestablish the central government in Jamestown. In the spirit of Stuart politics, he appointed favorites to the county courts and supported local cliques, which established property qualifications for voting and replaced popularly elected vestries with self-perpetuating vestries.

Berkeley consolidated his position by keeping the same loyal assembly in session for fifteen years. To the chagrin of the early colonial leaders, his favorites were new men who had come to Virginia during and after the English Civil War. They were frequently well trained and had political and economic connections in England. Bacon's chief lieutenants were older, established planters disgruntled at losing their former power and prestige. These frustrated colonists seized on the unsettled Indian conditions to voice political protests. At a hastily called assembly in June 1676, they passed laws, ''democratical'' in nature, aimed at breaking the power of Berkeley's county oligarchies and reasserting the position of the old settlers. What ultimately was intended is un-known. Bacon died, the rebellion collapsed, and Berkeley, going berserk, executed twenty men in what was the only political blood purge in American history.

Bacon's Rebellion produced no great Virginia victory over royal authority. Crown restraints in Virginia and other colonies grew greater in the 1680s. Governor Thomas Lord Culpeper (1677–83) and Lord Howard of Effingham (1684–88) both were selected representatives of Stuart imperial policies. Lord Howard, in particular, was a persistent, obedient servant of the Stuarts, a confirmed believer in the divine right of kings, and completely unsympathetic toward representative government. The assembly, he asserted, should meet only when called by the king, should consider business previously approved by the Crown, and should execute only laws scrutinized by royal attorneys. Had such a policy been carried out, colonial self-government would have been squelched. But this did not happen, because bitter opponents of the 1670s joined forces to isolate and neutralize the governors, thereby depriving them of the loyalty of a proroyalist political faction in Virginia.

The Stuart threat to representative government ended with the Glorious Revolution of 1688. Englishmen thrust James I from the throne and called William and Mary to be their monarchs. This bloodless coup brought significant changes to Virginia. Howard left the colony, and his able successors, if they did not always appreciate the assembly, respected its right to speak for the colony and relied heavily on it for direction. The Virginia Assembly, sensitive to the growing powers of Parliament, sought the same for itself. While stubbornly resisting direct royal influence in the 1680s, Virginia, after 1690, waged a subdued, unspectacular, and highly effective campaign to neutralize the governor's influence in domestic politics. By 1720, the campaign had succeeded.

Social and economic changes understandably paralleled and interacted with political change. By the early eighteenth century, the Indian threat had vanished, expansion without fear was possible, altered marketing conditions in Europe created new demands, and English and Scottish merchants turned to the Virginia market with new vigor. The colony was looked on as an economically underdeveloped area in need of credit. British merchants who controlled the tobacco trades extended credit with reasonable assurance of recovering their investment. Most of this credit went to the larger planters and their friends, who, in turn, acquired more land, expanded operations, upgraded their standard of living, and built the great plantations for which the colony became known.

The slave was the decisive difference between mid-seventeenth-century and mid-eighteenth-century Virginia. Before 1680, slavery on a large scale was rare, but it was commonplace thereafter. Slavery and mass-production methods characterized the tobacco plantation economy after 1720. Virginians condoned slavery as an established fact, though few defended it. The real sufferers, they thought, were not the slaves but the small planters and yeoman farmers who worked the fields with their families and with an occasional indentured servant. The yeoman might draw some satisfaction from knowing that the slave was permanently tied to the bottom rung of the social scale, but he also knew that his position was not much higher because of that same slave. While the same planter might buy a few slaves, he lacked the resources to match his more affluent neighbors, and he lost economic power and social position to the growing number of large slaveholding, landed gentry. Those who couldn't afford slaves tended to move west and south into Virginia or the Carolinas. Not surprisingly, these independent small farmers frequently became both antislave and anti-Negro in outlook.

One major change came after 1720, when thousands of Scots-Irish and German immigrants pushed down from Pennsylvania into the fertile Shenandoah Valley and into the western piedmont. Socially and religiously, these new settlers differed from settlers to the east. They were Presbyterians, Lutherans, Quakers, and German pietists—all dissenters from the established Church of England. Highly individualistic, they were alien to eastern traditions. Tobacco was not their king, since it could not be grown in the hilly back country. Yet, there was no sectionalism in colonial Virginia, no regulator uprisings similar to those of the Carolinas, no Paxton boys marching on Williamsburg as they did on Philadelphia, no tenant riots like those in New York and New Jersey. Unlike the Carolina frontier, the Virginia frontier was an overlay of new immigrants and old Virginians. At the same time that Germans and Scots-Irish were drifting south into the valley, settlers from eastern Virginia were moving west onto the piedmont, and speculators were making bold plans to sell western lands. Acting with dispatch, the Virginia General Assembly wisely established counties and extended representation to the new areas—leaving the settlers with none of the complaints about governmental inequities that upset inhabitants in the Carolinas and Pennsylvania. In an earlier day, the influx of dissenters might have caused serious problems, but religious fanaticism (never strong in Virginia) was on the wane by the eighteenth century, and toleration was on the rise. Some dissenters were harassed, but most were left free to worship as they pleased, provided they paid their tithes to the Anglican Church. Moreover, the colony's political leaders were also its leading land speculators. To sell land, they had to have settlers; to get settlers, they had to provide attractions. Their attractions were cheap land, available government, religious toleration, and a minimum of interference by spiritual and secular authorities. Most immigrants wanted no more than that. There were no sectionalism, for there were no sectional grievances. Sectionalism as a divisive force was not apparent until after the Revolution.

The golden age of the Virginia plantation

society ran from about 1720 to the eve of the Revolution. The populace—free and slave, native and immigrant—doubled, tripled, and then quadrupled in number. Tobacco was king, land was wealth. With the widest coastal plain in the colonies and fertile valleys just beyond the first mountain ridge, Virginians, unlike South Carolinians, had little difficulty in acquiring land. Dominating this society was the planter gentry—the first aristocracy of the rural South; the counterparts of Charleston's planter-merchants, the equals of Philadelphia and Boston merchants.

The first planter gentry of Virginia had been a score or so of men, primarily members of the council—the Carters, Randolphs, Byrds, Lees, Custises, Pages, and Ludwells—whose families in Virginia had found positions denied them in England and who had risen to the top through shrewd business practices and the accumulation of vast tracts of land. They had helped carve a civilization out of the wilderness with little help from the Crown; consequently, they often thought royal governors were interlopers gathering spoils after the labor had been done. By intermarriage, they had created a tight coterie of leaders that no governor could break. Sensitive to insult and quick to anger, they zealously guarded their interests through the distribution of Crown land, a function of the council. Generous in parceling land to themselves and their friends, they were equally generous in granting the king's land to all Virginians.

By the mid-eighteenth century, as the colony grew and tobacco trading flourished, the number of affluent planter families reaches several hundred. The council could no longer contain all the gentry families. Many burgesses not only were as wealthy as councilors but also were their social equals. As the lower house gained ascendancy over the upper house, the new generation of Randolphs, Harrisons, Lees, and Pages preferred to sit in the House of Burgesses alongside other rising gentry. No longer did small planters gain election to this "tobacco club." Neither did small farmers serve as justices or vestrymen, for offices at all levels were taken up by the gentry and their sons. Distinctions between classes, blurred in the seventeenth century, were much clearer in the eighteenth century.

Even though well-defined class lines existed in colonial Virginia, government by the gentry was not necessarily detrimental to the popular interests or so difficult to perform objectively as in a more diverse and complex social order. First, the common bond of land and farming gave the large and small cultivators similar economic interests and made the society homogeneous, at least east of the Blue Ridge Mountains. Second, the lesser farmer naturally elected his more affluent neighbors to the House of Burgesses, since the poorly run plantation was no recommendation for a public office that mainly promoted agricultural prosperity. Third, the hard-working small farmers lacked the time to serve in political offices. Finally, since social mobility was fairly fluid in a fast-growing society, the independent farmers and small slaveholders saw no reason to oust or destroy the larger planters. They wanted to join them.

The liberal humanism of the planter gentry did much to assure the people that they had little to fear from planter leadership. The gentry willingly served in government because they believed in *noblesse oblige*—with power and privilege went responsibility. Honor, duty, and devotion to class interest had called them to office, and they took the call seriously. Not without a certain amount of condescension, they thought that government would be run by persons less qualified if they refused to serve. They alone had the time, the financial resources, and the education necessary for public office. Moreover, they were the social leaders and were, therefore, expected to set an example in manners and morals, to uphold the church, to be generous with benevolences, to serve the government with enlightened self-interest, and in general to be paragons of duty and dignity.

Not surprisingly, they enjoyed the prestige that came with office. To be in a position of authority, to control government, to enact laws, to have the power of life and death over men are intangibles for which there can be no financial compensation. Not that such compensations were omitted from the scheme of things. The real advantage of political service to most officeholders came from the opportunity to acquire land and to extend their business acquaintances. It would not be remiss to say that the gentry had a split personality—one side governed by duty, the other side by lust for land. Perhaps this is what is meant by "enlightened self-interest."

Trained for public duties on their self-contained plantations, the gentry brought to office well-developed talents and tastes for wielding power. Though they remembered their own interests, they nevertheless believed that they were bound to respect and protect the interests of others. They held that sovereignty was vested in the people, who delegated certain powers to government. They extolled republicanism and willingly enfranchised the people. Their humanism was a product of experience, common sense, and the common law. Liberal humanism not only seemed the right and just attitude; equally important, it worked. Of course, the Virginia gentry were in a position to be charitable. They trusted the people because the people trusted them. One may speculate whether their view of individual liberties would have been so liberal had Virginia been less homogeneous in character or had the lower classes challenged their leadership.

The small farmers and slaveholders had one protection against gentry oligarchy: they were in the majority and they had the right to vote. True, they elected only the burgesses, but that single choice was an important guarantee of their rights, since the House of Burgesses was the strongest political body in Virginia. Thomas Jefferson once remarked that the election process tended to eliminate class conflicts and extremism; the aristocrat with no concern for the small farmer was not apt to be elected, and the man who demagogically courted the popular vote was ostracized by the gentry. Therefore, the House of Burgesses became, at the same time, the center of planter rule and popular government. It operated as a restraint of oligarchy.

Some historians believe that Virginia, like Massachusetts, was a democratic society. Economic, social, and political opportunity, they say, existed for all. Far from the gentry's dominating the society, the small- and middle-sized farmers and slaveholders may have deferred to their judgment, but the reverse was actually the case. Since the gentry were in a minority, they had to defer to the wishes of the majority—the small landholders—if they wanted to retain the reins of office. So say Robert and B. Kathryn Brown.

A comparison of the relative positions of the small landowners in the seventeenth and eighteenth centuries shows that without doubt they had immeasureably improved their economic lot while they were being socially outstripped by more affluent neighbors. Politically, they shifted from holders of office to a check on officeholders.

Yet, was this democracy? What good was majority vote when the majority had so little to vote for? Choosing a burgess to sit at the occasional meetings of the General Assembly in Williamsburg was not nearly so important as having a voice in county affairs, where most matters affecting small farmers were decided. Could a society be democratic when every official except one was appointed by self-perpetuating justices, vestrymen, councilors, and the royal governor, none of whom was responsible to the electorate? Could it be democratic when only men of means held office and when advancement seemed more dependent on wealth and birth than on talent? To a large extent, the small farmers were effectively separated from the power structure with little means of uniting in a rural society.

The gentry, a minority, were a group of like-minded men working in close alliance, careful not to disturb the social equilibrium. When they contested each other for a seat in the assembly, they offered the electorate only a choice between planter A and planter B, between Tweedledum and Tweedledee. They were the perfect example of what has been consistently true in American society: a cohesive minority dominating an amorphous majority. Perhaps the question that ought to be asked about this planter gentry government is not whether it was democratic but whether it was effective. William Penn once wrote, "governments depend on men rather than men upon governments, let them be good and government cannot be bad." If this is the primary question, then must not one say that the planter gentry, with their own type of consensus politics, provided eighteenth-century Virginia with enlightened and dynamic leadership? Could a society be democratic when 40 percent of its members were enslaved?

Or is the half-century of the golden age a period too short to judge the gentry society? After the Revolution, Virginia declined as the soil lost its richness, tobacco lacked foreign markets, and the younger generations moved west and south to more promising opportunities. When the planter aristocracy ceased to be infused and refreshed with the rising gentry, it became inert, lacking in insight, inbred, and distrustful of progress elsewhere. In the place of a masculine Washington or a visionary Jefferson, nineteenth-century leadership could offer as its spokesmen only an effete John Randolph and a myopic John Tyler. Equally significant, the lower class, having deferred so long to the excellent leadership of the eighteenth century, could not recapture what it had let atrophy—its political consciousness. Not until the 1960s did Virginia voters exercise their voting privileges in proportions equaling their colonial ancestors.

SUGGESTED READINGS

Boorstin, Daniel J. *The Americans: The Colonial Experience.* New York: Random House, 1958.

Brown, Robert, and B. Kathryn Brown. *Virginia, 1705–1786: Democracy or Aristocracy.* East Lansing: Michigan State University Press, 1964.

Craven, Wesley. *Southern Colonies in the Seventeenth Century.* Baton Rouge: Louisiana State University Press, 1949.

Greene, Jack P. *The Quest for Power: The Lower Houses of Assembly in the Southern Royal Colonies.* Chapel Hill: University of North Carolina Press, 1963.

Isaac, Rhys. *Transformation of Virginia, 1740–1790.* Chapel Hill: University of North Carolina Press, 1982.

Malone, Dumas. *Jefferson the Virginian.* Boston: Little Brown, 1948.

Edmund S. Morgan. *American Slavery-American Freedom; The Ordeal of Colonial Virginia.* New York: W. W. Norton, 1975.

Sydnor, Charles S. *Gentlemen Freeholders: Political Practices in Washington's Virginia.* Chapel Hill: University of North Carolina Press, 1952.

Washburn, Wilcomb. *The Governor and the Rebel.* Chapel Hill: University of North Carolina Press, 1957.

DOCUMENT 3.1
Nathaniel Bacon: Manifesto Concerning the Present Trouble in Virginia

After being declared a rebel by Governor William Berkeley, Nathaniel Bacon rallied his forces near Middle Plantation (Williamsburg) and issued a manifesto setting forth his reasons for taking up arms against all Indians, even Indians supposedly allied with Virginia. Bacon was careful to note that his greivance was with Berkeley, not the King, whom he felt certain

Source: *Virginia Magazine of History and Biography,* vol. 1 (1894), pp. 55–58.

would redress the rebels' greivances if he knew the true nature of the events.

If Verture be a sin, if Piety be giult, all the Principles of morality goodness and Justice be perverted, Wee must confesse That those who are now called Rebells may be in danger of those high imputations, Those loud and severall Bulls would affright Innocents and render the defence of our Brethren and the enquiry into our sad and heavy oppressions Treason. But if there bee as sure there is, a just God to appeal too, if Religion and Justice be a sanctuary here, If to plead ye cause of the oppressed, If sincerely to aime at his Majesties Honour and the Publick good without any reservation or by Interest, If to stand in the Gap after soe much blood of our dear Brethren bought and sold, If after the losse of a great part of his Majesties Colony deserted and dispeopled, freely with our lives and estates to indeavor to save the remaynders bee Treason God Almighty Judge and left guilty dye, But since wee cannot in our hearts find one single spott of Rebellion or Treason or that we have in any manner aimed at the subverting ye setled Government or attempting of the Person of any either magistrate or private man not with standing the severall Reproaches and Threats of some who for sinister ends were disaffected to us and censured our ino [cent] and honest designes, and since all people in all places where wee have yet bin can attest our civill quiet peaseable behaviour farre different from that of Rebellion and tumultuous persons let Trueth be bold and all the world know the real Foundations of pretended qiult, Wee appeale to the Country itselfe what and of what nature their Oppressions have bin or by what Caball and mistery the designs of many of those whom wee call great men have bin transacted and caryed on, but let us trace these men in Authority and Favour to whose hands the dispensation of the Countries wealth has been commited; let us observe the sudden Rise of

their Estates composed with the Quality in which they first entered this Country. Or the Reputation they have held here amongst wise and discerning men, And lett us see wither their extractions and Education have not bin vile, And by what pretense of learning and vertue they could soe soon into Imployments of so great Trust and consequence, let us consider their sudden advancement and let us also consider wither any Publick work for our safety and defence or for the Advancement and propogation of Trade, liberall Arts or sciences is here Extant in any [way] adequate to our vast chardg, now let us compare these things togit [her] and see what spounges have suckt up the Publique Treasure and wither it hath not bin privately contrived away by unworthy Favourites and juggling Parasites whose tottering Fortunes have been repaired and supported at the Publique chardg, now if it be so Judg what greater giult can bee then to offer to pry into these and to unriddle the misterious wiles of a powerfull Cabal let all people Judge what can be of more dangerous Import then to suspect the soe long Safe proceedings of Some of our Grandees and wither People may with safety open their Eyes in soe nice a Concerne.

DOCUMENT 3.2
Bacon's Rebellion: The King's View

King Charles II, uncertain about why his colony was in rebellion, dispatched a commission to investigate the source of the troubles. By the time the commissioners arrived, Bacon had died, the rebellion had ended, and Berkeley was back in control. The enraged governor refused to cooperate with the commission, which finally had to depose him and send him

---

Source: *A True Narrative of the Rise, Progresse, and Cessation of the Late Rebellion in Virginia . . . by his Majestys Commissioners, 1677.*

back to England. The commission report questioned the actions and motives of both Bacon and Berkeley.

The assembly mett March 1676 to consult for the Safety and defence of the Country ag't the Incursions and destructions of the Indians, dayly Comitted upon the Inhabitants of Virginia, there having beene within the space of about 12 months before, neer 300 Christian persons murder'd by the Indians Enemy. What care the Assembly tooke to prevent these massacres was onely to build Forts at the heads of each River and on the Frontiers and confines of the country, for erecting of w'ch and maintaining Guards on them a heavie leavy was laid by act of Assembly on the People; . . .

The unsatisfyed People finding themselves still lyable to the Indian Crueltyes, and the cryes of their wives and children growing grievous and intollerable to them, gave out in Speeches that they were resolved to Plant tobacco rather than pay the Tax for maintaining of Forts, and that the erecting of them was a great Grievance, Juggle and cheat, and of no more use or service to them than another Plantation with men at it, and that it was merely a Designe of the Grandees to engrosse all their Tobacco into their owne hands.

Thus the sense of this oppression and the dread of a common approaching calamity made the giddy-headed multitude madd, and precipitated them upon that rash overture of Running out upon the Indians themselves, at their owne voluntary charge and hazard of their Lives and Fortunes, onely they first by Petition humbly craved leave or comission to be ledd by any comander or comanders as the Governor should please to appoint over them. . . . But instead of Granting this Petition the Governor by Proclamation under great Penalty forbad the like Petitioning for the future. . . .

The Rout being got together now wanted nor waited for nothing but one to head and lead them out on their design. It soe happen'd

that one Nathaniel Bacon Junr, a person whose lost and desperate fortunes had thrown him into that remote part of the world about 14 months before, and fram'd him fitt for such a purpose, as by the Sequel will appeare, which may make a short character of him no impertinent Digression.

Hee was a person whose erratique fortune had carryed and shewne him many Forraigne Parts, and of no obscure Family. Upon his first comming into Virginia hee was made one of the Councill, the reason of that advancement (all on a suddain) being best known to the Governour [Bacon was Berkeley's cousin], which honor made him the more considerable in the eye of the Vulgar, and gave some advantage to his pernicious designes. Hee was said to be about four or five and thirty years of age [he was 29 years old], indifferent tall but slender, blackhair'd and of an ominous, pensive, melancholly Aspect, of a pestilent and prevalent Logical discourse tending to atheisme in most companyes, not given to much talke, or to make suddain replyes, of a most imperious and dangerous hidden Pride of heart, despising the wisest of his neighbours for their Ignorance, and very ambitious and arrogant. But all these things lay hidd in him till after hee was a councillor, and untill he became powerfull and popular. . . .

DOCUMENT 3.3
Virginia's Gentry and the Call to Duty

Sir John Randolph (1693–1737) was a speaker of the House of Burgesses and one of the few knighted Virginia gentry. At the opening of the House of Burgesses in 1736, Sir John felt constrained to remind the sitting members of their basic obligations to the people.

Source: *Journal of the House of Burgesses*, August 5, 1736.

We must consider ourselves chosen by all the People; sent hither to represent them, to give their Consent in the weightiest of their Concerns; and to bind them by Laws which may advance their Common Good. Herein they trust you with all that they have, place the greatest Confidence in your Wisdoms and Discretions, and testify the highest Opinion of your Virtue. And surely, a Desire of pleasing some, and the Fear of offending others; Views to little Advantages and Interests; adhering too fondly to ill-grounded Conceits; the Prejudices of Opinions too hastily taken up; and Affectation to Popularity; Private Animosities or Personal Resentments; which have often too much to do in Popular Assemblies, and sometimes put a Bias upon Mens Judgments can upon no Occasion, turn us aside in the Prosecution of this important Duty, from what shall appear to be the true Interest of the People: Tho' it may be often impossible to conform to their Sentiments, since, when we come to consider and compare them, we shall find them so various and irreconcileable.

The Honour of the House of Burgesses hath of late been raised higher than can be observed in former Times; and I am persuaded you will not suffer it to be lessened under your Management.

I will be watchful of your Privileges, without which we should be no more than a dead Body; and advertise you of every Incident that may have the least Tendency to destroy or diminish them. . . .

DOCUMENT 3.4
The People: A European Rediscovers Them in Virginia

The Marquis de Chastellux, a French nobleman and soldier, fought with the Americans in the

Source: Marquis Francis-Jean Chastellux, *Travels in North America in the Years 1780, 1781, and 1782*, trans. and ed. Howard C. Rice, Jr. (Chapel Hill: University of North Carolina Press, for the Institute of Early American History and Culture, 1963), vol. 2, pp. 397–98.

late stages of the Revolution and then traveled throughout the United States trying to discover who the Americans were. Like most Europeans, he found that the American was not simply a European peasant who had crossed the Atlantic but a new class altogether.

I continued on for seventeen miles more, the whole way in the defiles of the Western Mountains [the Blue Ridge near Charlottesville, Virginia] before finding a place where I could rest my horses. At last I stopped at a lonely house, belonging to an Irishman by the name of Macdonald where I found eggs, ham, chicken, and whiskey, and where I had an excellent dinner. He was an honest and obliging man, and his wife, who had a very agreeable and mild countenance, had nothing rustic either in her bearing or manners. For, in the midst of the woods and rustic tasks, a Virginian never resembles a European peasant: he is always a free man, who has a share in the government, and the command of a few Negroes. Thus he unites in himself the two distinct qualities of citizen and master, and in this respect clearly resembles the majority of the individuals who formed what were called *the people* in the ancient republics; a people very different from the people of our day, though the two are very improperly confused in the frivolous declamations of our half-philosophers, who, in comparing ancient with modern times, have invariably mistaken *the people* for mankind in general, and have praised the oppressors of humanity, thinking that they were defending its cause. How many ideas need to be rectified! How many words, whose meanings are still vague and indeterminate! The ''dignity of man'' has been urged a hundred times, and this expression has enjoyed great favor. The ''dignity of man,'' however, is a comparative matter. If taken as applying to individuals, dignity increases as a man considers his relationship to the classes beneath him. It is the plebeian who makes the dignity of the noble, the slave that of the free man, and the Negro that of the white. . . .

What then is the principle on which Reason . . . can finally rely? It is equality of rights, the general interest which rules all, private interest linked to the general good, social order as necessary as the symmetry of the beehive, etc., etc. If all this does not lend itself easily to eloquence, we must console ourselves, and prefer sound, to highsounding, morality.

I had reason to be pleased with the sound morality of Mr. Macdonald; he served me with the best he had, did not make me pay too dear, and gave me all the information I needed to continue on my way.

DOCUMENT 3.5
The Small Farmer

The Reverend Mr. Devereux Jarratt (1733– 1801), son of a small tidewater planter, became a minister in the Church of England. Near the end of his life he wrote an autobiographical letter to a friend, which tells us something about the attitude of the "simple" folk toward Virginia's gentry.

I was born in *New Kent,* a county in Virginia, about 25 miles below Richmond, on January 6th, 1732–3, O.S. I was the youngest child of *Robert Jarratt* and *Sarah* his wife. . . .

My father was brought up to the trade of a carpenter, at which he wrought till the very day before he died. He was a mild, inoffensive man, and much respected among his neighbors. . . . None of my ancestors, on either side, were either rich or great, but had the character of honesty and industry, by which they lived in credit among their neighbors, free from real want, and above the frowns of the world. This was also the habit, in which my parents were. They always had plenty of plain food and raiment, wholesome and good, suitable to their humble station, and the times in which they

---

Source: *Life of Devereux Jarratt* (Baltimore: 1806), pp. 12–16.

lived. Our food was altogether the produce of the farm, or plantation, except a little sugar, which was rarly used; and our raiment was altogether my mother's manufacture, except our hats and *shoes,* the *latter* of which we never put on, but in the winter season. We made no use of *tea* or *coffee* for breakfast, or at any other time; nor did I know a single family that made any use of them. Meat, bread and milk was the ordinary food of all my acquaintance. I suppose the *richer sort* might make use of *those* and other luxuries, but to such people I had no access. We were accustomed to look upon, what were called *gentle folks,* as beings of a superior order. For my part, I was quite shy of *them,* and kept off at a humble distance. A *periwig,* in those days, was a distinguishing badge of *gentle folk*—and when I saw a man riding the road, near our house, with a wig on, it would so alarm my fears, and give me such a disagreeable feeling, that, I dare say, I would run off, as for my life. Such ideas of the difference between *gentle* and *simple,* were, I believe, universal among all of my rank and age. . . .

My parents neither sought nor expected any titles honors, or great things, either for themselves or children. Their highest ambition was to teach their children to read, write, and understand the fundamental rules of arithmetic. I remember also, they taught us short prayers, and made us very perfect in repeating the *Church Catechism.* They wished us all to be brought up in some honest calling, that we might earn our bread, by the sweat of our brow, as they did. . . .

DOCUMENT 3.6
Class and Caste in the South: The Gentry Viewpoint

Few colonial Virginians were as cosmopolitan as William Byrd II of Westover (1674–1744). Indian trader, land speculator, planter, builder of one of the most beautiful homes in Virginia, politician, scholar, writer, and raconteur, Byrd also was an inveterate recorder of events. He had a concise, descriptive, often biting style, and his works have given us insights into many facets of Virginia class structure. This can be seen in the following three items—on the poor white subsistence farmer on the Carolina frontier, on the ostracism of a girl who has brought "shame" to her family by marrying below her class, and on the impact of slavery on the white population.

THE HISTORY OF THE DIVIDING LINE[1]

We landed at the Plantation of cornelius Keith, where I beheld the wretchedest Scene of Poverty I had ever met with in this happy Part of the World. The Man, his Wife and Six Small Children, liv'd in a Penn, like so many Cattle, without any Roof over their Heads but that of Heaven. And this was their airy Residence in the Day time, but then there was a Fodder Stack not far from this Inclosure, in which the whole Family shelter'd themselves a night's and in bad weather.

However, 'twas almost worth while to be as poor as this Man was, to be as perfectly contented. All his Wants proceeded from Indolence, and not from Misfortune. He had good Land, as well as good Health and good Limbs to work it, and, besides, had a Trade very useful to all the Inhabitants round about. He cou'd make and set up Quern Stones very well, and had proper Materials for that purpose just at Hand, if he cou'd have taken the pains to fetch them. . . .

I am sorry to say it, but Idleness is the general character of the men in the Southern Parts of this Colony as well as in North Carolina. The Air is so mild, and the Soil so fruitful,

that very little Labour is requir'd to fill their Bellies, especially where the Woods afford such Plenty of Game. These Advantages discharge the Men from the Necessity of killing themselves with Work, and then for the other Article of Raiment, a very little of that will suffice in so temperate a Climate. But so much as is absolutely Necessary falls to the good women's Share to provide. They all Spin, weave and knit, whereby they make a good Shift to cloath the whole Family; and to their credit be it recorded, many of them do it very completely, and thereby reproach their Husbands' Laziness in the most inoffensive way, that is to say, by discovering a better Spirit of Industry in themselves. . . .

A PROGRESS TO THE MINES[2]

The Widow smiled graciously upon me, and entertain'd me very handsomely. Here I learnt all the tragical Story of her Daughter's humble Marriage with her Uncle's Overseer. Besides the meanness of this mortal's Aspect, the Man has not one visible Qualification, except Impudence, to recommend him to a Female's Inclinations. But there is sometimes such a Charm in that Hibernian Endowment, that frail Woman cant withstand it, tho' it stand alone without any other Recommendation. Had she run away with a Gentleman or a pretty Fellow, there might have been some Excuse for her, tho' he were of inferior Fortune: but to stoop to a dirty Plebian, without any kind of merit, is the lowest Prostitution. I found the Family justly enraged at it; and tho' I had more good Nature than to join in her Condemnation, yet I cou'd devise no Excuse for so senceless a Prank as this young Gentlewoman had play'd. . . .

---

[1] Source: William Byrd II, *The History of the Dividing Line* (1728) in *The Westover Manuscripts* ed. Edmund Ruffin (Petersburg, Virginia, 1841).

[2] Source: William Byrd II, *A Progress to the Mines* (1732) in *The Westover Manuscripts* ed. Edmund Ruffin (Petersburg, Virginia, 1841).

WILLIAM BYRD TO JOHN PERCEVAL[3]

. . . Your Lordship's opinion concerning Rum & negroes is certainly very just & your excluding both of them from your colony of Georgia will be very Happy: tho' with Respect to Rum, the Saints of New England, I fear will find out some trick to evade your Act of Parliament. . . . I wish that we could be blessed with the same Prohibition. They import so many negro's hither, that I fear this Colony will sometime or other be confounded by the name of New Guinea. I am sensible of many bad consequences of multiplying these Ethiopians amongst us. They blow up the pride, & ruin the Industry of our White People, who Seeing a Rank of poor Creatures below them, detest work for fear it should make them look like Slaves. Then that poverty which will ever attend upon Idleness, disposed them, as much to pilfer as it dos the Portuguise, who account it much more like a gentleman to steal, than to dirty their hands with Labour of any kind. Another unhappy Effect of many Negroes is, the necessity of being severe. Numbers make them insolent & then foul Means must do what fair will not. We have however nothing like the Inhumanity here, that is practiced in the [West Indian] Islands & God forbid we ever shou'd. But these base Tempers require to be rid with a tort rein, or they will be apt to throw their Rider. Yet even this is terrible to a good natured Man, who must submit to be either a Fool or a Fury. And this will be more our unhappy case, the more the Negros are increast amongst us. But these private mischeifs are nothing, if compared to the publick danger. . . . It were, therefore, worth the consideration, of a British Parliament, My Lord, to put an end, to this unchristian Traffick, of making Merchandise of our Fellow Creatures. . . .

---

[3] Source: Letter from William Byrd to John Perceval, Earl of Egmont, July 12, 1736 *(Virginia Magazine of History and Biography)*.

Great Awakening and Enlightenment

Milton Cantor
University of Massachusetts

Ideas do not spring, like Athene, fully armed from the head of Zeus. They are victims and possessors of the past. The principal signposts of both the Great Awakening and the Enlightment in colonial America were rooted in the ideas of a host of European thinkers. Characterizing the overseas Enlightenment were persistent intellectual curiosity, philosophical and scientific speculation, and a desire to increase knowledge. Contrariwise, hostility to rationalism, formalism and skepticism, and distrust of anything resembling creedal Christianity had axial roles in the definition of evangelical religion. That Americans shared these ideas reveals their deep ties to the culture of their past. Yet, as we shall see, the themes of each are at the heart of the national heritage, and the American experience helped to order, clarify, sift, and reshape them.

Such a reshaping was inevitable. The New World was unique. It had a new setting and presented new necessities. It possessed a vast western domain, which held a means of achieving bliss without an appeal to heaven. Incorporating a dynamic and essentially unstratified society rather than a hereditary monarchy or a static caste system, it encouraged belief in salvation as an act of individual effort and in progress (both social and individual) within the framework of the existing social organiza-

tion. The Enlightenment and the Awakening drew their strength from these sources; both also shared the Puritan belief that God had a special destiny in store for the New World, though the Enlightenment often subtly secularized the Chosen People theme.

To return to the question of the transfer of values and culture, the Great Awakening had demonstrable ties with the Old World. Between 1730 and 1760, practically all of western Europe was swept by some kind of religious emotionalism. There were, for example, scattered awakenings in Wales and Scotland. In Germany, there was a mystical or quietistic pietism, an inner-light movement that was exported to America by means of various sects—Mennonites, Schwenkfelders, Moravians, Dunkers, and others. From England, where it existed in a more dramatic form, came the Awakening religion of Methodism, as proselytized by the Wesley brothers and George Whitefield. The colonial religious rising of the 1730s and 1740s, while somewhat attributable to forces at work on its own soil, was also part of an international movement.

The Enlightenment was equally cosmopolitan, a culmination of factors long at work in English and continental society. Both it and the Awakening, therefore, raise demanding and difficult questions. First and most important,

52

was there a unique American Enlightenment, a product of the special advance of the colonies? Given an affirmative response, could this Enlightenment be presented as a systematic and rigorously consistent body of thought? If, on the other hand, the answer is negative, was the intellectual ferment in the colonies little more than a pale imitation of European developments? Were there no differences? Did Americans contribute nothing at all to the Enlightenment?

Approximately the same questions may be asked of the Great Awakening. Was it in any way a unique phenomenon? Or was it a European flowering grafted onto a native plant? Assuming uniqueness, how was it special; that is, in what way did the American environment modify and reform the European experience? Why did the spark of any one local awakening, here or abroad, suddenly ignite a general conflagration? Finally, why did the Awakening—wherever it appeared—have such a great appeal to what we may call ordinary folk? And a related inquiry—why did the Enlightenment have such a selective attraction, generally to a highly literate middle and upper-middle class?

Given the implications of these questions, one is naturally surprised to find that, contrary to the general impression, the Enlightenment and the Awakening shared some common ground. Both favored religious freedom, fought for disestablishment of church and state, promoted humanitarian reform, and cooperated in the cause of educational improvement, particularly higher education. Both claimed that a providential design was operative in the New World. Both relied on experience rather than on tradition or authority. Both, finally, were far more hopeful than Calvinism, for each centered on the individual and his ability to make his own way to salvation. For evangelical preachers, people were "free" to accept or reject God's hand; for the votaries of Enlightenment, reason governed.

Although the Awakening was part of the international history of the eighteenth century, one may still ask: Why in America in the 1730s? Why first in the Middle Colonies? Why in a boorish and rough community dominated by the Dutch Reformed church? Why a revival stressing the piety of the heart rather than church attendance? And why at a time when colonial thinkers were beginning to write enlightened tracts?

Clearly, such reformation ideas as the universal priesthood of all believers and the individual's ability to make his own approach to God found a welcome in the New World. Any religious expression that insisted that human beings found grace alone, in a direct and unmediated relation with God, would be immensely attractive to those who stressed man's active participation in the drama of his destiny. So would any expression that satiated the spiritual hunger of those displeased or dissatisfied by Newton's demonstration of God's existence, which was derived from impregnable postulates regarding the nature of the universe.

What helped set the stage for revivalism was a growing awareness of religious decline. Gloomy forebodings overtook early eighteenth-century clerical leaders as New World religion became more institutionalized and less personal, as it became more an intellectual satisfaction than an emotional experience, as secularism and commercialism eroded piety. Their sermons lamented the loss of that purity known to their fathers. They deplored the rising spirit of gain and the dangers inherent in religious freedom. They pronounced imprecations on the impious—in a society that in 1720 contained more unchurched people than any other area of the Western world. They pointed to the many signs of God's displeasure—an epidemic of smallpox, a disastrous fire, "throat distemper," "a blast upon the wheat"—but the people went their material ways unperturbed, and a deadness settled on religion—whether Puritan or Presbyterian.

New England tried to check the decline with

the half-way covenant, but the measure failed. Its ministers then resorted to synodical strictures and jeremiads. The sermons were delivered and heard without feeling, a further reflection on the aridity and dullness that had begun to characterize cultural life, particularly in Congregational enclaves, where it mingled with enmity toward the rigidities and pessimism of Genevan doctrine. The Enlightenment seemed an urgent threat, especially when it encouraged Arminianism, an approach to religion that emphasized free will and man's role in his own salvation; and the growth of rationalism appeared to prefigure a further erosion of faith.

The time seemed ripe for some new religious emphasis and leadership. It called "for a type of preaching that would prick the conscience," Winthrop Hudson has asserted, "convict men of sin, and lead them through a crisis of individual decision into a personal experience of God's redeeming love." Given this situation, it is hardly surprising that revivalists, many of them intelligent and educated men, appealed to men's hearts with all the inspired rhetoric at their command.

The great revival that they set in motion has been described as a "tidal wave of religious fervor." It swept over the colonies and irremediably stained American culture. It offered religion to the masses in terms easily understood and appreciated. Its technique was revivalism; its practitioners were often volatile and passionate men describing the torments of hell in great detail and simultaneously offering the delights of heaven to those ready to avail themselves of God's grace.

This revival, free of denominational control, was directed to Protestants regardless of creedal allegiance. It elicited its most enthusiastic response in regions where religious traditions had weakened and the hold of the established church was negligible. Hence, we have the claim that revivalism was largely a frontier expression; or, as one scholar has stated, "a revolt of the back-country producers from the stringent con-

trols of the mercantile aristocracy which ruled from afar." While it is tempting to see the Awakening in terms of broad and simple opposites, it seems more likely that religious emotionalism knew no boundaries, that it was both urban and rural, as much a factor in the covenanted community as at the raw edge of wilderness, touching the lives of rich and poor alike.

Into Pennsylvania in the early eighteenth century came a German host, actually pouring out of Switzerland and Holland as well as western Germany. The first were Mennonites, followed by a group of Schwenkfelders who settled in the Philadelphia outskirts in the late 1720s. Their ranks were swelled by increasing numbers of Dunkers, Inspirationists, German Quakers, and others. They represented a new religious strain—one in reaction to formal religious beliefs such as Calvinism, one subordinating theology and doctrinal controversy to a religion of the heart and of inner spiritual light, one stressing Christianity as a way of life rather than as a creed, and one partially shaped by separation from Luther's church. The Mennonites, for instance, held separatist notions and believed that religion was an individual matter; so did the Amish, their schismatic brethren.

Clerical unity everywhere was shattered by the turbulent religious upheavals. The immediate antecedents of the New World Awakening may be found among four Dutch Reformed churches in the Raritan Valley of northern New Jersey. Their spiritual leader was a German-born pastor, Theodorus Frelinghuysen. Dismayed by the perfunctory orthodoxy of his parishioners, Frelinghuysen demanded a shattering experience of spiritual rebirth. His impassioned preaching, his advocacy of inner religion (in contrast to the mere outward performance of religious duties), and his rejection of gradual conversion brought a cleavage in Dutch Reformed churches in New Jersey and New York and brought charges of heresy against him.

Perhaps more important in New Jersey were

the efforts of William Tennent and his sons, all of whom were key figures in the Presbyterian revival, the Scots-Irish phase of the Awakening in the middle colonies. Tennent the elder was a preacher of great power, but he was known chiefly as the founder of the first Log College (at Neshaminy, Pennsylvania), a school that trained sixteen to eighteen ministers a year for over twenty years. Their principal distinction, like their mentor, was an inspired evangelical zeal. They hurled the charge of unregenerate at their opponents, and by tossing away stale scripts and speaking directly to the heart they contributed to the militant revival then careening through the colony.

Into this situation, in the autumn of 1739, came an eloquent, twenty-four-year-old Anglican minister, George Whitefield, who was already the mightiest preacher in Christendom. He had stepped ashore at Lewes, Delaware, on October 30, 1739, and immediately began an evangelical tour of the region. His extemporaneous preaching, marvelous voice, and keen sense of the histrionic made him a heaven-sent leader from the viewpoint of Presbyterian revivalism. Whole towns fell under the sway of this English pied piper, as some critics dubbed him. Yet, he was catalyst, not cause. The soil had been prepared in advance, and Whitefield truly reaped as he had sown. A harvest of souls turned the scattered revivals in Frelinghuysen and the Tennents into a Great Awakening.

Whitefield ranged up and down the colonies, preaching wherever opportunity offered and leaving audiences exhausted. "Some were struck pale as Death," one report stated, "others wringing their hands, others laying on the ground, others sinking into the arms of their friends, and most lifting up their eyes toward heaven, and crying out to God." Certainly his personal magnetism, "magic voice," and vivid dramatic power resulted in the conversion of countless thousands from 1739 to 1741.

Working closely with Whitefield and following in his tracks were the fiery Scots-Irish revivalists, and they committed the worse excesses. Gilbert Tennent, in particular, shouted and stamped and raged; and sobbing and cries of terror from the listeners punctuated his delivery. His rousing sermons, one listener stated, had no regard for the ears of his parishioners, "nor their Fancy with language; but to aim directly at their *Hearts* and *Consciences.*" These methods had startling success, making him the minister most responsible for the effectiveness of the Middle Colonies Awakening. Like Frelinghuysen, he clung to the bleak Calvinist picture of man's depravity and total dependence on God, yet he paradoxically affirmed the individual's ability to assist in his own salvation, a contradiction shared by so many revivalists.

Certainly, these diametically opposed convictions were held by Jonathan Edwards, the major figure in the New England Awakening. This Awakening began in 1724, mainly in the Connecticut valley of western Massachusetts, though some fairly flagrant scenes of emotional religion were also being enacted in Boston. Hatched in the quiet little town of Northampton, the revival raged and spread like a pestilence, moving irresistibly east and south, where it swept over Connecticut, splintering the colony's Congregationalists into New and Old Lights, and the New Lights into moderate and separatist wings. Everywhere it frightened conservatives, who believed it had to be suppressed. To them, Edwards was the archenemy, the anti-Christ, but to the ordinary parishioner, he was a great preacher.

Edwards' greatness consisted in his understanding of the Awakening's implications. He himself was no radical; he did not preach democracy; he was a Calvinist, accepting the notion of total depravity and man's inexorable tendency to sin. His temperament did not easily lend itself to revivalist methods or to direct appeals to his parishioners, and it was only his sense of mission that goaded him, despite misgivings, to emotionalism. He lived in an age when Puritanism had lost much of its inner power, when the problem of salvation was no longer urgent.

Above all others in New England, Edwards sought to turn men's hearts again to God and to hammer home to them the need for participatory rebirth. "Men no more regard warnings of future punishment because it don't seem real to them," he said, and he dedicated himself to that end. More than anyone else, he boldly used reason and would confine religion to the rational or speculative; yet, he battled the entire rationalist impulse, fearing Arminianism because it challenged the Calvinist idea of God's absolute sovereignty.

In this important sense, Edwards was indeed the belated and authentic voice of Puritanism, representing a purity of Calvinist belief exceeding anything known a century earlier. Humble before God, perpetually affirming "the absolute and immediate dependence which men have upon God," insistent that "true virtue or holiness has its seat chiefly in the heart, rather than in the head," his religion was personal, intuitive, spontaneous. Yet, he invariably resorted to reason, and he accepted Calvinist doctrine not because it was orthodox but because of the facts. He restored to an omnipotent God what Arminians and covenant theologians had taken from Him and given to man. His was a righteous God who needed no justification and who set the conditions for salvation.

Nor did the South escape. Revivalistic itinerants, like Samuel Davies, infiltrated most southern churches. Separatist Baptists decended from New England, and their extreme emotional appeal resulted in a striking Baptist growth in North Carolina. Methodism, the last phase of the Southern Awakening, also made many conversions in Virginia, where Presbyterians and Baptists had paved the way.

The awakenings, then, were generally interrelated and colonieswide. Their effects are less clear than the actual events. Certainly, revivalism divided the major denominations. But it did more. It split Baptists, like Presbyterians and Methodists, into Old Lights or Regulars and New Lights or Separates; it splintered Congregationalism into a multitude of separate churches and weakened the parish system; and it brought an astonishing growth in membership and, hence, in power to dissenting churches. It weakened the structure of the established social order, challenged religious authority, and contributed to freedom of religion everywhere. By its challenge to ministerial authority and theocratic government, it inevitably challenged civil authority as well. Finally, revivalism forced into the open an issue fundamental both to theology and to political-intellectual life—whether man's will is wholly free or wholly subject to God's will. In giving wide currency to the belief that all men were equal before God, it prepared the soil for the assumption that they were equal before their peers.

The Enlightenment, however, is rightly considered markedly different from the Great Awakening. We shall see that its values and outlook, even the small intellectual elite who were involved in the Enlightenment, sharply distinguished it from revivalism. Nonetheless, the revivalists contributed to the creation of a democratic ethos and they clearly had something in common with the reformist temper of the Enlightenment. Indeed, adherents of the Awakening and of the Enlightenment frequently overlooked their divergent views and stressed things shared in common: individualism, disregard of social status, emphasis on such terms as "liberty" and "freedom," interest in applied science, suspicion of theological doctrine, and enthusiasm for higher education.

Revulsion against the spiritual and emotional orgies of revivalism did, to be sure, cause some to seek other channels of religious and intellectual satisfaction. For this minority of disaffected who could not accept emotional religion, Enlightenment ideas were immensely attractive. In dealing with these ideas, we are caught up by the need to determine the extent of their transit to the New World and by the differences as well as the similarities at home and abroad.

In contemplating the Enlightenment, we again may affirm that ideas do not develop in a vacuum. Wherever they settle and build, individuals bring beliefs and institutions with them, though these are at least partially recast. Colonial thinkers, after all, had been reading the same books, drawing on the same sources, and sharing the same experiences as Europeans. They were also mightily impressed by Sir Isaac Newton and the implications of Newtonian mechanics. Newton, above all other European scientists and philosophers, cleared up arbitrary assumptions about God and the cosmos. He seemed to banish mystery from the universe. Alexander Pope's couplet expressed the high esteem in which Newton was held by the Enlightenment:

> Nature and Nature's laws lay hid in night,
> God said: "Let Newton be," and there was light.

After Newton, it seemed reasonable, though astonishing, to believe that the whole universe was subject to physical laws that could be reduced to mathematical equations. Since Newton had found a law of gravity that operated through all nature, it was assumed that other pervasive natural laws existed, equally discoverable by the use of scientific methods—laws governing society, human nature, political life, and economic affairs. Thanks to Newton, the colonists less frequently referred to Providence in order to explain natural events. Slowly being pushed outside man's universe, God was becoming more remote—a first cause—and the law of nature was replacing Him as the sole guide in human affairs.

Science encouraged speculation in the possibility of multiple worlds and systems. It encouraged the belief that the laws introduced by the Creator were accessible to individuals through their own reason. In this manner, scientific speculation did more than dispel the shadows of ancient superstition in other fields of human experience; it also eliminated the medieval idea that the function of thought was to accept, not to create—the idea of reason as the servant of revelation or as an accepted body of knowledge and truth. Science gave new functions to reason—to the mind of man—which were more important than the objective data it made accessible to that mind. Individuals began to look on reason as a kind of energy, a force understood by its effects, a *means* by which to do something. Colonial thinkers paid indiscreet obeisance at the shrines of reason and science. This worship led inexorably to the development of the three central propositions of the American Enlightenment: (1) man's reliance on reason to know himself and his world, (2) belief in the impersonal God of deism rather than the personal deity of Puritanism, and (3) confidence in man as an individual and in his perfectibility. A further look at the evolution of these doctrines is in order.

For colonial thinkers, first of all, enlightenment began as "the triumph of empirical fact," a thesis that led to John Locke. In his *Essay Concerning Human Understanding,* a work as revolutionary as his political studies, Locke claimed that the mind of man was like a blank tablet *(tabula rasa),* a "white paper, void of all characters, without any ideas." Since the mind contained nothing that had not previously been in the senses, knowledge ultimately depended on impressions received through the senses as a result of personal experiences. Hence, the practitioners of enlightenment insisted on a form of truth verifiable by empirical methods rather than subject to arbitrary postulates about the nature of things. Yet, they unhesitatingly endorsed such a priori truths as the natural right to life, liberty, and the pursuit of happiness, even though such "self-evident" theorems, essentially of a moral or philosophical nature, were not scientifically verifiable.

Lockean empiricism implied that man was merely a receiver of sensation, a creature rather than creator. These nonhumanistic implications notwithstanding, Locke's authority remained practically unchallenged in his age. He inspired generations of Americans who found that the proper study of mankind was man. Understandably, he appealed to a new nation that emphasized experimental knowledge, applied intelligence, and human ends. However, colonial thinkers again seemed indifferent to consistency. They were enamored of Locke, but they also professed faith in the individual's ability to know himself and his world and, in so doing, to transform both. Moreover, they contributed to their own humanistic convictions by stressing inductive methods and utilitarian ends. Experimentation rather than revelation was the way to an explanation of man's universe, according to Benjamin Franklin. Beautiful theories interested him only so far as he could see in them a possible application to human life.

Once colonists had been affected by the claims of natural science and the concept of a law-governed universe, they ceased to view divine government as a mystery only partially explained by revelation. Science, in this sense, became a tool in the creation of a new humanism. It caused men to doubt miracles, to give little credence to the Puritan insistence on human helplessness, and to become more interested in the affairs of this world rather than those of the next. God was not ignored: nearly all advanced thinkers found evidence of His existence in the grand design of nature. But design was a dangerous basis for belief in the reality and goodness of deity: glorifying God in nature was only one step from glorifying nature.

Contemporary reliance on science and reason made a reality of this hazard, and persuaded colonists that the universe, including man, was completely ruled by natural law. It was easy to shift emphasis from Newton's attempt on a beautifully harmonious natural and cosmic mechanism built by God to the conviction that human beings, by the use of the mind, could

unlock the mysteries of the universe. Such assurance, in turn, tended to integrate man within the fold of nature in general and within the animal kingdom in particular. Once again, the eighteenth-century humanists ignored a paradox: the individual was within nature, yet, because of unique characteristics, was set apart from other forms of natural life. There was, however, no gainsaying the importance given to human reason, human inquiry, and human will. The individual's responsibility increased, while reliance on divine will, divine guidance, and supernatural revelation was minimized.

Deism further accelerated the movement away from a God-centered universe. Although embraced by only a handful of Americans, it was representative of the effect of science on religious thought. Its native strain recognized no accepted ecclesiastical creed or authority. It stood on the rock of reason rather than on faith. For American deists, reason was the primary source of religious as well as natural truths, and science became increasingly the means to a rational approach to God and nature.

At the very least, the most temperate of colonial practitioners sought to humanize the Godlike conception of Christ. They asserted that God was rational, that He ruled a rational universe, and that He could not intervene in man's daily life. They found His true revelation in the visible creation—the world of nature. The more extreme scientific deists—Thomas Paine is one of their best representatives—unequivocally rejected Christian revelation, organized churches, Old Testament accounts of creation, and priestly pretensions to authority. But unlike Baron d'Holbach and other French atheists, they were antireligion rather than antiChristian. Paine expressed a belief in God, but his conception of Him derived from science and reason, not from revelation.

Deism was more than a sum of its parts. It was an attitude of mind—optimistic and confident, free and untrammeled, democratic and humanitarian. All true religion, American deists claimed, was personal rather than institutional. Man was not only *not* evil, he was good (unless corrupted by ignorance or prejudice); better yet, he had unlimited possibilities. He might expand his knowledge indefinitely without supernatural assistance. He could understand and manipulate his environment in order to create a better life on earth.

Optimism about man's moral and physical destiny was one element in the belief in progress. This optimism was less about human nature than about what could be done with human beings through the progress of science and through education.

After Locke, who denied predetermined human nature, the idea of progress was assisted by the belief that education could shape the lives of human beings, that they could control their environment, and that the human mind could be made the creature of a planned society. Thus, the idea of progress matured as a revolutionary concept—revolutionary not in any specific political tactic so much as in the attitude it implied toward the individual and society. It inevitably enrolled New World thinkers in the struggle to alleviate the human condition. They criticized the criminal code, the slave trade, imprisonment for debt, and inequitable laws of inheritance. In brief, they made humanitarian reform ancillary to the Enlightenment in America.

Confident about the future of American society and mankind, most colonists subscribed to the notion of progress. Their conviction was fortified by their own physical situation as well as by overseas impulses. Individuals who had hacked a civilization out of the wilderness, pushed forward the frontier of settlement, and built a nation where none existed before could readily imagine a brave new world. They needed no instruction from overseas mentors. Nor did they conceive of progress in purely philosophical terms, as did Europeans. They had the lessons of their unique experiences and concrete achievements. They were encouraged by a survey of man's savage past, which showed an unrelenting advance from darkness to light and suggested that this advance might continue indefinitely. They were excited by the American Revolution. The events of 1776 signaled the beginning of an era that would produce ever-increasing happiness for the whole human race and encouraged colonists to think in terms of human possibilities, of the individual as he might be rather than what he was or had been.

Not that progress was inevitable. It would be achieved only through the conscious efforts of rational individuals; its success depended on proper utilization of the forces of nature and on discovery of practical and scientific methods of directing human development. An earthly utopia was possible because the individual's increasing enlightenment freed him from bonds of superstition and enabled him to build society on the foundation of natural laws as revealed by human reason.

Belief in a rational reconstruction of society was shared by Enlightenment thinkers at home and abroad, but the native bloom had a less ambivalent attitude toward reason and education. For Jefferson, education was the panacea. It could prevent the individual from falling victim to superstition and ignorance; it was essential to the inculcation of morality and to the discovery of the laws of nature; it was, finally, the keystone in the arch of democratic government.

Thus, by the late eighteenth century, the shape of glorious things to come in America was founded on the bedrock of reason, education, and the advancement of science. All operated in the framework of human perfectibility. Ultimately, it was affirmed, these forces would create a heaven on earth, a golden age—one of the future and not of the past as had been thought overseas—and an inspiration for all peoples. More than just prophecy, this was a moral and philosophical postulate that inspired our greatest orators and noblest poets; and which lay at the core of American idealism. It stemmed from a faith in the future that still astonishes modern man.

In retrospect, one may claim that the European Enlightenment was the virus carrier, that the earliest settlers brought the spirit of optimism with them, and that their buoyancy and confidence were a force that made no wilderness prospect too bold and no speculation too reckless. But their experiences in a new land, so richly adorned with natural advantages that could only be reserved for the chosen people of God, also contributed to the vision of futurity. So it was with the other basic features of the Age of Reason in America. To what degree, for example, was the cis-Atlantic notion of equality shaped by the actual mobility of life in the New World, and to what degree by the writings of European intellectuals? The origins of the movement itself—the American Enlightenment—are as difficult to delineate as its component parts. No precisely assignable and altogether satisfactory meaning may be found for it or for the rhetoric that distinguished it. Words such as "reason" and "nature," thought to be immutable and transcendent in the eighteenth century—the same for all thinking peoples, all nations, and all cultures—have long since lost their unequivocal simplicity. Can we go much beyond our earlier explanations in the search for reliable and universally applicable meaning? Can we measure with precision and unfailing dependability the effect of the Enlightenment on the American Revolution or the American mind?

Certainly, these questions cannot be answered by simply letting the European philosophers speak for the colonial movement. There is no absolute coherence in eighteenth-century thought, and for this reason we must avoid hypothesizing the native development as part of a cosmopolitan and supranational unity. Indeed, we have found that there was not even logical consistency within the New World mind. Beliefs, after all, are articles of faith

and emotional drives that impel men to action. Subsequently, they present enormous problems to the student of ideas for precisely this reason. Books may be consistent, but men are not. The educated colonist could unblinkingly endorse contraries: deism and Anglicanism, humanism and materialism, self-evident truths and the critical spirit, hardheaded practices and an ethic of secular benevolence.

We know that late colonial thinkers weakened traditional religion and sought the advantages of life here on earth. They hoped for an attainable earthly paradise rather than a Christian Zion. But the American Enlightenment was not basically irreligious, and its strongest intellectual thrust lay not in its rejection of belief but, rather, in the new form of faith it proclaimed. Precisely here is its strongest affinity to the Awakening. Indeed, it might be argued that the Enlightenment represented a translation into secular terms of the objectives, and even the spirit, of the revivalist impulse. Both movements, in sum, are identical in that they fused European ideas with special experiences in the American environment; both made important contributions to their Old World expressions; both were, finally, marked by a desire to give individuals new meaning in the New World.

SUGGESTED READINGS

Becker, Carl. *The Declaration of Independence*. New York: Harcourt, Brace, 1922.

———. *The Heavenly City of the Eighteenth Century Philosophers*. New Haven, Conn.: Yale University Press, 1932.

Berlin, Isaiah. *The Age of Enlightenment*. New York: George Braziller, 1957.

Boorstin, Daniel J. *The Lost World of Thomas Jefferson*. New York: Henry Holt, 1948.

Bushman, Richard. *From Puritan to Yankee: Character and the Social Order in Connecticut*. Cambridge, Mass.: Harvard University Press, 1967.

Commager, Henry Steele. *The Empire of Reason.* Garden City, New York: Doubleday Publishing, 1977.

Curti, Merle E. *Probing Our Past.* New York: Harper, 1955.

Gaustad, Edwin S. *The Great Awakening.* New York: Harper, 1957.

Gay, Peter. *The Enlightenment.* 2 vols. New York: Alfred A. Knopf, 1966–69.

Goen, C. C. *Revivalism and Separatism in New England, 1740–1800.* New Haven, Conn.: Yale University Press, 1962.

Heimert, Alan. *Religion and the American Mind.* Cambridge, Mass.: Harvard University Press, 1966.

Hindle, Brooke. *The Pursuit of Science in Revolutionary America.* Chapel Hill: University of North Carolina Press, 1956.

McLoughlin, William. *Isaac Backus and the American Pietistic Tradition.* Boston: Little, Brown, 1967.

May, Henry. *The Enlightenment in America.* New York: Oxford University Press, 1976.

Morais, Herbert. *Deism in Eighteenth-Century America.* New York: Columbia University Press, 1934.

Nye, Russel. *The Cultural Life of the New Nation.* New York: Harper, 1960.

Tanis, James. *Dutch Calvinistic Pietism in the Middle Colonies.* The Netherlands: Nijhoff, 1968.

Willey, Basil. *The Eighteenth Century Background.* London: Chatto and Windus, 1940.

DOCUMENT 4.1
An Awakening Is Needed

Theoretically, the Awakening and the Enlightenment were both addressed to contrary impulses in man. The Awakening tugged at the heart; the Enlightenment appealed to the

Source: Jonathan Edwards, *A History of the Work of Redemption,* ed. E. Hickman. 10th ed., 2 vols., (London, 1865), vol. 1, pp. 470–72, 480–81, 492–93, 510–13.

head. Such simplicities are dangerous, however, since religious movements are complex and resistant to simple generalizations. Some of the complexities of revivalism, as well as the necessity for it, are suggested in this passage from Jonathan Edwards, pastor of the Northampton Massachusetts Congregational Church after 1729, and the minister whose preachings initiated the New England phase of the Awakening.

I proceed now to the last thing that was proposed to be considered, relating to the success of Christ's redemption during this space, viz., what the state of things is now in the world with regard to the church of Christ, and the success of Christ's purchase. And this I would do, by showing how things are now, compared with the first times of the Reformation. And, 1, I would show wherein the state of things is altered for the worse; and 2, How it is altered for the better.

(1.) I would show wherein the state of things is altered from what it was in the beginning of the Reformation, for the worse; and it is so especially in these three respects.

[1.] The Reformed church is much diminished. The Reformation, in the former times of it, as was observed before, was supposed to take place through one half of Christendom, excepting the Greek church, or that there were as many Protestants as Papists. But now it is not so; the Protestant church is much diminished. . . .

[2.] Another thing wherein the state of things is altered for the worse from what was in the former times of the Reformation, is the prevailing of licentiousness in principles and opinions. There is not now that spirit of orthodoxy which there was then; there is very little appearance of zeal for the mysterious and spiritual doctrines of Christianity; and they never were so ridiculed, and held in contempt, as they are in the present age; and especially in England, the principal kingdom of the Reformation. In this kingdom, those principles, on which the power of godliness depends, are in a great measure exploded; and Arianism, and Socinianism, and Arminianism, and Deism, are the things which prevail, and carry almost all before them. And particularly history gives no account of any age wherein there was so great an apostasy of those who had been brought up under the light of the gospel, to infidelity; never was there such a casting off of the Christian, and all revealed religion; never any age wherein was so much scoffing at, and ridiculing the gospel of Christ, by those who have been brought up under gospel light, nor any thing like it, as there is at this day.

[3.] Another thing wherein things are altered for the worse, is, that there is much less of the prevalency of the power of godliness, than there was at the beginning of the Reformation. There was a glorious outpouring of the Spirit of God that accompanied the first Reformation, not only to convert multitudes in so short a time from Popery to the true religion, but to turn many to God and true godliness. Religion gloriously flourished in one country and another, as most remarkably appeared in those times of terrible persecution, which have already been spoken of. But now there is an exceeding great decay of vital piety; yea, it seems to be despised, called *enthusiasm, whimsy,* and *fanaticism.* Those who are truly religious, are commonly looked upon to be crackbrained, and beside their right mind; and vice and profaneness dreadfully prevail, like a flood which threatens to bear down all before it. But I proceed now to show,

(2.) In what respect things are altered for the better from what they were in the first Reformation.

[1.] The power and influence of the Pope is much diminished. Although, since the former times of the Reformation, he has gained ground in extent of dominion; yet he has lost in degree of influence. . .

[2.] There is far less persecution now than

there was in the first times of the Reformation. You have heard already how dreadfully persecution raged in the former times of the Reformation; and there is something of it still. Some parts of the Protestant church are at this day under persecution, and so probably will be till the day of the church's suffering and travail is at an end, which will not be till the fall of Antichrist. But it is now in no measure as it was heretofore. There does not seem to be the same spirit of persecution prevailing; it is become more out of fashion even among the Popish princes. The wickedness of the enemies of Christ, and the opposition against his cause, seem to run in another channel. The humor now is, to despise and laugh at all religion; and there seems to be a spirit of indifferency about it. However, so far the state of things is better than it has been, that there is so much less of persecution.

[3.] There is a great increase of learning. In the dark times of Popery before the Reformation, learning was so far decayed, that the world seemed to be overrun with barbarous ignorance. Their very priests were many of them grossly ignorant. Learning began to revive with the Reformation, which was owing very much to the art of printing, which was invented a little before the Reformation; and since that, learning has increased more and more, and at this day is undoubtedly raised to vastly a greater height than ever it was before: and though no good use is made of it by the greater part of learned men, yet the increase of learning in itself is a thing to be rejoiced in, because it is a good, and, if duly applied, an excellent handmaid to divinity, and is a talent which, if God gives men a heart, affords them a great advantage to do great things for the advancement of the kingdom of Christ, and the good of the souls of men. . . . .

God in his providence now seems to be acting over again the same part which he did a little time before Christ came. The age wherein Christ came into the world, was an age wherein learning greatly prevailed, and was at a greater height than ever it had been before; and yet wickedness never prevailed more than then. God was pleased to suffer human learning to come to such a height before he sent forth the gospel into the world, that the world might see the insufficiency of all their own wisdom for the obtaining of the knowledge of God. . . . So now learning is at a great height at this day in the world, far beyond what it was in the age when Christ appeared; and now the world, by their learning and wisdom, do not know God; and they seem to wander in darkness, are miserably deluded, stumble and fall in matters of religion, as in midnight darkness. . . .

But yet, when God has sufficiently shown men the insufficiency of human wisdom and learning for the purposes of religion, and when the appointed time comes for that glorious outpouring of the Spirit of God, when he will himself by his own immediate influence enlighten men's minds; then may we hope that God will make use of the great increase of learning as a handmaid to religion, as a means of the glorious advancement of the kingdom of his Son. . . . And there is no doubt to be made of it, that God in his providence has of late given the world the art of printing, and such a great increase of learning, to prepare for what he designs to accomplish for his church in the approaching days of its prosperity. And thus the wealth of the wicked is laid up for the just, agreeable to Prov. xiii, 22. . . .

. . . there is nothing else that informs us what this scheme and design of God in his works is, but only the Holy Scriptures. Nothing else pretends to set in view the whole series of God's works of providence from beginning to end, and to inform us how all things were from God at first, and for what end they are, and how they were ordered from the beginning, and how they will proceed to the end of the world, and what they will come to at last, and how then all things shall be to God. Nothing else but the Scriptures has any pretence for

showing any manner of regular scheme or drift in those revolutions which God orders from age to age. Nothing else pretends to show what God would effect by the things which he has done, and is doing, and will do; what he seeks and intends by them. . . .

Reason shows that it is fit and requisite, that the intelligent and rational beings of the world should know something of God's scheme and design in his works; for they doubtless are the beings that are principally concerned. The thing that is God's great design in his works, is doubtless something concerning his reasonable creatures, rather than brute beasts and lifeless things. The revolutions by which God's great design is brought to pass, are doubtless revolutions chiefly among them, and which concern their state, and not the state of things without life or reason. And therefore surely it is requisite that they should know something of it; especially seeing that reason teaches that God has given his rational creatures reason and a capacity of seeing God in his works; for this end, that they may see God's glory in them, and give him the glory of them. But how can they see God's glory in his works, if they do not know what God's design in them is, and what he aims at by what he is doing in the world?

And further, it is fit that mankind should be informed something of God's design in the government of the world, because they are made capable of actively falling in with that design, and promoting of it, and acting herein as his friends and subjects; it is therefore reasonable to suppose, that God has given mankind some revelation to inform them of this: but this is nothing else that does it but the Bible. . . .

Here we are shown the connection of the various parts of the work of providence, and how all harmonizes, and is connected together in a regular, beautiful, and glorious frame. . . .

How rational, worthy, and excellent a revelation is this! And how excellent a book is the Bible, which contains so much beyond all other books in the world! And what characters are here of its being indeed a divine book! A book that the great Jehovah has given to mankind for their instruction, without which we should be left in miserable darkness and confusion.

From what has been said, we may see the glorious majesty and power of God in this affair of redemption: especially is God glorious in his power. His glorious power appears in upholding his church for so long a time, and carrying on this work; upholding it oftentimes when it was but as a little spark of fire, or as smoking flax, in which the fire was almost gone out, and the powers of earth and hell were combined to destroy it. Yet God has never suffered them to quench it, and finally will bring forth judgment unto victory. God glorifies his strength in his church's weakness; in causing his people, who are like a number of little infants, finally to triumph over all earth and hell; so that they shall tread on the lion and adder; the young lion and dragon shall they trample under foot. . . .

Let who will prevail now, let the enemies of the church exalt themselves as much as they will, these are the people that shall finally prevail. The last kingdom shall finally be theirs; the kingdom shall finally be given into their hands, and shall not be left to other people. . . .

DOCUMENT 4.2
The Dangers of Awakening Religion

Clerical establishment everywhere resented the intrusion, uninvited into their churches, of

Source: Charles Chauncy, *Enthusiasm described and caution'd against. A sermon Preach'd . . . the Lord's Day after the Commencement . . .* (Boston, 1742), pp. 1–27, abridged.

revivalists. This event simply confirmed their opinion that Awakening preachers were encouraging persons "subversive of Peace, Discipline and Government," But when Edwards observed "two armies, separated and drawn up in battle array," he referred not merely to clerical factions but to a fundamental cleavage within society as well. The governing elite—secular as well as spiritual—closed ranks against these enthusiasts and subversives, a reaction that contributed to the appearance of the Great Awakening as a democratic movement. Charles Chauncy, grandson of a Harvard president and a prestigious member of Boston's Congregational ministry, was actively opposed to the Awakening. He stood out as an antagonist of revivalism just as Edwards did as an apologist; and the protracted struggle between piety and enlightenment, faith and reason, mystery and clarity seemed to be personalized in these ministers. In the selection below, Chauncy relates something of the fears of the orthodox and the hopes of those who sought a commonsense religion.

. . . I shall take occasion to discourse to you upon the following Particulars.

I. I shall give you some account of *Enthusiasm,* in its *nature* and *influence.*

II. Point you to a rule by which you may judge of persons, whether they are under the influence of *Enthusiasm.*

III. Say what may be proper to guard you against this unhappy turn of mind.

The whole will then be follow'd with some suitable Application.

I. I am in the first place, to give you some account of *Enthusiasm.* And as this is a thing much talk'd of at present, more perhaps than at any other time that has pass'd over us, it will not be tho't unseasonable, if I take some pains to let you into a true understanding of it.

The word, from its Etymology, carries in

it a good meaning, as signifying *inspiration from God:* in which sense, the prophets under the old testament, and the apostles under the new, might properly be called *Enthusiasts.* For they were under a divine influence, spake as moved by the HOLY GHOST, and did such things as can be accounted for in no way, but by recurring to an immediate extraordinary power, present with them.

But the word is more commonly used in a bad sense, as intending an *imaginary,* not a *real* inspiration: according to which sense, the *Enthusiast* is one, who has a conceit of himself as a person favoured with the extraordinary presence of the *Deity.* He mistakes the workings of his own passions for divine communications, and fancies himself immediately inspired by the Spirit of God, when all the while, he is under no other influence than that of an over-heated imagination.

The cause of this *enthusiasm* is a bad temperament of the blood and spirits; 'tis properly a disease, a sort of madness: And there are few; perhaps none at all, but are subject to it, tho' none are so much in danger of it as those, in whom *melancholy* is the prevailing ingredient in their constitution. In these it often reigns; and sometimes to so great a degree, that they are really beside themselves, acting as truly by the blind impetus of a wild fancy, as tho' they had neither reason nor understanding.

And various are the ways in which their *enthusiasm* discovers itself.

Sometimes, it may be seen in their countenance. A certain wildness is discernable in their general look and air; especially when their imaginations are mov'd and fired.

Sometimes, it strangely loosens their tongues, and gives them such an energy, as well as fluency and volubility in speaking, as they themselves, by their utmost efforts, can't so much as imitate, when they are not under the enthusiastick influence.

Sometimes, it affects their bodies, throws them into convulsions and distortions, into quakings and tremblings. This was formerly common among the people called *Quakers.* I was myself, when a Lad, an eye witness to such violent agitations and foamings, in a bois-terous female speaker, as I could not behold but with surprize and wonder.

Sometimes, it will unaccountably mix itself with their conduct, and give it such a tincture of that which is freakish or furious, as none can have an idea of, but those who have seen the behavior of a person in a phrenzy.

Sometimes, it appears in their imaginary peculiar intimacy with heaven. They are, in their own opinion, the special favourites of God, have more familiar converse with him than other good men, and receive immediate, extraordinary communications from him. The tho'ts, which suddenly rise up in their minds, they take for suggestions of the Spirit; their very fancies are divine illuminations; nor are they strongly inclin'd to any thing, but 'tis an impulse from God, a plain revelation of his will.

And what extravagances, in this temper of mind, are they not capable of, and under the specious pretext too of paying obedience to the authority of God? Many have fancied themselves acting by immediate warrant from heaven, while they have been committing the most undoubted wickedness. There is indeed scarce any thing so wild, either in *speculation* or *practice,* but they have given into it: They have, in many instances, been blasphemers of God, and open disturbers of the peace of the world.

But in nothing does the *enthusiasm* of these persons discover it self more, than in the disre-gard they express to the Dictates of *reason.* They are above the force of argument, beyond conviction from a calm and sober address to their understandings. As for them, they are distinguish'd persons; God himself speaks in-wardly and immediately to their souls. ''They see [according to Locke] the light infused into their understandings . . . 'tis clear and visible there, like the light of bright sunshine; shews it self and needs no other proof but its own evidence. They feel the hand of God moving them within, and the impulses of his Spirit; and cannot be mistaken in what they feel. Thus they support themselves, and are sure reason hath nothing to do with what they see and feel. What they have a sensible experience of, admits no doubt, needs no probation.'' And in vain will you endeavour to convince such persons of any mistakes they are fallen into. They are certainly in the right, and know themselves to be so. They have the Spirit opening their understandings and revealing the truth to them. They believe only as he has taught them: and to suspect they are in the wrong is to do dishonour to the Spirit; 'tis to oppose his dictates, to set up their own wisdom in opposition to his, and shut their eyes against that light with which he has shined into their souls. They are not therefore capable of being argued with; you had as good reason with the wind.

And as the natural consequence of their being thus sure of every thing, they are not only infinitely stiff and tenacious, but impatient of contradiction, censorious and uncharitable: they encourage a good opinion of none but such as are in their way of thinking and speaking. Those, to be sure, who venture to debate with them about their errors and mistakes, their weaknesses and indiscretions, run the hazard of being stigmatiz'd by them as poor unconverted wretches, without the Spirit, under the government of carnal reason, enemies to God and religion, and in the broad way to hell.

They are likewise positive and dogmatical, vainly fond of their own imaginations, and invincibly set upon propagating them: And in the doing of this, their Powers being awakened, and put as it were, upon the stretch, from the strong impressions they are under, that they are authorized by the immediate command of God himself, they sometimes exert themselves

with a sort of *extatic* violence: And 'tis this that gives them the advantage, among the less knowing and judicious, of those who are modest, suspicious of themselves, and not too assuming in matters of conscience and salvation. The extraordinary fervour of their minds, accompanied with uncommon bodily motions, and an excessive confidence and assurance gains them great reputation among the populace; who speak of them as *men of GOD* in distinction from all others, and too commonly hearken to, and revere their dictates, as tho' they really were, as they pretend, immediately communicated to them from the Divine Spirit.

This is the nature of *Enthusiasm,* and this its operation, in a less or greater degree, in all who are under the influence of it. 'Tis a kind of religious Phrenzy, and evidently discovers it self to be so, whenever it rises to any great height.

And much to be pitied are the persons who are seized with it. Our compassion commonly works towards those, who, while under distraction, fondly imagine themselves to be Kings and Emperors: And the like pity is really due to those, who, under the power of *enthusiasm,* fancy themselves to be *prophets; inspired of God,* and *immediately called and commissioned by him to deliver his messages to the world:* And tho' they should run into disorders, and act in a manner that cannot but be condemned, they should notwithstanding be treated with tenderness and lenity; and the rather, because they don't commonly act so much under the influence of a *bad mind,* as a *deluded imagination.* And who more worthy of christian pity than those, who, under the notion of serving God and the interest of religion, are filled with zeal, and exert themselves to the utmost, while all the time they are hurting and wounding the very cause they take so much pains to advance. 'Tis really a pitiable case: And tho' the honesty of their intentions won't legitimate their bad actions, yet it very much alleviates their guilt: We should think as favourably of them as may be, and be dispos'd to judge with mercy, as we would hope to obtain mercy. . . .

'Tis indeed a powerful argument with many, in favour of these persons, their pretending to *impulses,* and a call from God; together with their insatiable thirst to do good to souls. And 'tis owing to such pretences as these, that encouragement has been given to the rise of such numbers of *lay-exhorters and teachers,* in one place and another, all over the land. But if 'tis one of the things wrote by the apostle as the *commandment of* God, that there should be *officers* in the church, an *order of men* to whom it should belong, as their *proper, stated work,* to exhort and teach, this cannot be the business of others: And if any who think themselves to be *spiritual,* are under *impressions* to take upon them *this ministry,* they may have reason to suspect, whether their *impulses* are any other than the workings of their own imaginations: And instead of being under any divine extra-ordinary influence, there are just grounds of fear, whether they are not acted from the vanity of their minds: Especially, if they are but beginners in religion; men of weak minds, babes in understanding: as is most commonly the case. The apostle speaks of *novices,* as in danger of being *lifted up with pride, and falling into the contamination of the devil:* And it is a seasonable caution to this kind of person. They should study themselves more, and they will see less reason to think their disposition to exhort and teach to be from the Spirit of God. And indeed, if the Spirit has bid men to *abide in their own callings,* 'tis not conceivable he should influence them to *leave their callings:* And if he has set a mark of disgrace upon *busy-bodies in other men's matters,* 'tis impossible he should put men upon *wandring about from house to house, speaking the things they ought not.*

And it deserves particular consideration, whether the suffering, much more the encouraging *women, yea, girls* to speak in the assemblies for religious worship, is not a plain breach of that *commandment of the Lord,* wherein it is said, *Let your women keep silence in the churches; for it is not permitted to them to speak—It is a shame: for women to speak in the church.* After such an express constitution, designedly made to restrain *women* from speaking in the church, with what face can such a practice be pleaded for? They may pretend, they are moved by the Spirit, and such a tho't of themselves may be encouraged by others; but if the apostle *spake by the* Spirit, when he delivered *this commandment,* they can't *act by the* Spirit, when they break it. 'Tis a plain case, these Female Exhorters are condemned by the apostle; and if 'tis the *commandment of the* Lord, that they should not speak, they are *spiritual* only in their own tho'ts, while they attempt to do so.

The last thing I shall mention as written by the apostle, is that which obliges to a *just decorum in speaking* in the *house of* God. . . .

But as the most suitable guard against the first tendencies towards *enthusiasm,* let me recommend to you the following words of counsel.

1. Get a true understanding of the *proper work of the* Spirit: and don't place it in those things wherein the gospel does not make it to consist. . . .

Herein, in general, consists the work of the Spirit. It does not lie in giving men *private revelations,* but in opening their minds to understand the *publick ones* contained in the scripture. It does not lie in *sudden impulses* and *impressions,* in *immediate calls* and *extraordinary missions.* Men mistake the business of the Spirit, if they understand by it such things as these. And 'tis, probably, from such unhappy mistakes, that they are at first betrayed into *enthusiasm.* Having a wrong notion of the *work of* the Spirit, 'tis no wonder if they take the uncommon sallies of their own minds for his influences.

You cannot, my brethern, be too well acquainted with what the *bible* makes the *work* of the Holy Ghost, in the affair of salvation: And if you have upon your minds a clear and distinct understanding of this, it will be a powerful guard to you against all *enthusiastical impressions*.

2. Keep close to the *Scripture,* and admit of nothing for an impression of the Spirit, but what agrees with that unerring rule. Fix it in your minds as a truth you will invariably abide by, that the *bible* is the grand test, by which every thing in religion is to be tried; and that you can, at no time, nor in any instance, be under the guidance of the Spirit of God, much less his *extraordinary* guidance, if what you are led to, is inconsistent with the things there revealed, either in point of *faith* or *practice*. And let it be your care to compare the motions of your minds, and the workings of your imaginations and passions, with the *rule* of God's *word*. And see to it, that you be imparital in this matter: Don't make the rule bend to your preconceiv'd notions and inclinations; but repair to the *bible,* with a mind dispos'd, as much as may be, to know the truth as it lies nakedly and plainly in the *scripture* it self. And whatever you are moved to, reject the motion, esteem it as nothing more than a vain fancy, if it puts you upon any method of *thinking,* or *acting,* that can't be evidently reconcil'd with the *revelations* of God in *his word*.

This adherence to the bible, my brethern is one of the best preservatives against *enthusiasm*. If you will but express a due reverence to this *book* of God, making it the great rule of judgment, even in respect of the Spirits *influences* and *operations,* you will not be in much danger of being led into delusion. Let that be your inquiry under all suppos'd *impulses* from the Spirit, *What saith the scripture? To the law, and to the testimony:* If your impressions,

and imagined spiritual motions agree not therewith, 'tis because there is no hand of the Spirit of God in them: They are only the workings of your own imaginations, or something worse; and must at once, without any more ado, be rejected as such.

3. Make use of the *Reason* and *Understanding* God has given you. This may be tho't an ill-advis'd direction, but 'tis as necessary as either of the former. Next to the *Scripture,* there is no greater enemy to *enthusiasm,* than *reason.* 'Tis indeed impossible a man shou'd be an *enthusiast,* who is in the just exercise of his understanding; and 'tis because men don't pay a due regard to the sober dictates of a well inform'd mind, that they are led aside by the delusions of a vain imagination. Be advised then to shew yourselves men, to make use of your reasonable powers; and not act as the *horse* or *mule,* as tho' you had no understanding.

'Tis true, you must not go about to set up your own *reason* in *opposition* to *revelation:* Nor may you entertain a tho't of making *reason your rule* instead of *scripture.* The bible, as I said before, is the *great rule* of religion, the grand test in matters of salvation: But then you must use your reason in order to understand the *bible:* Nor is there any other possible way, in which, as a reasonable creature, you shou'd come to an understanding of it.

You are, it must be acknowledged, in a corrupt state. The fall has introduc'd great weakness into your reasonable nature. You can't be too sensible of this; nor of the danger you are in of making a wrong judgment, thro' prejudice, carelessness, and the undue influence of sin and lust. And to prevent this, you can't be too solicitous to get your *nature sanctified:* Nor can you depend too strongly upon the divine grace to assist you in your search after truth: and 'tis in the way of due dependence on God, and the influences of his Spirit, that I advise you to the use of your reason:

And in this way, you must make use of it. How else will you know what is a revelation from God? What shou'd hinder your entertaining the same tho't of a *pretended* revelation, as of a *real* one, but your reason discovering the falshood of the one, and the truth of the other? And when in the enjoyment of an undoubted revelation from God, as in the case of the *scripture,* How will you understand its meaning, if you throw by your reason? How will you determine, that this, and not that, is its true sense, in this and the other place? Nay, if no reasoning is to be made use of, are not all the senses that can be put on scripture equally proper? Yea, may not the most contrary senses be receiv'd at the same time, since reason only can point out the inconsistency between them? And what will be sufficient to guard you against the most monstrous extravagancies, in *principle* as well as *practice,* if you give up your understandings? What have you left, in this case, to be a check to the wantoness of your imaginations? What shou'd hinder your following every idle fancy, 'till you have lost yourselves in the wilds of falshood and inconsistency? . . .

4. You must not lay too great stress upon the *workings* of your *passions* and *affections.* These will be excited, in a less or greater degree, in the business of religion: and 'tis proper they shou'd. The passions, when suitably mov'd, tend mightily to awaken the *reasonable powers,* and put them upon a lively and vigorous exercise. And this is their proper use: And when address'd to, and excited to this purpose, they may be of good service: whereas we shall mistake the right use of the passions, if we place our religion *only* or *chiefly,* in the heat and fervour of them. The *soul* is the *man:* And unless the *reasonable nature* is suitably wro't upon, the *understanding* enlightened, the *judgment* convinc'd, the *will* perswaded, and the *mind* intirely chang'd, it will avail but to little purpose; tho' the passions shou'd be set

all in a blaze. This therefore you shou'd be most concern'd about. And if while you are sollicitous that you may be in transports of affection, you neglect your more noble part, your reason and judgment, you will be in great danger of being carried away by your imaginations. This indeed leads directly to *Enthusiasm:* And you will in vain, endeavour to preserve yourselves from the influence of it, if you a'nt duly careful to keep your passions in their proper place, under the government of a well inform'd understanding. While the passions are uppermost, and bear the chief sway over a man, he is in an unsafe state: None knows what he may be bro't to . You can't therefore be too careful to keep your passions under the regimen of a *sober judgment.* 'Tis indeed a matter of necessity, as you would not be led aside by delusion and fancy.

5. In the last place here, you must not forget to go to God by *prayer.* This is a duty in all cases, but in none more than the present. If left to yourselves, your own wisdom and strength, you will be insufficient for your own security; perpetually in danger from your *imaginations,* as well as the other enemies of your *souls.* You can't be too sensible of this; nor can you, from a sense of it, apply with too much importunity to the Father *of mercies,* to take pity upon you, and send you such a supply of grace as is needful for you. You must not indeed think, that your duty lies in the business of prayer, and nothing else. You must use your own endeavours, neglect nothing that may prove a guard to you: But together with the use of other means, you must make known your request to God by prayer and supplication. You must daily commit the keeping of your soul to him; and this you must particularly be careful to do in times of more special hazard; humbly hoping in God to be your help: And if he shall please to undertake for you, no delusion shall ever have power over you, to seduce you. . . .

DOCUMENT 4.3
The Awakening in Virginia

From Maine to Georgia, the revivals were directed by men of great eloquence and feeling. New Side Presbyterians sent William Robinson of Tennent's Log College into Virginia and West Virginia, where a revival directed by laymen was already in progress. Samuel Davies, who here describes the work of Robinson, Whitefield, and other Awakening preachers, was the soul of the entire North Carolina and Virginia dissenting movement. Given the fierce Anglican opposition and his unwavering efforts in behalf of toleration, Davies can lay claim to being one of the little recognized heroes in securing religious freedom.

I have prevailed, Sir, on my good Friend before mentioned, who was the principal private Instrument of promoting the late Work, and therefore well acquainted with it, to write me a Narrative of its Rise & Progress from this Period 'till my Settlement here: and this, together with the Substance of what he and others have told me, I shall present to you without any material Alterations, and personate him, tho' I shall not exactly use his Words.

"The Reverend Mr. *Whitefield* had been in *Virginia,* I think, in the Year 1740, and at the Invitation of the Rev. Mr [James] *Blair,* our late Commissary, had preached in *Williamsburg,* our Metropolis, about 60 miles from *Hanover.* His Fame was much spread abroad, as a very warm and alarming Preacher; which made such of us in *Hanover* as had been awakened, very eager to see & hear him; but as he left the Colony before we heard of him, we had no Opportunity. But in the Year—43,

Source: Samuel Davies, *The State of Religion among the Protestant Dissenters, in Virginia, in a Letter to the Rev. Mr. Joseph Bellamy* . . . (Boston, 1751), pp. 4–38.

a young Gentleman arrived from Scotland with a Book of his Sermons preached in *Glasgow,* & taken from his Mouth in short Hand, which with Difficulty I procured. After I had read it with great Liking & Benefit, I invited my Neighbours to come & hear it; and the Plainness, Popularity, & Fervency of the Discourses, being peculiarly fitted to affect our unimproved Minds, and the Lord rendring the Word efficacious, many were convinced of their undone Condition, and constrained to seek deliverance with the greatest Solicitude. A considerable Number convened every Sabbath to hear these Sermons, instead of going to Church, and frequently on Week Days. The Concern of some was so passionate and violent, that they could not avoid crying out, weeping bitterly, &c. and that when such Indications of religious Concern were so strange and ridiculous, that they could not be occasioned by Example or Sympathy, and the Affectation of them would have been so unprofitable an Instance of Hypocrisy, that none could be tempted to it. My Dwelling-House at length was too small to contain the People; whereupon we determined to build a Meeting-House, meerly for Reading; for we knew of no Minister in the World whom we could get to preach to us according to our Liking; and having never been accustomed to social *extempore* Prayer, none of us durst attempt it in Company. By this single Mean sundry were solemnly awakened, and their Conduct ever since is a living Attestation of the Continuance and happy Issue of their Impressions. When the Report of these Sermons and the Effects occasioned by reading them was spread Abroad, I was invited to several Places to read them, at a considerable Distance; and by this Means the Concern was propagated.

* * * * *

I shall now re-assume the Person of my Informer and proceed in his Narrative—"On the 6th of July—43, Mr. [William] *Robinson* preached his first Sermon to us from *Luk.* 13.3.

and continued with us preaching four Days successively. The Congregation was large the first Day; and as the Report of him spread, it vastly encreas'd on the three ensuing. 'Tis hard for the liveliest Imagination to form an Image of the Condition of the Assembly on these glorious Days of the Son of Man. Such of us as had been hungring for the Word before, were lost in an agreable Confusion of various Passions, surprized, astonished, pleased, enraptured! so that we were hardly capable of Self-Government, and some could not refrain from publickly declaring their Transport: we were overwhelmed with the Tho'ts of the unexpected Goodness of God, in allowing us to hear the Gospel preached in a Manner that surpassed even our former Wishes, and much more our Hopes. Many that come thro' Curiosity were *pricked to the Heart;* and but few in the numerous Assemblies on these four Days appeared unaffected. They returned astonishd, alarmed with Apprehensions of their dangerous Condition, convinced of their former entire ignorance of Religion, and anxiously enquiring, what they should do to be saved; and there is Reason to believe there was as much Good done by these four Sermons, as by all the Sermons preached in these Parts before or since.

"Before Mr. *Robinson* left us, he successfully endeavoured to correct some of our *Antinomian* Mistakes, and to bring us to carry on the Worship of God more regularly at our Meetings. He advised us to meet to read good Sermons, and to begin & conclude with Prayer and singing of Psalms, which 'till then we had omitted. When we met next, we complied with his Directions; and when all the rest refused, I read and prayed with Trembling and Diffidence; which Method was observed in sundry Places 'till we were furnished with a Minister. The Blessing of God remarkably attended these more private Means; and it was really astonishing to observe the solemn Impressions begun or continued in many, by hearing good Discourses read. I had repeated invitations to come

to many Places round, some of them 30 or 40 Miles distant, to read; with which I generally comply'd. Considerable Numbers were won't to attend, with eager Attention and awful Solemnity; and sundry were, in a Judgment of Charity, Thoro'ly turned to God, and thereupon erected Meeting-Houses, and chose Readers among themselves, by which the Work was more extensively carried on.

"Soon after our Father, Mr. *Robinson,* left us, the Rev. Mr. *John Blair* paid us a short visit; and truly he came to us *in the Fulness of the Gospel of Christ.* Former Impressions were ripened, and new formed on many Hearts. One Night in particular a whole House-full of People was quite over-come with the Power of the Word, particularly of one pungent Sentence that dropt from his Lips; and they could hardly sit or stand, or keep their Passions under any proper Restraints, so general was the Concern during his Stay with us; and so ignorant were we of the Danger Persons in such a Case were in of Apostacy, which unhappy Observation has since taught us, that we pleased our selves with the Expectation of the *gathering* of more *People* to the divine *Shiloh* than now seem to have been actually gathered to him; tho' there be still the greatest Reason to hope that sundry bound themselves to the Lord in an everlasting Covenant, never to be forgotten.

"Some Time after this, the Rev. Mr. *John Roan,* was sent by the Presbytery of *New-Castle,* (under whose immediate Care we had voluntarily placed ourselves to suppy us.) He continued with us longer than either of the former; and the happy Effects of his Ministrations are still apparent in many Instances. He preached at sundry Places at the earnest Solicitations of the People, which was the happy Occasion of beginning and promoting the religious Concern, where there were little Appearances of it before. This, together with his speaking pretty freely about the Degeneracy of the Clergy in this Colony, gave a general Alarm, and some Measures were concerted to suppress us. To incense the Indignation of the Government the more, a perfidious Wretch deposed, he heard Mr. Roan use some blasphemous Expressions in his Sermon, and speak in the most shocking & reproachful Manner of the established Church. An Indictment was thereupon drawn up against Mr. Roan, (tho' by that Time he had departed the Colony) and some of the People who had invited him to preach at their Houses, were cited to appear before the general Court. . . .

". . . [Our] present Pastor, was sent by the Presbytery to supply us about six Week, in Spring, Anno 1747, when our Discouragements from the Government were renewed and multiplied: For on one Sunday the Governour's Proclamation was set up at our Meeting-House, *strictly requiring all Magistrates to suppress & prohibit, as far as they lawfully could, all itinerant Preachers, &c."* which occasion'd us to forebear Reading that Day, 'till we had Time to deliberate and consult what was expedient to do; but how joyfully were we surprized before the next Sabbath, when we unexpectedly heard that Mr. Davies was come to preach so long among us; and especially, that he had qualified himself according to Law, and obtained the Licensure of four Meeting-Houses among us, which had never been done before! Thus when our Hopes were expiring, and our Liberties more precarious than ever, we were suddenly advanced to a more secure Situation. *"Man's Extremity is the Lord's Opportunity."* For this seasonable Instance of the Interposition of divine Providence, we desire to offer our grateful Praises; and we importune the Friends of Zion generously to concur in the delightful Employ."

Thus, Sir, I have given you a brief Account of the Rise and Progress of Religion here 'till my first coming into the Colony; and the Facts themselves I know to be well attested, tho' the Order in which I have related them, is in some Instances preposterous.—I shall now proceed in my Narrative from my own Knowledge,

and inform you of the State of Affairs since *April 1747.*

The Dissenters here were under peculiar Disadvantages for want of a settled Minister. By this they were not only deprived of the stated Ministrations of the Gospel, but also exposed to great Difficulties from the Government, which could not be wholly removed while they continued vacant; for it was alledged, (this is no proper Place to enquire with how much Law or Reason) that 'till they were an organized Congregation, and had a Minister qualified, and their Meeting-Houses licens'd, according to Law, they could not claim the Liberties and Immunities of the Act of Toleration. . . .

DOCUMENT 4.4
Learning as a Preparation for Living

Samuel Harrison Smith (1772–1845) was an important Republican publisher. He expressed quite representative Jeffersonian sentiments when he urged that social utility should provide the standard for American education.

A tolerably correct idea of Geography would seem, in a Republic especially, to involve great advantages. The interest of the mercantile part of the community is closely connected with correct geographical knowledge. . . .

The cultivation of natural philosophy, particularly so far as it relates to agriculture and manufactures, has been heretofore almost entirely neglected. The benefits, however, which it would produce, are great, both as they regard the happiness of the individual, and as they regard national wealth. Many of the labours of the farmer and the mechanic, so far from forbidding reflection, invite it. . . .

Source: Samuel Harrison Smith, *Remarks on Education* (Philadelphia, 1798), pp. 44–45, 48–51.

This progressive improvement would be promoted, in the third place, by inspiring youth with a taste for, and an attachment to, science, so firm, that it should be almost impossible to eradicate it in the subsequent periods of life. . . .

Rendering, in the fourth place, knowledge as highly practical as possible.

This idea has been already noticed. But it merits a more extensive discussion. Next to the first object it claims the greatest notice.

All science ought to derive its rank from its utility. The real good which it actually does, or is capable of doing, is the only genuine criterion of its value. Man may indulge himself in sublime reveries, but the world will forever remain uninterested in them. It is only when he applies the powers of his mind to objects of general use, that he becomes their benefactor; until he does this he is neither entitled to their gratitude or applause.

He is the best friend of man, who makes discoveries involving effects which benefit mankind the most extensively. Moral truths are therefore of importance but little short of infinite. For they apply to numbers which almost evade enumeration, and to time which loses itself in eternity. These truths, all agree, are not to be fought in the cloister. They are only acquired by uniting the calm and patient reflection of retirement, with the bold and penetrating observation of active life.

In physics, the happiness of mankind is in the highest degree increased by discoveries and improvements connected with agriculture and manufactures. These two occupations employ nine-tenths of most communities, and a much larger proportion of others. Does it not then become an interesting enquiry, whether it be not expedient in infancy and youth to communicate to the mind the leading principles of nature and art in these departments of labour, not only by a theoretic exposition of them, but also by their practical development.

If almost the whole community be destined to pursue one or other of these avocations from necessity, and if it be the duty of an individual to support himself, whenever he can, by an exertion of his own powers; and if these can only yield a sure support from an ability to be acquired in youth to prosecute a particular branch of agriculture or mechanics, does it not seem to be the duty of society to control education in such a way as to secure to every individual this ability? If this ability existed, how much misery would be annihilated, how much crime would be destroyed? . . .

Naked speculation is either unintelligible or uninteresting to the young mind, while it delights in examining external appearances, and often in searching after their causes. . . .

DOCUMENT 4.5
Experimental Science in the Service of Truth

Benjamin Franklin (1706–90) was typical of a number of prominent colonists who contributed to the expansion of knowledge upon which the American Enlightenment rested. He, too, was affected by the claims of natural science, yielding the palm to it rather than to supernaturalism. Practical-minded and worldly, Franklin stressed observable facts and theories capable of verification—that is, the inductive method, rather than revelation, as the way of truth.

In 1746, being at Boston I met there with a Dr. Spence who was lately arrived from Scotland, and show'd me some electric experiments. They were imperfectly perform'd as he was not very expert but, being on a subject quite new to me, they equally surpris'd and

Source: Benjamin Franklin, "Autobiography," in *The Works of Benjamin Franklin* ed. John Bigelow (New York, 1904), vol. 1, pp. 289–93.

pleased me. Soon after my return to Philadelphia, our library company receiv'd from Mr. P. Collinson, Fellow of the Royal Society of London, a present of a glass tube with some account of the use of it in making such experiments. I eagerly seized the opportunity of repeating what I had seen at Boston; and, by much practice, acquir'd great readiness in performing those, also, which we had an account of from England, adding a number of new ones. I say much practice, for my house was continually full, for some time, with people who came to see these new wonders. . . .

Oblig'd as we were to Mr. Collinson for his present of the tube, etc., I thought it right he should be inform'd of our success in using it, and wrote him several letters containing accounts of our experiments. He got them read in the Royal Society where they were not at first thought worth so much notice as to be printed in their Transactions. One paper, which I wrote for Mr. Kinnersley, on the sameness of lightning with electricity, I sent to Dr. Mitchel, an acquaintance of mine and one of the members also of that society, who wrote me word that it had been read, but was laughed at by the connoisseurs. The papers, however, being shown to Dr. Fothergill, he thought they were of too much value to be stifled and advis'd the printing of them, Mr. Collinson then gave them to Cave for publication in his *Gentleman's Magazine;* but he chose to print them separately in a pamphlet. . . .

It was, however, some time before those papers were much taken notice of in England. A copy of them happening to fall into the hands of the Count de Buffon, a philosopher deservedly of great reputation in France, and, indeed, all over Europe, he prevailed with M. Dalibard to translate them into French, and they were printed at Paris. The publication offended the Abbé Nollet, preceptor in Natural Philosophy to the royal family, and an able experimenter, who had form'd and publish'd a theory of electricity, which then had the gen-

eral vogue. He could not at first believe that such a work came from America, and said it must have been fabricated by his enemies at Paris, to decry his system. Afterwards, having been assur'd that there really existed such a person as Franklin at Philadelphia, which he had doubted, he wrote and published a volume of "Letters," chiefly address'd to me, defending his theory, and denying the verity of my experiments and of the positions deduc'd from them.

I once purpos'd answering the abbé, and actually began the answer, but, on consideration that my writings contain'd a description of experiments which any one might repeat and verify, and if not to be verifi'd, could not be defended; or of observations offer'd as conjectures and not delivered dogmatically, therefore not laying me under any obligation to defend them; and reflecting that a dispute between two persons, writing in different languages, might be lengthened greatly by mistranslations and thence misconceptions of one another's meaning, much of one of the abbé's letters being founded on an error in the translation. I concluded to let my papers shift for themselves, believing it was better to spend what time I could spare from public business in making new experiments, than in disputing about those already made. I therefore never answered M. Nollet, and the event gave me no cause to repent my silence; for my friend M. le Roy, of the Royal Academy of Sciences, took up my cause and refuted him; my book was translated into the Italian, German, and Latin languages, and the doctrine it contain'd was by degrees universally adopted by the philosophers of Europe in preference to that of the abbé; so that he lived to see himself the last of his sect, except Monsieur B——, of Paris, his *élève* and immediate disciple.

What gave my book the more sudden and general celebrity, was the success of one of its proposed experiments, made by Messrs. Dalibard and De Lor at Marly, for drawing lightning from the clouds. This engaged the public attention every where. M. de Lor, who had an apparatus for experimental philosophy, and lectur'd in that branch of science, undertook to repeat what he called the *Philadelphia Experiments;* and, after they were performed before the king and court, all the curious of Paris flocked to see them. I will not swell this narrative with an account of that capital experiment, nor of the infinite pleasure I receiv'd in the success of a similar one I made soon after with a kite at Philadelphia, as both are to be found in the histories of electricity.

. . . Some members of the Society in London, particularly the very ingenious Mr. Canton, having verified the experiment of procuring lightning from the clouds by a pointed rod, and acquainting them with the success, they soon made me more than amends for the slight with which they had before treated me. . . .

DOCUMENT 4.6
The Voice of Deism

Thomas Paine (1737–1809), son of a corsetmaker to whose trade he had been apprenticed, was English born. After an unsettled early life, he migrated to America in 1774 and became a naturalized citizen, the leading revolutionary propagandist, and a confirmed deist. His plea for a rational Christianity, The Age of Reason (1794), *is the classic statement of American deism and possibly the most widely read deistic work of all times.*

I believe in one God, and no more; and I hope for happiness beyond this life.

I believe in the equality of man, and I believe

Source: Thomas Paine, "The Age of Reason," in *Writings of Thomas Paine* ed. Moncure D. Conway (New York, 1896), vol. 4, pp. 188–90.

that religious duties consist in doing justice, loving mercy, and endeavouring to make our fellow-creatures happy.

But, lest it should be supposed that I believe in many other things in addition to these, I shall, in the progress of this work, declare the things I do not believe, and my reasons for not believing them.

I do not believe in the creed professed by the Jewish church, by the Roman church, by the Greek church, by the Turkish church, by the Protestant church, nor by any church that I know of. My own mind is my church.

All national institutions of churches, whether Jewish, Christian, or Turkish, appear to me no other than human inventions set up to terrify and enslave mankind, and monopolize power and profit.

I do not mean by this declaration to condemn those who believe otherwise; they have the same right to their belief as I have to mine. But it is necessary to the happiness of man, that he be mentally faithful to himself. Infidelity does not consist in believing, or in disbelieving; it consists in professing to believe what he does not believe. . . .

If we consider the nature of our condition here, we must see there is no occasion for such a thing as *revealed religion*. What is it we want to know? Does not the creation, the universe we behold, preach to us the existence of an Almighty Power, that governs and regulates the whole? And is not the evidence that this creation holds out to our senses infinitely stronger than any thing we can read in a book, that any imposter might make and call the word of God? As for morality, the knowledge of it exists in every man's conscience.

Here we are. The existence of an Almighty Power is sufficiently demonstrated to us, though we cannot conceive, as it is impossible we should, the nature and manner of its existence. We cannot conceive how we came here ourselves, and yet we know for a fact that we are here. . . .

Deism then teaches us, without the possibility of being deceived, all that is necessary or proper to be known. The creation is the Bible of the Deist. He there reads, in the hand-writing of the Creator himself, the certainty of his existence, and the immutability of his power; and all other Bibles and Testaments are to him forgeries. The probability that we may be called to account hereafter, will, to reflecting minds, have the influence of belief; for it is not our belief or disbelief that can make or unmake the fact. As this is the state we are in, and which it is proper we should be in, as free agents, it is the fool only, and not the philosopher, nor even the prudent man, that will live as if there were no God.

But the belief of a God is so weakened by being mixed with the strange fable of the Christian creed, and with the wild adventures related in the Bible, and the obscurity and obscene nonsense of the Testament, that the mind of man is bewildered as in a fog. Viewing all these things in a confused mass, he confounds fact with fable; and as he cannot believe all, he feels a disposition to reject all. But the belief of a God is a belief distinct from all other things, and ought not to be confounded with any. The notion of a Trinity of Gods has enfeebled the belief of *one* God. A multiplication of beliefs acts as a division of belief; and in proportion as anything is divided, it is weakened.

Religion, by such means, becomes a thing of form instead of fact; of notion instead of principles; morality is banished to make room for an imaginary thing called faith, and this faith has its origin in a supposed debauchery; a man is preached instead of a God; an execution is an object for gratitude; the preachers daub themselves with the blood, like a troop of assassins, and pretend to admire the brilliancy it gives them; they preach a humdrum sermon on the merits of the execution; then praise Jesus Christ for being executed, and condemn the Jews for doing it. A man, by hearing all this nonsense lumped and preached together, confounds the God of the Creation with the imagined God of the Christians, and lives as if there were none.

Of all the systems of religion that ever were invented, there is none more derogatory to the Almighty, more unedifying to man, more repugnant to reason, and more contradictory in itself, than this thing called Christianity. Too absurd for belief, too impossible to convince, and too inconsistent for practice, it renders the heart torpid, or produces only atheists and fanatics. As an engine of power, it serves the purpose of despotism; and as a means of wealth, the avarice of priests; but so far as respects the good of man in general, it leads to nothing here or hereafter.

The only religion that has not been invented, and that has in it every evidence of divine originality, is pure and simple Deism. It must have been the first and will probably be the last that man believes. But pure and simple Deism does not answer the purpose of despotic governments. They cannot lay hold of religion as an engine but by mixing it with human inventions, and making their own authority a part; neither does it answer the avarice of priests, but by incorporating themselves and their functions with it, and becoming, like the government, a party in the system. It is this that forms the otherwise mysterious connection of church and state; the church human, and the state tyrannic.

Were a man impressed as fully and strongly as he ought to be with the belief of a God, his moral life would be regulated by the force of that belief; he would stand in awe of God, and of himself, and would not do the thing that could not be concealed from either. To give this belief the full opportunity of force, it is necessary that it acts alone. This is Deism. . . .

chapter 5

The Republican Revolution

Gordon S. Wood
Brown University

Because the American Revolution was not like other revolutions, it is not easily interpreted. Most of us cannot quite believe that we had a real revolution like other nations and peoples have had: where property was destroyed, people were killed, society was disrupted, and everything became different. The American Revolution had no reign of terror, and many of the leaders who began it were in control at its end. It does not appear to have the same kinds of social causes or social character that other revolutions have had. The American colonists were not an oppressed people; they had no crushing imperial chains to throw off. In fact, the colonists knew they were freer, more prosperous, and less burdened with cumbersome feudal and monarchical restraints than any part of mankind in the eighteenth century. To be sure, there were growing social distinctions in the colonies and increasing poverty in the provincial cities; but in eighteenth-century America, there was nothing remotely comparable to the fabulous wealth of the English nobility or the vile and violent slums of London. Hence, explaining the Revolution in social terms, as a class conflict or as an uprising of the poor against the rich, has been very difficult. The American Revolution does not seem to involve the sorts of social oppression or economic deprivation that lie behind other revolutions.

Consequently, much of our history writing has minimized the radical and social character of the American Revolution. Most often it has been viewed as an intellectual defense of American constitutional rights against British encroachment (''no taxation without representation''), fought not to change the existing social order, but to preserve it. Some historians have even seen the Revolution as nothing but a colonial war for independence. In short, our Revolution as we like to say, was a peculiarly conservative affair, exclusively concerned with politics and with political rights and, in comparison with the social purposes and social character of other revolutions, hardly a revolution at all.

Much of this is true enough; but the conservative, exclusively political interpretation of the Revolution is ultimately misleading. Of course, the American Revolution was different from other revolutions, but it was not less radical and social for being different. It was radical and social, however, in a very special eighteenth-century sense. No doubt much of the concerns and language of the premodern, pre-Marxian eighteenth century were almost entirely political. That was because men in that different, distant world could not conceive of society apart from politics. Social distinctions, social deprivations, and social evils were generally still regarded as rooted in the abuses of government. Titles of social rank, privileges and monopolies, even property and wealth of various sorts, all seemed ultimately to flow from connections to government, in the end, to royal authority. Hence, when eighteenth-century radicals on both sides of the Atlantic talked in what seem to be only political terms—of protecting liberty from royal power and privilege, purifying a corrupt constitution, and becoming republicans—they nevertheless had a decidedly social message. In our eyes, the American Revolutionaries appear to be absorbed in changing only their governments, not their society. But, in destroying monarchy and establishing republican governments they were changing their society, too, and they knew it. Republicanism implied a new kind of social order.

We cannot appreciate what republicanism meant for the Revolutionaries unless we understand something of the nature of the old society it replaced. Eighteenth-century Anglo-American society, as the English historian Harold Perkin describes it, was still essentially precapitalist, a society of personal influence and dependent relationships that sustained a world totally unlike that of nineteenth-century America or today. This old society was a hierarchy of different levels and ranks that ran from the king at the top to the black slaves on the bottom. In between there were various degrees of dependency, including large numbers of bonded white persons. Even a modest household was likely to have apprentices or indentured servants. In such a society "men were acutely aware of their exact relation to those immediately above and below them, but only vaguely conscious except at the very top of their connections with those of their own level." This society was bound together by vertical lines of interest and connection rather than by the horizontal solidarities of class and occupation that we are more familiar with. Individuals did not think in modern class terms—of society divided

into mutually hostile layers each united against the others by a common source of income or common occupation. The only horizontal cleavage of great importance was that between gentlemen and common people, and that was scarcely defined solely in economic terms. Up and down the social chains ran links of vertical connection—two-way relations between patrons and clients based on mutual trust—"a social nexus peculiar to the old society, less formal and inescapable than feudal homage, more personal and comprehensive than the contractual, employment relationships of the capitalist 'Cash Payment.' For those who lived within its embrace," says Perkin, this vertical relationship "was so much an integral part of the texture of life that they had no name for it save 'friendship.' "

In this old society, select individuals, gentlemen of property, were far more influential as patrons than is the case today. Eighteenth-century gentlemen, with their networks of kin and connections, their easier access to markets and to political and legal authority, played crucial mediating roles for numerous clients and dependents, and they reinforced the assumption that superiority of all sorts was unitary and indivisible. Who you were and whom you knew were far more important than what you could do. In the absence of the impersonal selection procedures and institutions that we take for granted, patronage and personal influence inevitably formed the vertical links and loyalties that held the social hierarchy together and made things work. Appointments to government offices, the securing of military commissions or judgeships, the awarding of land or contracts—all were the political aspects of a personal system of recruitment and attachment that ramified throughout the society. Creditors and debtors, masters and apprentices, husbands and wives, landlords and tenants, teachers and students—all were tied together by strings of interest and dependency, and social relations at all levels were determined by personal selection and influence. When men moved up within the hierarchy, it was not usually because they had worked hard and saved money and gone to college; rather, it was because they had obtained the "friendship" of someone who had power and influence—whether it was the governor appointing a Justice of the Peace, or a merchant lending money, or a minister helping someone's son go to Yale.

We are too apt to think of eighteenth-century America in terms of Benjamin Franklin, printer, making it. But Franklin's career was extraordinary, to say the least; and in his lifetime, at least before the Revolution, he was never celebrated in America as the common man who made good. In fact, Franklin spent most of his lifetime seeking patronage and place within English society and politics, and he really did not become an American until the late 1760s, when all hopes for an English position were squashed. His *Autobiography* was written after he had abandoned his English political and social ambitions, and it became a kind of justification of his failure, a salve for his disillusionment, and ultimately, to readers of the nineteenth century—who actually established Franklin's modern bourgeois "Poor Richard" reputation—a vindication of the American Revolution and the changes it had made in the old patronage society.

Such patronage was, of course, most evident in politics. The key to Sir Lewis Namier's great success as a historian in opening up the nature of eighteenth-century politics for us in the twentieth century was his perception of the special character of these vertical relationships, and his understanding of the peculiar behavior of the politicians in whom the vertical chains of patronage and "friendship" converged. Politics in this society was highly personal, dependent on face-to-face relations or on the widespread use of personal correspondence. Such politics—more like faculty politics today in departments or colleges than in a democratic society—such politics involved a great deal of personal contacts, personal maneuvering and

manipulation, and put a premium on certain traits of character—on circumspection, caution, prudence, and calculation. It was this personal structure of politics, this prevalence of numerous vertical links and loyalties, and not simply men's abhorrence of division, that explains the absence of organized political parties in the eighteenth century. We now know that it was not really any sort of extensive legal restrictions on the suffrage that kept most colonists from political participation. As yet, only a few members of the society thought of politics as a means by which the problems of their lives could be resolved. Some historians have grasped at the notion of deference to explain the willing acceptance by most eighteenth-century men of elite gentry rule; but "deference" seems too simple a concept to explain the complexity of these innumerable ties of dependency, patronage, and connection. When, in 1743, Henry Beekman, a large New York landowner, interceded on behalf of several small freeholders of his county who were faced with an ejectment suit, he exercised the power of patronage available in his dominant position. Although he told the beneficiaries of his aid that he would "expect no other reward for this than your friendship," he clearly expected such friendship to manifest itself in political allegiance at election time.

In the end, for America and for Great Britain, it was the disintegration of this older patronage society of dependent relationships that prepared the way for the emergence of the liberal, modern, capitalistic world of the early nineteenth century. In America, the disintegration had begun early. The reordering of colonial life in the first century and a half of American history had either prohibited or inhibited a duplication of the normal social patterns of the mother country. To the extent that the colonists had already destroyed or had never established this traditional society, to the degree that Americans were splintered by religious and ethnic diversity and were more independent, more resentful and mistrustful of one another—to that extent, eighteenth-century America was already more modern than England.

Not only did colonial society lack a titled nobility, but the American upper level of gentlemen was weak and thin in comparison with the English gentry. The American "aristocracy," such as it was, was far more bourgeois in its nature and far more precariously based in the economy. It consequently had to scramble for its wealth and symbols of distinction far more greedily than the more stable gentry of England. Hence, the American gentlemanly leaders always appeared far more mercenary than did the English squirearchy; they were never able to duplicate the paternalism, the mutual protection and allegiance between superiors and inferiors that made the English aristocracy so relatively secure.

The use of personal influence in religion, in the economy, or in politics was never as deeply entrenched in America as it was in England. Militia officers were often selected by their companies; ministers were hired by their congregations; and many politicians were elected by an extremely broad electorate. Landed tenantry was rare in America, and yeoman farmers, in contrast to England, maintained a remarkable degree of independence. Everywhere multiplying religions and ethnic groups—whether Baptists in New England or Germans in Pennsylvania—sought the support of their own kind, and they often cut through traditional lines of interest and patronage. Mistrust, jealousy, and competition among individuals and groups were always more extensive in America than in England. All sorts of privileges and monopolies, from military contracts to tavern licenses, which made sense in the hierarchical patronage society of the mother country, were continually suspect in the colonies. The recipients of such privileges—those in whom the lines of personal influence were supposed to converge—were never as readily identifiable in America. In fact, the very weakness of the patronage society in the colonies only made the bonds of personal influence that did exist seem more arbitrary and unjust, and hence, more vulnerable to challenge.

By the middle of the eighteenth century, what remained of this older paternalistic world in the colonies was steadily eroding. Not only were new commercial arrangements—like the Scottish factorage system in the Chesapeake—emerging to break apart older personal marketing and credit relationships, but new immigration and the internal movement of tens of thousands of settlers—down the Appalachian valley into the Carolinas, up the Connecticut river into Vermont—shattered traditional communal and kinship ties.

It was in politics, however, where the erosions of the old society were most manifest; and it was in politics where the battle lines were drawn. During the middle decades of the eighteenth century, colonial politics became increasingly popularized as opposition groups in the colonial assemblies resorted to making more and more appeals to the people, as a counterweight to the use of royal authority by the governors. The weakening of older connections, and the further fragmentation of colonial interests, forced Crown officials and other conservatives into strenuous efforts to tighten up the society and to lessen popular participation in politics. Some of them attempted to restrict the expansion of popular representation in the assemblies, to limit the meetings of the assemblies, and to control the laws passed by the assemblies. Others toyed with plans for remodeling the colonial governments, for making the salaries of royal officials independent of the colonial legislatures, and for strengthening the royal councils or upper houses in the legislatures. Some even suggested introducing a titled nobility into America in order to stabilize colonial society. But most royal officials simply tried to use whatever traditional instruments of political patronage and influence they had available to them to curb popular disorder and pressure—relying on intricate maneuvering and personal manipulation of individuals in place of appeals to the people.

In the 1760s, all of these efforts became hopelessly entangled in the British government's attempts to extract revenue from the colonists and to reform the awkwardly structured empire. Everything came together to threaten each American's expanding expectations of liberty and independence. In the emotionally charged atmosphere of the 1760s and 70s, all the British and royal efforts at reform seemed to be an evil extension of what was destroying liberty in England itself. Through the manipulation of puppets or placemen in the House of Commons, the Crown—since 1760 in the hands of a new young Tory king, George III—unhinged the English constitution and sapped the strength of popular representation in Parliament. As events in the 1760s and 70s show, the Crown with the aid of a pliant Parliament was trying to reach across the Atlantic to corrupt Americans in the same way.

Already in some colonies this corruption, this use of patronage and preferments, had created tiny pockets of Crown influence, even among some of the royally commissioned justices of the peace. It had turned much of America into a dumping ground for worthless English place-seekers, and allowed even native Americans, like the clan of Thomas Hutchinson in Massachusetts, to pile up offices to the exclusion of those who, John Adams and James Otis felt, were better men. The prevailing revulsion against this sort of corruption even spilled over to affect those who were unconnected with royal authority, and it explains some of the anger of Virginians, like Thomas Jefferson, James Madison, Patrick Henry, and Richard Henry Lee, against the older clique of tidewater planters who tended to look after one another and to restrain the entry of others into their inner circle. Nothing was worse, Virginia critics of this clique said, than that "dreaded foe to public virtue, warm and private friendship."

Although the focus of American thinking in the 1760s and 70s was on politics, such attacks on "friendship" could not be confined to government or even to Crown officials.

In this peculiar eighteenth-century context, one can best understand the Revolutionaries' appeal for independence—not just the independence of the United States, but the independence of different parts of the government from one another (particularly the independence of the legislature from the executive) and, most importantly, the independence of individuals from personal influence and "warm and private friendship." The republican ideology that American leaders invoked in their struggle with Great Britain was centrally concerned with independence and the elimination of corruption. It drew on a Western tradition stretching back to the classical times of ancient Greece and Rome. As developed and refined by eighteenth-century English radicals, this republican heritage could be used to explain and to justify American resistance and revolution as well as the erection of new independent governments. In the new revolutionary constitutions of 1776, nearly all the states struck out at corruption in government and forbade members of the executive from simultaneously holding seats in the legislatures (which forever prohibited the development of parliamentary cabinet government in America). Everywhere, Americans sought to reduce the artificial influence of government over the shape of their society.

By invoking republicanism and by attacking corruption, however, Americans were not simply expressing their resentment toward particular political practices that had denied some of them the highest offices of government. They were actually tearing at the bonds holding the traditional society together. Their assault was therefore as much social as it was political. But the social meaning was not one of class conflict; it grew out of that distinctive eighteenth-century society. The great social antagonists of the pre-Revolutionary period were not the poor versus the rich, or even democrats versus aristocrats, but rather patriots versus courtiers. Courtiers were persons whose position or rank came artificially from above—from personal connections and influence that ultimately flowed from the Crown or court. Patriots, though, were those who not only loved their country but were free of independent connections and influence; their position or rank came naturally from their talent, from below, and from recognition by the people.

A society of patriots was in effect a republic. Hence, the Americans' eventual resort to republicanism in 1776 flowed naturally from their goals and possessed immense social significance—a significance that for the eighteenth century was as radical as Marxism to the nineteenth century. Republicanism presumed, as the Virginia Declaration of Rights stated in 1776, that men would be "equally free and independent." Citizens in a republic would relate to each other and to the state voluntarily and equally. Unlike monarchies, whose corrupting influence and numerous dependent ranks maintained public order, even over a large and diverse populace, republics had to be held together by the people's willingly offered service, from patriotism or, as the eighteenth century called it, from "virtue."

From this belief, heightened by the knowledge of what had happened to the republics of antiquity, it is not surprising that Americans would become obsessed with their own morality.

This morality or virtue demanded independent individuals. For, as Jefferson said, "dependence begets subservience and venality, suffocates the germ of virtue, and prepares fit tools for the designs of ambition." Hence, the sturdy independent yeomen, Jefferson's "chosen people of God," were regarded as the most incorruptible and therefore the best citizens for a republic. The celebration of the farmer in the years following the Revolution was not a literary conceit but a scientifically based imperative of republican government.

In such a world of free independent men, slavery, which had existed for over a century without substantial criticism, suddenly became an excruciating anomaly. Since the seventeenth century, most colonists had taken slavery for granted as simply the most base and dependent status in a hierarchy of different dependent ranks. But republican equality now compelled Americans to confront the aberration of slavery in their midst as they never had to before, and if they were to retain it, to defend and justify it as a "peculiar institution."

Despite republicanism's stress on equality, the Revolutionaries did not intend to level their society. Jefferson still envisioned social and economic distinctions; only now these distinctions would be based, not on private connections or governmental influence, but on merit. Republicanism was opposed to all legal privileges and unequal and artifically created inheritance patterns; but equality did not mean a redistribution of property. Although excessive wealth might be dangerous in a republic, the individual possession of property was central to a republic. For property, particularly landed property, guaranteed a man's independence. Jefferson feared the rabble of the cities precisely because they were propertyless and dependent. All dependents, such as women and young men, could be denied the vote, because, as a convention of Essex County, Massachusetts, declared in 1778, they were "so situated as to have no wills of their own." Jefferson was so keen on this equation of property with citizenship that he proposed in 1776 that the new state of Virginia grant fifty acres of land to every man who did not have as much.

Of course, the Revolution in the end went farther than most American leaders in 1776 intended. Indeed, republicanism created a society, in some respects, the exact opposite of what was hoped for. The republican stress on equality was expanded and was soon used to question the natural distinctions the Revolutionary leaders had taken for granted. Even as early as the 1780s, the claim that one man was as good as any other seemed to breed licentiousness in the states and to require a restrengthening of governmental and executive authority. Independent patriots were not supposed to become selfish, moneymaking individualists; but the permissiveness of republicanism made it difficult to restrain individualistic and capitalistic pressures. By freeing persons from older social connections and dependencies, and by making them the independent shapers of their destinies, republicanism helped to create the nineteenth-century acquisitive society of scrambling self-made men that Tocqueville described. Yet, for all of its unanticipated consequences, republicanism summed up the meaning of the American Revolution. It identified us as a people and defined most of our noblest ideals and values. It gave us our sense, that we were in the vanguard of history, pointing the way toward a society different from what men had ever known—where people were freer, more independent, more equal, and more able to achieve their aspirations.

SUGGESTED READINGS

Bailyn, Bernard. *The Ideological Origins of the American Revolution.* Cambridge, Mass.: Harvard University Press, 1967.

Bailyn, Bernard. *The Ordeal of Thomas Hutchinson.* Cambridge, Mass.: Harvard University Press, 1974.

Christie, Ian R., and Benjamin W. Labaree. *Empire or Independence, 1760–1776.* New York: Norton, 1976.

Foner, Eric. *Tom Paine and Revolutionary America.* New York: Oxford University Press, 1976.

Gipson, Lawrence H. *The Coming of the Revolution, 1763–1775.* New York: Harper, 1954.

Jameson, J. Franklin. *The American Revolution Considered as a Social Movement.* Princeton, N.J.: Princeton University Press, 1926.

Jensen, Merrill. *The Founding of a Nation.* New York: Oxford University Press, 1968.

Henretta, James A. *The Evolution of American Society, 1700–1815.* Lexington, Mass.: D. C. Heath, 1973.

Namier, Sir Lewis. *England in the Age of the American Revolution.* London: Macmillan, 1930.

Olson, Alison Gilbert. *Anglo-American Politics, 1660–1775.* New York: Oxford University Press, 1973.

Palmer, Robert R. *The Age of the Democratic Revolution: A Political History of Europe and America, 1760–1800.* 2 vols. Princeton, N.J.: Princeton University Press, 1959, 1964.

Perkin, Harold J. *The Origins of Modern English Society, 1780–1880.* London: Routledge & Kegan Paul, 1969.

Pole, J. R. *Political Representation in England and the Origins of the American Republic.* New York: Macmillan, 1966.

Wood, Gordon S. *The Creation of the American Republic, 1776–1787.* Chapel Hill: University of North Carolina Press, 1969.

Young, Alfred F., ed. *The American Revolution.* De Kalb, Ill.: Northern Illinois University Press, 1976.

DOCUMENT 5.1
The Ladder of Social Dependency

Henry Fielding in this passage from his great comic novel, The Adventures of Joseph Andrews *(1742), succinctly captures the particularly vertical nature of eighteenth-century English society. Although colonial society lacked all the intricate calibrations of English society, it was similarly organized.*

. . . It may not be unpleasant to survey the picture of dependence like a kind of ladder; as, for instance: early in the morning arises the postilion, or some other boy, which great families, no more than great ships, are without, and falls to brushing the clothes and cleaning the shoes of John the footman; who, being drest himself, applies his hands to the same labours for Mr. Second-hand, the squire's gentleman; the gentleman in the like manner, a

Source: Henry Fielding, *The Adventures of Joseph Andrews* (London, 1742), bk. 2, chap. 13.

little later in the day, attends the squire; the squire is no sooner equipped than he attends the levee of my lord; which is no sooner over than my lord himself is seen at the levee of the favourite, who, after the hour of homage is at an end, appears himself to pay homage to the levee of his sovereign. Nor is there, perhaps, in this whole ladder of dependence, any one step at a greater distance from the other than the first from the second; so that to a philosopher the question might only seem, whether you would choose to be a great man at six in the morning, or at two in the afternoon. And yet there are scarce two of these who do not think the least familiarity with the persons below them a condescension, and, if they were to go one step farther, a degradation.

DOCUMENT 5.2
Tyrants and Courtiers

Perhaps no Revolutionary leader was more resentful of Lieutenant Governor Thomas Hutchinson of Massachusetts and those connected with him than the young, ambitious lawyer John Adams. In his diary and writings, Adams often revealed just how attractive and tempting power and position could be.

1765

. . . [L]et us ask a few questions. Has not his Honor the Lieutenant-Governor discovered to the people, in innumerable instances, a very ambitious and avaricious disposition? Has he not grasped four of the most important offices in the Province into his own hands? Has not his brother-in-law, Oliver, another of the greatest places in government? Is not a brother of the Secretary, a judge of the superior court? Has not that brother a son in the House? Has

Source: *The Works of John Adams*, ed., C. F. Adams (Boston, 1850–51), vol. 2, pp. 150–51; 293–95, vol. 4, p. 43.

not the Secretary a son in the House, who is also a judge in one of the counties? Did not that son marry the daughter of another of the Judges of the Superior Court? Has not the Lieutenant-Governor a brother, a Judge of the pleas in Boston, and a namesake and near relation who is another Judge? Has not the Lieutenant-Governor a near relation who is register of his own court of probate, and deputy secretary? Has he not another near relation who is Clerk of the House of Representatives? Is not this amazing ascendency of one family foundation sufficient on which to erect a tyranny? Is it not enough to excite jealousies among the people?

1772

"If I would but go to hell, for an eternal moment or so, I might be knighted."

Shakspeare.

Shakspeare, that great master of every affection of the heart and every sentiment of the mind, as well as of all the powers of expression, it sometimes fond of a certain pointed oddity of language, a certain quaintness of style that is an imperfection in his character. The motto prefixed to this paper may be considered as an example to illustrate this observation.

Abstracted from the point and conceit in the style, there is sentiment enough in these few words to fill a volume. It is a striking representation of that struggle which I believe always happens between virtue and ambition, when a man first commences a courtier. By a courtier, I mean one who applies himself to the passions and prejudices, the follies and vices of great men, in order to obtain their smiles, esteem, and patronage, and consequently their favors and preferment. Human nature, depraved as it is, has interwoven in its very frame a love of truth, sincerity, and integrity, which must be overcome by art, education, and habit, before the man can become entirely ductile to the will of a dishonest master. When such a master requires of all who seek his favor an implicit resignation to his will and humor, and these require that he be soothed, flattered, and assisted in his vices and follies, perhaps the blackest crimes that men can commit, the first thought of this will produce in a mind not yet entirely debauched, a soliloquy something like my motto, as if he should say,—

"The Minister of State or the Governor would promote my interest, would advance me to places of honor and profit, would raise me to titles and dignities that will be perpetuated in my family; in a word, would make the fortune of me and my posterity forever, if I would but comply with his desires, and become his instrument to promote his measures. But still I dread the consequences. He requires of me such compliances, such horrid crimes, such a sacrifice of my honor, my conscience, my friends, my country, my God, as the Scriptures inform us must be punished with nothing less than hell-fire, eternal torment; and this is so unequal a price to pay for the honors and emoluments in the power of a Minister or Governor, that I cannot prevail upon myself to think of it. The duration of future punishment terrifies me. If I could but deceive myself so far as to think eternity a moment only, I could comply and be promoted."

Such as these are probably the sentiments of a mind as yet pure and undefiled in its morals; and many and severe are the pangs and agonies it must undergo, before it will be brought to yield entirely to temptation.

Notwithstanding this, we see every day that our imaginations are so strong, and our reason so weak, the charms of wealth and power are so enchanting, and the belief of future punishment so faint, that men find ways to persuade themselves to believe any absurdity, to submit to any prostitution, rather than forego their wishes and desires. Their reason becomes at last an eloquent advocate on the side of their passions, and they bring themselves to believe that black is white, that vice is virtue, that folly is wisdom, and eternity a moment.

1775

. . . The nature of the encroachment upon the American constitution is such, as to grow every day more and more encroaching. Like a cancer, it eats faster and faster every hour. The revenue creates pensioners, and the pensioners urge for more revenue. The people grow less steady, spirited, and virtuous, the seekers more numerous and more corrupt, and every day increases the circles of their dependents and expectants, until virtue, integrity, public spirit, simplicity, and frugality, become the objects of ridicule and scorn, and vanity, luxury, foppery, selfishness, meanness, and downright venality swallow up the whole society.

DOCUMENT 5.3
Republican Resentment

In one of his many satires, William Livingston, governor of the newly independent state of New Jersey, explored the sense of political and social deprivation that lay behind the resentment of many patriot Whigs against the Tory courtiers and royal officials.

TO THE PRINTER OF THE NEW-JERSEY GAZETTE.

Sir,

Several essays have been published in your Gazette, and in other News-papers, calculated to prove the superior excellence of our independence to that of our subordination of Great-Britain. But as the lion told the man, who showed him the statue of a human figure with

---

Source: Trenton *New Jersey Gazette*, Sept 9, 1778, in *New Jersey Archives* ed., Francis B. Lee 2nd ser. (Trenton, 1903), vol. 2, pp. 416–20.

that of a lion at his feet, "that men were the only statuaries;" and that if *lions* understood the art of carving images, they would represent the "man prostrate before the lion"—So I may venture to say that all those essays are the compositions of warm *whigs,* who are intoxicated with the imaginary charms of democracy: and that were the *friends of government* to handle the subject, they could easily shew its superiority to all our republican and levelling systems. This talk I have undertaken in a firm reliance of being allowed that freedom of sentiment to which, according to our professed ideas of liberty, every man seems to be clearly entitled—I shall, therefore, without any apprehensions of exposing myself to a legal prosecution, and with the greatest decorum and impartiality, proceed to particularize some eminent advantages peculiar to the old government, of which we are most lamentably deprived by our independency and republicanism. . . .

That the vulgar should be flattered by our muggletonian, tatterdemalion governments, is not to be wondered at, considering into what importance those whimsical raggamuffin constitutions have elevated the heretofore dispicable and insignificant mobility. But I am astonished that men of fashion and spirit should prefer our hotchpotch, oliverian, oligargical anarchies, to the beautiful, the *constitutional,* the *jure divino,* and the heaven-descended monarchy of Britain. For pray how are the better sort amidst our universal *levelism,* to get into offices? During the halcyon days of *royalty* and *loyalty,* if a gentleman was only blessed with a handsome wife or daughter, or would take the trouble of informing the ministry of the disaffection of the colonies, suggesting at the same time the most proper measures for reducing them to parliamentary submission, (the inexhaustible source of all peace and felicity) he was instantly rewarded with some lucrative appointment, his own disqualifications and the maledictions of the rabble notwithstanding. But how is a gentleman of family, who is al-

ways entitled to a fortune, to be promoted to a post of profit, or station of eminence in these times of *unsubordination* and *fifth monarchynism?* Why, he must deport himself like a man of virtue and honor, (which abridges him of a thousand innocent liberties) and would in almost any other employment yield him ten times the amount of his emoluments. He must moreover pretend to be a patriot, and to love his country, and he must consequently be a hypocrite, and act under perpetual restraint, or he is detected and discarded with infamy. Besides, it is not only the smallness of our salaries, and the necessity of having an adequate degree of merit to get into office, (a condition never exacted by the generosity of monarchs) but the comparative scarity of offices themselves, that must make every man of laudable ambition eternally regret our revolt from the *mother country:* For the present governments being manufactured by the populace, who have worked themselves into a pursuasion of I know not what, of public weal and public virtue, and the interest of one's country, it has been ridiculously imagined that there ought to be no more offices in a state than are absolutely requisite for what these *deluded creatures* call the benefit of the commonwealth. Under the old constitution, on the contrary, whenever the crown was graciously disposed to oblige a gentleman, (and the royal coffers at the happy juncture of princely munificence happened to shew rather too much of their bottoms) an office was instantly invented for the purpose; and both land and water, earth and sea should be ransacked, but his Majesty would create a *Surveyor of Woods* and a *Sounder of Coasts.* Thus every humble suitor who had a proper introduction was always sure of being genteely provided for, without either consulting a mob, or losing any time about the wild chimera of public utility. . . .

We have irretrievably lost, by our fatal revolt, another important advantage, I mean the late useful and uninterrupted influx of the British gallantry, and all the politeness of the Court of London. While we received our governors and other principal officers immediately from the fountain-head of high life and polish'd manners, it was impossible for us to degenerate into our primitive clownishness and rusticity. But these being now unfortunately excluded, we shall gradually reimmerse into plain hospitality, and downright honest sincerity; than which nothing can be more insipid to a man of breeding and *politesse*. Alas, how often shall we recall to mind those jovial and delicious hours, when our bucks experienced the inimitable *conviviality,* and our belles the not-to-be-told-of endearments of a *Dunmore*[1] and a Sparks![2] And with respect to that unnecessary and *rebellious* innovation in the ancient and *constitutional* colour of the British military uniform, which Congress have wantonly transformed into all the multifarious discolorations of *Joseph's coat;* I *pertest,* were I a woman, I should instantly turn tory in revenge of the dismal prospect of our not having, by next Christmas, a single *red-coat* on the continent.

Our printers, I am confident, will universally join me in my lamentation over our unfortunate secession. These gentlemen, in conformity to the principles of our civil establishments, (probably indeed coincident with their own, but that renders foreign restraints not the less arbitrary or irksome) are cruelly restricted to plain truth and decency; while their brother-craftsmen in the enemy's lines, with the whole typographical fraternity on the *constitutional* island, are gen-

erously permitted to range uncontrolled thro' the boundless fields of imagination, and to exert all the powers of inventive genius in embellishing their publications with the *marvellous;* which has ever been deemed a capital beauty in composition, and affects the mind in the most agreeable manner, by its unexpected surprize and novelty.

Thus have I endeavoured to point out the most essential defects of our republican government, and have, in my humble opinion, offered sufficient reasons to induce every dispassionate American to wish for a speedy reconciliation with the *parent state, consistent with that union of force, on which the safety of our common religion and liberty depends.*

I ought, however, candidly to acknowledge that many gentlemen are of opinion that we have gained one very material advantage over Great-Britain by our separation from her. I mean that no persons employed by the States are mistrusted for imitating her example in peculation, and defrauding their country in any [of] the departments committed to their management, and that all continental property is husbanded with the greatest economy; but this, without any predilection for Old England, I shrewdly suspect wants confirmation.

Hortentius

DOCUMENT 5.4
Forming Republics

By the early months of 1776, independence was only a matter of time, and writers were busy discussing the advantages of the different kinds of governments. Although there was never much doubt that the colonies would soon become republics, Americans, like this publicist, realized that republicanism was a much-criticized and problematical form of government in the eighteenth century.

---

[1] Last royal Governor of Virginia.

[2] *A most accomplished* royal *governor in the West-Indies who, by his peculiar tenderness for everything in petticoats, whether* feme sole *or* feme covert, *occasioned a most* unnatural *conspiracy of a number of husbands and fathers, who rushed into his room and* traiterously *slew him upon the spot—An indignity to the regal appointment, which Great-Britain—from her* parental affection *for the* colonies, plantations and provinces—*was too indulgent to punish as a rebellion against the* supremacy of parliament.

Source: *American Archives. . . ,* ed. Peter Force 4th ser. (Washington, D. C., 1844), vol. 5, pp. 180–83.

TO THE PEOPLE OF NORTH-AMERICA ON THE DIFFERENT KINDS OF GOVERNMENT.

Pure Monarchy is that form of Government which is framed for the exaltation of the Prince alone, and his interest and grandeur are of primary consideration; the people are only of consequence so far as their welfare is involved in his. The grand monarch is the only being known to the Constitution; who, like the Divinity, (pardon the comparison,) derives every power from himself; from whom the other members of the community derive every privilege they possess, and on whose will they depend for their continuance. Aristocracy divides all the privileges of the State among the grandees of the nation; and constituting them the sole legislators and executors, lodges all power in their hands. Oligarchy distributes the powers of Government into a few hands, who are generally the leaders of so many factions, which exist in the State. In all these forms the people are but of small, if of any consideration, and the farther they diverge from pure Monarchy, the more intolerable they become. Popular Government—sometimes termed Democracy, Republick, or Commonwealth—is the plan of civil society wherein the community at large takes the care of its own welfare, and manages its concerns by representatives elected by the people out of their own body.

Seeing the happiness of the people is the true end of Government; and it appearing by the definition, that the popular form is the only one which has this for its object; it may be worth inquiring into the causes which have prevented its success in the world. In this inquiry it would ill become us to sit down contented with the accounts given by Royal ambassadors, or men of ambition, who can never arrive to the height they aspire to in a Republick. With such men, it is impossible for a Commonwealth to confer happiness on its members. Were they honestly to investigate the subject, perhaps they would alter their opinions. The necessity of mutual defence first gave rise to social connections, which were, consequently, of the military kind. Thus very great distinctions between the members of the same community were incorporated into the very Constitution of the State, and formed an insuperable obstacle to a perfect Republick. Every nation which has hitherto attempted to set up a Republick, entered on the measure too late. They were the convulsed remains of some Government erected upon military principles; and finding it hard to content those with the simple rights of freemen who were once possessed of all power, they too easily gave way to claims of a superior nature, whereby they admitted an interest separate and distinct from, and inconsistent with, the general welfare of the people. This interest forever clashing with that of the community, produced continual confusions, until the people, wearied out with the struggle, gave up to the aristocratical party, or blindly following some popular leader, in confidence of his attachment to their interest, gave all power into his hands, which generally ended in tyranny.

The inexperience of mankind was another cause of the decay of popular Governments. Being unacquainted with legislative representation, established on the principles of a free, uninfluenced, and general election, they met in large, and, consequently, tumultuous assemblies. This gave ambitious and designing men, to whom such a form of Government is always unfavourable, great opportunities of breeding disturbance, and creating factions, which generally terminate in its dissolution. Besides this manner of conducting publick affairs, not suiting extensive dominion, the privileges of the society were continually confined to the precincts of the capital; and as soon as their territories extended beyond these bounds, slavery took place; which, inducing the necessity of standing armies, laid a foundation for overturning itself. The feuds and animosities attendant on this mode of managing publick affairs, gave great opportunities to those whose ambitious designs were incompatible with the good of the society, to bring it into dislike and contempt. Far from trying to remedy any defects in the system, or to put an end to factions and disturbances, they used their utmost abilities and cunning to heighten the old, or excite new; until the minds of the people were so torn to pieces and worn out by feuds and confusions, that they were ready to submit to anything which could relieve them from their unhappy situation. Then artfully charging the troubles themselves had occasioned to the fault of the Constitution, they easily obtained such a change in its form as was more favorable to their designs.

Political writers, either mistaking the true causes of the uneasinesses which are found in ancient popular Governments, or willing to make court to Princes, have greatly contributed to bring the Republican forms of Government into discredit. This has been carried to such a length with many, that the mentioning a Democracy constantly excites in them the idea of anarchy; and few, except such as have emancipated themselves from the shackles of political bigotry and prejudice, can talk of it with patience, and hearken to anything offered in its defence.

One or all of the foregoing causes have, to one time or other, contributed to the destruction of Republicks; but of all others, the first has done most. Where two or more separate interests exist in a Government, there contention will remain until one becomes master. A nation must consist of all Kings, all nobles, or all simple freemen, to prevent such confusions, and preserve its privileges. Every attentive reader of history must perceive this. The history of the *Roman* Commonwealth, abating for its foreign wars, is little else but a relation of feuds, factions, and animosities, occasioned by the existence of a rank of nobles, whose interest was unconnected with the plebeians. They formed schemes, and adopted plans, to balance the powers, and reconcile the interests of these two ranks. But all to no purpose; tyr-

anny at last destroyed them both. The irreconcilableness of these two interests did more to prevent the formation of a Republick in *Great Britain,* than all the ambition of a *Cromwell;* and, if I mistake not, *Ludlow,* in his Memoirs, charges its failure to this cause alone. Where no King is, that body must enjoy his power, or be annihilated: they must and will hang together. To a man of reflection, this will readily appear, and fully explain the reasons why a Parliament that dethroned a King, voted a House of Lords useless. They will be an everlasting plague to the society which has not a King; for they will always be aiming at kingly authority. And where there is a King, their dignity and consequence will flow from him, and they will be his tools, if he makes no attack on their peculiar privileges.

Two or more distinct interests can never exist in society, without finally destroying the liberties of the people. The best plans will fail in accomplishing this, until mankind shall have learned to do to others as they would be done unto. The whole wisdom of the *British* nation, at a time when its virtue and wisdom was at the highest, exerted its utmost efforts to form a perfect plan of political freedom, and to preserve and secure the rights of the three distinct classes, of King, Lords, and Commons; and it was thought they had effected it; but later experience has proved the contrary. The Crown of *Great Britain* is now as absolute in the legislature as the Crown of *France,* and were it not for the Habeas Corpus Act, and Trial by Jury, the consequences of offending it would be full as fatal.

Kings and nobles are artificial beings, for whose emolument civil society was never intended; and notwithstanding they have had the good fortune to escape general censure from the world, yet I will boldly affirm that nine-tenths of all the publick calamities which ever befell mankind, were brought on by their means. The protest which the Almighty entered against Kings, when the *Jews* demanded one, shows in what estimation they are held by the

Divinity. Point me out the King that does not verify the description, and I will begin to suspect the divinity of the Bible. Wicked Kings and Governours make up the history of the Old Testament, and the chief part of the labour of the Prophets was to keep them within bounds. It is thought to be vastly in favour of Kings, that we are commanded to pray for them; but if the nature or design of prayer were attended to, it would certainly make against them. If the wickedest of men stand most in need of prayers, it is no wonder that so many clergymen are continually sending up petitions for Kings; but it is certainly much against them that all these prayers do them so little good.

Mankind never suffered so much during the existence of a Republick as they have suffered in the short reigns of many Kings. A *Harry* VIII. did more mischief to his subjects than any Republick ever did to its members, notwithstanding they were so illy constituted. But the true principles of republicanism are at present so well understood, and the mode of conducting such a Government so simple and easy, and *America* so fit for its reception, that a dozen of wise heads and honest hearts might, in one day, form a plan for the United Colonies which would as much excel any one now existing, as the *British* Constitution does that of *Caffraria*.

When I seriously consider this, and take a survey of the state of civil Government throughout the world, the modes whereby they acquired their present forms, and the causes which gave rise to them, I cannot help cherishing a secret hope that *God* has destined *America* to form the last and best plan that can possibly exist; and that he will gradually carry those who have long been under the galling yoke of tyranny in every other quarter of the globe, into the bosom of perfect liberty and freedom in *America*. Were the great men of the present day, and all those who choose to interfere in publick affairs, only to set before them the Godlike pleasure of conferring the most lasting and complete state of happiness human nature is capable of, in a state of civil society, on millions yet unborn, and the eternal reward which must attend the doing so much good; I cannot help thinking but contracted views, partial interest, and party factions, would sink under, and yield to considerations of so greatly superior a nature.

Few opportunities have ever been offered to mankind of framing an entire Constitution of Government, upon equitable principles. All modern authors on this subject agree, that mankind are entitled to freedom by birth, and that they are independent of, and on a level with, each other when they enter into society. This being the case, it is evident that where great distinctions exist in a community before its Constitution is formed, its members do not enter on equally advantageous terms; and it will be difficult, if not impossible to frame an equitable plan. *Rome* had her *Patres,* and *Patres Conscripti,* before she attempted it; and the consequence was, an eternal clashing of interest, which kept their Constitution so fluctuating, that they never could be said to have anything permanent, but their hatred to Kings; and this was the only stable principle which preserved the Commonwealth as long as it lasted.

Whenever any rank in society is invested with more than an equal share of the privileges and powers of the society, it must be at the expense of the other ranks. Men, naturally on a level, ought to remain so by the constitution of the society, if they will secure the liberty and welfare of the community, and every civil and necessary distinction, as that of legislator and magistrate; and the other civil officers should be so settled as never to remain long in one family, otherwise it will end in the enslaving of that people. All natural distinctions—such as weak and strong, wise and foolish; and every accidental or adventitious one—such as learned or unlearned, rich and poor; may safely exist in the community, without interrupting its peace and felicity; but every family distinction which a society creates, will finally prove destructive to that society. Princes of the blood, Princes of the empire, and Peers of the realm, ever have been, are now, and ever will be, the convenient and necessary tools of Royal tyrants, scattered up and down the community, for the more ready accomplishing his will who created them. All political distinctions ought to be the gift of the free people at large, and continually to revert to them at the end of the political year, to be renewed or otherwise, as they shall think proper.

Almost every civil Constitution now existing in the world is partly the spurious offspring of some former very defective one. Perhaps *America* is the only country in the world wholly free from all political impediments, at the very time they are under the necessity of framing a civil Constitution. Having no rank above that of freemen, she has but one interest to consult, and that interest, (blessed be *God* for it,) is the true and only interest of men as members of society.

Salus Populi

DOCUMENT 5.5
Republican Constitutions

All the new state constitutions drafted in the months immediately following the Declaration of Independence contained many provisions growing out of the colonists' fears and concerns brought to the fore during the previous decade. The following articles from state constitutions are representative of the Revolutionaries' republican sentiments.

PENNSYLVANIA CONSTITUTION (1776)

Sec. 36. As every freeman to preserve his independence (if without a sufficient estate) ought to have some profession, calling, trade or farm, whereby he may honestly subsist, there can

Source: *The Federal and State Constitutions . . .* ed. Francis N. Thorp (Washington, 1909), pp. 1547, 1410, 1313, 1864.

be no necessity for, nor use in establishing offices of profit, the usual effects of which are dependence and servility unbecoming freemen, in the possessors and expectants; faction contention, corruption, and disorder among the people.

NORTH CAROLINA CONSTITUTION (1776) DECLARATION OF RIGHTS

XXII. That no hereditary emoluments, privileges or honors ought to be granted or conferred in this State.

XXIII. That perpetuities and monopolies are contrary to the genius of a free State, and ought not to be allowed.

NEW JERSEY CONSTITUTION (1776)

XX. That the legislative department of this government may, as much as possible, be preserved from all suspicion of corruption, none of the Judges of the Supreme or other Courts, Sheriffs, or any other person or persons possessed of any post of profit under the government, other than Justices of the Peace, shall be entitled to a seat in the Assembly: but that, on his being elected, and taking his seat, his office or post shall be considered as vacant.

VERMONT CONSTITUTION (1777)

XXXIV. The future legislature of this State, shall regulate entails, in such manner as to prevent perpetuities.

DOCUMENT 5.6
The Chosen People of God

More than any other Revolutionary leader, Thomas Jefferson rested his faith in republicanism on the virtue of the farmer.

Source: Thomas Jefferson, *Notes on the State of Virginia* (1785) in *The Writings of Thomas Jefferson* ed. Paul L. Ford (New York, 1894), vol. 3, pp. 268–69.

The political economists of Europe have established it as a principle, that every State should endeavour to manufacture for itself; and this principle, like many others, we transfer to America, without calculating the difference of circumstance which should often produce a difference of result. In Europe the lands are either cultivated, or locked up against the cultivator. Manufacture must therefore be resorted to, of necessity, not of choice, to support the surplus of their people. But we have an immensity of land courting the industry of the husbandman. Is it best then that all our citizens should be employed in its improvement, or that one half should be called off from that to exercise manufactures and handicraft arts for the others? Those who labour in the earth are the chosen people of God, if ever he had a chosen people; whose breasts he has made his peculiar deposit for substantial and genuine virtue. It is the focus in which he keeps alive that sacred fire, which otherwise might escape from the face of the earth. Corruption of morals in the mass of cultivators is a phenomenon of which no age nor nation has furnished an example. It is the mark set on those, who not looking up to heaven, to their own soil and industry, as does the husbandman, for their subsistence, depend for it on casualties and caprice of customers. Dependance begets subservience and venality, suffocates the germ of virtue, and prepares fit tools for the designs of ambition. This, the natural progress and consequence of the arts, has sometimes perhaps been retarded by accidental circumstances: but, generally speaking the proportion which the aggregate of the other classes of citizens bears in any state to that of its husbandmen, is the proportion of its unsound to its healthy parts, and is a good enough barometer whereby to measure its degree of corruption. While we have land to labour then, let us never wish to see our citizens occupied at a workbench, or twirling a distaff. Carpenters, masons, smiths, are wanting in husbandry: but, for the general operations of manufacture, let our work-shops remain in Europe. It is better to carry provisions and materials to work-men there, than bring them to the provisions and materials, and with them their manners and principles. The loss by the transportation of commodities across the Atlantic will be made up in happiness and permanence of government. The mobs of great cities add just so much to the support of pure government, as sores do to the strength of the human body. It is the manners and spirit of a people which preserve a republic in vigour. A degeneracy in these is a canker which soon eats to the heart of its laws and constitution.

DOCUMENT 5.7
The Promise of America

In this Fourth of July oration of 1778, David Ramsay, physician of Charleston, South Carolina, offered Americans an inspired and widely shared vision of the Revolution's meaning.

We are now celebrating the anniversary of our emancipation from British tyranny; an event that will constitute an illustrious era in the history of the world, and which promises an extension of all those blessings to our country, for which we would choose to live, or dare to die.

Our present form of government is every way preferable to the royal one we have lately renounced. It is much more favorable to purity of morals, and better calculated to promote all our important interests. Honesty, plain-dealing, and simple manners, were never made the patterns of courtly behavior. Artificial manners always prevail in kingly governments; and royal courts are reservoirs, from whence insincerity, hypocrisy, dissimulation, pride, luxury,

Source: H. Niles, ed., *Principles and Acts of the Revolution in America* (Baltimore, 1822), pp. 64–72.

and extravagance, deluge and overwhelm the body of the people. On the other hand, republics are favorable to truth, sincerity, frugality, industry, and simplicity of manners. Equality, the life and soul of commonwealth, cuts off all pretensions to preferment, but those which arise from extraordinary merit: Whereas, in royal governments, he that can best please his superiors, by the low arts of fawning and adulation, is most likely to obtain favor.

It was the interest of Great Britain to encourage our dissipation and extravagance, for the two-fold purpose in *increasing the sale of her manufactures,* and of *perpetuating our subordination.* In vain we sought to check the growth of luxury, by sumptuary laws; every wholesome restraint of this kind was sure to meet with the royal negative. While the whole force of example was employed to induce us to copy the dissipated manners of the country from which we sprung. If, therefore, we had continued dependent, our frugality, industry, and simplicity of manners, would have been lost in an imitation of British extravagance, idleness, and false refinements.

How much more happy is our present situation, when necessity, co-operating with the love of our country, compels us to adopt both public and private economy? Many are now industriously clothing themselves and their families in sober home-spun, who, had we remained dependent, would have been spending their time in idleness, and strutting in the costly robes of British gaiety.

The arts and sciences, which languished under the low prospects of subjection, will now raise their drooping heads, and spread far and wide, till they have reached the remotest parts of this untutored continent. It is the happiness of our present constitution, that all offices lie open to men of merit, of whatever rank or condition; and that even the reins of state may be held by the son of the poorest man, if possessed of abilities equal to the important station. We are no more to look up for the blessings of government to hungry courtiers, or the needy dependents of British nobility; but must educate our own children for these exalted purposes. When subjects, we had scarce any other share in government, but to obey the arbitrary mandates of a British parliament: But honor, with her dazzling pomp, interest, with her golden lure, and patriotism, with her heart-felt satisfaction, jointly call upon us now to qualify ourselves and posterity for the bench, the army, the navy, the learned professions, and all the departments of civil government. The independence of our country holds forth such generous encouragement to youth, as cannot fail of making many of them despise the syren calls of luxury and mirth, and pursue heaven-born wisdom with unwearied application. A few years will now produce a much greater number of men of learning and abilities, than we could have expected for ages in our boyish state of minority, guided by the leading strings of a parent country.

How trifling the objects of deliberation that came before our former legislative assemblies, compared with the great and important matters, on which they must now decide! They might then, *with the leave of the king,* his governors and councils, make laws about *yoking hogs, branding cattle,* or *making rice;* but they are now called upon to determine on peace and war, treaties and negociations with foreign states, and other subjects interesting to the peace, liberty, sovereignty, and independence of a wide extended empire. No wonder that so little attention has been paid to learning; for ignorance was better than knowledge, while our abject and humiliating condition so effectually tended to crush the exertions of the human mind, and to extinguish a generous ardor for literary pre-eminence.

The times in which we live, and the governments we have lately adopted, all conspire to fan the sparks of genius in every breast, and kindle them into flame. . . .

Every circumstance concurs to make it prob-

able, that the arts and sciences will be cultivated, extended, and improved, in independent
America. They require a fresh soil, and always
flourish most in new countries. A large volume
of the book of nature, yet unread, is open before
us, and invites our attentive perusal. Many useful plants, unknown to the most industrious
botanist, waste their virtues in our desert air.
Various parts of our country, hitherto untrod
by the foot of any chymist, abound with different minerals. We stand on the shoulders of
our predecessors, with respect to the arts that
depend on experiment and observation. The
face of our country, intersected by rivers, or
covered by woods and swamps, gives ample
scope for the improvement of mechanics, math-
ematics, and natural philosophy. Our free governments are the proper nurseries of rhetoric,
criticism, and the arts which are founded on
the philosophy of the human mind. In monarchies, an extreme degree of politeness disguises
the simplicity of nature, and "sets the looks
at variance with the thoughts;" in republics,
mankind appear as they really are, without any
false coloring: In these governments, therefore,
attentive observers have an opportunity of
knowing all the avenues to the heart, and of
thoroughly understanding human nature. The
great inferiority of the moderns to the ancients
in fine writing, is to be referred to this veil
cast over mankind by the artificial refinements
of modern monarchies. From the operation of
similar causes, it is hoped, that the free governments of America will produce poets, orators,
critics and historians, equal to the most celebrated of the ancient commonwealths of Greece
and Italy. . . .

In monarchies, favor is the source of preferment; but, in our new forms of government,
no one can command the suffrages of the people, unless by his superior merit and capacity. . . .

We are the first people in the world who
have had it in their power to choose their own
form of government. Constitutions were forced

on all other nations, by the will of their conquerors, or, they were formed by accident, caprice,
or the overbearing influence of prevailing parties or particular persons: But, happily for us,
the bands of British government were dissolved
at a time when no rank above that of freemen
existed among us, and when we were in a
capacity to choose for ourselves among the
various forms of government, and to adopt that
which best suited our country and people. Our
deliberations, on this occasion, were not directed by the overgrown authority of a conquer-
ing general, or the ambition of an aspiring nobility, but by the pole-star of public good,
inducing us to prefer those forms that would
most effectually secure the greatest portion of
political happiness to the greatest number of
people. We had the example of all ages for
our instruction, and many among us were well
acquainted with the causes of prosperity and
misery in other governments.

In times of public tranquility, the mighty
have been too apt to encroach on the rights
of the many: But it is the great happiness of
America, that her independent constitutions
were agreed upon by common consent, at a
time when her leading men needed the utmost
support of the multitude, and therefore could
have no other object in view, but the formation
of such constitutions as would best suit the
people at large, and unite them most heartily
in repelling common dangers. . . .

It is difficult to compute the number of advantages arising from our present glorious
struggle; harder still, perhaps impossible, precisely to ascertain their extent. It has attracted
the attention of all Europe to the nature of
civil liberty, and the rights of the people. Our
constitutions, pregnant with the seeds of liberty
and happiness, have been translated into a variety of languages, and spread far and wide.
Who can tell what great events, now concealed
in the womb of time, may be brought into
existence by the nations of the old world emu-
lating our successful efforts in the cause of

liberty? The thrones of tyranny and despotism will totter, when their subjects shall learn and know, by our example, that the happiness of the people is the end and object of all government. The wondering world has beheld the smiles of Heaven on the numerous sons of America, resolving to die or be free: Perhaps this noble example, like a wide spreading conflagration, may catch from breast to breast, and extend from nation to nation, till tyranny and oppression are utterly extirpated from the face of the earth. . . .

Our independent constitutions, formed on the justest principles, promise fair to give the most perfect protection to life, liberty and property, equally to the poor and the rich. As at the conflagration of Corinth, the various melted metals running together, formed a new one, called Corinthian brass, which was superior to any of its component parts; in like manner, perhaps it is the will of Heaven, that a new empire should be here formed, of the different nations of the old world, which will rise superior to all that have gone before it, and extend human happiness to its utmost possible limits. None can tell to what perfection the arts of government may be brought. May we not therefore expect great things from the patriots of this generation, jointly co-operating to make the new born republic of America as complete as possible? Is it not to be hoped, that human nature will here receive her most finished touches? That the arts and sciences will be extended and improved? That religion, learning, and liberty, will be diffused over this continent? and in short, that the American editions of the human mind will be more perfect than any that have yet appeared? Great things have been achieved in the infancy of states; and the ardor of a new people, rising to empire and renown, with prospects that tend to elevate the human soul, encourages these flattering expectations. . . .

It has never yet been fairly tried how far the equal principles of republican government would secure the happiness of the governed. The ancients, unacquainted with the present mode of taking the sense of the people by representatives, were too apt, in their public meetings, to run into disorder and confusion. The distinction of *patricians,* and *plebians,* laid the foundation of perpetual discord in the Roman commonwealth. If the free states of Greece had been under the control of a common superintending power, similar to our continental congress, they could have peaceably decided their disputes, and probably would have preserved their freedom and importance to the present day. Happily for us, warned by experience, we have guarded against all these evils. No artificial distinction of ranks has been suffered to take place among us. We can peaceably convene a state in one small assembly of deputies, representing the whole in an equal proportion. All disputes between the different states, and all continental concerns, are to be managed by a congress of representatives from each. What a security for liberty, for union, for every species of political happiness! Small states are weak, and incapable of defence, large ones are unwieldly, greatly abridge natural liberty, and their general laws, from a variety of clashing interests, must frequently bear hard on many individuals: But our confederation will give us the strength and protection of a power equal to that of the greatest; at the same time that, in all our internal concerns, we have the freedom of small independent commonwealths. We are in possession of constitutions that contain in them the excellencies of all forms of government, free from the inconveniences of each; and in one word, we bid fair to be the happiest and freest people in the world for ages yet to come. . . .

Ever since the flood, true religion, literature, arts, empire and riches, have taken a slow and gradual course from east to west, and are now about fixing their long and favorite abode in this new western world. Our sun of political happiness is already risen, and hath lifted its head over the mountains, illuminating our hemisphere with liberty, light, and polished life. Our independence will redeem one quarter of the globe from tyranny and oppression, and consecrate it the chosen seat of truth, justice, freedom, learning and religion. We are laying the foundation of happiness for countless millions. Generations yet unborn will bless us for the blood-bought inheritance, we are about to bequeath them. Oh happy times! Oh glorious days! Oh kind, indulgent, bountiful Providence, that we live in this highly favored period, and have the honor of helping forward these great events, and of suffering in a cause of such infinite importance!

DOCUMENT 5.8
Disillusionment

As early as 1782 some of the most zealous patriots like Charles Lee of Virginia were beginning to doubt their fellow-Americans' capacity to sustain republicanism. Were Americans sufficiently different from Europeans? Did they have enough virtue to be republicans? These were questions that continued to lie at the heart of the American experience.

. . . I know not what is the cause my dear friend, but of late I find myself much affected in my health—perhaps it is my state of rustication, perhaps the embarrassment of my private affairs, and perhaps in great measure the dis-

Source: Charles Lee to Robert Morris, August 15, 1782, in "Lee Papers," New York Historical Society, *Collections* (New York, 1875), vol. 4, pp. 26–27.

agreeable aspect of public affairs, for with submission the prospect is not only disagreeable but hideous, at least to a man of my feelings and sanguine expectation. I have ever from the first time I read Plutarch been an Enthusiastick for liberty and (to my cost I now find) for liberty in a republican garb—indeed it is natural to a young person whose chief companions are the Greek and Roman Historians and Orators to be dazzled with the splendid picture—but alas I now find this perfect kind of liberty could be only supported by qualities, not possess'd by the individuals of the modern world—a public and patriotick spirit reigning in the breast of every individual superceding all private considerations—it was this spirit alone that carried several of the Grecian states and the Roman Republick triumphantly through so many ages—for as to the formal literal construction of their Governments, they were defective to absurdity—it was virtue that supported them—All writers agree that virtue must be the basis of republics and most of all Federal Republics—have the Americans this necessary virtue? On the contrary are they not on these setting out more corrupted than the oldest people in Europe—And it is no wonder—They are corrupted by the laws themselves, which Mr Montesquieu says is a corruption incurable because the evil is in the remedy itself—but to shorten my sermon, the Empire of Britain is overturned and the situation of America neither promises happiness security nor glory—the House of Bourbon alone can cry out le triumphe—this you will say I ought to have seen before—I confess it and the sense of my want of foresight perhaps concurs strongly to the uneasy situation of my mind and of course so sensibly affects my health and spirits.

chapter **6**

The Founding Fathers: Radicals or Conservatives?

Stanley Elkins
Smith College

For well over a generation, the dominant image of the Founding Fathers has been a conservative one. Whereas the nineteenth century saw an assembly of Olympian sages whose only concern was the welfare of the nation, we now tend to see a group of tough-minded realists, suspicious of popular democracy and acutely concerned with the security of private property. Moreover, the entire movement to create a strong national government is usually described, in equally conservative terms, as a reaction against the radicalism of the Revolution—an effort to limit and restrain the sometimes irresponsible but generally democratic state governments. For some historians, the meeting at Philadelphia actually takes on the overtones of a right-wing plot.

On the face of it, this conservative, antidemocratic picture of the Fathers is not an easy one to challenge. The men who drafted the Constitution and engineered its ratification *were* toughminded and realistic, and few, if any, would have qualified as good democrats. To this extent, historians like Charles A. Beard, Vernon Parrington, and Merrill Jensen have some justification for insisting that the supporters of the Constitution were a distinctly conservative lot. The major difficulty with their argu-

ment is not that it is wrong, but that the description is equally appropriate for the men who opposed the Constitution—the Anti-Federalists. George Clinton and Patrick Henry, both deeply hostile to the Constitution, were no more willing to trust the innate virtue of the people nor any less concerned with the sanctity of property than was Alexander Hamilton.

To describe the Fathers as conservatives, therefore, may tell something about the eighteenth-century mind (and even more about the twentieth-century mind), but it tells little about the aims, motives, and intentions of the men themselves. Moreover, it tends to blur the differences between the Federalists and the Anti-Federalists that *were* meaningful—for example, the basic disagreement over the existence of a national interest that might transcend the needs and desires of any particular state. Federalists such as Madison and Hamilton not only believed that such an interest did exist, but they were also convinced that it could only be properly fostered and cared for by a strong unitary government. To Clinton and Henry, this was a dangerously utopian idea. Unable or unwilling to project either their loyalties or their vision of the future beyond the borders of their home states, they could see little point

to a government that would extend over a third
of a continent. They recognized instinctively
that such a government would limit not only
the sovereign power of the states but also their
own power within those states. They would
be forced to adjust to a new political entity
that would include all sorts of interests and
people that were outside their immediate
knowledge and experience. The Federalists
might view such an entity as a great stage for
new and brilliant careers, but the Anti-Federalists could see it only as a threat. One might
well argue that the Founding Fathers were the
radicals, and their opponents were striving to
maintain the *status quo.*

"Radical" might seem a curious term for
describing the Fathers, but consider for a moment what these men hoped to do. They were
determined to change a loose coalition of virtually sovereign communities into a unified republic, stretching from Maine to Georgia and
from the Mississippi River to the Atlantic
Ocean. The very success of their efforts makes
it difficult for us today to appreciate just how
bold a scheme this was. Though Americans
spoke the same language and shared the same
customs, they had little sense of themselves
as a nation or even as a potential nation. Only
rarely did their energies, their interests, or their
loyalties extend much beyond the borders they
had known as colonies; even at the height of
the Revolution, Washington could never hope
to hold more than a portion of his troops when
he crossed from one state to another. For the
majority of Americans, to defend one's country
meant simply to defend one's state. Yet, somehow, these people had to be persuaded to grant
extensive powers to a nation that in their minds
hardly existed.

Merrill Jensen has argued that the Federalists
(or the "Nationalists," as he accurately calls
them) were not only opposed to some of the
radical ideas generated by the Revolution, but
that, by and large, they also had been reluctant
supporters of the Revolution itself, joining it

only when it was clear that a break with Britain
was inevitable. It might be argued that just
the reverse was true: the Federalists' dream
of a unified republic did not develop out of
any reluctance to accept the Revolution but,
rather, was a direct result of the profoundest
sort of involvement in it.

One tends to forget that there were actually
two sides to the Revolution—a state side and
a continental side. For many men, probably
most, the state side was much more concrete:
the real business that concerned them was the
independence of their own states. But the other
side of the Revolution was its character as a
continental war effort, and it is surprising to
discover how many of the men who would
later become Federalists were deeply engaged
in this continental side of the movement. A
significant proportion of them served in the
Continental Army, as diplomats representing
the *United States,* as key administrative officers
of the *national* government, or as members
of the Continental Congress and its war committees. The experience they underwent, the
difficulties they faced, and the problems they
had to solve must have added up to a special
attitude of mind with regard to the ultimate
aims of the Revolution, one differing in certain
very significant ways from that of the men
who, during the war period, were concerned
principally with state affairs.

These men—these future Federalists—were
coming to think more easily and readily in
national rather than in local terms. By 1783,
the name America had come to mean more
to them than simply a loose coalition of former
colonies struggling to free themselves from
British control. Probably the full significance
of this change was still generally unrecognized
at the time the Treaty of Paris was signed.
The basic goal of the Revolution had been independence, and independence was achieved. But
there is strong reason to believe that by the
middle of that same decade, the 1780s, the
apparent collapse of all hope that the Confeder-

ation might some day assume true national attributes helped goad many of the men most intimately connected with the continental war effort into decisive, far-reaching, and drastic action.

Thus, the continental conceptions of the Federalist leaders—Madison, Hamilton, Jay, Knox, and the others—had had their birth in a revolutionary setting. Not only were their ideas radical for the setting and the times; so were their methods. The constitutional movement they launched in the late 1780s fairly takes the breath away with its energy, its adroitness in maneuver, its daring, thrust, and dash. If, moreover, one party or the other is to be shown in the role of conservatives, then the Anti-Federalists—those who opposed the Constitution—are far better qualified for it than the Federalists; they represented reversion to the old provincial ways, the urge to rest, to drift, to turn back the clock.

Indeed, to a large proportion of Americans in that decade it was not absolutely obvious that they were living through a critical period—not nearly so obvious as it would appear in retrospect to historians a century later. Much depended on the point of view, and points of view were multiple and diverse; Americans were simply not yet accustomed to conceiving their welfare in national terms. Nor were the economic and military problems of the several postwar state governments all of the same sort. Those of some were certainly serious; for others, it was not self-evident that outside help was indispensable. A national point of definition for thinking about these matters was not ready-made and waiting; it had to be created, and the first steps required labor, persuasion, and an intensely committed leadership.

However, to the men who would constitute that leadership, things looked very different. Viewing the states collectively, as a nation with the Confederation government as its one expression, they saw with despair that this government was approaching the point of impotence.

That side of the story is familiar enough to us: because it had no guaranteed income and was all but bankrupt, it was often unable to sit for lack of a quorum, it was chronically blocked by what amounted to a state veto and, thus, powerless either to regulate commerce amid conflicting state interests or to enforce its own treaty obligations, the morale and effectiveness of Congress had reached about zero. And yet, by definition, this state of things could be seen as critical only by those who cared; it was, after all, the very policy of neglect, of the states' paying less and less attention to Congress and going their separate ways, that had brought the situation into being. It would thus take considerable will and energy to redefine the problems and discontents of diverse groups and localities in such a way that a series of national solutions would make the clearest, most obvious sense.

This was the setting in which the first consequential step—the Annapolis Convention of 1786—was taken to strengthen the continental government. Madison and Hamilton were the leading spirits in arranging a meeting of delegates to discuss the commercial problems of the several states. The Convention itself was a failure—only five states sent delegates—but the dozen men who did turn up at Annapolis seized the occasion to lay plans for what became the Constitutional Convention of Philadelphia.

Only its eventual brilliant success has obscured the revolutionary character of this move. Those dozen men, exploiting the superficial legitimacy of a partially constituted interstate meeting, took it on themselves to prepare a call to all the states, which they persuaded Congress to transmit, for a convention of delegates whose purpose would be to revise the Articles of Confederation. The Articles made no allowance for such a procedure, and the legal basis for sweeping change was thus created ad hoc. The intimation, therefore, that the Fathers deliberately subverted the Confederation is not without basis.

Yet, by this time the balance had already begun to tip somewhat, and there were indications that the plot might count on a growing basis of support, at least to the all-important point of allowing such a convention to meet. The decisive factors, which began were beginning now to take on an interrelated quality, included: the growing awareness by eastern merchant groups that commercial retaliation against Great Britain by separate state action was useless; the refusal of New York to accept a national impost (which meant that without assured revenues a national government for any purpose might as well go out of existence); the chaotic condition of public finance in the state of Rhode Island; and, finally, Shays's Rebellion in western Massachusetts during the winter of 1786–87. The combined impact of these developments conferred a growing importance on the coming meeting at Philadelphia, scheduled for May 1787. At the very least, it had to be taken seriously, regardless of whether anything might be accomplished. It was thus that even New York—although a strong new national government was hardly to its interest or liking—did not quite dare to boycott the Convention. Every state except one sent delegates, and the men who assembled at Philadelphia in the spring of 1787 turned out to be an exceptionally able and intelligent lot.

What went on inside the Convention during the next months does not really belong in a discussion of either Federalism versus Anti-Federalism or radicalism versus conservatism. The proceedings were not all sweetness and harmony, but a majority of the delegates were already committed to a new frame of government and became progressively more committed the longer they worked together. One might even go further and say that their very nationalism—the momentum of their commitment to a significantly strengthened national instrument—holds the key not only to the ingenuity of the Convention's major compromises but even to some of its ironies. They resolved the small state–large state tensions by giving the small states equal representation in one branch of the legislature and thus secured their support not only for a national government but for one strong enough to curb their potentially aggressive larger neighbors. With the seemingly cumbersome device of the Electoral College, they balanced a whole series of divergent convictions about how the people ought to choose their executive, what the executive-legislative relation ought to be, and how the character of the executive branch should be defined— at the same time providing the new Republic with a strong and independent chief executive. In deciding that the national government might act directly upon the body of citizens, though only in a specified number of areas, they brilliantly avoided the seemingly insoluble problem of divided sovereignty—one of the very problems that had brought on the Revolution.

But it was the delegates' growing nationalism, perhaps even more than their skill, that brought them over these multiple difficulties. Indeed, it led them at one point—on the question of the slave trade—into deceiving themselves, into making a ''compromise'' that was no compromise at all. A number of them understood the potentially disruptive force of slavery, but they would not risk the fruits of their labors either by dealing with the expansion of slavery into the West or by challenging South Carolina and Georgia on the extension of the slave trade. So they devised a compromise whereby on the one hand the national government might levy a tax on imported slaves, and, on the other, no limit would be placed on the trade until at least the year 1808. The deceptiveness of this as a ''settlement'' is suggested by the way in which the parties to it reported back to their constituents. The Carolinians assured theirs that slavery now had nothing to fear from a national government, while Northerners told theirs that slavery was now on its way to extinction.

But with this exception, the document having been completed and with the Federalists girding for the fight over ratification, the essentially revolutionary quality of the constitutional movement once more becomes apparent.

The vested interests of ruling cliques in the various state capitals was better served, at least in the short run, by guarding the status quo, and several such groups used their influence in support of Anti-Federalism. (Patrick Henry in Virginia and George Clinton in New York, as noted above, were outstanding examples of this conservative impulse.) Yet, the Federalists' strategic position had drastically altered for the better: they now had the advantages of initiative and momentum. Moreover, they had shown great astuteness in planning the process of ratification, and would show equal astuteness, combined with prodigious energy, in staging the campaign.

The ratifying would be done through elected state conventions, which meant that the existing state governments would be circumvented, that the people could be directly bombarded with Federalist propaganda, and that the delegates, if not already disposed toward ratification, might be subjected to powerful persuasions and pressures from the Federalist committees now springing up everywhere. Besides, the Constitution would go into effect after only nine states approved it. This meant that vetoes from one or two states could no longer hamstring the enterprise, that before the worst battles (in New York and Virginia) had to be fought, the old Confederation would have gone out of existence, and that the most difficult states, being the last to fall in line, would by the same token be those subject to the most intense pressures.

That was about the way things worked out during the crucial months of 1787–88. The Anti-Federalists, moving always too late and with too little, lost every crucial test. Their best argument was the lack of a bill of rights, yet it seems to have been generally felt that such a problem was hardly irremediable. Five of the states, well softened up in advance, rati-

fied almost immediately. The Federalists swung Massachusetts after the most exhausting efforts. By mid-1788, eight had come around, and on June 21, New Hampshire made the ninth. The labors of Madison and the known sentiments of Washington finally made the difference in Virginia, despite the thunderous anti-Constitution oratory of Patrick Henry.

New York had a powerful and prestigious Anti-Federalist governor and a two-to-one Anti-Federalist majority in its ratifying convention. In light of these great initial advantages, we can only conclude that it must have taken a combination of lightning-raid tactics and sheer attrition to demoralize New York's Anti-Federalist defenses. With ten states already in, the moral pressures on New York were terrific, and the Federalist delegates exploited them to the full. They had worked to delay the vote until New Hampshire and Virginia acted; meanwhile, Madison and Hamilton had made special arrangements to rush the Virginia news northward as swiftly as possible. The tireless Federalists refused to debate the Constitution as a whole, but argued its merits point by point, which meant that their detailed knowledge of each section could operate to the most impressive advantage. Finally, Hamilton and his friends set afoot the rumor that New York City, in the event of nonratification, was ready to secede from the state. By July 16, 1788, the exhausted Anti-Federalists had had enough, and on that day New York approved the federal Constitution by a margin of three votes. A government of the United States under the Constitution was assured.

SUGGESTED READINGS

Beard, Charles E. *An Economic Interpretation of the Constitution of the United States.* New York: Macmillan, 1913.

Beeman, Richard, Stephen Botein, and Edward Carter, eds. *Beyond Confederation: The Origins of the Constitution and American National Identity.* Chapel Hill: University of North Carolina Press, 1987.

Brown, Robert E. *Charles Beard and the Constitution.* Princeton, N.J.: Princeton University Press, 1956.

DePauw, Linda Grant. *The Eleventh Pillar: New York State and the Federal Constitution.* Ithaca, N.Y.: Cornell University Press, 1966.

Jensen, Merrill. *The New Nation.* New York: Alfred A. Knopf, 1950.

Lynd, Staughton. *Class Conflict, Slavery, and the United States Constitution: Ten Essays.* Indianapolis: Bobbs-Merrill, 1968.

McDonald, Forrest. *E Pluribus Unum: The Formation of the American Republic, 1776–1790.* Boston: Houghton Mifflin, 1965.

Main, Jackson Turner. *The Antifederalists: Critics of the Constitution.* Chapel Hill: University of North Carolina Press, 1961.

Robinson, Donald L. *Slavery in the Structure of American Politics: 1765–1820.* New York: Harcourt Brace Jovanovich, 1970.

Rossiter, Clinton. *1787: The Grand Convention.* New York: Macmillan, 1966.

Rutland, Robert. *Ordeal of the Constitution: The Antifederalists and the Ratification Struggle of 1787–1788.* Norman, Okla.: University of Oklahoma Press, 1966.

Warren, Charles. *The Making of the Constitution.* Boston: Little, Brown, 1937.

Wills, Garry. *Explaining America: The Federalist.* New York: Doubleday, 1981.

Wood, Gordon. *The Creation of the American Republic.* Chapel Hill: University of North Carolina Press, 1969.

DOCUMENT 6.1
The Articles of Confederation

The Articles of Confederation served as the first government charter for the new United

Source: James D. Richardson, ed., *Messages and Papers of the Presidents* (New York, 1897), vol. 1, pp. 5–14.

States. They were the work of a committee of the Continental Congress and when complete were reported to the Congress by John Dickinson on July 12, 1776. The Congress adopted the Articles on November 15, 1777. During 1778 and 1779, representatives of the states signed the Articles. Only Maryland held out because of the question of western lands. Finally, on March 1, 1781, the Articles were approved and became the law of the land.

To all to whom these Presents shall come, we the undersigned Delegates of the States affixed to our Names send greeting. Whereas the Delegates of the United States of America in Congress assembled did on the fifteenth day of November in the Year of our Lord One Thousand Seven Hundred and Seventy seven, and in the Second Year of the Independence of America agree to certain articles of Confederation and perpetual Union between the States of Newhampshire, Massachusetts-bay, Rhode-island and Providence Plantations, Connecticut, New York, New Jersey, Pennsylvania, Delaware, Maryland, Virginia, North-Carolina, South-Carolina and Georgia in the Words following, viz. ''Articles of Confederation and perpetual Union between the states of Newhampshire, Massachusetts-bay, Rhodeisland and Providence Plantations, Connecticut, New York, New Jersey, Pennsylvania, Delaware, Maryland, Virginia, North-Carolina, South-Carolina and Georgia.

Art. I. The Stile of this confederacy shall be ''The United States of America.''

Art. II. Each state retains its sovereignty, freedom and independence, and every Power, Jurisdiction and right, which is not by this confederation expressly delegated to the United States, in Congress assembled.

Art. III. The said states hereby severally enter into a firm league of friendship with each other, for their common defence, the security of their Liberties, and their mutual and general welfare, binding themselves to assist each other, against all force offered to, or attacks made upon them, or any of them, on account of religion, sovereignty, trade, or any other pretence whatever.

Art. IV. The better to secure and perpetuate mutual friendship and intercourse among the people of the different states in this union, the free inhabitants of each of these states, paupers, vagabonds and fugitives from Justice excepted, shall be entitled to all privileges and immunities of free citizens in the several states; and the people of each state shall have free ingress and regress to and from any other state, and shall enjoy therein all the privileges of trade and commerce, subject to the same duties, impositions and restrictions as the inhabitants thereof respectively, provided that such restriction shall not extend so far as to prevent the removal of property imported into any state, to any other state of which the Owner is an inhabitant; provided also that no imposition, duties or restriction shall be laid by any state, on the property of the united states, or either of them.

If any Person guilty of, or charged with treason, felony, or other high misdemeanor in any state, shall flee from Justice, and be found in any of the united states, he shall upon demand of the Governor or executive power, of the state from which he fled, be delivered up and removed to the state having jurisdiction of his offence.

Full faith and credit shall be given in each of these states to the records, acts and judicial proceedings of the courts and magistrates of every other state.

Art. V. For the more convenient management of the general interests of the united states, delegates shall be annually appointed in such manner as the legislature of each state shall direct, to meet in Congress on the first Monday in November, in every year, with a power reserved to each state, to recal its delegates, or any of them, at any time within the year, and to send others in their stead, for the remainder of the Year.

No state shall be represented in Congress by less than two, nor by more than seven Members; and no person shall be capable of being a delegate for more than three years in any term of six years; nor shall any person, being a delegate, be capable of holding any office under the united states, for which he, or another for his benefit receives any salary, fees or emolument of any kind.

Each state shall maintain its own delegates in a meeting of the states, and while they act as members of the committee of the states.

In determining questions in the united states, in Congress assembled, each state shall have one vote.

Freedom of speech and debate in Congress shall not be impeached or questioned in any Court, or place out of Congress, and the members of congress shall be protected in their persons from arrests and imprisonments, during the time of their going to and from, and attendance on congress, except for treason, felony, or breach of the peace.

Art. VI. No state without the Consent of the united states in congress assembled, shall send any embassy to, or receive any embassy from, or enter into any conference, agreement, or alliance or treaty with any King, prince or state; nor shall any person holding any office of profit or trust under the united states, or any of them, accept of any present, emolument, office or title of any kind whatever from any king, prince or foreign state; nor shall the united states in congress assembled, or any of them, grant any title of nobility.

No two or more states shall enter into any treaty, confederation or alliance whatever between them, without the consent of the united states in congress assembled, specifying accurately the purposes for which the same is to be entered into, and how long it shall continue.

No state shall lay any imposts or duties, which may interfere with any stipulations in treaties, entered into by the united states in congress assembled, with any king, prince or state, in pursuance of any treaties already proposed by congress, to the courts of France and Spain.

No vessels of war shall be kept up in time of peace by any state, except such number only, as shall be deemed necessary by the united states in congress assembled, for the defence of such state, or its trade; nor shall any body of forces be kept up by any state, in time of peace, except such number only, as in the judgment of the united states, in congress assembled, shall be deemed requisite to garrison the forts necessary for the defence of such state; but every state shall always keep up a well regulated and disciplined militia, sufficiently armed and accoutred, and shall provide and constantly have ready to use, in public stores, a due number of field pieces and tents, and a proper quantity of arms, ammunition and camp equipage.

No state shall engage in any war without the consent of the united states in congress assembled, unless such state be actually invaded by enemies, or shall have received certain advice of a resolution being formed by some nation of Indians to invade such state, and the danger is so imminent as not to admit of a delay, till the united states in congress assembled can be consulted: nor shall any state grant commissions to any ships or vessels of war, nor letters of marque or reprisal, except it be after a declaration of war by the united states in congress assembled, and then only against the kingdom or state and the subjects thereof, against which war has been so declared, and under such regulations as shall be established by the united states in congress assembled, unless such state be infested by pirates, in which case vessels of war may be fitted out for that occasion, and kept so long as the danger shall continue, or until the united states in congress assembled shall determine otherwise.

Art. VII. When land-forces are raised by any state for the common defence, all officers of or under the rank of colonel, shall be appointed by the legislature of each state respectively by whom such forces shall be raised, or in such manner as such state shall direct, and all vacancies shall be filled up by the state which first made the appointment.

Art. VIII. All charges of war, and all other expences that shall be incurred for the common defence or general welfare, and allowed by the united states in congress assembled, shall be defrayed out of a common treasury, which shall be supplied by the several states, in proportion to the value of all land within each state, granted to or surveyed from any Person, as such land and the buildings and improvements thereon shall be estimated according to such mode as the united states in congress assembled, shall from time to time direct and appoint. The taxes for paying that proportion shall be laid and levied by the authority and direction of the legislatures of the several states within the time agreed upon by the united states in congress assembled.

Art. IX. The united states in congress assembled, shall have the sole and exclusive right and power of determining on peace and war, except in the cases mentioned in the sixth article—of sending and receiving ambassadors—entering into treaties and alliances, provided that no treaty of commerce shall be made whereby the legislative power of the respective states shall be restrained from imposing such imposts and duties on foreigners, as their own people are subjected to, or from prohibiting the exportation or importation of any species of goods or commodities whatsoever—of establishing rules for deciding in all cases, what captures on land or water shall be legal, and in what manner prizes taken by land or naval forces in the service of the united states shall be divided or appropriated—of granting letters of marque and reprisal in times of peace—appointing courts for the trial of piracies and felonies committed on the high seas and establishing courts for receiving and determining finally appeals in all cases of captures, provided that no member of congress shall be appointed a judge of any of the said courts.

The united states in congress assembled shall also be the last resort on appeal in all disputes and differences now subsisting or that hereafter may arise between two or more states concerning boundary, jurisdiction or any other cause whatever; which authority shall always be exercised in the manner following. Whenever the legislative or executive authority or lawful agent of any state in controversy with another shall present a petition to congress, stating the matter in question and praying for a hearing, notice thereof shall be given by order of congress to the legislative or executive authority of the other state in controversy, and a day assigned for the appearance of the parties by their lawful agents, who shall then be directed to appoint by joint consent, commissioners or judges to constitute a court for hearing and determining the matter in question: but if they cannot agree, congress shall name three persons out of each of the united states, and from the list of such persons each party shall alternately strike out one, the petitioners beginning, until the number shall be reduced to thirteen; and from that number not less than seven, nor more than nine names as congress shall direct, shall in the presence of congress be drawn out by lot, and the persons whose names shall be so drawn or any five of them, shall be commissioners or judges, to hear and finally determine the controversy, so always as a major part of the judges who shall hear the cause shall agree in the determination: and if either party shall neglect to attend at the day appointed, without shewing reasons, which congress shall judge sufficient, or being present shall refuse to strike, the congress shall proceed to nominate three persons out of each state, and the secretary of congress shall strike in behalf of such party absent or refusing; and the judgment and sentence of the court to be appointed, in the manner

before prescribed, shall be final and conclusive; and if any of the parties shall refuse to submit to the authority of such court, or to appear to defend their claim or cause, the court shall nevertheless proceed to pronounce sentence, or judgment, which shall in like manner be final and decisive, the judgment or sentence and the other proceedings being in either case transmitted to congress, and lodged among the acts of congress for the security of the parties concerned: provided that every commissioner, before he sits in judgment, shall take an oath to be administered by one of the judges of the supreme or superior court of the state, where the cause shall be tried, ''well and truly to hear and determine the matter in question, according to the best of his judgment, without favour, affection or hope of reward:'' provided also that no state shall be deprived of territory for the benefit of the united states.

All controversies concerning the private right of soil claimed under different grants of two or more states, whose jurisdictions as they may respect such lands, and the states which passed such grants are adjusted, the said grants or either of them being at the same time claimed to have originated antecedent to such settlement of jurisdiction, shall on the petition of either party to the congress of the united states, be finally determined as near as may be in the same manner as is before prescribed for deciding disputes respecting territorial jurisdiction between different states.

The united states in congress assembled shall also have the sole and exclusive right and power of regulating the alloy and value of coin struck by their own authority, or by that of the respective states—fixing the standard of weights and measures throughout the united states—regulating the trade and managing all affairs with the Indians, not members of any of the states, provided that the legislative right of any state within its own limits be not infringed or violated—establishing and regulating post-offices from one state to another, throughout all the united states, and exacting such postage on the papers passing thro' the same as may be requisite to defray the expences of the said office—appointing all officers of the land forces, in the service of the united states, excepting regimental officers—appointing all the officers of the naval forces, and commissioning all officers whatever in the service of the united states—making rules for the government and regulation of the said land and naval forces, and directing their operations.

The united states in congress assembled shall have authority to appoint a committee, to sit in the recess of congress, to be denominated "A Committee of the States," and to consist of one delegate from each state; and to appoint such other committees and civil officers as may be necessary for managing the general affairs of the united states under their direction—to appoint one of their number to preside, provided that no person be allowed to serve in the office of president more than one year in any term of three years; to ascertain the necessary sums of Money to be raised for the service of the united states, and to appropriate and apply the same for defraying the public expences—to borrow money, or emit bills on the credit of the united states, transmitting every half year to the respective states an account of the sums of money so borrowed or emitted,—to build and equip a navy—to agree upon the number of land forces, and to make requisitions from each state for its quota, in proportion to the number of white inhabitants in such state; which requisition shall be binding, and thereupon the legislature of each state shall appoint the regimental officers, raise the men and cloath, arm and equip them in a soldier like manner, at the expence of the united states, and the officers and men so cloathed, armed and equipped shall march to the place appointed, and within the time agreed on by the united states in congress assembled: But if the united states in congress assembled shall, on consideration of circumstances judge proper

that any state should not raise men, or should raise a smaller number than its quota, and that any other state should raise a greater number of men than the quota thereof, such extra number shall be raised, officered, cloathed, armed and equipped in the same manner as the quota of such state, unless the legislature of such state shall judge that such extra number cannot be safely spared out of the same, in which case they shall raise officer, cloath, arm and equip as many of such extra number as they judge can be safely spared. And the officers and men so cloathed, armed and equipped, shall march to the place appointed, and within the time agreed on by the united states in congress assembled.

The united states in congress assembled shall never engage in a war, nor grant letters of marque and reprisal in time of peace, nor enter into any treaties or alliances, nor coin money, nor regulate the value thereof, nor ascertain the sums and expences necessary for the defence and welfare of the united states, or any of them, nor emit bills, nor borrow money on the credit of the united states, nor appropriate money, nor agree upon the number of vessels of war, to be built or purchased, or the number of land or sea forces to be raised, nor appoint a commander in chief of the army or navy, unless nine states assent to the same: nor shall a question on any other point, except for adjourning from day to day be determined, unless by the votes of a majority of the united states in congress assembled.

The congress of the united states shall have power to adjourn to any time within the year, and to any place within the united states, so that no period of adjournment be for a longer duration than the space of six Months, and shall publish the Journal of their proceedings monthly, except such parts thereof relating to treaties, alliances or military operations as in their judgment require secrecy; and the yeas and nays of the delegates of each state on any question shall be entered on the Journal, when it is desired by any delegate; and the delegates of a state, or any of them, at his or their request shall be furnished with a transcript of the said Journal, except such parts as are above excepted, to lay before the legislatures of the several states.

Art. X. The committee of the states, or any nine of them, shall be authorised to execute, in the recess of congress, such of the powers of congress as the united states in congress assembled, by the consent of nine states, shall from time to time think expedient to vest them with; provided that no power be delegated to the said committee, for the exercise of which, by the articles of confederation, the voice of nine states in the congress of the united states assembled is requisite.

Art. XI. Canada acceding to this confederation, and joining in the measures of the united states, shall be admitted into, and entitled to all the advantages of this union: but no other colony shall be admitted into the same, unless such admission be agreed to by nine states.

Art. XII. All bills of credit emitted, monies borrowed and debts contracted by, or under the authority of congress, before the assembling of the united states, in pursuance of the present confederation, shall be deemed and considered as a charge against the united states, for payment and satisfaction whereof the said united states, and the public faith are hereby solemnly pledged.

Art. XIII. Every state shall abide by the determinations of the united states in congress assembled, on all questions which by this confederation are submitted to them. And the Articles of this confederation shall be inviolably observed by every state, and the union shall be perpetual; nor shall any alteration at any time hereafter be made in any of them; unless such alteration be agreed to in a congress of the united states, and be afterwards confirmed by the legislatures of every state.

And Whereas it hath pleased the Great Governor of the World to incline the hearts of the legislatures we respectively represent in congress, to approve of, and to authorize us to ratify the said articles of confederation and perpetual union. Know Ye that we the undersigned delegates, by virtue of the power and authority to us given for that purpose, do by these presents, in the name and in behalf of our respective constituents, fully and entirely ratify and confirm each and every of the said articles of confederation and perpetual union, and all and singular the matters and things therein contained: And we do further solemnly plight and engage the faith of our respective constituents, that they shall abide by the determinations of the united states in congress assembled, on all questions, which by the said confederation are submitted to them. And that the articles thereof shall be inviolably observed by the states we respectively represent, and that the union shall be perpetual. In Witness whereof we have hereunto set our hands in Congress. Done at Philadelphia in the state of Pennsylvania the ninth Day of July in the Year of our Lord one Thousand seven Hundred and Seventy-eight, and in the third year of the independence of America.

DOCUMENT 6.2
The Failure of the Confederation

James Madison wrote regularly to Edmund Pendleton, a former Virginia jurist and a respected elder statesman. Here, he describes current efforts to strengthen the Confederation.

New York, Feb[y] 24, 1787

. . . The only step of moment taken by Cong[s]., since my arrival has been a recommendation of the proposed meeting in May for revising the federal articles. Some of the States, consid-

Source: Gaillard Hunt, ed., *The Writings of James Madison, 1783–1787* (New York: G. P. Putnam's Sons, 1901), vol. 2, pp. 317–20.

ering this measure as an extra-constitutional one, had scruples ag[st]. concurring in it without some regular sanction. By others it was thought best that Cong[s]. should remain neutral in the business, as the best antidote for the jealousy of an ambitious desire in them to get more power into their hands. This suspense was at length removed by an instruction from this State to its delegates to urge a Recommendatory Resolution in Congress which accordingly passed a few days ago. Notwithstanding this instruction from N. York, there is room to suspect her disposition not to be very federal, a large majority of her House of delegates having very lately entered into a definite refusal of the impost, and the instruction itself having passed in the Senate by a casting vote only. In consequence of the sanction given by Cong[s]., Mass[ts]. it is said will send deputies to the Convention, and her example will have great weight with the other N. England States. The States from N. C[a]. to N. Jersey inclusive have made their appointments, except Mary[d]., who has as yet only determined that she will make them. The gentlemen here from S. C[a]. & Georgia, expect that those States will follow the general example. Upon the whole therefore it seems probable that a meeting will take place, and that it will be a pretty full one. What the issue of it will be is among the other arcana of futurity and nearly as inscrutable as any of them. In general I find men of reflection much less sanguine as to the new than despondent as to the present System. Indeed the Present System neither has nor deserves advocates; and if some very strong props are not applied, will quickly tumble to the ground. No money is paid into the public Treasury; no respect is paid to the federal authority. Not a single State complies with the requisitions; several pass them over in silence, and some positively reject them. The payments ever since the peace have been decreasing, and of late fall short even of the pittance necessary for the Civil list of the Confederacy. It is not possible that a government can last long under

these circumstances. If the approaching convention should not agree on some remedy, I am persuaded that some very different arrangement will ensue. The late turbulent scenes in Mass[ts]. & infamous ones in Rhode Island, have done inexpressible injury to the republican character in that part of the U. States; and a propensity towards Monarchy is said to have been produced by it in some leading minds. The bulk of the people will probably prefer the lesser evil of a partition of the Union into three more practicable and energetic Governments. The latter idea I find after long confinement to individual speculations & private circles, is beginning to shew itself in the Newspapers. But tho' it is a lesser evil, it is so great a one that I hope the danger of it will rouse all the real friends of the Revolution to exert themselves in favor of such an organization of the confederacy as will perpetuate the Union, and redeem the honor of the Republican name. . . .

DOCUMENT 6.3
The Disorders Which Have Arisen in These States

Henry Knox had been chief of artillery during the Revolution and secretary of war during the later years of the Confederation. This letter from George Washington, written in answer to Knox's lurid account of Shays's Rebellion, gives some sense of the impact of this event on many of the men who would soon play leading roles in the movement for the Constitution.

Mount Vernon, December 26, 1786

. . . Lamentable as the conduct of the Insurgents of Massachusetts is, I am exceedingly

Source: John C. Fitzpatrick, ed., *The Writings of George Washington* (Washington, D.C.: U.S. Government Printing Office, 1939), vol. 29, pp. 121–24.

obliged to you for the advices respecting them; and pray you, most ardently, to continue the acct. of their proceedings; because I can depend upon them from you without having my mind bewildered with those vague and contradictory reports which are handed to us in Newspapers, and which please one hour, only to make the moments of the next more bitter. I feel, my dear Genl. Knox, infinitely more than I can express to you, for the disorders which have arisen in these States. Good God! who besides a tory could have foreseen, or a Briton predicted them! were these people wiser than others, or did they judge of us from the corruption, and depravity of their own hearts? The latter I am persuaded was the case, and that notwithstanding the boasted virtue of America, we are far gone in every thing ignoble and bad.

I do assure you, that even at this moment, when I reflect on the present posture of our affairs, it seems to me to be like the vision of a dream. My mind does not know how to realize it, as a thing in actual existence, so strange, so wonderful does it appear to me! In this, as in most other matters, we are too slow. When this spirit first dawned, probably it might easily have been checked; but it is scarcely within the reach of human ken, at this moment, to say when, where, or how it will end. There are combustibles in every State, which a spark might set fire to. In this State, a perfect calm prevails at present, and a prompt disposition to support, and give energy to the federal System is discovered, if the unlucky stirring of the dispute respecting the navigation of the Mississippi does not become a leaven that will ferment, and sour the mind of it.

The resolutions of the prest. Session respecting a paper emission, military certificates, &ca., have stamped justice and liberality on the proceedings of the Assembly, and By a late act, *it* seems very desirous of a General Convention to revise and amend the federal Constitution. Apropos, what prevented the Eastern States from attending the September meeting at Annapolis? Of all the States in the Union it should have seemed to me, that a measure of this sort (distracted as they were with internal commotions, and experiencing the want of energy in the government) would have been most pleasing to them. What are the prevailing sentiments of the one now proposed to be held at Philadelphia, in May next? and how will it be attended? . . .

The Maryland Assembly has been violently agitated by the question for a paper emission. It has been carried in the House of Delegates, but what has, or will be done with the Bill in the Senate I have not yet heard. The partisans in favor of the measure in the lower House, threaten, it is said, a secession if it is rejected by that Branch of the Legislature. Thus are we advancing. In regretting, which I have often done with the deepest sorrow, the death of our much lamented frd. General Greene, I have accompanied it of late with a quaery, whether he would not have prefered such an exit to the scenes which it is more than probable many of his compatriots may live to bemoan. . . .

That G. B. will be an unconcerned Spectator of the present insurrections (if they continue) is not to be expected. That she is at this moment sowing the Seeds of jealousy and discontent among the various tribes of Indians on our frontier admits of no doubt, in my mind. And that she will improve every opportunity to foment the spirit of turbulence within the bowels of the United States, with a view of distracting our governments, and promoting divisions, is, with me, not less certain. Her first Maneuvres will, no doubt, be covert, and may remain so till the period shall arrive when a decided line of conduct may avail her. Charges of violating the treaty, and other pretexts, will not then be wanting to colour overt acts, tending to effect the grt. objects of which she has long been in labour. A Man is now at the head of their American Affairs well calculated to conduct measures of this kind, and more than probably was selected for the purpose. We ought not therefore to sleep nor to slumber. Vigilance in watching, and vigour in acting, is, in my opinion, become indispensably necessary. If the powers are inadequate amend or alter them, but do not let us sink into the lowest state of humiliation and contempt, and become a by-word in all the earth. I think with you that the Spring will unfold important and distressing Scenes, unless much wisdom and good management is displayed in the interim. . . .

DOCUMENT 6.4
Storms in the Political World Are Necessary

In the following selection, Jefferson confides his feelings about Shays's Rebellion. This letter to Madison, January 30, 1787, tells us something about his philosophy of government and his attitude toward popular "turbulence."

. . . I am impatient to learn your sentiments on the late troubles in the Eastern states. So far as I have yet seen, they do not appear to threaten serious consequences. Those states have suffered by the stoppage of the channels of their commerce, which have not yet found other issues. This must render money scarce, and make the people uneasy. This uneasiness has produced acts absolutely unjustifiable: but I hope they will provoke no severities from their governments. A consciousness of those in power that their administration of the public affairs has been honest, may perhaps produce too great a degree of indignation: and those characters wherein fear predominates over hope may apprehend too much from these instances of irregularity. They may conclude too hastily that nature has formed man insusceptible of any other government but that of force, a con-

clusion not founded in truth, nor experience. Societies exist under three forms sufficiently distinguishable. 1. Without government, as among our Indians. 2. Under governments wherein the will of every one has a just influence, as in the case in England in a slight degree, and in our states in a great one. 3. Under governments of force: as in the case in all other monarchies and in most of the other republics. To have an idea of the curse of existence under these last, they must be seen. It is a government of wolves over sheep. It is a problem, not clear in my mind, that the 1st. condition is not the best. But I believe it to be inconsistent with any great degree of population. The second state has a great deal of good in it. The mass of mankind under that enjoys a precious degree of liberty and happiness. It has it's evils too: the principal of which is the turbulence to which it is subject. But weigh this against the oppressions of monarchy, and it becomes nothing. *Malo periculosam libertatem quam quietam servitutem.* [I prefer perilous liberty to quiet servitude.] Even this evil is productive of good. It prevents the degeneracy of government, and nourishes a general attention to the public affairs. I hold it that a little rebellion now and then is a good thing, and as necessary in the political world as storms in the physical. Unsuccessful rebellions indeed generally establish the incroachments on the rights of the people which have produced them. An observation of this truth should render honest republican governors so mild in their punishment of rebellions, as not to discourage them too much. It is a medicine necessary for the sound health of government. If these transactions give me no uneasiness, I feel very differently at another piece of intelligence, to wit, the possibility that the navigation of the Mississippi may be abandoned to Spain. I never had any interest Westward of the Alleghaney; and I never will have any. But I have had great opportunities of knowing the character of the people who inhabit that country. And I will

Source: Paul L. Ford, ed., *The Writings of Thomas Jefferson* (New York: G. P. Putnam's Sons, 1894), vol. 4, pp. 361–63.

venture to say that the act which abandons the navigation of the Missisipi is an act of separation between the Eastern and Western country. It is a relinquishment of five parts out of eight of the territory of the United States, an abandonment of the fairest subject for the paiment of our public debts, and the chaining those debts on our own necks *in perpetuum*. . . .

DOCUMENT 6.5
Northern and Southern Versions of the Same "Compromise"

Here one may see, from the debates in two of the state ratifying conventions, how the proponents of ratification could defend the slave trade clause from diametrically opposed viewpoints. Among the several speakers represented here, Pinckney and Wilson are of particular interest, both were strong nationalists and major figures at the Philadelphia Convention.

SOUTH CAROLINA

The general [Charles Cotesworth Pinckney] then said he would make a few observations on the objections which the gentleman had thrown out on the restrictions that might be laid on the African trade after the year 1808. On this point your delegates had to contend with the religious and political prejudices of the Eastern and Middle States, and with the interested and inconsistent opinion of Virginia, who was warmly opposed to our importing more slaves. I am of the same opinion now as I was two years ago, when I used the expressions the gentleman has quoted—that, while

Source: Jonathan Elliott, ed., *The Debates in the Several State Conventions of the Adoption of the Federal Constitution* (Washington, 1836), vol. 2, pp. 107–108, 452; vol. 4, 285–86, 296–97.

there remained one acre of swamp-land uncleared of South Carolina, I would raise my voice against restricting the importation of negroes. I am as thoroughly convinced as that gentleman is, that the nature of our climate, and the flat, swampy situation of our country, obliges us to cultivate our lands with negroes, and that without them South Carolina would soon be a desert waste.

You have so frequently heard my sentiments on this subject, that I need not now repeat them. It was alleged, by some of the members who opposed an unlimited importation, that slaves increased the weakness of any state who admitted them; that they were a dangerous species of property, which an invading enemy could easily turn against ourselves and the neighboring states; and that, as we were allowed a representation for them in the House of Representatives, our influence in government would be increased in proportion as we were less able to defend ourselves. "Show some period," said the members from the Eastern States, "when it may be in our power to put a stop, if we please, to the importation of this weakness, and we will endeavor, for your convenience, to restrain the religious and political prejudices of our people on this subject." The Middle States and Virginia made us no such proposition; they were for an immediate and total prohibition. We endeavored to obviate the objections that were made in the best manner we could, and assigned reasons for our insisting on the importation, which there is no occasion to repeat, as they must occur to every gentleman in the house: a committee of the states was appointed in order to accommodate this matter, and, after a great deal of difficulty, it was settled on the footing recited in the Constitution.

By this settlement we have secured an unlimited importation of negroes for twenty years. Nor is it declared that the importation shall be then stopped; it may be continued. We have a security that the general government can never emancipate them, for no such authority is granted; and it is admitted, on all hands, that the general government has no powers but what are expressly granted by the Constitution, and that all rights not expressed were reserved by the several states. We have obtained a right to recover our slaves in whatever part of America they may take refuge, which is a right we had not before. In short, considering all circumstances, we have made the best terms for the security of this species of property it was in our power to make. We would have made better if we could; but, on the whole, I do not think them bad.

* * * * *

PENNSYLVANIA

Mr. JAMES WILSON. . . . With respect to the clause restricting Congress from prohibiting the *migration or importation of such persons* as any of the states now existing shall think proper to admit, prior to the year 1808, the honorable gentleman says that this clause is not only dark, but intended to grant to Congress, for that time, the power to admit the importation of *slaves*. No such thing was intended. But I will tell you what was done, and it gives me high pleasure that so much was done. Under the present Confederation, the states may admit the importation of slaves as long as they please; but by this article, after the year 1808, the Congress will have power to prohibit such importation, notwithstanding the disposition of any state to the contrary. I consider this as laying the foundation for banishing slavery out of this country; and though the period is more distant than I could wish, yet it will produce the same kind, gradual change, which was pursued in Pennsylvania. It is with much satisfaction I view this power in the general government, whereby they may lay an interdiction on this reproachful trade: but an immediate advantage is also obtained;

for a tax or duty may be imposed on such importation, not exceeding ten dollars for each person; and this, sir, operates as a partial prohibition; it was all that could be obtained. I am sorry it was no more; but from this I think there is reason to hope, that yet a few years, and it will be prohibited altogether; and in the mean time, the *new* states which are to be formed will be under *the control* of Congress in this particular, and slaves will never be introduced amongst them. . . .

DOCUMENT 6.6
Benjamin Franklin Urges Compromise

Franklin's observations on constitution-making at Philadelphia (September 17, 1787) are typical of the man; they are reasonable and modest in spirit and suggest his commonsense approach as well as the spirit of accommodation that guided many of the delegates.

I confess that there are several parts of this constitution which I do not at present approve, but I am not sure I shall never approve them: For having lived long, I have experienced many instances of being obliged by better information, or fuller consideration, to change opinions even on important subjects, which I once thought right, but found to be otherwise. It is therefore that the older I grow, the more apt I am to doubt my own judgment, and to pay more respect to the judgment of others. Most men indeed as well as most sects in Religion, think themselves in possession of all truth, and that wherever others differ from them it is so far error. Steele a Protestant in a Dedication tells the Pope, that the only difference between

Source: Gaillard Hunt, ed., *The Writings of James Madison* (New York: G. P. Putnam's Sons, 1903), vol. 4, pp. 472–75, 482–83.

our Churches is their opinions of the certainty of their doctrines is, the Church of Rome is infallible and the Church of England is never in the wrong. But though many private persons think almost as highly of their own infallibility as of that of their sect, few express it so naturally as a certain french lady, who in a dispute with her sister, said "I don't know how it happens, Sister but I meet with no body but myself, that's always in the right—*Il n'y a que moi qui a toujours raison.*"

In these sentiments, Sir, I agree to this Constitution with all its faults, if they are such; because I think a general Government necessary for us, and there is no form of Government but what may be a blessing to the people if well administered, and believe farther that this is likely to be well administered for a course of years, and can only end in Despotism, as other forms have done before it, when the people shall became so corrupted as to need despotic Government, being incapable of any other. I doubt too whether any other Convention we can obtain, may be able to make a better Constitution. For when you assemble a number of men to have the advantage of their joint wisdom, you inevitably assemble with those men, all their prejudices, their passions, their errors of opinion, their local interests, and their selfish views. From such an assembly can a perfect production be expected? It therefore astonishes me, Sir, to find this system approaching so near to perfection as it does; and I think it will astonish our enemies, who are waiting with confidence to hear that our councils are confounded like those of the Builders of Babel; and that our States are on the point of separation, only to meet hereafter for the purpose of cutting one another's throats. Thus I consent, Sir, to this Constitution because I expect no better, and because I am not sure, that it is not the best. The opinions I have had of its errors, I sacrifice to the public good. I have never whispered a syllable of them abroad. Within these walls they were born, and here they shall die. If every one of us in returning to our Constituents were to report the objections he has had to it, and endeavor to gain partizans in support of them, we might prevent its being generally received, and thereby lose all the salutary effects & great advantages resulting naturally in our favor among foreign Nations as well as among ourselves, from our real or apparent unanimity. Much of the strength & efficiency of any Government in procuring and securing happiness to the people, depends, on opinion, on the general opinion of the goodness of the Government, as well as of the wisdom and integrity of its Governors. I hope therefore that for our own sakes as a part of the people, and for the sake of posterity, we shall act heartily and unanimously in recommending this Constitution (if approved by Congress & confirmed by the Conventions) wherever our influence may extend, and turn our future thoughts & endeavors to the means of having it well administered.

On the whole, Sir, I can not help expressing a wish that every member of the Convention who may still have objections to it, would with me, on this occasion doubt a little of his own infallibility, and to make manifest our unanimity, put his name to this instrument. . . .

DOCUMENT 6.7
The Anti-Federalist Argument

The essay that follows, strongly attacking the proposed Constitution, was at one time attributed to Elbridge Gerry. Subsequent scholarship, however, has identified it as the work of Mercy Warren, sister of the Massachusetts revolutionary patriot, James Otis.

Source: Paul L. Ford, ed., *Pamphlets on the Constitution of the United States, Published during its Discussion by the People, 1787–1788* (Privately printed; Brooklyn, N.Y., 1888), pp. 1–23.

Some gentlemen, with laboured zeal, have spent much time in urging the necessity of government, from the embarrassments of trade—the want of respectability abroad and confidence of the public engagements at home:—These are obvious truths which no one denies; and there are few who do not unite in the general wish for the restoration of public faith, the revival of commerce, arts, agriculture, and industry, under a lenient, peaceable and energetick government: But the most sagacious advocates for the party have not by fair discussion, and rational argumentation, evinced the necessity of adopting this many headed monster; of such motley mixture, that its enemies cannot trace a feature of Democratick or Republican extract; nor have its friends the courage to denominate a Monarchy, an Aristocracy, or an Oligarchy, and the favoured bantling must have passed through the short period of its existence without a name, had not Mr. *Wilson,* in the fertility of his genius, suggested the happy epithet of a *Federal Republic.*—But I leave the field of general censure on the secresy of its birth, the rapidity of its growth, and the fatal consequences of suffering it to live to the age of maturity, and will particularize some of the most weighty objections to its passing through this continent in a gigantic size.—It will be allowed by every one that the fundamental principle of a free government is the equal representation of a free people— . . . And when society has thus deputed a certain number of their equals to take care of their personal rights, and the interest of the whole community, it must be considered that responsibility is the great security of integrity and honour; and that annual election is the basis of responsibility.—Man is not immediately corrupted, but power without limitation, or amenability, may endanger the brightest virtue—whereas a frequent return to the bar of their Constituents is the strongest check against the corruptions to which men are liable, either from the intrigues of others of more subtle genius, or the propensities of their own

hearts,—and the gentlemen who have so warmly advocated in the late Convention of the Massachusetts, the change from annual to biennial elections; may have been in the same predicament, and perhaps with the same views that Mr. *Hutchinson* once acknowledged himself, when in a letter to *Lord Hillsborough,* he observed, ''that the grand difficulty of making a change in government against the general bent of the people had caused him to turn his thoughts to a variety of plans, in order to find one that might be executed in spite of opposition,'' and the first he proposed was that, ''instead of annual, the elections should be only once in three years:''. . .

DOCUMENT 6.8
The Constitution of the United States

Framed at a constitutional convention in Philadelphia in 1787, the Constitution was ratified in June 1788 when New Hampshire, the ninth state needed to put the Constitution into effect, gave its approval. The new government of the United States under the Constitution began March 4, 1789.

We the People of the United States, in Order to form a more perfect Union, establish Justice, insure domestic Tranquility, provide for the common defence, promote the general Welfare, and secure the Blessings of Liberty to ourselves and our Posterity, do ordain and establish this Constitution for the United States of America.

ARTICLE I

Sec. 1. All legislative Powers herein granted shall be vested in a Congress of the United States, which shall consist of a Senate and House of Representatives.

Source: James D. Richardson, ed., *Messages and Papers of The Presidents* (New York, 1897), vol. 1, pp. 15–30.

Sec. 2. The House of Representatives shall be composed of Members chosen every second Year by the People of the several States, and the Electors in each State shall have the Qualifications requisite for Electors of the most numerous Branch of the State Legislature.

No Person shall be a Representative who shall not have attained to the Age of twenty five Years, and been seven Years a Citizen of the United States, and who shall not, when elected, be an Inhabitant of that State in which he shall be chosen.

Representatives and direct Taxes shall be apportioned among the several States which may be included within this Union, according to their respective Numbers, which shall be determined by adding to the whole Number of free Persons, including those bound to Service for a Term of Years, and excluding Indians not taxed, three fifths of all other Persons. The actual Enumeration shall be made within three Years after the first Meeting of the Congress of the United States, and within every subsequent Term of ten Years, in such Manner as they shall by Law direct. The Number of Representatives shall not exceed one for every thirty Thousand, but each State shall have at Least one Representative; and until such enumeration shall be made, the State of New Hampshire shall be entitled to chuse three, Massachusetts eight, Rhode-Island and Providence Plantations one, Connecticut five, New-York six, New Jersey four, Pennsylvania eight, Delaware one, Maryland six, Virginia ten, North Carolina five, South Carolina five, and Georgia three.

When vacancies happen in the Representation from any State, the Executive Authority thereof shall issue Writs of Election to fill such Vacancies.

The House of Representatives shall chuse their Speaker and other Officers; and shall have the sole Power of Impeachment.

Sec. 3. The Senate of the United States shall be composed of two Senators from each State, chosen by the Legislature thereof, for six Years; and each Senator shall have one Vote.

Immediately after they shall be assembled in Consequence of the first Election, they shall be divided as equally as may be into the three Classes. The Seats of the Senators of the first Class shall be vacated at the Expiration of the second Year, of the second Class at the Expiration of the fourth Year, and of the third Class at the Expiration of the sixth Year, so that one third may be chosen every second Year; and if Vacancies happen by Resignation, or otherwise, during the Recess of the Legislature of any State, the Executive thereof may make temporary Appointments until the next Meeting of the Legislature, which shall then fill such Vacancies.

No Person shall be a Senator who shall not have attained to the Age of thirty Years, and been nine Years a Citizens of the United States, and who shall not, when elected, be an Inhabitant of that State for which he shall be chosen.

The Vice President of the United States shall be President of the Senate, but shall have no Vote, unless they be equally divided.

The Senate shall chuse their other Officers, and also a President pro tempore, in the Absence of the Vice President, or when he shall exercise the Office of President of the United States.

The Senate shall have the sole Power to try all Impeachments. When sitting for that Purpose, they shall be on Oath or Affirmation. When the President of the United States is tried, the Chief Justice shall preside: And no Person shall be convicted without the Concurrence of two thirds of the Members present.

Judgment in Cases of Impeachment shall not extend further than to removal from Office, and disqualification to hold and enjoy any Office of honor, Trust or Profit under the United States: but the Party convicted shall nevertheless be liable and subject to Indictment, Trial, Judgment and Punishment, according to Law.

Sec. 4. The Times, Places and Manner of holding Elections for Senators and Representatives, shall be prescribed in each State by the Legislature thereof; but the Congress may at any time by Law make or alter such Regulations, except as to the Places of chusing Senators.

The Congress shall assemble at least once in ever Year, and such Meeting shall be on the first Monday in December, unless they shall by Law appoint a different Day.

Sec. 5. Each House shall be the Judge of the Elections, Returns, and Qualifications of its own Members, and a Majority of each shall constitute a Quorum to do Business; but a smaller Number may adjourn from day to day, and may be authorized to compel the Attendance of absent Members, in such Manner, and under such Penalties as each House may provide.

Each House may determine the Rules of its Proceedings, punish its Members for disorderly Behaviour, and, with the Concurrence of two thirds, expel a Member.

Each House shall keep a Journal of its Proceedings, and from time to time publish the same, excepting such Parts as may in their Judgment require Secrecy; and the Yeas and Nays of the Members of either House on any question shall, at the Desire of one fifth of those Present, be entered on the Journal.

Neither House, during the Session of Congress, shall, without the Consent of the other, adjourn for more than three days, not to any other Place than that in which the two Houses shall be sitting.

Sec. 6. The Senators and Representatives shall receive a Compensation for their Services, to be ascertained by Law, and paid out of the Treasury of the United States. They shall in all Cases, except Treason, Felony and Breach of the Peace, be privileged from Arrest during their Attendance at the Session of their respective Houses, and in going to and returning from the same; and for any Speech or Debate in either House, they shall not be questioned in any other Place.

No Senator or Representative shall, during the Time for which he was elected, be appointed to any civil Office under the Authority of the United States which shall have been created, or the Emoluments whereof shall have been encreased during such time; and no Person holding any Office under the United States, shall be a Member of either House during his Continuance in Office.

Sec. 7. All Bills for raising Revenue shall originate in the House of Representatives; but the Senate may propose or concur with Amendments as on other Bills.

Every Bill which shall have passed the House of Representatives and the Senate, shall, before it become a Law, be presented to the President of the United States; If he approve he shall sign it, but if not he shall return it, with his Objections to that House in which it shall have originated, who shall enter the Objections at large on their Journal, and proceed to reconsider it. If after such Reconsideration two thirds of that House shall agree to pass the Bill, it shall be sent, together with the Objections, to the other House, by which it shall likewise be reconsidered, and if approved by two thirds of that House, it shall become a Law. But in all such Cases the Votes of both Houses shall be determined by yeas and Nays, and the Names of the Persons voting for and against the Bill shall be entered on the Journal of each House respectively. If any Bill shall not be returned by the President within ten Days (Sundays excepted) after it shall have been presented to him, the Same shall be a Law, in like Manner as if he had signed it, unless the Congress by their Adjournment prevent its Return, in which Case it shall not be a Law.

Every Order, Resolution, or Vote to which the Concurrence of the Senate and House of Representatives may be necessary (except on a question of Adjournment) shall be presented to the President of the United States; and before the Same shall take Effect, shall be approved by him, or being disapproved by him, shall be repassed by two thirds of the Senate and House of Representatives, according to the

Rules and Limitations prescribed in the Case of a Bill.

Sec. 8. The Congress shall have Power To lay and collect Taxes, Duties, Imposts and Excises, to pay the Debts and provide for the common Defence and general Welfare of the United States; but all Duties, Imposts and Excises shall be uniform throughout the United States;

To borrow Money on the credit of the United States;

To regulate Commerce with foreign Nations, and among the several States, and with the Indian Tribes;

To establish an uniform Rule of Naturalization, and uniform Laws on the subject of Bankruptcies throughout the United States;

To coin Money, regulate the Value thereof, and of foreign Coin, and fix the Standard of Weights and Measures;

To provide for the Punishment of counterfeiting the Securities and current Coin of the United States;

To establish Post Offices and post Roads;

To promote the Progress of Science and useful Arts, by securing for limited Times to Authors and Inventors the exclusive Right to their respective Writings and Discoveries;

To constitute Tribunals inferior to the supreme Court;

To define and punish Piracies and Felonies committed on the high Seas, and Offences against the Law of Nations;

To declare War, grant Letters of Marque and Reprisal, and make Rules concerning Captures on Land and Water;

To raise and support Armies, but no Appropriation of Money to that Use shall be for a longer Term than two Years;

To provide and maintain a Navy;

To make rules for the Government and Regulation of the land and naval Forces;

To provide for calling forth the Militia to execute the Laws of the Union, suppress Insurrections and repel Invasions;

To provide for organizing, arming, and disciplining, the Militia, and for governing such Part of them as may be employed in the Service of the United States, reserving to the States respectively, the Appointment of the Officers, and the Authority of training the Militia according to the discipline prescribed by Congress;

To exercise exclusive Legislation in all Cases whatsoever, over such District (not exceeding ten Miles square) as may, by Cession of particular States, and the Acceptance of Congress, become the Seat of the Government of the United States, and to exercise like Authority over all Places purchased by the Consent of the Legislature of the State in which the Same shall be, for the Erection of Forts, Magazines, Arsenals, dock-Yards, and other needul Buildings;—And

To make all Laws which shall be necessary and proper for carrying into Execution the foregoing Powers, and all other Powers vested by this Constitution in the Government of the United States, or in any Department or Officer thereof.

Sec. 9. The Migration or Importation of such Persons as any of the States now existing shall think proper to admit, shall not be prohibited by the Congress prior to the Year one thousand eight hundred and eight, but a Tax or duty may be imposed on such Importation, not exceeding ten dollars for each Person.

The Privilege of the Writ of Habeas Corpus shall not be suspended, unless when in Cases of Rebellion or Invasion the public Safety may require it.

No Bill of Attainder or ex post facto Law shall be passed.

No Capitation, or other direct, Tax shall be laid, unless in Proportion to the Census or Enumeration herein before directed to be taken.

No Tax or Duty shall be laid on Articles exported from any State.

No Preference shall be given by any Regulation of Commerce or Revenue to the Ports of one State over those of another: nor shall Vessels bound to, or from, one State, be obliged to enter, clear, or pay Duties in another.

No Money shall be drawn from the Treasury, but in Consequence of Appropriations made by Law; and a regular Statement and Account of the Receipts and Expenditures of all public Money shall be published from time to time.

No Title of Nobility shall be granted by the United States: And no Person holding any Office of Profit or Trust under them, shall, without the Consent of the Congress, accept of any present, Emolument, Office, or Title, of any kind whatever, from any King, Prince or foreign State.

Sec. 10. No State shall enter into any Treaty, Alliance, or Confederation; grant Letters of Marque and Reprisal; coin Money; emit Bills of Credit; make any Thing but gold and silver Coin a Tender in Payment of Debts; pass any Bill of Attainder, ex post facto Law, or Law impairing the Obligation of Contracts, or grant any Title of Nobility.

No State shall, without the Consent of the Congress, lay any Imposts or Duties on Imports or Exports, except what may be absolutely necessary for executing it's inspection Laws: and the net Produce of all Duties and Imposts, laid by any State on Imports or Exports, shall be for the Use of the Treasury of the United States; and all such Laws shall be subject to the Revision and Controul of the Congress.

No State shall, without the Consent of Congress, lay any Duty of Tonnage, keep Troops, or Ships of War in time of Peace, enter into any agreement or Compact with another State, or with a foreign Power, or engage in War, unless actually invaded, or in such imminent Danger as will not admit of delay.

ARTICLE II

Sec. 1. The executive Power shall be vested in a President of the United States of America. He shall hold his Office during the Term of four Years, and, together with the Vice Presi-

dent, chosen for the same Term, be elected, as follows

Each State shall appoint, in such Manner as the Legislature thereof may direct, a Number of Electors, equal to the whole Number of Senators and Representatives to which the State may be entitled in the Congress: but no Senator or Representative, or Person holding an Office of Trust or Profit under the United States, shall be appointed an Elector.

The Electors shall meet in their respective States, and vote by Ballot for two Persons, of whom one at least shall not be an Inhabitant of the same State with themselves. And they shall make a List of all the Persons voted for, and of the Number of Votes for each; which List they shall sign and certify, and transmit sealed to the Seat of the Government of the United States, directed to the President of the Senate. The President of the Senate shall, in the Presence of the Senate and House of Representatives, open all the Certificates, and the Votes shall then be counted. The Person having the greatest Number of Votes shall be the President, if such Number be a Majority of the whole Number of Electors appointed; and if there be more than one who have such Majority, and have an equal Number of Votes, then the House of Representatives shall immediately chuse by Ballot one of them for President; and if no person have a Majority, then from the five highest on the List and the said House shall in like Manner chuse the President. But in chusing the President, the Votes shall be taken by States, the Representation from each State having one Vote; A quorum for this Purpose shall consist of a Member or Members from two thirds of the States, and a Majority of all the States shall be necessary to a Choice. In every Case, after the Choice of the President, the Person having the greatest Number of Votes of the Electors shall be the Vice President. But if there should remain two or more who have equal Votes, the Senate shall chuse from them by Ballot the Vice President.

The Congress may determine the Time of chusing the Electors, and the Day on which they shall give their Votes; which Day shall be the same throughout the United States.

No Person except a natural born Citizen, or a Citizen of the United States, at the time of the Adoption of this Constitution, shall be eligible to the Office of President; neither shall any Person be eligible to that Office who shall not have attained to the Age of thirty five Years, and been fourteen Years a Resident within the United States.

In Case of the Removal of the President from Office, or of his Death, Resignation, or Inability to discharge the Powers and Duties of the said Office, the Same shall devolve on the Vice President, and the Congress may by Law provide for the Case of Removal, Death, Resignation or Inability, both of the President and Vice President, declaring what Officer shall then act accordingly, until the Disability be removed, or a President shall be elected.

The President shall, at stated Times, receive for his Services, a Compensation, which shall neither be encreased nor diminished during the Period for which he shall have been elected, and he shall not receive within that Period any other Emolument from the United States, or any of them.

Before he enter on the Execution of his Office, he shall take the following Oath or Affirmation:—''I do solemnly swear (or affirm) that I will faithfully execute the Office of President of the United States, and will to the best of my Ability, preserve, protect and defend the Constitution of the United States.''

Sec. 2. The President shall be Commander in Chief of the Army and Navy of the United States, and of the Militia of the several States, when called into the actual Service of the United States; he may require the Opinion, in writing, of the principal Officer in each of the executive Departments, upon any Subject relating to the Duties of their respective Offices, and he shall have Power to grant Reprieves and Pardons for Offences against the United States, except in Cases of Impeachment.

He shall have Power, by and with the Advice and Consent of the Senate, to make Treaties, provided two thirds of the Senators present concur; and he shall nominate, and by and with the Advice and Consent of the Senate, shall appoint Ambassadors, other public Ministers and Consuls, Judges of the supreme Court, and all other Officers of the United States, whose Appointments are not herein otherwise provided for, and which shall be established by Law: but the Congress may by Law vest the Appointment of such inferior Officers, as they think proper, in the President alone, in the Courts of Law, or in the Heads of Departments.

The President shall have Power to fill up all Vacancies that may happen during the Recess of the Senate, by granting Commissions which shall expire at the End of their next Session.

Sec. 3. He shall from time to time give to the Congress Information of the State of the Union, and recommend to their Consideration such Measures as he shall judge necessary and expedient; he may, on extraordinary Occasions, convene both Houses, or either of them, and in Case of Disagreement between them, with Respect to the Time of Adjournment, he may adjourn them to such Time as he shall think proper; he shall receive Ambassadors and other public Ministers; he shall take Care that the Laws be faithfully executed, and shall Commission all the Officers of the United States.

Sec. 4. The President, Vice President and all civil Officers of the United States, shall be removed from Office on Impeachment for, and Conviction of, Treason, Bribery, or other high Crimes and Misdemeanors.

ARTICLE III

Sec. 1. The judicial Power of the United States, shall be vested in one supreme Court, and in

such inferior Courts as the Congress may from time to time ordain and establish. The Judges, both of the supreme and inferior Courts, shall hold their Offices during good Behaviour, and shall, at stated Times, receive for their Services, a Compensation, which shall not be diminished during their Continuance in Office.
Sec. 2. The judicial Power shall extend to all Cases, in Law and Equity, arising under this Constitution, the Laws of the United States, and Treaties made, or which shall be made, under their Authority;—to all Cases affecting Ambassadors, other public Ministers and Consuls;—to all Cases of admiralty and maritime Jurisdiction;—to Controversies to which the United States shall be a Party;—to Controversies between two or more States;—between a State and Citizens of another State;—between Citizens of different States,—between Citizens of the same State claiming Lands under Grants of different States, and between a State, or the Citizens thereof, and foreign States, Citizens or Subjects.

In all Cases affecting Ambassadors, other public Ministers and Consuls, and those in which a State shall be Party, the supreme Court shall have original Jurisdiction. In all the other Cases before mentioned, the supreme Court shall have appellate Jurisdiction, both as to Law and Fact, with such Exceptions, and under such Regulations as the Congress shall make.

The Trial of all Crimes, except in Cases of Impeachment, shall be by Jury; and such Trial shall be held in the State where the said Crimes shall have been committed; but when not committed within any State, the Trial shall be at such Place or Places as the Congress may by Law have directed.
Sec. 3. Treason against the United States, shall consist only in levying War against them, or in adhering to their Enemies, giving them Aid and Comfort. No Person shall be convicted of Treason unless on the Testimony of two Witnesses to the same overt Act, or on Confession in open Court.

The Congress shall have Power to declare the Punishment of Treason, but no Attainder of Treason shall work Corruption of Blood, of Forfeiture except during the Life of the Person attainted.

ARTICLE IV

Sec. 1. Full Faith and Credit shall be given in each State to the Public Acts, Records, and judicial Proceedings of every other State. And the Congress may by general Laws prescribe the Manner in which such Acts, Records and Proceedings shall be proved, and the Effect thereof.
Sec. 2. The Citizens of each State shall be entitled to all Privileges and Immunities of Citizens in the several States.

A Person charged in any State with Treason, Felony, or other Crime, who shall flee from Justice, and be found in another State, shall on Demand of the executive Authority of the State from which he fled, be delivered up, to be removed to the State having Jurisdiction of the Crime.

No Person held to Service or Labour in one State, under the Laws thereof, escaping into another, shall, in Consequence of any Law or Regulation therein, be discharged from such Service or Labour, but shall be delivered up on Claim of the Party to whom such Service or Labour may be due.
Sec. 3. New States may be admitted by the Congress into this Union; but no new States shall be formed or erected within the Jurisdiction of any other State; nor any State be formed by the Junction of two or more States, or Parts of States, without the Consent of the Legislatures of the States concerned as well as of the Congress.

The Congress shall have Power to dispose of and make all needful Rules and Regulations respecting the Territory or other Property belonging to the United States; and nothing in this Constitution shall be so construed as to Prejudice any Claims of the United States, or of any particular State.

Sec. 4. The United States shall guarantee to every State in this Union a Republican Form of Government, and shall protect each of them against Invasion; and on Application of the Legislature, or of the Executive (when the Legislature cannot be convened) against domestic Violence.

ARTICLE V

The Congress, whenever two thirds of both Houses shall deem it necessary, shall propose Amendments to this Constitution, or, on the Application of the Legislatures of two thirds of the several States, shall call a Convention for proposing Amendments, which, in either Case, shall be valid to all Intents and Purposes, as Part of this Constitution, when ratified by the Legislatures of three fourths of the several States, or by Conventions in three fourths thereof, as the one or the other Mode of Ratification may be proposed by the Congress; Provided that no Amendment which may be made prior to the Year One thousand eight hundred and eight shall in any Manner affect the first and fourth Clauses in the Ninth Section of the first Article; and that no State, without its Consent, shall be deprived of it's equal Suffrage in the Senate.

ARTICLE VI

All Debts contracted and Engagements entered into, before the Adoption of this Constitution, shall be as valid against the United States under this Constitution, as under the Confederation.

This Constitution, and the Laws of the United States which shall be made in Pursuance

thereof; and all Treaties made, or which shall be made, under the Authority of the United States, shall be the supreme Law of the Land; and the Judges in every State shall be bound thereby, any Thing in the Constitution or Laws of any State to the Contrary notwithstanding.

The Senators and Representatives before mentioned, and the Members of the several State Legislatures, and all executive and judicial Officers, both of the United States and of the several States, shall be bound by Oath or Affirmation, to support this Constitution; but no religious Test shall ever be required as a Qualification to any Office or public Trust under the United States.

ARTICLE VII

The Ratification of the Conventions of nine States, shall be sufficient for the Establishment of this Constitution between the States so ratifying the Same.

Done in Convention by the Unanimous Consent of the States present the Seventeenth Day of September in the Year of our Lord one thousand seven hundred and Eighty seven and of the Independence of the United States of America the Twelfth. In witness whereof We have hereunto subscribed our Names,

G° Washington—Presid[t]
and deputy from Virginia

Delaware	Geo:Read
	Gunning Bedford jun
	John Dickinson
	Richard Basset
	Jaco:Broom

Maryland	James M[c]Henry
	Dan of S[T] Tho[S] Jenifer
	Dan[L] Carroll

Virginia	John Blair
	James Madison Jr.

North Carolina $\left\{\begin{array}{l}\text{W}^{\text{M}}\text{ Blount}\\\text{Rich}^{\text{D}}\text{ Dobbs}\\\quad\text{Spaight}\\\text{Hu Williamson}\end{array}\right.$

South Carolina $\left\{\begin{array}{l}\text{J. Rutledge}\\\text{Charles Cotesworth}\\\quad\text{Pinckney}\\\text{Charles Pinckney}\\\text{Pierce Butler}\end{array}\right.$

Georgia $\left\{\begin{array}{l}\text{William Few}\\\text{Abr Baldwin}\end{array}\right.$

New Hampshire $\left\{\begin{array}{l}\text{John Langdon}\\\text{Nicholas Gilman}\end{array}\right.$

Massachusetts $\left\{\begin{array}{l}\text{Nathaniel Gorham}\\\text{Rufus King}\end{array}\right.$

Connecticut $\left\{\begin{array}{l}\text{W}^{\text{M}}\text{ Sam}^{\text{L}}\text{ Johnson}\\\text{Roger Sherman}\end{array}\right.$

New York $\left\{\text{Alexander Hamilton}\right.$

New Jersey $\left\{\begin{array}{l}\text{Wil:Livingston}\\\text{David Brearley}\\\text{W}^{\text{M}}\text{ Paterson}\\\text{Jona:Dayton}\end{array}\right.$

Pensylvania $\left\{\begin{array}{l}\text{B Franklin}\\\text{Thomas Mifflin}\\\text{Rob}^{\text{T}}\text{ Morris}\\\text{Geo. Clymer}\\\text{Tho}^{\text{s}}\text{ FitzSimons}\\\text{Jared Ingersoll}\\\text{James Wilson}\\\text{Gouv Morris}\end{array}\right.$

Articles in addition to, and Amendment of the Constitution of the United States of America, proposed by Congess, and ratified by the Legislatures of the several States, pursuant to the fifth Article of the original Constitution.

[The first ten amendments went into effect November 3, 1791]

ARTICLE I

Congress shall make no law respecting an establishment of religion, or prohibiting the free exercise thereof; or abridging the freedom of speech, or of the press; or the right of the people peaceably to assemble, and to petition the government for a redress of grievances.

ARTICLE II

A well regulated Militia, being necessary to the security of a free State, the right of the people to keep and bear Arms, shall not be infringed.

ARTICLE III

No Soldier shall, in time of peace be quartered in any house, without the consent of the Owner, nor in time of war, but in a manner to be prescribed by law.

ARTICLE IV

The right of the people to be secure in their persons, houses, papers, and effects, against unreasonable searches and seizures, shall not be violated, and no Warrants shall issue, but upon probable cause, supported by Oath or affirmation, and particularly describing the place to be searched, and the persons or things to be seized.

ARTICLE V

No person shall be held to answer for a capital, or otherwise infamous crime, unless on a presentment or indictment of a Grand Jury, except in cases arising in the land or naval forces, or in the Militia, when in actual service in time of War or public danger; nor shall any person be subject for the same offence to be twice put in jeopardy of life or limb; nor shall be compelled in any criminal case to be a witness against himself, nor be deprived of life, liberty, or property, without due process of law; nor shall private property be taken for public use, without just compensation.

ARTICLE VI

In all criminal prosecutions, the accused shall enjoy the right to a speedy and public trial, by an impartial jury of the State and district wherein the crime shall have been committed, which district shall have been previously ascertained by law, and to be informed of the nature and cause of the accusation; to be confronted with the witnesses against him; to have compulsory process for obtaining witnesses in his favor, and to have the Assistance of Counsel for his defence.

ARTICLE VII

In Suits at common law, where the value in controversy shall exceed twenty dollars, the right of trial by jury shall be preserved, and no fact tried by a jury, shall be otherwise re-examined in any Court of the United States, than according to the rules of the common law.

ARTICLE VIII

Excessive bail shall not be required, nor excessive fines imposed, nor cruel and unusual punishments inflicted.

ARTICLE IX

The enumeration in the Constitution, of certain rights, shall not be construed to deny or disparage others retained by the people.

ARTICLE X

The powers not delegated to the United States by the Constitution, nor prohibited by it to the States, are reserved to the States respectively, or to the people.

DOCUMENT 6.9
Hamilton Advises New York Federalists

The following letters were written by Alexander Hamilton on the eve of the New York ratification convention. They concern the tactics that would enable the heavily outnumbered Federalist delegation to snatch victory from what appeared to be inevitable defeat.

TO GOUVERNEUR MORRIS

New York, May 19, 1788

. . . Your account of the situation of Virginia was interesting, and the present appearances as represented here justify your conjectures. It does not however appear that the adoption of the Constitution can be considered as out of doubt in that State. Its conduct upon the occasion will certainly be of critical importance.

In this State, as far as we can judge, the elections have gone wrong. The event, however, will not certainly be known till the end of the month. Violence rather than moderation is to be looked for from the opposite party. Obstinacy seems the prevailing trait in the character of its leader. The language is that if all the other States adopt, this is to persist in refusing the Constitution. It is reduced to a certainty that Clinton has in several conversations declared the *Union* unnecessary—though I have the information through channels which do not permit a public use to be made of it.

We have, notwithstanding this unfavorable complexion of things, two sources of hope: one, the chance of a ratification by nine States before we decide, and the influence of this upon the firmness of the *followers;* the other, the probability of a change of sentiment in

Source: Henry Cabot Lodge, ed., *The Works of Alexander Hamilton* (New York: G. P. Putnam's Sons, 1904), vol. 9, pp. 428–35.

the people, auspicious to the Constitution. . . .

TO JOHN SULLIVAN, ESQ., PRESIDENT OF THE STATE OF NEW HAMPSHIRE

New York, June 6, 1788

You will no doubt have understood that the Anti-Federal party has prevailed in this State by a large majority. It is therefore of the utmost importance that all external circumstances should be made use of to influence their conduct. This will suggest to you the *great advantage* of a speedy decision in your State, if you can be sure of the question, and a prompt communication of the event to us. With this view, permit me to request that the instant you have taken a decisive vote in favor of the Constitution, you send an express to me at Poughkeepsie. Let him take the *shortest route* to that place, change horses on the road, and use all possible diligence. I shall with pleasure defray all expenses, and give a liberal reward to the person. As I suspect an effort will be made to precipitate us, all possible *safe* dispatch on your part, as well to obtain a decision as to communicate the intelligence of it, will be desirable.

TO JAMES MADISON, JUNIOR

New York, June 8, 1788

In my last, I think, I informed you that the elections had turned out, beyond expectation, favorable to the Anti-Federal party. They have a majority of two thirds in the Convention, and, according to the best estimate I can form, of about four sevenths in the community. The views of the leaders in this city are pretty well ascertained to be turned towards a *long* adjournment—say, till next spring or summer. Their incautious ones observe that this will give an opportunity to the State to see *how* the government works, and to act according to *circumstances*.

My reasonings on the fact are to this effect: The leaders of the party hostile to the Constitution are equally hostile to the Union. They are, however, afraid to reject the Constitution at once, because that step would bring matters to a crisis between this State and the States which had adopted the Constitution, and between the parties in the State. A separation of the Southern District from the other parts of the State, it is perceived, would become the object of the Federalists and of the neighboring States. They therefore resolve upon a long adjournment as the safest and most artful course to effect their final purpose. . . .

TO JAMES MADISON, JUNIOR

New York, May 19, 1788

Some days since I wrote to you, my dear sir, inclosing a letter from a Mr. Vanderkemp, etc.

I then mentioned to you that the question of a majority for or against the Constitution would depend upon the County of Albany. By the later accounts from that quarter, I fear much that the issue there has been against us.

As Clinton is truly the leader of his party, and is inflexibly obstinate, I count little on overcoming opposition by reason. Our only chances will be the previous ratification by nine States, which may shake the firmness of his followers; and a change in the sentiments of the people, which have, for some time, been travelling towards the Constitution, though the first impressions, made by every species of influence and artifice, were too strong to be eradicated in time to give a decisive turn to the elections. We shall leave nothing undone to cultivate a favorable disposition in the citizens at large.

The language of the anti-Federalists is, that if all the other States adopt, New York ought still to hold out. I have the most direct intelligence, but in a manner which forbids a public use being made of it, that Clinton has, in several conversations, declared his opinion of the *inutility* of the Union. . . . We think here that the situation of your State is critical. Let me know what you now think of it. I believe you meet nearly at the time we do. It will be of vast importance that an exact communication should be kept up between us at that period; and the moment *any decisive* question is taken, if favorable, I request you to dispatch an express to me, with pointed orders to make all possible diligence, by changing horses, etc. All expense shall be thankfully and liberally paid. I executed your commands respecting the first volume of the *Federalist*. I sent forty of the common copies and twelve of the finer ones, addressed to the care of Governor Randolph. The printer announces the second volume in a day or two, when an equal number of the two kinds shall also be forwarded. . . .

chapter 7

Antiparty Party Builders: The Federalists and Republicans

Roger H. Brown
American University

The first American political parties organized on a national scale were founded by men who were opposed to political parties. Neither the Federalists, who organized the Federalist party when they managed the central government, from 1789 to 1801, nor the Jeffersonian Republicans, who built their opposition party in the 1790s and then held power from 1801 to 1829, wanted, expected, or welcomed the political parties that had been organized. Far from regarding their party organizations as constructive forces that would be permanent, Federalist and Republican politicians looked on each others' parties as dangerous entities that must be contained, battled, and put out of business. This done, their own party, a necessary evil, could then be disbanded and dissolved. Concerned that permanent parties threatened the nation's stability and security, they built the first modern political parties not out of the conviction that parties were a positive good, but because stern necessity compelled them to be organized.

How did antiparty assumptions guide the Federalists and the Jeffersonian Republicans when they controlled the central government? How did they shape the Federalists' handling of domestic and foreign issues during the

1790s, and the Federalists' response to the emergent Jeffersonian Republican opposition? How did the Federalists try to counter the Republican party opposition and its challenges to their leadership and policies? How, in turn, did the Republicans, after defeating the Federalists in 1800, view them as an opposition party? How did this view guide the Jeffersonian Republicans as they dealt with the Federalists? When and how did antiparty attitudes change into a more positive view of party and pave the way for the second American party system?

The Revolutionary generation derived its ideas about parties from history and experience. Republican Rome, seventeenth-century England, and colonial, Revolutionary, and Confederation America afforded ample proof that political parties were detrimental and dangerous. "Formed" party opposition made men partisan when they should be disinterested; party competition distorted judgment, kept men from acting for the public good, and even led them into treason. By dividing and polarizing the people, rival political organizations undermined and weakened government's operation. They inflamed passions and sometimes prompted insurrection and revolution. Because party opposition could easily translate into sedition, Federalists and Jeffersonian Republicans equated their rivals and their rivals' party-forming behavior with "faction," an eighteenth-century term meaning a seditious party.

The Revolutionary generation hoped for a political order that would be free from political parties. Both Federalist and Republican party-leaders, until after the War of 1812, believed their rivals comprised an opposition "faction" that would weaken and possibly destroy the Republic. When Federalist-Republican party competition in the 1790s and early 1800s did not yield the predicted dangers and the Republic survived and prospered, the national climate towards parties grew more favorable.

By contrast, political parties today do not have to justify themselves. Because modern political parties are fully accepted as having a legitimate, beneficial, and essential role in the political system, they are taken for granted as a constructive force in our political life. Competing political parties are said to provide the electorate with practical choices among various candidates and policies; they bring the principles of democratic self-government closer to reality. In a competitive party system, opposition parties keep watch over persons in power, which keeps them honest and responsible. A healthy party competition checks extremism, promotes compromise, and encourages politicians to follow a middle way: since parties must attract the widest possible range of voters, they have powerful incentives to steer between extremes. Competition between parties stabilizes the body politic by enlisting voters in the political system and providing a legitimate means of expressing opposition that is neither subversive nor violent.

The Federalist and Republican parties emerged in the 1790s out of political battles over Federalist domestic and foreign policy. During their period of power, from 1789 to 1801, the Federalists made securing the new Republic, with its more centralized government established by the Constitution, their top prior-

ity. But Federalist policies produced the very evils they were designed to prevent. Designed to build national unity around and support for the Republic's newly established central government, these policies produced criticism, opposition, and the Jeffersonian Republican party—the first truly national political party. The Federalists then organized their party to combat Republican adversaries.

The financial and economic measures of Federalist Secretary of the Treasury Alexander Hamilton first gave the Republicans impetus to organize. Proposed and given statutory force early in President George Washington's first administration, these measures included the central government's funding of the Revolutionary War debt of the Confederation government, its assumption and funding of the states' debts, a national bank, and encouragement of manufacturing. Hamilton's purpose was both to establish the new government's credit and to build a climate of business and commercial confidence in its operations and policies. Everyone, rich and poor alike, he believed, would eventually benefit from the new government's policies and give their respect and support. The most immediate beneficiaries would be the wealthy—the merchants, financiers, speculators, and manufacturers who held the largest proportion of the public debt and who would invest in national bank stock and obtain bank loans. But other groups also would prosper as benefits resulting from investor confidence and new capital worked their way down and out through the whole society. Similarly, by encouraging manufacturing, Hamilton wanted not only to make the United States independent of foreign nations in military supplies and other essentials, but to gather support for the new government by creating a larger home market for agricultural goods, increasing employment, and stimulating national productivity and prosperity.

Despite these intentions, Hamilton's efforts precipitated a storm of criticism and opposition.

Hamilton's program seemed preferential treatment for wealthy merchants, financiers, and speculators at the expense of the small farmer and planter. Yet the latter must support the Republic if it were to survive and flourish. But, as Hamilton's policies developed, the Virginia planter-statesmen Thomas Jefferson, James Madison, and others grew genuinely fearful that such policies were undermining the new nation. Knowing that Hamilton doubted the Republic's practical strength and that at the Constitutional Convention he had advocated a system similar to Britain's, Jefferson and Madison alleged that Hamilton was secretly working to transform the government into a British-style monarchy by consolidating its power and corrupting its legislators.

Such suspicions and allegations outraged Hamilton and his Federalist supporters. Believing that their measures would promote the new government's prosperity and success, they denounced criticism as rank demagoguery and equated opposition to administration policies with acts that would discredit and destroy the new central government's very structure. No less than the President himself made this equation. Any organized opposition to administration measures, Washington reasoned, constituted opposition to the government's existence. When new Democratic-Republican Societies stirred local opinion against administration measures, he condemned these "self-created societies" as "the most diabolical attempts to destroy the best fabric of human government and happiness that has ever been presented for the acceptance of mankind." If their agitation continued, he warned, "they would shake the government to its foundation." Then, when western Pennsylvania farmers, in 1794, refused to pay the whiskey tax and defied its collection, Washington blamed the Democratic Societies. The Whiskey Rebellion threatened "the very existence of Government and the fundamental principles of social order;" and as defiance of the law continued, Washington called up

12,000 militia and marched them into western Pennsylvania. To demonstrate further the government's strength, the ringleaders were seized, brought back to Philadelphia, and tried for insurrection. Such, in Washington's eyes, had been "the first *formidable* fruit" of political party opposition. Unless such opposition was broken, "we may bid adieu to all government in this country, except mob and club government."

Federalist foreign policy, which sought to enhance the new government's authority and unite the country, gave political parties additional impetus. Sometimes portrayed as biased against France and attached to England, Federalist leaders tried to maintain peace with both powers, which they believed would allow the nation to develop and prosper. Accordingly, Washington's famous neutrality policy sought to avoid war abroad and controversy at home. Likewise, John Jay's mission to England early in 1794 attempted to settle the two most explosive issues between that country and the United States: (1) continued British possession of the northwest posts, and (2) acceptable British limitations on the American export trade to France and on the American carrying trade between France and France's West Indies possessions. Unfortunately, Jay brought back a treaty that, although it transferred the posts to the United States, failed to establish the American claim to rights in the carrying and export trades. It also committed the United States not to retaliate against England by commercial restrictions. Republicans immediately denounced the Jay Treaty as a sellout to England and a betrayal of the nation's right to carry on trade with a former ally and friend. Federalists, fearing that Republican demagogues would stampede the nation into war with England unless these issues were resolved, swung to the Treaty's support and secured its ratification.

As Republican opponents predicted, Jay's treaty led to a dangerous confrontation with the Directory, France's ruling body. France, after all, depended on American carriers in the trade between home ports and the West Indies, as well as on American food products. The Jay Treaty had tacitly all but surrendered this trade to British control. Consequently, the Directory tried to force the Federalists either to repudiate the treaty or be themselves repudiated and driven from office by a presumably pro-French electorate. Hence, American diplomats in France were insulted, war was threatened, and Yankee vessels were seized. Resolved not to yield to these crude pressures, President John Adams undertook a carefully limited, undeclared maritime war against the Directory and ordered America's tiny navy into action against French warships and privateers. In the tense summer days of 1798, when a French invasion seemed likely, Adams considered proposing a formal war declaration to rally the nation and deter the enemy. But the British navy's defeat of the French fleet at the Battle of the Nile dispelled the invasion threat, and the President saw great danger in launching a full-scale war that did not have defense of the nation as its object. At a time when Republicans were denouncing the Federalists for mismanaging relations with France, an all-out war against French maritime depredations and insults might invite open Republican resistance and precipitate civil war. At the very least, the heavy weight of war taxes, the increased debt, and an enlarged army would produce a "compleat revolution of sentiment" against the Federalists, bring the Republicans to power, and then produce war with Great Britain. To head off these possibilities, Adams courageously dispatched a new mission to France to make peace, presided over the dismantling of the new army voted by the Federalist congressional majority, purged his Cabinet of its most bellicose members, and pardoned leaders of the Fries Rebellion who were arrested in Pennsylvania for obstructing the war program.

A handful of Federalist extremists rejected these presidential actions. Rather than unify the nation by compromise and conciliation, Alexander Hamilton, Theodore Sedgwick, Timothy Pickering, Oliver Wolcott, Jr., and others tried, by intimidation and force, to suppress their Republican adversaries, whom they now considered, in an obvious analogy to the revolutionary extremists in France, to be "Jacobin" seditionists and terrorists. Accordingly, they urged a vigorous military buildup, passed and enforced the Sedition Law, attempted to deport aliens, and sought to discredit and crush the Republicans by provoking them into rebellion. Hamilton, in the most questionable period of his career, suggested marching the Federalist-controlled army into Virginia, where he thought the danger was most acute. Hamilton also urged nonnaturalized aliens be ordered out of the country and even recommended that large states under Republican control be subdivided into small units so that they might not challenge the national government. Federalists took other extraordinary precautions against an anticipated Republican-inspired insurrection: armed patrols walked the streets of Philadelphia; President Adams stored arms in his residence; and North Carolina Federalists requested weapons from the federal arsenal "to keep a certain class of people in order."

Yet, despite their anxious preoccupation with the rising Republican opposition, the Federalists were slow to confront it where its challenge was greatest—at the level of local party organization. Whether because of their distaste for politics of this kind, or because they felt the government could withstand the pressure, the Federalists not only failed to keep up with their rivals in organizing local party structures but also angrily denounced the Republican tactics as divisive and disruptive. It was a fatal mistake. By the end of the 1790s, the Republicans had created a national system of state and local party organization that, throughout the union—especially in the rural middle and southern states—had gained them strong popular support. Although some Federalists attempted to match the Republicans in building local party organizations, their efforts were intermittent and scattered; Federalist strength centered only in the commercial northeast and in seaports. Not until after their defeat in the presidential and congressional elections of 1800 did the Federalist leadership face necessity and begin to organize local party structures.

Even then the Federalists acted with much reluctance. "A party," asserted the Federalist Jeremiah Smith, "must do the very thing we condemn, prefer their friends to the public good." Should Federalist newspapers discredit Republicans by direct attacks on their characters? According to Fisher Ames, a Federalist newspaper should always be "fastidiously polite and well bred. It should whip Jacobins as a gentlemen would a chimney-sweeper, at arm's length, and keeping aloof from his soot." But Ames to the contrary, Federalist newspapers were soon the equal of the Republicans in the use of invective and scurrility. Should Federalist party leaders seek votes through means other than dignified discussion and transmission of accurate information? Not according to Federalist election instructions: since "it is only from the class of honest and mistaken men, that we can hope to increase the numbers of Federalists," only "fair means" should be used to convince men "of the justice of the federal cause." By 1811, however, even Massachusetts Federalists were holding mass rallies, instructing colleagues how to manage these affairs, and advocating "popular addresses," "animating" speeches, and exhortatory resolutions. Pressing even further, some Federalists threatened their employees with dismissal if they voted Republican, distributed food and liquor on election day, enrolled and purged voters illegally, and transported persons to the polls to vote—eligible or not.

Explanations for this grudging conversion to party politics will miss much if they concentrate on a Federalist hunger to recover power for its own sake. Although any political party

inevitably includes men who want power and office alone, a better explanation must seize on the Federalist conviction that the Republic faced great danger and possible destruction if the Republicans continued at the helm. From the Federalist perspective, the Republican ascendency meant that the nation was in the hands of irresponsible politicians whose overriding concern was popularity and power. Hence, from the first Jeffersonian attempts to curtail government spending and replace Federalist officeholders with loyal Republicans, to the declaration of the controversial War of 1812, the Federalists assigned corrupt and sinister motives to their adversaries. Small wonder that Federalists felt they must organize and electioneer. The Republic must not be sacrificed on the altar of consistency, political purity, or fears about the evils of party.

Nor is it strange that a Federalist minority espoused nullification, resistance, and secession. By 1804, Federalist extremists like Timothy Pickering of Massachusetts and Roger Griswold, Uriah Tracy, and James Hillhouse of Connecticut were plotting to establish a Federalist-led Northern Confederation. By 1809, disgruntled Federalist clergy and Connecticut Valley leaders were calling on their constituents to defy and ignore the embargo. By 1814, press and pulpit rang with calls for nullification, a separate peace with Great Britain, resistance to the federal government's authority, and withdrawal from the Union. Persuaded that any of these attempts would plunge the nation into civil war, moderate Federalist leaders like George Cabot and Harrison Gray Otis of Massachusetts, in a move to head off this danger, organized the Hartford Convention. Determined, as Cabot put it, "to allay the ferment and prevent a crisis," they won the Convention's approval of a program that would, through amendment of the Federal Constitution, enable the Federalist congressional minority to veto war declarations, embargoes, and the admission of new states, and that would reduce the numerical representation of the Republican South in the House of Representatives.

Like the Federalists, Republican party builders did not intend their party to be permanent. "The early parties, unlike modern parties," one scholar concludes, "were not machines whose primary function was to win office; they were patriotic associations of minute-men springing to the defence of freedom, like the Sons of Liberty of the Revolution, and like the revolutionary associations too they could disband when the danger was passed." When a narrow election victory over the Federalists in 1800 gave them control of Congress and the presidency, President-elect Thomas Jefferson and other Republican leaders knew the battle was only half won. Having been defeated and ousted from power, the Federalists must be kept from regaining power. This implied policy that would please the largest number of voters and alienate the fewest. Although some Jeffersonian Republicans urged that radical populistic-agrarian measures be adopted, their leader flexibly pursued a moderate course that would appeal to the many and offend only the few. Rather than alienate the entire financial-business community and disrupt the economy, Jefferson decided that most existing Federalist economic policies should be quietly retained—including the funding-assumption program, the Bank, and even moderately protective duties on imported foreign manufactures. More dramatically, Jefferson reduced the army and navy and American legations abroad—cuts that made it possible to repeal the direct taxes of the previous Adams administration. A show of the plain, frugal republican style was also made. Jefferson abandoned the personal address to Congress of his predecessors, which smacked too much of kingship. He dressed with artful simplicity, and gave up quasi-royalist ceremonies like the levee and diplomatic precedence at presidential dinner parties. When the stunning prize of the Louisiana Purchase fell into his lap, Jefferson put

aside preferred constitutional and budgetary principles and engineered the acquisition treaty with Napoleon. His strict construction principles were thus breached and the national debt was appreciably increased, but the benefits for the nation and the party were immense.

Jefferson's anti-Federalist party strategy became apparent when he moved to quash Federalist press attacks and coax bankers and financiers into the Republican camp. Early in his administration, Jefferson secretly urged Republican state officials in Pennsylvania to prosecute local Federalist newspapers under the existing common law of sedition. Since the 1798 federal Sedition Law had expired, and since widespread prosecution of Federalist newspapers might backfire on the Republicans, Jefferson wanted the seditious libel prosecution to be at state initiative and selectively targeted. Moreover, in a preview of later Jacksonian "pet bank" policy, Jefferson pressed his Treasury Secretary, Albert Gallatin, to deposit federal funds among Republican state banks in order to build political support for his party within the banking community.

The concern of Republican leaders that the Republic be upheld and that the Federalists be kept from recapturing power, if they could not be entirely destroyed as a political force, surfaced again during the difficult years of the Embargo and the War of 1812. When the two European powers, Great Britain and France, resumed hostilities, they declared each others' coastlines in blockade and seized American ships and sailors trading with the enemy. Jefferson and his party asserted, more forcefully than the Federalists during the 1790s had done, that international law prohibited such practices. Confident that the weapons of economic pressure would force England, France, or both into concessions, Jefferson engineered the famous self-denying ban on exports—the Embargo—as a bargaining counter against British and French blockades and impressments. To a small minority of Republican agrarian ideologues, the Embargo seemed folly. By committing government prestige to the defense of merchants and shipowners, Jefferson, they charged, was putting both nation and party on the road to war or disgrace; far better, said John Randolph of Roanoke and John Taylor of Caroline, to let American ships fend for themselves and suffer the privations of a temporarily reduced foreign commerce. But Jefferson and other Republicans were considering maritime and commercial interests and they feared a possible Federalist resurgence if the government and party did not stand up for commerce. Moreover, the prestige and future of the nation and the Republican party required that the government actively defend maritime commerce. Ironically, Republicans championed maritime rights, while Federalists denounced the series of Republican measures taken to uphold these rights—the Embargo (1807–09), the Nonintercourse law (1809–10), Macon's Bill No. 2 (1810–11), and the Nonimportation law (1811-12).

The War of 1812, which followed when Republican measures failed, saw the Republican-Federalist interparty conflict reach a climax. Midway through 1811, President James Madison and Republican congressional leaders regretfully concluded that diplomacy and economic coercion would not work, and that war or submission were the only available policy alternatives. Blocked and stymied by Britain's unyielding refusal to soften blockades, the Republican congressional majority, led by Henry Clay and John C. Calhoun, with Madison prompting from backstage, took the United States into the war for ''Free Trade and Sailors' Rights.'' Among the motives leading to their 1812 declaration of war, concern for the nation's prestige and standing, and for the political fate of the Republican party ranked high, perhaps highest. The still unproved ''experiment'' in Republican government, born in Revolution and strengthened by the Federal Consti-

tution, needed to demonstrate its viability and standing among nations by declaring and fighting a war; otherwise, its prestige both at home and abroad would be severely, perhaps fatally, wounded. Founded to protect the nation against Federalist policies and management and still the only reliable custodian of the country's best interests, Republican leaders thought, the party must not be turned out of power by a reduced but still dangerous Federalism. Yet the latter opposed the war. Misconstruing the war's true origins, Federalists held that the Republicans had declared war because they desired to conquer Canada, because Napoleon had bribed them to join him against England, or because they had trapped themselves into a no exit position and feared an election defeat.

Soon after the War of 1812 ended, the first American party system began to disintegrate. A minority party since its defeat in the 1800 election, the Federalists had been in decline before the conflict, while the Republicans, with superior organization, greater popular appeal, and a larger natural constituency, gained in strength and numbers. The War of 1812 accelerated this process. Partisan Federalist charges that the Republicans were friends of France and incapable of waging offensive war, rang hollow, especially after Plattsburg, Baltimore, and New Orleans. Federalist obstructionism and the Hartford Convention not only discredited the party, but raised doubts about *its* patriotism. In the immediate postwar era, the Republicans legislated those favorite Federalist measures of the prewar period—the protective tariff, a Second Bank of the United States, and a larger navy. Its leadership discredited and its program preempted, the Federalist party further declined. Interparty paranoia—the basic fuel of the party before the War of 1812—also waned. In 1817, when Republican President James Monroe was entertained by Massachusetts Federalists on a visit to Boston, a Federalist editor hailed the event as symbolizing "An Era of Good Feelings"—indirect verbal testimony that interparty hostility had diminished. Yet, President Monroe, antiparty like his Virginia predecessors and determined to end the Federalist party once and for all, appointed only loyal Republicans to federal office; Federalists deserted their party in droves. By 1820, Federalists were too weak to field a presidential candidate; Monroe ran for a second term unopposed.

With the Federalists removed as a national political force, the Republican party disintegrated. By the 1824 election, five Republicans of various regional and ideological hues were active presidential candidates for whom votes were cast: Andrew Jackson, John Quincy Adams, Henry Clay, John C. Calhoun, and William H. Crawford. When Jackson won a plurality but not a majority of electoral votes, the choice fell to the House of Representatives, which chose Adams by a narrow margin.

By the mid-1820s, however, a new political generation was coming to power. First appearing on the political stage when the first American parties formed and competed, younger men like Martin Van Buren made their careers as party organizers; they were much more comfortable with the party and party competition than the previous generation. A resourceful and energetic Jeffersonian Republican party loyalist, Van Buren owed his political career to the party, took pleasure in party activity and, together with his allies in New York's Albany Regency, publicly celebrated the party and its benefits. In 1827, Van Buren helped to found the new Jacksonian Democratic party and helped to launch the second American party system. Alarmed by sectional conflict between pro and antislavery politicians in Congress, Van Buren held that a new national party, committed to strict constructionism and democracy, would enhance national unity and save the Union by encompassing northern and southern men in the same party and taking the slavery issue off the national agenda. A more hospitable era that accepted and celebrated the party and its benefits was dawning.

SUGGESTED READINGS

Banner, James M. *To the Hartford Convention: the Federalists and the Origins of Party Politics in Massachusetts, 1789–1815*. New York: Alfred A. Knopf, 1970.

Banning, Lance. *The Jeffersonian Persuasion: Evolution of a Party Ideology*. Ithaca N.Y.: Cornell University Press, 1978.

Brown, Roger H. *The Republic in Peril: 1812*. New York: W. W. Norton, 1971.

Buel, Richard. *Securing the Revolution: Ideology in American Politics, 1789–1815*. Ithaca, N.Y.: Cornell University Press, 1972.

Chambers, William N. *Political Parties in a New Nation: the American Experience, 1778–1800*. New York: Oxford University Press, 1963.

Fischer, David Hackett. *The Revolution of American Conservatism: The Federalist Party in the Era of Jeffersonian Democracy*. New York: Harper & Row, 1965.

Heale, M. L. *The Making of American Politics: 1750–1850*. New York: Longman, 1977.

Hofstadter, Richard. *The Idea of a Party System: the Rise of Legitimate Opposition in the United States, 1780–1840*. Berkeley: University of California Press, 1970.

Kurtz, Stephen G. *The Presidency of John Adams: the Collapse of Federalism, 1795–1800*. Philadelphia: University of Pennsylvania Press, 1957.

Levy, Leonard. *Jefferson and Civil Liberties: the Darker Side*. Cambridge, Mass.: Harvard University Press, 1963.

Miller, John C. *The Federalist Era: 1789–1801*. New York: Harper & Row, 1960.

Remini, Robert V. *Martin Van Buren and the Making of the Democratic Party*. New York: Columbia University Press, 1959.

Smelser, Marshall. *The Democratic-Republic: 1801–1815*. New York: Harper & Row, 1968.

Young, James Sterling. *The Washington Community: 1800–1828*. New York: Columbia University Press, 1968.

DOCUMENT 7.1
President Washington Warns Against Party Opposition

In the Farewell Address, President George Washington warns his countrymen against engaging in party opposition. Obviously aimed at the emergent Republican opposition party, Washington's warning reflects the prevailing antiparty attitudes of a preparty eighteenth-century America.

FAREWELL ADDRESS

17 September 1796

I have already intimated to you the danger of Parties in the State, with particular reference to the founding of them on Geographical discriminations. Let me now take a more comprehensive view, and warn you in the most solemn manner against the baneful effects of the Spirit of Party, generally.

This spirit, unfortunately, is inseperable from our nature, having its root in the strongest passions of the human Mind. It exists under different shapes in all Governments, more or less stifled, controuled, or repressed; but, in those of the popular form it is seen in its greatest rankness and is truly their worst enemy.

The alternate domination of one faction over another, sharpened by the spirit of revenge natural to party dissention, which in different ages and countries has perpetrated the most horrid enormities, is itself a frightful despotism. But this leads at length to a more formal and perma-

Source: George Washington, "Farewell Address," in *The Writings of George Washington* (Worthington C. Ford, ed., New York, 1892), vol. 8, pp. 301–302, 304–305.

nent despotism. The disorders and miseries, which result, gradually incline the minds of men to seek security and repose in the absolute power of an Individual: and sooner or later the chief of some prevailing faction more able or more fortunate than his competitors, turns this disposition to the purposes of his own elevation, on the ruins of Public Liberty.

Without looking forward to an extremity of this kind (which nevertheless ought not to be entirely out of sight) the common and continual mischiefs of the spirit of Party are sufficient to make it the interest and the duty of a wise People to discourage and restrain it.

It serves always to distract the Public Councils and enfeeble the Public administration. It agitates the Community with ill founded jealousies and false alarms, kindles the animosity of one part against another, foments occasionally riot and insurrection. It opens the door to foreign influence and corruption, which find a facilitated access to the government itself through the channels of party passions. Thus the policy and and [*sic*] the will of one country, are subjected to the policy and will of another.

There is an opinion that parties in free countries are useful checks upon the Administration of the Government and serve to keep alive the spirit of Liberty. This within certain limits is probably true, and in Governments of a Monarchical cast Patriotism may look with endulgence, if not with favour, upon the spirit of party. But in those of the popular character, in Governments purely elective, it is a spirit not to be encouraged. From their natural tendency, it is certain there will always be enough of that spirit for every salutary purpose. And there being constant danger of excess, the effort ought to be, by force of public opinion, to mitigate and assuage it. A fire not to be quenched; it demands a uniform vigilance to prevent its bursting into a flame, lest instead of warming it should consume.

DOCUMENT 7.2
The Threat to the Republic: the Hamiltonian View

The emerging Republican opposition to the Hamiltonian economic program awakened fears within the Washington administration that the new government would not be stable enough to carry out its policies. Alexander Hamilton, in a letter to Colonel Edward Carrington of Virginia, pessimistically assesses this prospect.

To Colonel Edward Carrington

Philadelphia, May 26, 1792

A word on another point. I am told that serious apprehensions are disseminated in your state as to the existence of a Monarchical party meditating the destruction of State & Republican Government. If it is possible that so absurd an idea can gain ground it is necessary that it should be combatted. I assure you on my *private faith* and *honor* as a Man that there is not in my judgment a shadow of foundation of it. A very small number of men indeed may entertain theories less republican than Mr. Jefferson & Mr. Madison; but I am persuaded there is not a Man among them who would not regard as both *criminal & visionary* any attempt to subvert the republican system of the Country. Most of these men rather *fear* that it may not justify itself by its fruits, than feel a predilection for a different form; and their fears are not diminished by the factions & fanatical politics which they find prevailing among a certain set of Gentlemen and threatening to disturb the tranquility and order of the the Government.

As to the destruction of State Governments, the *great* and *real* anxiety is to be able to pre-

serve the National from the too potent and counteracting influence of those Governments. As to my own political Creed, I give it to you with the utmost sincerity. I am *affectionately* attached to the Republican theory. I desire *above all things* to see the *equality* of political rights exclusive of all *hereditary* distinction firmly established by a practical demonstration of its being consistent with the order and happiness of society.

As to the State Governments, the prevailing byass of my judgment is that if they can be circumscribed within bounds consistent with the preservation of the National Government they will prove useful and salutary. If the States were all the size of Connecticut, Maryland or New Jersey, I should decidedly regard the local Governments as both safe & useful. As the thing now is, however, I acknowledge the most serious apprehensions that the Government of the U States will not be able to maintain itself against their influence. I see that influence already penetrating into the National Councils & preverting their direction.

Hence a disposition on my part towards a liberal construction of the powers of the National Government and to erect every fence to guard it from depredations, which is, in my opinion, consistent with constitutional propriety. . . . I said, that I was *affectionately* attached to the Republican theory. This is the real language of my heart which I open to you in the sincerity of friendship; & I add that I have strong hopes of the success of that theory; but in candor I ought also to add that I am far from being without doubts. I consider its success as yet a problem.

It is yet to be determined by experience whether it be consistent with that *stability* and *order* in Government which are essential to public strength & private security and happiness. On the whole, the only enemy which Republicanism has to fear in this Country is in the Spirit of faction and anarchy. If this

Source: Harold C. Syrett and Jacob E. Cooke, eds., *The Papers of Alexander Hamilton* (New York: Columbia University Press, 1961), vol. 11, pp. 426–45.

will not permit the ends of Government to be attained under it—if it engenders disorders in the community, all regular and orderly minds will wish for a change—and the demagogues who have produced the disorder will make it for their own agrandizement. This is the old Story.

If I were disposed to promote Monarchy & overthrow State Governments, I would mount the hobby horse of popularity—I would cry out usurpation—danger to liberty &c. &c.—I would endeavour to prostrate the National Government—raise a ferment—and then "ride in the Whirlwind and direct the Storm." That there are men acting with Jefferson & Madison who have this in view I verily believe. I could lay my finger on some of them. That Madison does not mean it I also verily believe, and I rather believe the same of Jefferson; but I read him upon the whole thus— "A man of profound ambition & violent passions."

DOCUMENT 7.3
Hamilton Surveys His Public Career

By 1802, Hamilton had become more convinced than ever of what he had anticipated at the time of the Constitutional Convention—that a republican government, no matter what its particular composition, was inherently weak and unstable. In this letter to Gouverneur Morris, Hamilton expresses this view and indicates personal discouragement not only because his efforts to support the Republic have been misunderstood and vilified but also because the pernicious doctrines of the

Source: Henry Cabot Lodge, ed., *The Works of Alexander Hamilton* (New York: G. P. Putnam's Sons, 1903), vol. 10, pp. 425–26.

Jeffersonian Republicans have been firmly entrenched in the popular mind.

To Gouverneur Morris

New York, Feb. 27, 1802

. . . Mine is an odd destiny. Perhaps no man in the United States has sacrificed or done more for the present Constitution than myself; and contrary to all my anticipations of its fate, as you know from the very beginning, I am still laboring to prop the frail and worthless fabric. Yet I have the murmurs of its friends no less than the curses of its foes for my reward. What can I do better than withdraw from the scene? Every day proves to me more and more, that this American world was not made for me.

The suggestions with which you close your letter suppose a much sounder state of the public mind than at present exists. Attempts to make a show of a general *popular* dislike of the pending measures of the government, would only serve to manifest the direct reverse. Impressions are indeed making, but as yet within a very narrow sphere.

The time may erelong arrive when the minds of men will be prepared to make an effort to *recover* the Constitution, but the many cannot now be brought to make a stand for its preservation. We must wait a while.

DOCUMENT 7.4
A Federalist Congressman Defends the Sedition Law

An extreme Federalist, Congressman John Allen of Connecticut ardently defended this famous act to curb Republican criticism of the

Source: *Annals of the Congress of the United States,* 5th Cong., 2d sess., July 5, 1798, pp. 2093–2100.

Federalists and their policies. Arguing in Congress that the Sedition Law was necessary to ensure the federal government's survival, Allen branded the Republican opposition to the Federalists as a conspiracy directed against the central government's structure.

Mr. Allen—I hope this bill will not be rejected. If ever there was a nation which required a law of this kind, it is this. Let gentlemen look at certain papers printed in this city and elsewhere, and ask themselves whether an unwarrantable and dangerous combination does not exist to overturn and ruin the Government by publishing the most shameless falsehoods against the Representatives of the people of all denominations, that they are hostile to free Governments and genuine liberty, and of course to the welfare of this country; that they ought, therefore, to be displaced, and that the people ought to raise an *insurrection* against the Government.

In the *Aurora,* of the 28th of June last, we see this paragraph: "It is a curious fact, America is making war with France for *not* treating, at the very moment the Minister for Foreign Affairs fixes upon the very day for opening a negotiation with Mr. Gerry. What think you of this, Americans!"

Such paragraphs need but little comment. The public agents are charged with crimes, for which, if true, they ought to be hung. The intention here is to persuade the people that peace with France is in our power; nay, that she is sincerely desirous of it, on proper terms, but that we reject her offers, and proceed to plunge our country into a destructive war. . . .

Gentlemen contend for the liberty of opinions and of the press. Let me ask them whether they seriously think the liberty of the press authorizes such publications? The President of the United States is here called "a person without patriotism, without philosophy, and a mock monarch," and the free election of the people

is pronounced "a jostling him into the Chief Magistracy by the ominous combination of Old Tories with old opinions, and old Whigs with new."

If this be not a conspiracy against Government and people, I know not what to understand from the "threat of tears, execrations, derision, and contempt." Because the Constitution guaranties the right of expressing our opinions, and the freedom of the press, am I at liberty to falsely call you a thief, a murderer, an atheist? Because I have the liberty of locomotion, of going where I please, have I a right to ride over the footman in the path? The freedom of the press and opinions were never understood to give the right of publishing falsehood and slanders, nor of exciting sedition, insurrection, and slaughter, with impunity. A man was always answerable for the malicious publication of falsehood; and what more does this bill require?

In the *Aurora,* of last Tuesday, is this paragraph:

> Where a law shall have been passed in violation of the Constitution, making it criminal to expose the crimes, the official vices or abuses, or the attempts of men in power to usurp a despotic authority, is there any alternative between an abandonment of the Constitution and resistance?

The gentlemen [Mr. Livingston] makes his proclamation of war on the Government in the House on Monday, and this infamous printer [Bache] follows it up with the tocsin of insurrection on Tuesday. While this bill was under consideration in the Senate, an attempt is made to render it odious among the people. "Is there any alternative," says this printer, "between an abandonment of the Constitution and resistance?" He declares what is unconstitutional, and then invites the people to "resistance." This is an awful, horrible example of "the liberty of opinion and freedom of the press."

Can gentlemen hear these things and lie quietly on their pillows? Are we to see all these acts practiced against the repose of our country, and remain passive? Are we bound hand and foot that we must be witnesses of these deadly thrusts at our liberty? Are we to be the unresisting spectators of these exertions to destroy all that we hold dear? Are these approaches to revolution and Jacobinic domination, to be observed with the eye of meek submission? No, sir, they are indeed terrible; they are calculated to freeze the very blood in our veins. Such liberty of the press and of opinion is calculated to destroy all confidence between man and man; it leads to a dissolution of every bond of union; it cuts asunder every ligament that unites man to his family, man to his neighbor, man to society, and to Government. God deliver us from such liberty, the liberty of vomiting on the public floods of falsehood and hatred to everything sacred, human and divine! If any gentlemen doubts the effects of such a liberty, let me direct his attention across the water; it has there made slaves of thirty millions of men.

DOCUMENT 7.5
Jefferson Soothes His Federalist Adversaries

In this famous passage from Jefferson's first inaugural address, the new president plays down party differences and courts Federalist support. Federalists, he promises, will not be molested by his administration even if they wish to dissolve the Union or change its republican form.

Let us then, fellow citizens, unite with one heart & one mind; let us restore to social intercourse that harmony & affection, without which

Liberty, & even Life itself, are but dreary things.

And let us reflect that hav^g banish^d f^{rm} our land y^t religious intol^{ce} und^r wch mankind so long bled & suffered we h^{ve} yet gain^d little, if we counte^{nce} a politic^l intolr^{ce}, as despot^c as wick^d & capable of as bitter & bloody persecution.

During the throes and convulsions of the antient world, dur^g the agonis^d spasms of infuriat^d man, seeking through blood & slaughter his long lost liberty, it was not wonderful that the agitation of the billows should reach even this distant & peaceful shore: that y^s sh^d be more felt & fear^d by some, & less by others, & sh^d divide opinions as to measures of safety.

But every difference of opinion, is not a difference of principle. We have called, by different names, brethren of the same principle. We are all republicans: we are all federalists.

If there be any among us who wish to dissolve this union, or to change its republican form, let them stand undisturbed, as monuments of the safety wth wch error of opin^n m b tolerat^d wh^{re} reas^n is left free to combat it.

I know ind^d y^t some honest men h^{ve} fear^d y^t a republican govm^t cann^t be strong; y^t this govm^t is not strong enough. But w^d the honest patriot, in the full tide of successf^l experimen^t abandon a govm^t wch h^s so far kept us free & firm on ye theoretic & visionary fear y^t y^s govmt, the world's best hope m, by possibil^{ty}, want energy to preserve itself?

I trust not. I believe this, on the contrary, the strongest government on earth.

I believe it the only one where every man, at the call of the law, would fly to the standard of the law; would meet invasions of public order, as his own personal concern.

Some times it is said y^t Man cann^t be trust^d wth ye govmt of himself.—Can he y^n be trust^d wth ye govmt of others? Or have we found angels in ye form of kings to govern him?— Let History answ^r this question.

Source: Thomas Jefferson, *The Writings of Thomas Jefferson*, P. L. Ford, ed. (New York, G. P. Putnam's Sons, 1905), vol. 9, pp. 193–200.

DOCUMENT 7.6
Jefferson Tries to Eliminate His Federalist Adversaries

Here President Jefferson urges that the Federalist press be curbed and that merchants and monied men be detached from Federalism and drawn into the Republican party. The most hostile Federalist newspapers should be prosecuted, and any commercial bank that shows loyalty to the Republican party should be rewarded with federal government deposits.

To Governor Thomas McKean

February 19, 1803

On the subject of prosecutions, what I say must be entirely confidential, for you know the passion for torturing every sentiment and word which comes from me. The federalists having failed in destroying the freedom of the press by their gag-law, seem to have attacked it in an opposite form, that is by pushing its licentiousness and its lying to such a degree of prostitution as to deprive it of all credit. And the fact is that so abandoned are the tory presses in this particular that even the least informed of the people have learnt that nothing in a newspaper is to be believed. This is a dangerous state of things, and the press ought to be restored to its credibility if possible. The restraints provided by the laws of the states are sufficient for this if applied. And I have therefore long thought that a few prosecutions of the most prominant offenders would have a wholesome effect in restoring the integrity of the presses. Not a general prosecution, for that would look like a persecution; but a selected one. The paper I now enclose appears to me

to offer as good an instance in every repect to make an example of, as can be selected.

To Secretary of the Treasury Albert Gallatin

July 12, 1803

As to the patronage of the Republican Bank at Providence, I am decidedly in favor of making all the banks Republican, by sharing deposits among them in proportion to the dispositions they show; if the law now forbids it, we should not permit another session of Congress to pass without amending it. It is material to the safety of Republicanism to detach the mercantile interests from its enemies and incorporate them into the body of its friends.

DOCUMENT 7.7
Separatism and States' Rights

In these letters, Timothy Pickering, a Massachusetts Federalist notorious for his extremist tendencies, advocates separatism and nullification as strategies for regaining power.

To George Cabot

January 29, 1804

The Federalists are dissatisfied, because they see the public morals debased by the corrupt and corrupting system of our rulers. Men are tempted to become apostates, not to Federalism merely, but to virtue and to religion and to good government. Apostasy and original depravity are the qualifications for official honors and emoluments, while men of sterling worth are displaced, and held up to popular contempt and scorn. And shall we sit still, until this system shall universally triumph? until even

Source: Thomas Jefferson, *The Writings of Thomas Jefferson*, P. L. Ford, ed. (New York: G. P. Putnam's Sons, 1905), vol. 9, pp. 449–52, vol. 10, pp. 15–16.

Source: Timothy Pickering to George Cabot, January 29, 1804; Timothy Pickering to Christopher Gore, January 8, 1809. Pickering Papers, published by permission of the Massachusetts Historical Society.

in the Eastern States the principles of genuine Federalism shall be overwhelmed? Mr. Jefferson's plan of destruction has been gradually advancing. If at once he had removed from office all the Federalists, and given to the people such substitutes as we generally see, even his followers (I mean the mass) would have been shocked. He is still making progress in the same course; and has the credit of being the real source of all the innovations which threaten the subversion of the Constitution, and the prostration of every barrier erected by it for the protection of the *best,* and therefore to him the most obnoxious, part of the community. His instruments manifest tempers so malignant, so inexorable, as convince observing Federalists that the mild manners and habits of our countrymen are the only security against their extreme vengeance. How long we shall enjoy even this security, God only knows. And must we with folded hands wait the result, or timely think of other protection? This is a delicate subject. The principles of our Revolution point to the remedy,—a separation.

To Christopher Gore

January 8, 1809

It is scarcely conceivable that Mr. Jefferson should so obstinately persevere in the odious measure of the embargo, which he cannot but see has impaired his popularity and hazards its destruction, if he were not under secret engagements to the French emperor; unless you can suppose that he would run that hazard and the ruin of his country, rather than that a measure which he explicitly recommended should be pronounced unwise. . . . When we advert to the real character of Mr. Jefferson, there is no nefarious act of which we may not suppose him capable. He would *rather the United States should sink than change the present system of measures.* This is not opinion, but history. . . .

New England must be united in whatever great measure shall be adopted. During the approaching session of our legislature, there may be such farther advances in mischief as may distinctly point out the course proper to be adopted. A convention of delegates from those States, including Vermont, seems obviously proper and necessary. . . . A strong and solemn address, stating as concisely as will consist with perspicuity the evil conduct of our administration as manifested in their measures, ought to be prepared to be laid before our legislature when they meet, to be sent forth by their authority to the people. . . .

Pray look into the Constitution, and particularly to the 10th article of the amendments. How are the powers reserved to the States respectively, or to the people, to be maintained, *but by the respective States judging for themselves and putting their negative on the usurpations of the general government?*

DOCUMENT 7.8
The Convention as a Means of Containing Federalist Extremists

In this letter to a Connecticut Federalist, Harrison Gray Otis rejects nullification and secession and outlines alternative strategies. One of his suggestions—a convention to put forth proposals for revision of the federal Constitution—became the moderate Federalist strategy at Hartford in 1814, a meeting that Otis helped to organize and guide.

To Roger Griswold

Boston, January 4, 1809

Unless however this whole section is smitten providentially with blindness or stupified by infatuation, the madness of our rulers and the

Source: [Harrison Gray Otis?] to Roger Griswold, January 4, 1809. Published by permission of Yale University Library.

sufferings of the Country must rouse them to action, and it is of immense consequence to give a sure and temperate impulse to this action when they are prepared for it. To prevent insurrection, civil commotion, fruitless opposition, or a convulsive severance of the union, must be objects of immense importance, and I wish the system could be devised, matured and promulgated by your State. It is most obvious that the administration calculate upon the existence of such minorities in the Eastern States as will paralyze all our measures and leave them at full liberty to try out their experiments untill a State of war growing out of their measures shall enable them to enforce them by military power, and penal sentences, and hitherto they have but too much ground for such confidence. Nothing would more effectually undeceive them than a well concerted plan for convening and ascertaining the sentiments of the Eastern States upon their own peculiar interests. We have therefore thought, that it will be indispensable for our legislature, in some mode, to address the people, and to publish under the sanction of authority, a clear analysis of the causes of our difficulties, a review of leading measures, with temperate reflections upon the motives and unequivocal warnings of the tendencies & effects. Still the difficulty of the remedy, of the ultimate measures, recurs. Shall means be devised for calling a convention of the Eastern States & inviting N York to join (for the purpose of *more efficient remonstrance and more certain amendment to the Constitution*) by the present legislatures? Or shall they merely express their opinions of the expediency of this course and recommend to the people to make their next elections with that view? Or shall they forthwith declare certain laws unconstitutional and not binding on their citizens? This last would in my opinion be imprudent and in all views improper. I have rather thought something like the second would be advisable, and our friends here generally concur. We think that an authentic statement

of our situation from authority, published in all our towns and read in all our churches would open the eyes of a great majority & secure a great ascendancy in our legislature, or prove that we are devoted to ruin by the judgments of God, &, that of consequence opposition would be vain.

I repeat that if in this, or some similar course of proceedings you would lead, you would be supported with alacrity & firmness, and we should have the best reason for acceding to your proposals. We should avoid the cry of mad dog, and New Hampshire, Vermont & Rhode Island would follow with less jealousy and repugnance. This might be concerted. The plan of a convention to meet at *Hartford* or elsewhere for the purpose of procuring amendments to the Constitution essential to our best interests, and if these could not be effected at our joint instance, *other consequences,* might be met with prudence, circumspection, and such preparation as would avert violent commotions & civil war.

This my friend, are as you see, but *crude* hints for you to improve upon. Let your central Comm'ee write to ours without reserve. Or which would be better, let two or three of them come to Boston for a couple of days. No time should be lost.

DOCUMENT 7.9
Martin Van Buren Advocates Reviving the Republican Party

In this letter to Richmond, Virginia editor Thomas Ritchie, Martin Van Buren proposes that the old Republican party, virtually defunct, be revived. As an initial step, Van Buren urges that a national presidential nominating convention be held. Not only would a

Source: Martin Van Buren to Thomas Ritchie, January 13, 1827, Van Buren Mss, Library of Congress.

convention be "more in union with the spirit of the times," but it would be "the best and probably the only practicable mode of concentrating the entire vote of the opposition & of effecting what is of still greater importance, the substantial reorganization of the old Republican Party." Van Buren's preferred presidential candidate is war hero Andrew Jackson who, Van Buren believes, needs Republican party identification and revived organization to win election. In advocating this course, Van Buren values the national political party as a check to sectional conflict over slavery.

13 January 1827

[A presidential nominating convention] would be highly salutary on your section of the Union by the revival of the old party distinctions. We must always have party distinctions and the old ones are the best of which the nature of the case admits. Political combinations between the inhabitants of the different states are unavoidable & the most natural & beneficial to the country is that between the planters of the South and the plain Republicans of the north. The country has once flourished under a party thus constituted (& may again). It would take longer than our lives (even if it were practicable) to create new party feelings to keep those masses together. If the old ones were suppressed, Geographical divisions founded on local interests or, what is worse prejudices between free & slave holding states will inevitably take their place. Party attachment in former times furnished a complete antidote for sectional prejudices by producing counteracting feelings. It was not until that defence had been broken down that the clamour agt Southern Influence and African Slavery could be made effectual in the North. Those in the South who assisted in producing the change are, I am satisfied, now deeply sensible of their errour. Every honest Federalist of the South therefore should (and would if he duly reflected upon the subject) prefer the revival of old party feelings to any other state of things he has a right to expect. Formerly, attacks upon Southern Republicans were regarded by those of the north as assaults upon their political brethren & resented accordingly. This all powerful sympathy has been much weakened, if not, destroyed by the amalgamating policy of Mr. Monroe. It can & ought to be revived and the proposed convention would be eminently serviceable in effecting that object.

Jacksonian Democracy

Edward Pessen
Baruch College and the Graduate Center of the City University of New York

No aspect of American history has provoked such varied and frequently contradictory interpretations as Jacksonian democracy. Where one school sees Andrew Jackson
as man of the people and humble westerner
of rude origins, another school stresses his considerable wealth, horses, slaves, properties,
and high-placed friends. Jackson's beliefs—
they could hardly be called theories—prior to
his ascendancy to the Presidency have been
adjudged democratic and humane by some persons, narrow and conservative by others. His
political success has been ascribed, on the one
hand, to the rise of the West and the greater
prominence of American back-country farmers,
and on the other hand to the enthusiastic support
his allegedly radical program evoked from eastern or urban workers. (Critics of the latter view
have shown that he broke a strike and that
most workers apparently voted against him.)

Jackson believed that successful performance in high office required only ordinary
intelligence and diligence, but later critics concluded that in turning over too many positions
to men of precisely such mediocrity his spoils
system had a corrupting and deleterious effect
on government service. Nevertheless, some
modern scholars have noted the democratic implications both in the wholesale turnover of
political officeholders and in the new system
of party financing that went with it. His election
has been attributed to a sharp expansion of
the suffrage—a democratic upsurge to which
he allegedly contributed significantly and from
which he justifiably profited substantially. Another interpretation, however, holds that the
broadening of suffrage antedated Jackson's
rise, owed nothing to his policies, and brought
few benefits to him.

Depending on the author consulted, the Jackson administrations hammered out a broad program based on the president's sincere belief
in certain principles, or his policies were guided
by sheer expediency and opportunism. His program either was anticapitalistic in the agrarian
and anti-Bank tradition of John Taylor of Caroline, or it was clearly in the interest of expanding capitalism and of the new men on the make
who sought to profit from it. Either Jacksonian
democracy was a fitting title for a broad reform
movement led by the chief executive and his
aides; or, according to a recent study, it should
be discarded as a useless myth, not least because the Jackson government had little sympathy for the reforms it supposedly championed.
Nor do these divergences exhaust the list.

What is the significance of these widely differing interpretations? Undoubtedly, they testify, in part, only to the essentially contrary
points of view and political philosophies of

those who hold them. In this sense, Jacksonian democracy serves only as a convenient medium whose discussion enables the critic to develop his own ideas. But the broad range of views suggests as well the complexity of the era and the many facets it presents to the student who would try to understand it.

The era that Andrew Jackson so well symbolized was a most complex one. American life was being transformed—to a large extent, by developments that were not abetted by or even affected by the acts of Jackson and his administration. Important economic, social, and intellectual changes had been set in motion well before Old Hickory went to Washington— changes that hardly could be traced to any one political administration. Yet, to understand the impact that the vigorous Indian fighter did, in fact, have on his time, it is necessary to assess the way in which these changes affected the era and created its issues.

George Rogers Taylor, an economic historian, has suggestively entitled his study of the period *The Transportation Revolution*. Manufacturing, labor, farming, finance and banking, investment, the organization of business, population and immigration—all were affected significantly by a boom in transportation. The need for improved methods of transport and their lure of great profits attracted both private and government (local or state) capital, with resulting booms in turnpikes, steamboats, canal construction, and, toward the end of the period, railroads. Technical difficulties, high costs, terrible accidents that destroyed many lives as well as investments could not discourage the speculative boom in transportation methods that accounted for the bulk of state debts. Tocqueville's observation that Americans were always on the move is best understood against the background of Jacksonian America's frenzied building and experimenting in new ways of transporting people and things.

The era was also marked by feverish land speculation due in large part to the appreciation of values resulting from innovations in transportation. A growing need for currency was met primarily by state banks—some managed privately, others publicly. Various issues of bank paper differed widely in market value; they had in common only a tendency to promote both speculation and inflation. In the absence of federal requirements on specie reserves, the main brake on the banks' tendency to simply print money was the policy of the second Bank of the United States to demand specie from the banks of origin for state bank notes that it invariably accumulated. Tariff and public land payments—the federal government's chief means of raising money during the era—were usually made in such notes. At a time when money was desperately needed and speculative profits beckoned, few men sympathized with such restrictive ideas as high specie reserves, a stable price level, or a limited currency.

The production of manufactured goods came increasingly under control either of the merchant-capitalist, with his command of labor, materials, and markets, or of the factory owner, with his money-saving economies. Both tendencies seemed to constitute a threat to the status of workingmen and helped to produce a reaction in the form of a labor movement. A strange movement it was, composed mainly of skilled artisans led by well-to-do reformers, a number of whom had themselves never labored, and preoccupied with issues that had as much to do with the aspirations of the spirit as with the needs of the stomach.

Moreover, machinery was beginning to have important effects on agriculture, especially in the North and the West. Southern agriculture, though more diversified than is commonly believed, turned to staples and slavery rather than to mechanization. Land hunger led to renewed agitation for a liberalization of government land disposal policy. (Controversy about this issue touched off the historic Webster-Hayne debate in the Senate.) The economic innocence of the age is perhaps best indicated by the fact that a major issue concerned the disposition of the national government's Treasury surplus. In view of this surplus, a tariff was needed less for revenue than for protection of native industries. John C. Calhoun spoke for a South determined to buy its manufactured products—which it now knew it would not itself produce—in an unprotected market.

American society was in flux, according to both foreign and native observers. The period's sharp increase in population was caused largely by the flow of European immigrants. According to the merchant Philip Hone, immigration would always bring wretchedness and want, and the United States would be well advised to cease being almshouse and refuge for the poor of other countries. Some even blamed the immigrants for the cholera outbreak in 1832. Irish immigrants, in particular, suffered from poor housing, menial work at low pay, and a religious bigotry that did not confine itself to harsh words alone.

New York City emerged as the most populous of the nation's cities, followed closely by Philadelphia and, more distantly, by Baltimore, Boston, Charleston, New Orleans, Cincinnati, and Albany. Urbanism meant not only growth but also problems. Conservatives noted a decline in morality and an increase in prostitution. Hone attributed the many building accidents in New York City to the questionable values and rampant commercialism of an age that valued quick profits and, therefore, shoddy methods and materials over honest workmanship and respect for life. New York had its counterparts both in its slums and street-roaming gangs. The local constabulary, we are told, often hesitated to interfere with the Plug Uglies, the Forty Thieves, the Swamp Angels, or the Slaughterhouse Boys. Public health was a particularly crucial issue to an era when garbage disposal was left largely to pigs who rooted about in the streets, and when medical practice relied on bloodletting and cathartics. At the same time, however, improvements in lighting

and plumbing abetted material comfort, while new developments in amusements and dress warmed the spirit. Pantaloons became the vogue. (Mr. Taney not only introduced certain Jacksonian economic notions to the highest court but also the innovation of long trousers.)

An important, if undramatic, development of the era was municipal governments' increasing assumption of responsibility for street improvements, waterworks, gas mains and improved street lighting. Taxes were increased and unprecedented debts run up in order to finance these reforms. Contemporary observers found much that was crudely unattractive in American society and in the personal traits of Americans. They pointed, however, to the prevalence of a degree of social equality, equality of opportunity, and absence of social hierarchy and restraining tradition—social conditions that amazed those to whom the contours of European society were both the norm and the ideal. Mrs. Frances Trollope was repelled by the boastfulness, the mediocrity, the vulgarity, the low standards in food and taste. Michael Chevalier was revolted by the naïve preoccupation with material advancement. Jacksonians, he said, were ambitious without any grand ambition. Tocqueville, long before Thorstein Veblen, explained the American love of conspicuous display as a result of insecurity and the desire to impress one's neighbors with the visible signs of a wealth that in all probability had been acquired only recently and might just as quickly be lost. The physical and geographical mobility, which even Mrs. Trollope conceded was a major achievement of American civilization, was believed to be paralleled by an evident social mobility that allowed men to move as freely up and down the social ladder as they did across the physical landscape. On the other hand, there is reason to believe that foreign travelers paid too much attention to the egalitarianism on the surface of American society and not enough attention to inequalities beneath. The influence of class and wealth were great even in the newer cities of the West. In Boston and Philadelphia, class distinctions were so complicated that it was popularly said only a mathematician could analyze them.

Evidence drawn from rural and urban communities in all parts of the country indicates that Jacksonian America was not an egalitarian society—as it was long believed. Wealth was distributed unequally, the rich were rarely the ''self-made men'' Henry Clay and Alexis de Tocqueville claimed they were, class barriers were rarely breached, and the common man had little influence over politics or society for all the flattery directed at him by shrewd publicists and orators. The egalitarian *ideals* that flourished in the antebellum United States camouflaged a most inegalitarian social reality.

Egalitarian ideals influenced art and thought as well as society. The Jacksonian painter found the most precious in the most common. A movement to expand educational opportunity for working people resulted in the transformation of the common schools, no longer stigmatized as pauper schools. Free, tax-supported public schools greatly increased, while teacher training and instruction were substantially strengthened. Reformers experimented with new educational methods, influenced by Enlightenment-inspired European ideals, which in some cases antedated the vaunted progressivism of several generations later. The widespread desire for education was met, in part, by a flourishing library movement and by the rise of the lyceum, which saw such eminent personages as Horace Mann, Ralph Waldo Emerson, Daniel Webster, and Wendell Phillips giving lectures on a wide range of topics. In the late 1830s, tax-supported libraries established by state laws began to supplement the private libraries created by such philanthropists as the Astors, the Lawrences, and the Peabodys. Leveling tendencies were also manifested in journalism. New technological processes that made both paper and printing cheaper brought about the era of the penny

press, which was marked by greater coverage, livelier writing, a preoccupation with scandal, and a much larger newspaper-reading public than had been known before.

Important changes also occurred in American politics. While an older view attributed to the Jacksonian movement many of the political reforms of the period, modern scholarship has tended to show that Jackson was the beneficiary rather than the initiator of the democratic political developments. Well before his election in 1828, most states had ended all restrictions on the suffrage of adult white males. In eastern and western states, the choice of presidential electors had been removed from control of the state legislatures and placed in the hands of the voters.

The democratization of politics, as of society, did not mean the victory either of idealism or high-mindedness. On the state level, politics was often a sordid business. In New York and Tennessee, Massachusetts and Mississippi, practical men of affairs had organized efficient vote-getting machines perfectly capable of appealing to the electorate in lofty rhetoric while in fact, addressing themselves to no higher objective than getting or remaining in office. Nor is the word ''machine'' a misnomer for the tightly knit organizations that formed around nuclei of influential officeholders. The caucus was used as a device both for mapping out strategy and for enforcing discipline. Where the term ''caucus'' was in bad repute, as C. M. Snyder wrote in *The Jacksonian Heritage: Pennsylvania Politics 1833–1848,* Democratic local leaders would ''issue the call for a meeting, now termed a convention, but differing little from the traditional caucus . . . prepare a ticket in advance, and usually secure its acceptance from the assembled party members.''

On the national scene, able and opportunistic men sought to take advantage of the ending of the Virginia dynasty. The favorite son—a child of the era—was usually a man who had built up a powerful personal following on the basis of a congressional, military, or local political career. He sought the highest office generally by playing down his own wealth and influence, and by extolling the "sovereign people." It seemed to be an era of many parties: Republicans, National Republicans, Democrats, Republican Friends of the Administration, Anti-Masons, People's Party, the Working Men, and others. Certainly, there were many candidates; yet, each of them tended to assert his Republicanism and the kinship of his political credo with that of the revered Jefferson.

Actually, beliefs or political philosophy had little to do with the electoral contests of the period. The campaigns of 1824 and, above all, of 1828 were bitter, indeed; but the heat was generated by personality, not by ideology. In 1828, Jackson was denounced as an "adulterer, a gambler, a cock fighter, a brawler, and drunkard and a murderer." His friends, replying in kind, called John Quincy Adams a sensualist(!), a decadent aristocrat, immoral. The real issues of the contest were difficult to detect, for the good reason that the candidates' views on important political matters were similar or unknown.

As the geographical distribution of the votes makes clear, Jackson's success was not so much a victory for principles as it was a victory for the South. Although Jackson's ownership of many slaves and his proslavery attitudes no doubt enhanced his image in the eyes of southern voters, the election of 1828 is better interpreted as a clash of personality and sectional "favorite sons" rather than a pivotal or "transitional election." To be sure, some historians have stressed the alleged clash of political and social principles in the party contests of the era. But since separate groups of rich men, extreme conservatives, business leaders, occasional prodebtors, and even radicals were ranged in support of each of the leading candidates, it is hard to disagree with the conclusion of Glyndon Van Deusen that "the political conflicts of the Jacksonian period were fought more often with a view to gaining control of the government than out of devotion to diametrically opposed political and social ideals."

Whether a distinct ideological entity or not, the Jacksonians had a lasting impact on American politics, as much for their manner of administering as for the substance of their program. Jacksonian democracy represented presidential power and leadership. Andrew Jackson rates high in the judgment of political scientists, largely because of his dynamic use of the presidential office, a policymaking rather than a mere law-executing office in his hands. Whether one agrees with either his policies or his interpretation of his office, the modern concept of presidential leadership unquestionably owes much to him. He exercised this power whether dealing with the legislative or judicial branches of government, with friends or enemies, or with other governments. He vetoed twelve congressional bills and pocket-vetoed others, justifying the vetoes by a broad reasoning in which expediency was held sufficient. (An alert modern scholar points out that, like Jackson, another great vetoer, Grover Cleveland, was a Presbyterian—which may foreshadow a new religious interpretation of the executive negative.) *He* knew better than either the Congress or the courts—not only what was good for the country but also what was constitutional. Regarding a Supreme Court ruling he chose to ignore, he was said to have remarked: "John Marshall has made his decision; now let him enforce it." He respected neither judicial precedent nor the doctrine of judicial review. He treated his Cabinet as arbitrarily. When one Secretary of the Treasury after another would not accede to his plan to remove federal deposits from the Bank of the United States, he simply removed secretary after secretary until he found an acquiescent man.

The old Indian fighter and frontier duelist often responded to issues in personal terms. During the Bank War, for instance, he told his heir-apparent: "The Bank, Mr. Van Buren, is trying to kill me, *but I will kill it.*" The President's attitude toward men seemed to be based little on their philosophies and much on their loyalty to him. He ruled and was ruled by a code of personal conduct according to which men were judged by one simple criterion—where they stood with regard to Andrew Jackson. "Who is not for me must be considered against me," he said. He broke with his Vice President, John C. Calhoun, when he discovered that as Secretary of War Calhoun had a decade before urged the censure of the then General Jackson for his violation of the Florida border. He turned against and dismissed his Cabinet because several of their wives had snubbed the notorious wife of a long-time crony. Van Buren's loyalty on this seemingly inconsequential issue led Jackson to groom him as his successor. The President had a long list of bitter enemies, both in the government and out. Unfortunately for those scholars who would have it that he was a man dedicated to certain political principles, each enmity was evidently based on purely personal considerations. His favorite method for resolving such clashes was force, whenever possible. We are told that "most of the cabinet stood in some fear of the President." There was good reason, since he had slain a number of men and whipped or wounded others. He is supposed to have said once that the two great regrets of his life were that he had not shot Clay and had not hanged Calhoun. One marvels at the intrepidity of political opponents who dared criticize this steely-eyed, steel-nerved man of action.

Depending on the point of view, Jacksonian democracy meant rotation in office or the spoils system. The turnover of federal officials, however, was not nearly so great as was once believed. Modern research has disclosed that less than 1,000 out of more than 10,000 officeholders had been removed after Jackson's first eighteen months in office; relatively few additional removals occurred thereafter. Yet, the earlier concept of relative permanence of tenure in office unquestionably was overthrown. Jackson himself provided a lofty rationale for the new policy when, in his first message to Congress, he alluded to the consonance of rotation with republican principles, the tendency of long tenure in office to foster corruption, and the right of the citizenry to hold office. His lieutenants, however, spoke dryly of rewarding the faithful, building the party, and distributing the spoils of political war. Van Buren was to remove men for disloyalty to himself. (For all his talk of the common man, however, Jackson, like his aristocratic predecessors, appointed men of unusual wealth and social eminence to high government posts.)

That this new policy accorded with the spirit of the times is indicated by the eagerness with which the Whigs, ardent opponents of the spoils system as long as they were out of office, embraced it once in power. Its effects were varied and, in some cases, unanticipated. American politics was profoundly altered as major parties increasingly came to rely on the financial contributions of newly appointed officeholders. Patronage created the modern democratic party organization, fostered the pragmatic rather than ideological tendencies of American parties, placed success at the polls over principle, and in many instances led to a deterioration in the efficiency of various federal agencies, not to mention a decline in the prestige of the individuals staffing them.

Jackson stood for neither a strict nor a loose construction of the Constitution but rather, for a mixed construction. His policies regarding the Constitution, his interpretation of his own proper role under it, were tinctured with opportunism, notwithstanding the high tone he adopted. He was the strict constructionist when it suited him. Thus, he vetoed the Maysville project and the recharting of the Bank of the United States—the bank, among other reasons, for its "unconstitutional" stretching of congressional power. Yet, he asserted the doctrine that every official interpreted the Constitution for himself. The Supreme Court's decisions could be disregarded, a Treasury surplus could be "distributed" to the states despite the absence of constitutional justification, and Indian rights solemnly based on law and treaty could be treated with contempt. The record of the Old General on such issues as the tariff and government road building was anything but consistent. His views appeared to be changeable and subtly influenced by political considerations of the moment. For example, the administration's decision to restrict the mail privileges for abolitionist literature seemed dictated more by expediency than by proslavery sentiment.

The Jackson administration was militantly nationalistic in its foreign policy. It catered to the currently popular sentiment that the land of the free was morally right in lecturing to the decadent states of Europe and strong enough to get away with it. What was harder to do, and more praiseworthy, was its success in carrying off this policy. And political capital earned at home seemed more than deserved in view of the undoubted increase in respect that Jackson won for the United States. On balance, there was much to validate the self-praise heaped on the administration by its gray eminence, Amos Kendall, who claimed the Old General had won for the nation free trading rights in Colombia, secured commercial privileges in the Bosphorus, made a treaty with Austria, reinstituted a suspended treaty with Mexico, obtained an indemnity from Denmark, garnered trading rights with the British West Indies, and collected the spoliation claims from France—all from a diplomacy that neatly blended guile, righteousness, wrath, and muscle. It can also be argued, however, that Jackson's hot temper and penchant for bluster brought the nation unnecessarily to the brink of war.

At home, Jacksonian nationalism meant support for territorial expansion in the Northwest and Southwest, unremitting conquest of Indian territories, and stern opposition to nullification and its doctrine of state sovereignty—no matter how Calhoun sought to make such sovereignty constitutionally respectable. Reacting angrily to a protective tariff that was economically hurtful to South Carolina's planter interests, John C. Calhoun induced that state in November 1832 to hold a "nullification convention" that upheld the state's right to declare "null and void" the offending, allegedly unconstitutional law. Measure provoked countermeasure. In a "Proclamation to the People of South Carolina" prepared by his Secretary of State Edward Livingston, Andrew Jackson warned that "disunion by armed force was treason," and that the federal laws would be enforced. In early 1833 the administration prepared a Force Bill that was promptly nullified and derided by South Carolina as the Bloody Bill. The issue was finally resolved in the passage of a compromise tariff and a mutual exchange of defiant pronunciamentos by the federal and South Carolina governments. But there is little reason to doubt the integrity of the President's unionism, his sincerity in making his Jefferson Day Dinner pledge, or his willingness to invoke the Force Bill and to hang traitors. Nor is there any doubt of the general popularity of this policy.

Paradoxically, nationalistic Jacksonian democracy also meant states' rights. One of the arguments the President used against the bank was that its charter improperly limited the taxing power of the states. Similarly, the Maysville veto and the administration's reaction to the High Court's decisions in *Worcester* v. *Georgia* and *Cherokee* v. *Georgia* signified solicitude for the powers and the interests of individual states. The decisions of the Taney Court, most of whose members, including the Chief Justice, were Jackson appointees, were notably significant for their assertion of broad state powers to issue money and promote the general welfare.

It is a commonplace of recent interpretation

that the Jacksonians fostered the growth of a capitalism free of artistocratic and other restraints that interfered with freedom of opportunity. The relationship between Jacksonian democracy and the business community was complex and, in some respects, paradoxical. A wealthy man with interests in slaves and speculative land ventures, Jackson was at the same time suspicious of sharp commercial practices. An unhappy personal experience in business had convinced him that debt and inflation were twin evils. Undoubtedly, an anticommercial animus in part inspired his war on the second Bank, as well as a sincere belief that the Bank was a prime source of currency inflation, an unfair monopoly, a means of enabling a few speculative eastern insiders to wax fat at the expense of honest labor and the West. Old Hickory believed in sound or hard money. Unfortunately, however, the defeat of the Bank was sought by many of his allies precisely because, under Nicholas Biddle, it had become the one great obstacle to the inflationary ambitions of the state banks. Convinced that he was slaying the monster of "rag money," in accomplishing the Bank's downfall Jackson actually got rid of the one agency that had the power to limit reckless currency expansion. The result was precisely the opposite of what he intended, much to the satisfaction of state bankers, "trade Democrats," numerous rich men—whether Democratic or Whig—and large numbers of Americans of a speculative temper. Radicals who opposed banking in general, and who were either too dull or too innocent of knowledge of the intricacies of finance to understand what was going on, also rejoiced in the slaying of the dragon.

An interesting feature of the Jackson program was the way in which it could, for different reasons, satisfy speculators and men of property as well as radicals and spokesmen for labor. What labor might regard as an egalitarian attack on an aristocratic privilege, as in the call for general rather than special laws of incorporation, was, in fact, a requirement of a capitalistic society. By and large, the Jacksonians stood for a policy of laissez-faire, under which the elite would obtain no favors and every man might have the opportunity to compete in business. That the President himself evidently wanted the competition to be waged soberly did not inhibit men who wanted it frenzied.

Easily the most significant Jacksonian influences on the growth of business were the decisions of the Taney Court. Construed by some as an assertion of human rights over property rights, they actually upheld property rights while warning that the right to amass could not be confined, either explicitly or by implication, to a small vested group. Neither Jackson nor his Chief Justice sympathized with debtors or with the bankruptcy laws passed by a number of states to help relieve debtors of their obligations. A lofty rhetoric in one famous case, which seemed to speak of the community interest as the very highest, evidently blinded some contemporaries and later scholars to the fact that this same Court also broadened the rights of private corporations and safeguarded property rights and contracts—even if granted corruptly. A growing capitalistic society needed more bridges, more currency, more opportunities for investment; and a Jacksonian judiciary eased the way for all of these.

Finally, Jacksonian democracy represented a close tie between the executive and the people. Jackson spoke to the electorate over the heads of his enemies. A brilliant propagandist, he depicted issues in black-and-white terms—reducing complex issues to a clash between aristocracy (or parasites, the wicked, and the privileged) and the people (or honest labor, the virtuous, and the industrious). When many of his own supporters voiced doubts about his plan to remove the federal deposits from one relatively sound bank to a number of precarious ones, he retorted: "The people will understand." That they understood the real issues is questionable, but they evidently did understand as he meant them to. They shared, even gloried, in his dramatic oversimplifications; and they threw their political support not only to him but, in later generations, to others who, like him, spoke their language and fought the good fight versus the forces of darkness—even where the warfare might be confined to the field of rhetoric.

SUGGESTED READINGS

Aronson, Sidney H. *Status and Kinship in the Higher Civil Service.* Cambridge, Mass.: Harvard University Press, 1964.

Benson, Lee. *The Concept of Jacksonian Democracy.* Princeton, N.J.: Princeton University Press, 1961.

Hammond, Bray. *Banks and Politics in America: From the Revolution to the Civil War.* Princeton, N.J.: Princeton University Press, 1957.

McCormick, Richard P. *The Second American Party System.* Chapel Hill: University of North Carolina Press, 1966.

Meyers, Marvin. *The Jacksonian Persuasion.* Stanford, Cal.: Stanford University Press, 1957.

Pessen, Edward. *Jacksonian America: Society, Personality, and Politics.* Chicago: Dorsey Press, 1978.

———. *Riches, Class, and Power Before the Civil War.* Lexington, Mass.: D. C. Heath, 1973.

———, ed. *New Perspectives on Jacksonian Parties and Politics.* Boston: Allyn Bacon, 1969.

———. *Most Uncommon Jacksonians: The Radical Leaders of the Early Labor Movement.* Albany, N.Y.: State University of New York Press, 1967.

Remini, Robert V. *Andrew Jackson and the Bank War.* New York: W. W. Norton, 1968.

Schlesinger, Arthur M., Jr. *The Age of Jackson.* Boston: Little, Brown, 1945.

Smith, Walter B. *Economic Aspects of the Second Bank of the United States.* Cambridge, Mass.: Harvard University Press, 1953.

Taylor, George Rogers. *The Transportation Revolution.* New York: Holt, Rinehart & Winston, 1951.

Temin, Peter. *The Jacksonian Economy.* New York: W. W. Norton, 1969.

Tocqueville, Alexis de. *Democracy in America.* 2 vols. New York: Vintage, 1954.

Van Deusen, Glyndon. *The Jacksonian Era, 1828–1848.* New York: Harper, 1959.

Ward, John W. *Andrew Jackson: Symbol for an Age.* New York: Oxford University Press, 1955.

White, Leonard D. *The Jacksonians.* New York: Macmillan, 1954.

DOCUMENT 8.1
Convey the Favorable Voter

The following circular indicates that Andrew Jackson's friends did not have a monopoly on political know-how. Distributed by Indiana supporters of John Quincy Adams in 1828, it specifies in detail the practical steps to be taken to assure victory.

Centreville, July 19th, 1828

Dear Sirs—You were appointed at a county meeting of the friends of the Administration, held in this place, in May, 1827, a committee of vigilance for your district, and being uncertain whether you have been informed of that appointment, we beg leave now to notify you of it, and at the same time to solicit your co-operation and unremitting exertions to the duties which will be required of you. It is probably not unknown to you, that our opponents are daily making privately, as well as publicly, the most strenuous efforts, and unless we meet them in a correspondent manner, *showing an imposing front,* and a *bold, determined courage,* we may be defeated, although we believe that a great majority of the people of the county, and electoral district, are with us. The importance *of securing the delegation* to the Assem-

---

Source: William Chambers, Chairman Committee of Correspondence, *The Centreville Circular* (Centreville, Indiana, July 19, 1828).

bly in October is so obvious, and known to possess *so powerful a bearing* on that which is *to follow in November,* that we think it unnecessary to dwell on that subject; we would however, remark; that four gentlemen of undoubted abilities and unquestionable integrity have been selected by the general committee; for the promotion of whose election the friends of the administration have pledged themselves to give their individual and united support.

It is proposed and *will become a part of your duty to endeavor to discover the political sentiments of every voter in your district, to take down the names of all,* designating *for whom* they intend to *vote,* the *objections* of those opposed to the re-election of Mr. ADAMS, *and the cause of those objections;* on the other hand, *you are to acquaint yourselves with the reasons* of those *who prefer* General JACKSON, and endeavor to *put them right.* The list of persons so made out, to which you will add all voters deemed *doubtful,* and to whom GREAT *and* POINTED *attention must be paid,* is to be given in to the chairman of your district committee, or to the secretary with whom each committee man is frequently to communicate during the canvass, whose duty it will be to report their communications personally, together with all other information, to the corresponding committee at Centreville, every other Saturday in August. The chairman of the district committee, and the secretary must urge upon the several committee men *the necessity to see that all voters known to be favorable, and those who may be deemed* DOUBTFUL, BE FURNISHED WITH THE MEANS OF CONVEYANCE, *to the polls, and when there* KEPT IN VIEW *by the persons who convey them,* UNTIL THEY HAVE VOTED; *each committee man* to be as active and industrious as possible on the day of election, *a part of whom, the* MOST POWERFUL, *both in* PERSONAL STRENGTH *and* COURAGE, not less than six, must be appointed to stand constantly at the polls for the purpose as well of defending the rights

of our friends, as to object to illegal voters, many of whom, particularly young men, nearly of age, will no doubt be pushed forward. The chairman and secretary ought immediately to add to your number of committee men, at least twenty, or more if necessary—*taking them out of every neighborhood* in the district, and also *taking care to select as many young and active men as possible.* We beg leave also to recommend to the chairman and secretary *to have frequent and* PRIVATE *meetings, taking always such precautions that we may act completely and fully organized before those in opposition to us are* AWARE OF WHAT WE ARE ABOUT. We cannot close this communication *without urging it as of the* UTMOST *importance,* that this and all other matters connected with our arrangements, should be kept ENTIRELY TO OURSELVES, at any rate until the ORGANIZATION of our PLANS *is fully matured.*—When you get well under way, sub-committees would essentially, we think, aid our cause, they might then be formed for each neighborhood, under the direction of the chairman and secretary of the district committee. The committee of correspondence will give all the aid in their power in furnishing political papers and documents as they may be wanting. We beg leave, also, to impress on you the policy of a calm and temperate deportment towards those on whom you wish *to make an impression,* believing likewise, that towards those who are our determined adversaries the same line of conduct is the preferable one to pursue. We feel assured that you fully appreciate the cause in which we are engaged, and consider it of such vital importance to the existence of our republican institutions, that your exertions will be used and your *ingenuity* exercised to insure success.

We are with great esteem, very respectfully, Your most obedient servants,

WM. CHAMBERS, *Chairman Committee of Correspondence*

DOCUMENT 8.2
A Plea for Democratic Government

The following passage from Andrew Jackson's first annual message to Congress (1829) contains his arguments on behalf of what his friends called rotation in office. His enemies called it the spoils system.

There are, perhaps, a few men who can for any great length of time enjoy office and power without being more or less under the influence of feelings unfavorable to the faithful discharge of their public duties. Their integrity may be proof against improper considerations immediately addressed to themselves, but they are apt to acquire a habit of looking with indifference upon the public interests and of tolerating conduct from which an unpracticed man would revolt. Office is considered as a species of property, and government rather as a means of promoting individual interests than as an instrument created solely for the service of the people. Corruption in some and in others a perversion of correct feelings and principles divert government from its legitimate ends and make it an engine for the support of the few at the expense of the many. The duties of all public officers are, or at least admit of being made, so plain and simple that men of intelligence may readily qualify themselves for their performance; and I can not but believe that more is lost by the long continuance of men in office than is generally to be gained by their experience. I submit, therefore, to your consideration whether the efficiency of the Government would not be promoted and official industry and integrity better secured by a general extension of the law which limits appointments to four years.

In a country where offices are created solely for the benefit of the people no one man has any more intrinsic right to official station than another. Offices were not established to give support to particular men at the public expense. No individual wrong is, therefore, done by removal, since neither appointment to nor continuance in office is matter of right. The incumbent became an officer with a view to public benefits, and when these require his removal they are not to be sacrificed to private interests. It is the people, and they alone, who have a right to complain when a bad officer is substituted for a good one. He who is removed has the same means of obtaining a living that are enjoyed by the millions who never held office. The proposed limitation would destroy the idea of property now so generally connected with official station, and although individual distress may be sometimes produced, it would, by promoting that rotation which constitutes a leading principle in the republican creed, give healthful action to the system. . . .

DOCUMENT 8.3
The President States the Case against Mr. Biddle's Bank

Jackson's bank veto message of July 10, 1832, was as much a political document as it was a reasoned economic or constitutional analysis. The following excerpts indicate the breadth of his argument.

The bill "to modify and continue" the act entitled "An act to incorporate the subscribers to

Source: James D. Richardson, ed., *A Compilation of the Messages and Papers of the Presidents, 1789–1897* (Washington, D.C., 1896), vol. 2, pp. 448–49.

Source: James D. Richardson, ed., *A Compilation of the Messages and Papers of the Presidents, 1789–1897* (Washington, D.C., 1896), vol. 2, pp. 576–77, 590–91.

the Bank of the United States'' was presented to me on the 4th July instant. Having considered it with that solemn regard to the principles of the Constitution which the day was calculated to inspire, and come to the conclusion that it ought not to become a law, I herewith return it to the Senate, in which it originated, with my objections.

A bank of the United States is in many respects convenient for the Government and useful to the people. Entertaining this opinion, and deeply impressed with the belief that some of the powers and privileges possessed by the existing bank are unauthorized by the Constitution, subversive of the rights of the States, and dangerous to the liberties of the people, I felt it my duty at an early period of my Administration to call the attention of Congress to the practicability of organizing an institution combining all its advantages and obviating these objections. I sincerely regret that in the act before me I can perceive none of those modifications of the bank charter which are necessary, in my opinion, to make it compatible with justice, with sound policy, or with the Constitution of our country.

The present corporate body, denominated the president, directors, and company of the Bank of the United States, will have existed at the time this act is intended to take effect in twenty years. It enjoys an exclusive privilege of banking under the authority of the General Government, a monopoly of its favor and support, and, as a necessary consequence, almost a monopoly of the foreign and domestic exchange. The powers, privileges, and favors bestowed upon it in the original charter, by increasing the value of the stock far above its par value, operated as a gratuity of many millions to the stockholders.

An apology may be found for the failure to guard against this result in the consideration that the effect of the original act of incorporation could not be certainly foreseen at the time of its passage. The act before me proposes another

gratuity to the holders of the same stock, and in many cases to the same men, of at least seven millions more. This donation finds no apology in any uncertainty as to the effect of the act. On all hands it is conceded that its passage will increase at least 20 or 30 per cent more the market price of the stock, subject to the payment of the annuity of $200,000 per year secured by the act, thus adding in a moment one-fourth to its par value. It is not our own citizens only who are to receive the bounty of our Government. More than eight millions of the stock of this bank are held by foreigners. By this act the American Republic proposes virtually to make them a present of some millions of dollars. For these gratuities to foreigners and to some of our own opulent citizens the act secures no equivalent whatever. They are the certain gains of the present stockholders under the operation of this act, after making full allowance for the payment of the bonus.

Every monopoly and all exclusive privileges are granted at the expense of the public, which ought to receive a fair equivalent. The many millions which this act proposes to bestow on the stockholders of the existing bank must come directly or indirectly out of the earnings of the American people. It is due to them, therefore, if their Government sell monopolies and exclusive privileges, that they should at least exact for them as much as they are worth in open market. The value of the monopoly in this case may be correctly ascertained. The twenty-eight millions of stock would probably be at an advance of 50 per cent, and command in market at least $42,000,000, subject to the payment of the present bonus. The present value of the monopoly, therefore, is $17,-000,000, and this act proposes to sell for three millions, payable in fifteen annual installments of $200,000 each.

It is not conceivable how the present stockholders can have any claim to the special favor of the Government. The present corporation has enjoyed its monopoly during the period stipulated in the original contract. If we must have such a corporation, why should not the Government sell out the whole stock and thus secure to the people the full market value of the privileges granted? Why should not Congress create and sell twenty-eight millions of stock, incorporating the purchasers with all the powers and privileges secured in this act and putting the premium upon the sales into the Treasury?

But this act does not permit competition in the purchase of this monopoly. It seems to be predicated on the erroneous idea that the present stockholders have a prescriptive right not only to the favor but to the bounty of Government. It appears that more than a fourth part of the stock is held by foreigners and the residue is held by a few hundred of our own citizens, chiefly of the richest class. For their benefit does this act exclude the whole American people from competition in the purchase of this monopoly and dispose of it for many millions less than it is worth. This seems the less excusable because some of our citizens not now stockholders petitioned that the door of competition might be opened, and offered to take a charter on terms much more favorable to the Government and country.

But this proposition, although made by men whose aggregate wealth is believed to be equal to all the private stock in the existing bank, has been set aside, and the bounty of our Government is proposed to be again bestowed on the few who have been fortunate enough to secure the stock and at this moment wield the power of the existing institution. I can not perceive the justice or policy of this course. . . .

It is to be regretted that the rich and powerful too often bend the acts of government to their selfish purposes. Distinctions in society will always exist under every just government. Equality of talents, of education, or of wealth can not be produced by human institutions. In the full enjoyment of the gifts of Heaven and the fruits of superior industry, economy,

and virtue, every man is equally entitled to protection by law; but when the laws undertake to add to these natural and just advantages artificial distinctions, to grant titles, gratuities, and exclusive privileges, to make the rich richer and the potent more powerful, the humble members of society—the farmers, mechanics, and laborers—who have neither the time nor the means of securing like favors to themselves, have a right to complain of the injustice of their Government. There are no necessary evils in government. Its evils exist only in its abuses. If it would confine itself to equal protection, and, as Heaven does its rains, shower its favors alike on the high and the low, the rich and the poor, it would be an unqualified blessing. In the act before me there seems to be a wide and unnecessary departure from these just principles.

Nor is our Government to be maintained or our Union preserved by invastions of the rights and powers of the several States. In thus attempting to make our General Government strong we make it weak. Its true strength consists in leaving individuals and States as much as possible to themselves—in making itself felt, not in its power, but in its beneficence; not in its control, but in its protection; not in binding the States more closely to the center, but leaving each to move unobstructed in its proper orbit.

Experience should teach us wisdom. Most of the difficulties our Government now encounters and most of the dangers which impend over our Union have sprung from an abandonment of the legitimate objects of Government by our national legislation, and the adoption of such principles as are embodied in this act. Many of our rich men have not been content with equal protection and equal benefits, but have besought us to make them richer by act of Congress. By attempting to gratify their desires we have in the results of our legislation arrayed section against section, interest against interest, and man against man, in a fearful commotion which threatens to shake the foundations of our Union. It is time to pause in our career to review our principles, and if possible revive that devoted patriotism and spirit of compromise which distinguished the sages of the Revolution and the fathers of our Union. If we can not at once, in justice to interests vested under improvident legislation, make our Government what it ought to be, we can at least take a stand against all new grants of monopolies and exclusive privileges, against any prostitution of our Government to the advancement of the few at the expense of the many, and in favor of compromise and gradual reform in our code of laws and system of political economy.

I have now done my duty to my country. If sustained by my fellow-citizens, I shall be grateful and happy; if not, I shall find in the motives which impel me ample grounds for contentment and peace. In the difficulties which surround us and the dangers which threaten our institutions there is cause for neither dismay nor alarm. For relief and deliverance let us firmly rely on that kind Providence which I am sure watches with peculiar care over the destinies of our Republic, and on the intelligence and wisdom of our countrymen. Through *His* abundant goodness and *their* patriotic devotion our liberty and Union will be preserved.

Andrew Jackson

DOCUMENT 8.4
Jackson Comes under Attack

The following selections are from the diary of Philip Hone for 1833 and 1834. Hone was an influential conservative who lived in New York City during the period. His comments are typical of the reaction of many in the

Source: Allan Nevins, ed., *The Diary of Philip Hone, 1828–1851* (New York: Dodd, Mead, 1927), vol. 1, pp. 106–7, 112–13.

business community to the Jacksonian financial measures.

Friday, Dec. 20.—General Jackson's ill-advised measure of removing the public money from the Bank of the United States has occasioned great distress among those who unfortunately depend upon their credit to pay their debts. His out and out partisans attribute the difficulty to the operations of the bank, which they say ought to increase its discounts. . . . Money cannot be obtained at seven percent on bond and mortgage, and for less permanent loans the borrower is completely at the mercy of the lender. Stocks have fallen prodigiously, particularly railroad and canal company stock. I hold $50,000 of stock in the Delaware & Hudson, the Camden & Amboy, and Boston & Providence companies which is not worth so much by ten or twelve thousand as it was three months since.

Friday, Dec. 27.—The holidays are gloomy, the weather is bad, the times are bad, stocks are falling, and a panic prevails which will result in bankruptcies and ruin in many quarters where a few short weeks since the sun of prosperity shone with unusual brightness. It will be worse before it is better.

Monday, Dec. 30.—The times are dreadfully hard. The supererogatory act of tyranny which the President exercised in removing the deposits has produced a state of alarm and panic unprecedented in our city. The friends of the United States Bank on the one side, and the whole array of Jackson men, together with the friends of the Pet Banks, on the other, mutually accuse each other of being the cause of the pressure; and so between them both, the community groans under the distress which these misunderstandings have created. "A plague on both your houses!" say I. The truth is, we are smarting under the lash which the vindictive ruler of our destinies has inflicted upon us as a penalty for the sin which Nicholas Biddle committed in opposing his election. My share of punishment amounts to $20,000, which I have lost by the fall of stocks in the last sixty days. Delaware & Hudson Canal stock has fallen suddenly from 125 per cent to 75 per cent; Boston & Providence Railroad from 115 per cent to 88 per cent; Camden & Amboy from 150 per cent to 125 per cent. Delaware and Hudson fell 20 per cent in two days, owing principally to the failure of Shipman & Corning, brokers, who have been gambling in the stock. . . . The removal of the deposits I believe to be the great cause of the pecuniary distress, to which may be added the operation of cash duties on woolens, which brings a large amount of payments into the Treasury. The gambling in stocks which has been carried on by the brokers to an extent disgraceful to the commercial character of the city is another cause of the distress.

Friday, Jan. 31.—*Another Failure.* Wall Street was thrown into consternation this morning by the failure of John G. Warren & Son, a house in good credit and one of the most extensive in their line as brokers. This unexpected event is attributed to the unprecedented fall in stocks occasioned by the derangement of the money concerns of the city. If Gen. Jackson had visited Wall Street this morning, he might have been regaled with a sight similar to that of the field of battle at New Orleans. His killed and wounded were to be seen in every direction, and men enquiring with anxious solicitude, ''Who is to fall next?''

Friday, Feb. 7.—. . . *Great meeting.*—A public meeting having been called by a notice signed by 174 respectable names of ''the citizens who are opposed to the removal of the deposits from the Bank of the United States, and who are in favor of a sound currency by means of a national bank,'' an immense concourse assembled at twelve o'clock at the place of meeting—the park. The number is computed at from twelve to fifteen thousand. I was waited upon by a committee and requested to officiate as chairman. When I came on the ground precisely at twelve o'clock I found an immense crowd already assembled, consisting principally of the most respectable mechanics and others in the city—men of character, respectability, and personal worth, with a few miscreants who went, perhaps of their own accord, but were more probably sent there to excite disturbance and disturb the proceedings. The rabble had gotten possession of the chair, and it required some hard thumps to clear the way sufficiently for me to come forward. I attempted to address the meeting, but the yells of the mob, and the noise of better disposed persons in attempting to command silence, rendered all my efforts unavailing; so I put the question upon the resolutions, which were carried by an immense majority, and then adjourned the meeting; but the mob did not disperse for a considerable time afterwards. This apparently organized outrage upon the freedom of our citizens cannot fail to strengthen our cause.

DOCUMENT 8.5
The President Replies to South Carolina

The following excerpts from President Jackson's proclamation of December 10, 1832, contain his description of South Carolina's nullification measures as well as his nationalistic response to them.

Whereas a convention assembled in the State of South Carolina have passed an ordinance by which they declare ''that the several acts and parts of acts of the Congress of the United States purporting to be laws for the imposing of duties and imposts on the importation of foreign commodities, and now having actual operation and effect within the United States,

---

Source: James D. Richardson, ed., *A Compilation of the Messages and Papers of the Presidents, 1789–1897* (Washington, D.C., 1896), vol. 2, pp. 640–42.

and more especially'' two acts for the same purposes passed on the 29th of May, 1828, and on the 14th of July, 1832, ''are unauthorized by the Constitution of the United States, and violate the true meaning and intent thereof, and are null and void and no law,'' nor binding on the citizens of that State or its officers; and by the said ordinance it is further declared to be unlawful for any of the constituted authorities of the State or of the United States to enforce the payment of the duties imposed by the said acts within the same State, and that it is the duty of the legislature to pass such laws as may be necessary to give full effect to the said ordinance; and

Whereas by the said ordinance it is further ordained that in no case of law or equity decided in the courts of said State wherein shall be drawn in question the validity of the said ordinance, or of the acts of the legislature that may be passed to give it effect, or of the said laws of the United States, no appeal shall be allowed to the Supreme Court of the United States, nor shall any copy of the record be permitted or allowed for that purpose, and that any person attempting to take such appeal shall be punished as for contempt of court; and, finally, the said ordinance declares that the people of South Carolina will maintain the said ordinance at every hazard, and that they will consider the passage of any act by Congress abolishing or closing the ports of the said State or otherwise obstructing the free ingress or egress of vessels to and from the said ports, or any other act of the Federal Government to coerce the State, shut up her ports, destroy or harass her commerce, or to enforce the said acts otherwise than through the civil tribunals of the country, as inconsistent with the longer continuance of South Carolina in the Union, and that the people of the said State will thenceforth hold themselves absolved from all further obligation to maintain or preserve their political connection with the people of the other States, and will forthwith proceed to organize a sepa-

rate government and do all other acts and things which sovereign and independent states may of right do; and

Whereas the said ordinance prescribes to the people of South Carolina a course of conduct in direct violation of their duty as citizens of the United States, contrary to the laws of their country, subversive of its Constitution, and having for its object the destruction of the Union—that Union which, coeval with our political existence, led our fathers, without any other ties to unite them than those of patriotism and a common cause, through a sanguinary struggle to a glorious independence; the sacred Union, hitherto inviolate, which, perfected by our happy Constitution, has brought us, by the favor of Heaven, to a state of prosperity at home and high consideration abroad rarely, if ever, equaled in the history of nations:

To perserve this bond of our political existence from destruction, to maintain inviolate this state of national honor and prosperity, and to justify the confidence my fellow-citizens have reposed in me, I, Andrew Jackson, President of the United States, have thought proper to issue this my proclamation, stating my views of the Constitution and laws applicable to the measures adopted by the convention of South Carolina and to the reasons they have put forth to sustain them, declaring the course which duty will require me to pursue, and, appealing to the understanding and patriotism of the people, warn them of the consequences that must inevitably result from an observance of the dictates of the convention.

Strict duty would require of me nothing more than the exercise of those powers with which I am now or may hereafter be invested for preserving the peace of the Union and for the execution of the laws; but the imposing aspect which opposition has assumed in this case, by clothing itself with State authority, and the deep interest which the people of the United States must all feel in preventing a resort to stronger measures while there is a hope that anything will be yielded to reasoning and remonstrance, perhaps demand, and will certainly justify, a full exposition to South Carolina and the nation of the views I entertain of this important question, as well as a distinct enunciation of the course which my sense of duty will require me to purpose.

The ordinance is founded, not on the indefeasible right of resisting acts which are plainly unconstitutional and too oppressive to be endured, but on the strange position that any one State may not only declare an act of Congress void, but prohibit its execution; that they may do this consistently with the Constitution; that the true construction of that instrument permits a State to retain its place in the Union and yet be bound by no other of its laws than those it may choose to consider as constitutional. It is true, they add, that to justify this abrogation of a law it must be palpably contrary to the Constitution; but it is evident that to give the right of resisting laws of that description, coupled with the uncontrolled right to decide what laws deserve that character, is to give the power of resisting all laws; for as by the theory there is no appeal, the reasons alleged by the State, good or bad, must prevail. If it should be said that public opinion is a sufficient check against the abuse of this power, it may be asked why it is not deemed a sufficient guard against the passage of an unconstitutional act by Congress? There is, however, a restraint in this last case which makes the assumed power of a State more indefensible, and which does not exist in the other. There are two appeals from an unconstitutional act passed by Congress—one to the judiciary, the other to the people and the States. There is no appeal from the State decision in theory, and the practical illustration shows that the courts are closed against an application to review it, both judges and jurors being sworn to decide in its favor. But reasoning on this subject is superfluous when our social compact, in express terms, declares that the laws of the United States, its Constitution,

and treaties made under it are the supreme law of the land, and, for greater caution, adds ''that the judges in every State shall be bound thereby, anything in the constitution or laws of any State to the contrary notwithstanding.'' And it may be asserted without fear of refutation that no federative government could exist without a similar provision. Look for a moment to the consequence. If South Carolina considers the revenue laws unconstitutional and has a right to prevent their execution in the port of Charleston, there would be a clear constitutional objection to their collection in every other port; and no revenue could be collected anywhere, for all imposts must be equal. It is no answer to repeat that an unconstitutional law is no law so long as the question of its legality is to be decided by the State itself, for every law operating injuriously upon any local interest will be perhaps thought, and certainly represented, as unconstitutional, and, as has been shown, there is no appeal.

If this doctrine had been established at an earlier day, the Union would have been dissolved in its infancy. The excise law in Pennsylvania, the embargo and nonintercourse law in the Eastern States, the carriage tax in Virginia, were all deemed unconstitutional, and were more unequal in their operation than any of the laws now complained of; but, fortunately, none of those States discovered that they had the right now claimed by South Carolina. The war into which we were forced to support the dignity of the nation and the rights of our citizens might have ended in defeat and disgrace, instead of victory and honor, if the States who supposed it a ruinous and unconstitutional measure had thought they possessed the right of nullifying the act by which it was declared and denying supplies for its prosecution. Hardly and unequally as those measures bore upon several members of the Union, to the legislatures of none did this efficient and peaceable remedy, as it is called, suggest itself. The discovery of this important feature in our Constitution was reserved to the present day. To the statesmen of South Carolina belongs the invention, and upon the citizens of that State will unfortunately fall the evils of reducing it to practice.

If the doctrine of a State veto upon the laws of the Union carries with it internal evidence of its impracticable absurdity, our constitutional history will also afford abundant proof that it would have been repudiated with indignation had it been proposed to form a feature in our Government.

DOCUMENT 8.6
There Can Be No Equality

There were dissenters. Champions of the "laboring masses" challenged the prevailing consensus. Middle and upper class nay-sayers were more rare. James Fenimore Cooper, always sensitive to the deficiencies of what he feared was a dehumanizing new order, found varied traces of inequality in the United States. As this passage indicates, Cooper believed that inequalities were not only inevitable but, in some cases, desirable.

ON AMERICAN EQUALITY

The equality of the United States is no more absolute than that of any other country. There may be less inequality in this nation than in most others, but inequality exists, and, in some respects, with stronger features than it is usual to meet with in the rest of christendom.

The rights of property being an indispensable condition of civilization, and its quiet possession every where guarantied, equality of condition is rendered impossible. One man must labor, while another may live luxuriously on his means; one has leisure and opportunity to cultivate his tastes, to increase his information, and to refine his habits, while another is compelled to toil, that he may live. One is reduced to serve, while another commands, and, of course, there can be no equality in their social conditions.

The justice and relative advantage of these differencies, as well as their several duties, will be elsewhere considered.

By the inequality of civil and political rights that exists in certain parts of the Union, and the great equality that exists in others, we see the necessity of referring the true character of the institutions to those of the states, without a just understanding of which, it is impossible to obtain any general and accurate ideas of the real polity of the country.

The same general exceptions to civil and political equality, that are found in other free countries, exist in this, though under laws peculiar to ourselves. Women and minors are excluded from the suffrage, and from maintaining suits at law, under the usual provisions, here as well as elsewhere. None but natives of the country can fill many of the higher offices, and paupers, felons and all those who have not fixed residences, are also excluded from the suffrage. In a few of the states property is made the test of political rights, and, in nearly half of them, a large portion of the inhabitants, who are of a different race from the original European occupants of the soil, are entirely excluded from all political, and from many of the civil rights, that are enjoyed by those who are deemed citizens. A slave can neither choose, nor be chosen to office, nor, in most of the states, can even a free man, unless a white man. A slave can neither sue nor be sued; he can not hold property, real or personal, nor can he, in many of the states be a witness in any suit, civil or criminal.

It follows from these facts, that absolute equality of condition, of political rights, or of civil rights, does not exist in the United States, though they all exist in a much greater

Source: James Fenimore Cooper, *The American Democrat,* pp. 39-43.

degree in some states than in others, and in some of the states, perhaps, to as great a degree as is practicable. In what are usually called the free states of America, or those in which domestic slavery is abolished, there is to be found as much equality in every respect as comports with safety, civilization and the rights of property. This is also true, as respects the white population, in those states in which domestic slavery does exist; though the number of the bond is in a large proportion to that of the free.

As the tendency of the institutions of America is to the right, we learn in these truths, the power of facts, every question of politics being strictly a question of practice. They who fancy it possible to frame the institutions of a country, on the pure principles of abstract justice, as these principles exist in theories know little of human nature, or of the restraints that are necessary to society. Abuses assail us in a thousand forms, and it is hopeless to aspire to any condition of humanity, approaching perfection. The very necessity of a government at all, arises from the impossibility of controlling the passions by any other means than that of force.

The celebrated proposition contained in the declaration of independence is not to be understood literally. All men are not "created equal," in a physical, or even in a moral sense, unless we limit the signification to one of political rights. This much is true, since human institutions are a human invention, with which nature has had no connection. Men are not born equals, physically, since one has a good constitution, another a bad; one is handsome, another ugly; one white, another black. Neither are men born equals morally, one possessing genius, or a natural aptitude, while his brother is an idiot. As regards all human institutions men are born equal, no sophistry being able to prove that nature intended one should inherit power and wealth, another slavery and want. Still artificial inequalities are the inevitable

consequences of artificial ordinances, and in founding a new governing principle for the social compact, the American legislators instituted new modes of difference.

The very existence of government at all, infers inequality. The citizen who is preferred to office becomes the superior of those who are not, so long as he is the repository of power, and the child inherits the wealth of the parent as a controlling law of society. All that the great American proposition, therefore, can mean, is to set up new and juster notions of natural rights than those which existed previously, by asserting, in substance, that God has not instituted political inequalities, as was pretended by the advocates of the Jus Divinum, and that men possessed a full and natural authority to form such social institutions as best suited their necessities.

There are numerous instances in which the social inequality of America may do violence to our notions of abstract justice, but the compromise of interests under which all civilized society must exist, renders this unavoidable. Great principles seldom escape working injustice in particular things, and this so much the more, in establishing the relations of a community, for in them many great, and frequently conflicting principles enter, to maintain the more essential features of which sacrifices of parts become necessary. If we would have civilization and the exertion indispensable to its success, we must have property; if we have property, we must have its rights; if we have the rights of property, we must take those consequences of the rights of property which are inseparable from the rights themselves.

The equality of rights in America, therefore, after allowing for the striking exception of domestic slavery, is only a greater extension of the principle than common, while there is no such thing as an equality of condition. All that can be said of the first, is that it has been carried as far as a prudent discretion will at all allow, and of the last, that the inequality is the simple result of civilization, unaided by any of those factitious plans that have been elsewhere devised in order to augment the power of the strong, and to enfeeble the weak.

Equality is no where laid down as a governing principle of the institutions of the United States, neither the word, nor any inference that can be fairly deduced from its meaning, occurring in the constitution. As respect the states, themselves, the professions of an equality of rights are more clear, and slavery excepted, the intention in all their governments is to main-

tain as far as practicable, though equality of condition is no where mentioned, all political economists knowing that it is unattainable, if, indeed, it be desirable. Desirable in practice, it can hardly be, since the result would be to force all down to the level of the lowest.

All that a good government aims at, therefore, is to add no unnecessary and artificial aid to the force of its own unavoidable consequences, and to abstain from fortifying and accumulating social inequality as a means of increasing political inequalities.

chapter 9

Antebellum Reform

Ronald G. Walters
Johns Hopkins University

"Nothing has more remarkably distinguished the Present Age," Ralph Waldo Emerson declared in 1840, "than the great harvest of projects it has yielded for the reform of domestic, social, civil, literary, and ecclesiastical institutions." He had in mind a thunderous wave of reform that swept across America between 1815 and the outbreak of the Civil War in 1861. It touched all regions, although it affected the North far more than the South, and it encompassed a wonderful profusion of causes—each designed to make the world and its people better, perhaps even perfect. Some of these crusades seem noble by modern standards, such as the antislavery and the women's rights movements; others seem naive, silly, or scarcely reforms at all, such as phrenology, the belief that analyzing the shape of an individual's head could lead to personal improvement.

Taken together, however, Emerson's "great harvest of projects" comprise what historians call "antebellum reform," and they raise important questions about social and political change in the United States. How, for example, did antebellum reformers differ from earlier reformers? What effect did their causes and crusades have on American life? Is reform a necessary part of democracy—a kind of stabilizing mechanism that enables the system to

adjust to changing conditions—or is it a disruptive phenomenon, the product of malcontented troublemakers? What causes periods of intense reform activity like the antebellum decades or, in our own century, the 1960s? Does reform serve the interests of some classes or groups at the expense of others or does it serve the broad public interest? What tactics are available to reformers in a democratic society? Many of these questions are of as much significance in the twentieth century as they were in the nineteenth century, but each owes much of its importance to the actions of the men and women whose energies defined antebellum reform.

There had been reformers in America before there was antebellum reform, although neither in such large numbers nor of the same type. In the eighteenth century a few Quakers, like John Woolman, campaigned long and courageously against slavery. Civic-minded individuals like Benjamin Franklin engaged in projects to improve their communities and citizens. Most early reformers, nonetheless, differed from their antebellum counterparts in striking ways. They were generally not part of organized mass movements, as antebellum reformers were. Few of them, moreover, made reform their primary occupation. Like Franklin, they did their good deeds while working at other trades. By contrast, some antebellum reformers supported themselves for years as advocates of unpopular causes, through income as editors of reformist newspapers, and as professional lecturers. For such men and women, reform was a career.

Antebellum reformers also differed from their predecessors in their approach. Eighteenth-century reformers tended to be moderate and conciliatory—often seeking to ameliorate a problem rather than eradicate it. They thought the world could be made into a better place— but not an ideal one and not transformed all at once. Many antebellum reformers saw things differently. They frequently pursued an ''ultraist'' course that struck critics as the most unreasonable sort of extremism. To them, moderation implied the unthinkable: tolerating sin and conciliating wrongdoers. In their eyes, slavery, drinking, and other evils had to be ended immediately and absolutely—not gradually and conditionally, as their eighteenth-century counterparts had believed. They did not merely want to improve things, as Franklin had, but to make them right, without compromise or delay.

The ''ultraist'' mentality was one of the legacies of religion influencing antebellum reform. It largely derived from evangelical Protestantism of a style associated with Charles G. Finney, whose great revivals swept from western New York toward the Atlantic seaboard in the 1820s. Although far from the first or only antebellum evangelist, he had the greatest influence on reformers of the 1830s and 1840s.

Finney's followers gave new life to two old—and sometimes heretical—beliefs in Christian thought, millennialism and perfectionism. Millennialism comes in many varieties, but the type prevalent among antebellum reformers maintained that a reign of God's law—a time of justice, peace, and plenty— would come on earth before the final judgement.

Perfectionism similarly takes many forms in religious thought, including ones leading to quite unreligious behavior. In antebellum reform, nonetheless, it was seldom more formal than an assumption that human beings could become perfect, meaning free from sin, on earth.

Finney's religion was aggressive in that it enjoined men and women to show that they had been saved (and perhaps even to bring salvation about) by doing good deeds. In describing genuine Christians, Finney said ''To the universal reformation of the world they stand committed.'' Combined with millennialism and perfectionism, this call to action gave life to a powerful vision of human possibility: it promised nothing less than heaven on earth and lay behind the impatience of antebellum reformers with partial solutions and gradual approaches.

Millennialism and perfectionism were not the only legacies of religion to antebellum reform. Some of the earliest nineteenth-century crusades were mounted by the churches to spread religion and morality, either by combating particular sins, such as swearing and dueling, or—more ambitiously—by sending Bibles, tracts, and missionaries to convert the heathen, many located in the western territories. The latter included Indians, of course, but also, and perhaps more disturbing for the fate of the nation, a distressingly large number of unchurched or heretical whites.

By 1830, the largest missionary organizations, including the American Tract Society and the American Bible Society, were major components of a ''benevolent empire'' of formidable proportions. Although the relationship was sometimes a tense one, these organizations contributed mightily to antebellum reform. Some of the connections were direct, through individuals like wealthy New York merchants Arthur and Lewis Tappan, who gave money and time to reforms within and without the benevolent empire. Occasionally, a religious organization like the American Tract Society would even use its resources to distribute temperance or antislavery literature.

The most important contribution of the benevolent empire may have been the model it provided for reforms that followed. It demonstrated that deeply committed individuals could create an effective propaganda machine, built upon central leadership, local auxiliaries, and use of new technologies. The latter cut the cost of printing and through canals, turnpikes, and (later) railroads, it improved transportation to the point where ideas and lecturers could cover the land. The same techniques that brought Bibles to infidels carried antebellum reform to the countryside and small towns of nineteenth-century America.

It would be a mistake to think of antebellum reform as simply an outgrowth of evangelical Protestantism and the benevolent empire. Even in the realm of ideas, there were other secular traditions from which reformers drew, particularly the political ideas of the American Revolution. When, for example, a small group of early feminists met at Seneca Falls, New York, in 1848 to press for women's rights, the declaration they produced was modeled after the Declaration of Independence, with the tyrant changed from George III to "man." Science—as understood in the nineteenth century—also provided fuel for reformers. When they claimed that Americans could be improved by proper diet, or by following certain other rules of good health, or that insanity could be cured in a well-run asylum, they phrased arguments in terms of "natural" laws of biology.

In reality, of course, few antebellum reformers saw contradictions between God's law, the ideology of the American Revolution, and the laws of nature—each merged into a powerful rationale for bringing about perfect humans and a perfect society. The essential point, however, is that important as religious revivalism and Protestant organizations were in inspiring antebellum reform, there were other traditions that also shaped it and other causes that produced it.

At first glance, it is the variety, not the uniformity, of antebellum reform that is most impressive.

At one extreme were the communitarians, small groups of men and women who gathered together to create approximately a hundred little utopian communities between the Revolution and the Civil War, each designed as a model of correct principles and proper social organization. Religious communitarian societies dated back to the eighteenth century and continued to appear throughout the antebellum period. Although many communities were the work of German immigrants, one such group, the Shakers, was the creation of an Englishwoman, Mother Ann Lee, and it especially fascinated nineteenth-century reformers because of its successful organization and odd customs, which included celibacy and the strange dancing ritual that gave the group its name.

More distinctive to the antebellum period, however, was the appearance of communitarian societies of largely secular origin—not religious retreats from the world but blueprints for the rest of humankind to follow. Among the most famous of these was Brook Farm, located outside Boston, begun in 1841 and devastated by a fire in 1846. The product of New England literary and intellectual ferment, it represented an earnest effort to combine the life of the mind with honest toil close to nature. Although many participants regarded it, in retrospect, as a charming interlude when they and their ideals were young, it inspired one famous alumnus, Nathaniel Hawthorne, to write a fictionalized account of it, *The Blithedale Romance,* as an attack on the egotism of reformers.

In spite of Brook Farm's fame, it had less influence on antebellum communitarians than the ideas of two European visionaries, Robert Owen, a British factory owner and philanthropist, and Charles Fourier, a French utopian who found a greater audience in America than in his native land. The views of the two men differed in many respects, but each proclaimed that a new social order could be built on rational principles and embodied in small communities held together by common interests and, in the case of Fourier, by joint ownership of property.

Owen arrived in America in 1824 predicting that the northern states would be converted to his ideas by 1827. His great experiment was New Harmony, Indiana, which he purchased from a German religious community at the beginning of 1825. Its rise and fall were spectacular, costly, and the result of Owen's inconsistent leadership, which extended to vagueness about the property relationships that might prevail in his ideal society.

Owen's failure, nearly total by 1827, did not destroy communitarianism. By 1840, it had new prophets, among them a former clergyman, John Humphrey Noyes, who blended religious and secular ideas in his upstate New York Oneida community, best known for unorthodox sexual practices. No communitarian thinker, however, had greater influence than Charles Fourier, whose strange ideas were domesticated by a tireless and persuasive American disciple, Albert Brisbane. Fourier, as Brisbane interpreted him, provided an intricate plan for small communities of men and women to take advantage of particular personal characteristics and create a harmonious social unit. Fourier inspired several communities—even Brook Farm adopted some of his ideas in its final phase—including a moderately successful one in Red Bank, New Jersey.

In the end, the utopias died, sometimes because of tragedies, such as fires at Brook Farm and Red Bank, but more often because of internal dissension, lack of funds and commitment, and unrealistic expectations about the power of communities to transform individuals and the world. They stood as ruined monuments on the landscape of antebellum reform, memorials to the belief that social relationships could be changed—perfected—totally and instantly.

Less sweeping in scope than communitarianism, but of far more interest to twentieth-century historians, was the antislavery movement, treated in greater detail elsewhere in this book. Beginning in 1831, the crusade against slavery took new form with the doctrine of "immediate emancipation," proclaimed with vehemence and intransigence that year by William Lloyd Garrison's Boston newspaper, the *Liberator*. Repudiating gradual approaches to slavery, including ones that would have colonized free blacks outside the United States, immediate emancipationists exemplified the ultraist spirit of antebellum reform and its eagerness to confront sin rather than negotiate with sinners.

Antislavery likewise exemplified other aspects of antebellum reform, including institutional instability. For a time in the 1830s, abolitionists combined forces to put together a formidable propaganda campaign in defiance of public hostility—including mob violence. But, by 1840, as Bertram Wyatt-Brown observed, the movement's organizational structure was in shambles, thanks to conflicts over issues such as the proper role of women in the movement and whether or not to engage in political action. Regarding the latter, many Abolitionists believed the only appropriate tactics were those of "moral suasion"—converting the hearts and minds of individuals. By 1840, some of their colleagues had rethought the issue and arrived at the conclusion that political action was appropriate after all. Their handiwork was the Liberty Party.

The real influence of abolitionists and other antebellum reformers, however, usually came less from traditional politics than from stirring controversy where apathy once prevailed and from creating powerful symbols and phrases (like the idea of a "slave power conspiracy," which Wyatt-Brown discusses,) that passed into the political language of the day.

Whatever its influence on politics, antislavery had a close relationship to two other significant reforms. The least well-known of these was the peace movement, which predated Garrison's call for immediate emancipation and followed the common path toward ultraism, in this case evolving from opposition to offensive wars to opposition to all wars, even defensive ones, and finally to complete repudiation of all kinds of force. The latter position, called nonresistance, was embodied in the American Peace Society, founded in 1828. Although never dominating mainstream pacifism, nonresistance did, however, take hold among some New England abolitionists, including Garrison, and it informed their opposition to slavery, which they saw as the supreme example of the wickedness of force. That view, and the association between abolition and pacifism, suffered severe strain with the Civil War, a tragedy of immoral means—violence—used for a moral end, the eradication of slavery. When the cruel choice came with the outbreak of war in 1861, it was the principle of peace that most commonly gave way.

Antislavery's linkage to the women's rights movement was even closer than to pacifism and less challenged by later events. Women were heavily involved in the crusade against slavery from the beginning, and disputes over their activities as speakers and leaders rocked the movement in the 1830s. In addition to provoking controversy, their participation led to unanticipated conclusions. The resistance they met from men forced them to consider the restraints society put upon them. The powerlessness of blacks, they came to realize, mirrored the powerlessness of women—they even shared a common oppressor in the white male. "The investigation of the rights of the slave," Angelina Grimke wrote, "has led me to a better understanding of my own." For some, that understanding led to Seneca Falls in 1848 and eventually into an organized campaign for greater legal, economic, and political rights for women.

In the antebellum years, nonetheless, women's rights was more a movement in the making (and one closely associated with antislavery) than the full-fledged crusade it became after 1865, when it focused upon the more limited objective of securing the vote for women.

Far greater in numbers than the women's rights movement was the temperance crusade, the largest of all antebellum reforms. The campaign against alcohol had its roots both in the formidable drinking habits of American men and in a combination of medical and religious objections to alcohol. A great evangelist, Lyman Beecher, served as a catalyst for previously scattered and sporadic efforts to eliminate drunkenness when he preached six horrifying sermons on the subject in 1825. Partly in answer to his call, a national organization, the American Society for the Promotion of Temperance, appeared the following year. It was the pioneer—but far from the last—of its kind.

In common with virtually every other antebellum reform of any size, the temperance movement was riddled with feuds and differences over ideology and tactics. The most moderate position—repudiated by Beecher—maintained that limited use of alcohol was acceptable, particularly use of wine or beer. By the late 1820s, it had been eclipsed by the extreme position that any use of alcohol, even communion wine, was evil.

Temperance took several particularly significant turns in the antebellum period. In its original form, it made little effort to proselytize drunkards and found its firmest home among the middle classes. That began to change in 1840, when hard-drinking patrons of a Baltimore tavern went to a temperance lecture as a jest and ended up converted. Their creation was the Washington Temperance Society, which quickly mushroomed into a major organization reaching out to drinkers and beyond the respectable middle classes.

While the Washingtonians brought new life (and new constituencies) to the campaign against alcohol, others took it in another direction—into politics. Many temperance advocates shared the misgivings of abolitionists and other reformers about politics. They felt that partisan political activity was in the hands of immoral men (like the ex-duelist Andrew Jackson) and that it subordinated principles to success at the polls. In addition to disliking how the political system operated, such reformers further thought that it was wrong, under any circumstances, to compel men and women to behave properly through use of governmental power. True morality, they believed, depended on the hearts of individuals—not on coercive legislation.

As early as the 1830s, however, some temperance advocates turned to legislation to achieve their aims, winning restrictions on the sale of alcohol in Massachusetts in 1838. Their most impressive victory occurred in Maine in 1851, with a law entirely prohibiting the sale and consumption of alcohol within the state. The so-called "Maine Law" served as a model for successful and nearly successful campaigns in other states, including the unlikely case of gold-rush California, where the margin of defeat was less than might have been expected. By the end of the Civil War, most Maine Laws were gone, victims of court challenges, political counterattacks, and poor enforcement. What antebellum temperance legislation demonstrated was not so much the success of political action—prohibition's grandest victories and greatest defeat lay ahead in the twentieth century—as the willingness of some reformers to move beyond moral suasion to active coercion.

Coercion, in fact, lay at the heart of another major cluster of reform activity, efforts to persuade normally parsimonious state legislatures to build costly institutions to reform and uplift youthful and errant citizens. These institutions ranged from public school systems, including such innovations as high schools and compulsory attendance, to insane asylums and prisons. By 1831, American penitentiaries were such wonders that they attracted European visitors,

including Alexis de Tocqueville, better known as a student of American democracy than of American incarceration.

Although quite different in most respects, schools, asylums, and prisons had a common rationale. In the rhetoric of the reformers who promoted them, they were instruments to instill proper virtues in individuals. Behind that notion lay an image of the model citizen—punctual, disciplined, self-controlled, and committed to all the Protestant pieties. Twentieth-century critics of antebellum reform charge that this represented an attempt at social control through imposition of middle-class values upon the working classes and the poor. The goal—so the argument runs—was to turn them into docile workers and orderly citizens in a system that did not especially serve their interests.

Certainly some—but definitely not all—working class men and women (particularly Catholics) had their suspicions about the efforts of reformers, largely because of their heavily Protestant bias. Yet, it is a mistake to see institution-building as nothing more than a middle-class Protestant plot to create a docile working class. For instance, the values of reformers and the working classes were not always diametrically opposed. Education, for example, was high on the list of demands of many working-class organizations (although compulsory school attendance did cut into family income by withdrawing children from the labor force). Also, reformers genuinely believed that their endeavors, whether reflected in school systems, model prisons, or better insane asylums, would benefit everyone. They thought that, within the proper environment, the recalcitrant school child could be turned into a perfect citizen, the insane could be healed, and the hardened criminal could be brought to repentance. These millennialistic expectations inevitably ran afoul of grim realities and many of the institutions (perhaps including schools) became more custodial than reforming; but the vision of the men and women who created them was far nobler than the end result.

The efforts of institution-builders—however they may have turned out—represented a different approach from most antebellum reformers; it forecast the direction of American reform at the end of the nineteenth century. Like later reformers, they assumed that public institutions and government agencies, including coercive ones, were proper instruments of social betterment. This was in conflict with the view of some of their contemporary reformers (most notably the nonresistants, who repudiated coercion for any purpose), but it was a course of action that would become integral to twentieth-century reform.

If institution-builders lay somewhat outside the mainstream of antebellum reform in their choice of tactics, another group, labor reformers, lay equally far outside it by virtue of their social origins. Most participants in the other major movements of the day—antislavery, temperance in its non-Washingtonian aspects, women's rights, communitarianism, and the rest—came from the middle levels of society, with a sprinkling of support from a few wealthy but pious individuals and from artisans. Labor agitation in the antebellum period, by contrast, attracted a few middle-class reformers (Robert Owen's son among them), but rested firmly on the discontents and aspirations of artisans. Although the term is still in use, nineteenth-century artisans have no exact counterpart in twentieth-century America. They were an extremely important element, both in numbers and sometimes in political terms, in antebellum cities. They worked in small shops or small groups and had their own hierarchy—stretching from the apprentice through the journeyman (who had learned the trade and possessed his own tools), to the master artisan who employed them. They were skilled workers who—in some trades such as shoemaking—were squeezed by new modes of production that reduced them

to factory hands and by the demands of their employers for greater productivity.

One important exception to the rule that artisans were at the heart of labor agitation were protests mounted by women factory workers in New England mills, most notably at the large ones in Lowell, Massachusetts, in the 1830s and 1840s. Drawing upon their heritage as descendants of sturdy New England stock, they conducted strikes in 1834 and 1836—wrapping around them the mantle of the American revolution and recalling the "spirit of our Patriotic Ancestors, who preferred privation to bondage." In the next decade, their tactics broadened to include political agitation and joint efforts with other New England workers—including men.

More characteristic of antebellum labor agitation were strikes and protests by artisans in major American cities throughout the antebellum period—most often coordinated by various kinds of workingmen's associations. The grievances were many, although mostly due to the transfer of work from small shops to factories. Like the Lowell mill women, male artisans used religious language less frequently than the rhetoric of the American Revolution—in their case, to defend a dying world of small producers in which camaraderie, respect for labor, personal relations between employer and employee, and political participation prevailed. With the notable exception of the few genuine radicals among them, their goals were more limited than those of middle-class utopians and reformers like Garrison, who envisioned a millennium. They sought fair wages, education for their children, adequate leisure time, and freedom from laws that favored their employers over them.

For a brief moment in the late 1820s, artisans put together their own workingmen's political parties—the closest America has come to having a Labor Party. With their failure, workers reattached themselves to the major parties, thereby attaching themselves to a political system that did not always represent their interests. In contrast to some middle-class reformers, who mistrusted the political system for its moral failings, artisans may have had greater faith in its beneficence than results warranted. However that may be, labor agitation stands as a reminder that there was a deep layer of economic and social discontent barely touched by such largely middle-class reforms as temperance and antislavery, whose leaders mostly ignored or deprecated the grievances of artisans and factory workers.

Any brief catalogue of antebellum causes and crusades fails to do justice to its variety, and slights such interesting characters as Sylvester Graham, a former clergyman who sparked a health reform movement through advocacy of a vegetarian diet as a cure for moral and physical ailments. Even so, it is probably easier to describe antebellum reform than to explain its causes. To some extent reformers were responding to real problems: slavery, alcoholism, oppression of women, ignorance, crime, and insanity all existed. Yet, none of these issues was new in the antebellum period. Something suddenly spurred men and women to perceive them as problems with available solutions.

Part of the answer lies in the realm of ideas. Revivalism, the American Revolution, and secular modes of thought like those of Owen and Fourier provided ideologies for social change: each gave a standard for judging what ought to be and a hope that human effort could achieve it. The notion of human perfectability was deeply ingrained in the thought of the day, consistent with what Americans saw as the mission of their nation, and seemingly borne out by the rapid pace of change in the first half of the nineteenth century.

The ideas upon which reform rested would have been meaningless without techniques for reaching mass audiences. Innovations in organizational structure, growing out of the benev-

olent empire, and better, cheaper means of communications provided the necessary mechanisms. In addition, reformers were resourceful at staging public festivals and at using such instruments of popular culture as the melodrama for their purposes. (Staged versions of literary classics like *Uncle Tom's Cabin* and the temperance novel *Ten Nights in a Bar-Room* presumably left audiences in tears and converted).

Ultimately, antebellum reform depended on reformers—men and women who had the time, resources, and world view to engage in movements to change their society. Most of them came from what we now consider the middle classes; all were deeply concerned about the transformation of American society, were involved in it, and were convinced that its evils could be rectified and its potential fulfilled.

Most reformers usually looked to voluntary efforts by people like themselves, not to the political system, for leadership. This was an approach that rested in part on discomfort with the results of democracy in America. Moreover, many aimed for a definition of themselves and their place in society. This was particularly apparent in the case of middle-class women, who formed a considerable part of every antebellum reform. Cultural stereotypes told them that they were naturally more moral and sympathetic to the downtrodden than were men. Yet, social practice denied them political power and defined the home as the primary arena within which they were to exercise their moral authority. Involvement in reform meant a public role—generally an acceptable one because it did not directly involve participation in the political process—and permitted a coded criticism of the world men had built. Most of the sins attacked by antebellum reformers were, after all, traditionally masculine ones such as slaveholding, war, and drunkenness. For many middle-class women, reform gave both an identity and a forum for a variety of grievances.

Reform served other purposes for reformers

including men. It brought them together in little communities of like-minded individuals—often knit by strong bonds of commitment and affection. If American democracy isolated humans, as observers such as Alexis de Tocqueville claimed, reforming and perfecting it brought them together in common cause.

Above all, reform was a response to the extraordinary economic and demographic transformation of America prior to the Civil War. A person born in 1800 and still alive in 1861 would have seen the United States change from a weak nation, bounded by the Mississippi River on the west, to a mighty one, more than double in area, stretching from the Atlantic to the Pacific. He or she would have seen technological marvels: creation of canals, steamboats, railroads, the telegraph, and wondrous machinery. This mythical American would also have witnessed extraordinary population growth—the spectacle of a nation simultaneously peopling a frontier *and* creating great cities—as well as the introduction of large numbers of immigrants, a significant portion of them Catholic rather than members of the Protestant majority. Finally, this fictitious American would have seen the beginnings of industrialization—the transformation from a world of farms, small shops, and maritime commerce to a manufacturing capacity great enough to fight a frightful modern war. Reform, in these decades of growth, provided a means of understanding and perhaps guiding the extraordinary changes in American life. Many of the growing pains of this transformation filled reformers with dread and inspired particular crusades, such as those aimed at crime and alcoholism, but the faith and optimism of reformers also told them that the process of change was not out of control and might, in fact, mark the beginning of God's reign on earth.

Antebellum reform now seems naïve in its millennialism and perfectionism—that belief in a perfect new world—and yet it had considerable consequences, both for its own time and for the future. Some of these are obvious. Antebellum reformers, for instance, helped cut the rate of alcohol consumption (at least temporarily), shaped American education, and built the massive, gloomy asylums and penitentiaries that dotted the nineteenth-century landscape.

There were other, less apparent ways in which antebellum reform influenced events. In crusades as different as workingmen's movements and antislavery, reformers helped define and redefine the language of political debate. Workers did this by insisting that the equal rights rhetoric of the American Revolution was a weapon against the privileges of their employers, just as it had been a weapon against the British in 1776. Abolitionists did the same by painting a picture of Southern despotism that made more and more sense to nonabolitionists as they tried to comprehend the seemingly aggressive behavior of Southern leaders in the 1840s and 1850s. In these cases, reformers did not necessarily settle issues or even win great victories. Instead, they framed the way in which other Americans understood themselves and the events of the day. That was not always the most satisfying kind of power, since it did not inevitably bring victory, but it is an important power possessed by reformers and radicals from the antebellum period to the present.

Antebellum reform shaped the future in other ways as well. It began the shift from religious to secular justifications of reform when it focused on the body (as temperance and health reform did) or looked to institutions like schools and asylums rather than to the soul of the individual as the source of social change. In addition, antebellum movements marked emergence of reform as a social role—a career that could be pursued for a considerable portion of one's adult life. On this score, the activities of asylum-builders and educational reformers were particularly significant. Through the enduring networks they created, and the institutions they built, they helped initiate the process of professionalizing social services and of creating social service bureaucracies.

By lobbying state legislatures for schools and asylums, and by pressing for antialcohol legislation, antebellum reformers also brought reform squarely into the political process—contrary to the views of many other crusaders, who felt that their job was to change hearts and minds, not to jockey for votes.

Whatever their differences on political action—and they were considerable—antebellum reformers of all sorts have two major kinds of significance from the perspective of the twentieth century. The first is that they found many of the fault lines of their society, the points of slippage between values and behavior, and presented alternatives for public debate. In doing so, reformers—who are, by definition, exceptional people—help us see what was wrong and what was *possible* within their culture. The second kind of significance comes from the responsibility pre-Civil War reformers bear for making reform a part of the normal process by which America adjusts to changes and to social pressures. From their time to now, Americans would accept the notion that the democratic process can tolerate—and may require—groups of private citizens who care deeply about issues and argue about them loudly, persistently, and even abrasively. That may be the most valuable heritage of contentious men and women who believed, as few of us do now, that God's will and human effort could make America paradise on earth.

SUGGESTED READINGS

Bestor, Arthur E. *Backwoods Utopias: The Sectarian and Owenite Phases of Communitarian Socialism in America, 1663–1829*. Philadelphia: University of Pennsylvania Press, 1950.

Cross, Whitney. *The Burned-Over District: The Social and Intellectual History of Enthusiastic Reli-*

gion in Western New York, 1800–1850. Ithaca, N.Y.: Cornell University Press, 1950.

Kaestle, Carl F. *Pillars of the Republic: Common Schools and American Society, 1780–1860*. New York: Hill and Wang, 1983.

Kanter, Rosabeth Moss. *Commitment and Community: Communes and Utopias in Sociological Perspective*. Cambridge, Mass.: Harvard University Press, 1972.

Rothman, David J. *Discovery of the Asylum: Social Order and Disorder in the New Republic*. Boston: Little, Brown, 1972.

Tyler, Alice Felt. *Freedom's Ferment: Phases of American Social History to 1860*. Minneapolis: University of Minnesota Press, 1944.

Tyrell, Ian R. *Sobering Up: From Temperance to Prohibition in Antebellum America, 1800–1860*. Westport, Conn.: Greenwood Press, 1979.

Walters, Ronald G. *American Reformers: 1815–1860*. New York: Hill and Wang, 1978.

Wilentz, Sean. *Chants Democratic: New York City and the Rise of the American Working Class, 1788–1850*. New York: Oxford University Press, 1984.

DOCUMENT 9.1
One Cheer for Reform

Ralph Waldo Emerson, the great Transcendentalist, appreciated the moral fervor of New Englanders who engaged in reform, but he went to an even greater extreme, and expressed with greater sophistication, the view that change begins with the individual. For him, that implied sympathy for reform but detachment from reform movements.

These Reforms are our contemporaries; they are ourselves; our own light, and sight, and conscience; they only name the relation which

Source: Ralph Waldo Emerson, "Lecture on the Times," in *Nature, Addresses, and Lectures* (Boston: Houghton Mifflin, 1883), pp. 262–65.

subsists between us and the vicious institutions which they go to rectify. They are the simplest statements of man in these matters; the plain right and wrong. I cannot choose but allow and honor them. The impuse is good, and the theory; the practice is less beautiful. The Reformers affirm the inward life, but they do not trust it, but use outward and vulgar means. . . . The love which lifted men to the sight of . . . better ends was the true and best distinction of this time, the disposition to trust a principle more than a material force. I think *that* is the soul of reform; the conviction that not sensuality, not slavery, not war, not imprisonment, not even government, are needed,—but in lieu of them all, reliance on the sentiment of man, which will work best the more it is trusted; not reliance on numbers, but, contrariwise, distrust of numbers and the feeling that then are we strongest when most private and alone. . . .

The Reforms have their high origin in an ideal justice, but they do not retain the purity of an idea. They are quickly organized in some low, inadequate form, and present no more poetic image to the mind than the evil tradition which they reprobated. They mix the fire of the moral sentiment with personal and party heats, with measureless exaggerations, and the blindness that prefers some darling measure to justice and truth. Those who are urging with most ardor what are called the greatest benefits of mankind, are narrow, self-pleasing, conceited men, and affect us as the insane do. They bite us, and we run mad also. . . . Whilst therefore I desire to express the respect and joy I feel before this sublime connection of reforms now in their infancy around us, I urge the more earnestly the paramount duties of self-reliance. I cannot find language of sufficient energy to convey my sense of the sacredness of private integrity. All men, all things, the state, the church, yea the friends of the heart are phantasms and unreal beside the sanctuary of the heart. . . .

DOCUMENT 9.2
Reform in a Democratic Society: A Reformer's View

Although best known as an abolitionist orator, Wendell Phillips' career as an agitator spanned a variety of causes and endured past the Civil War. Well-born and well-educated, he was— in spite of the flamboyance of his rhetoric—a thoughtful and perceptive observer of history and politics. In his view, reformers like himself were a crucial part of American democracy.

In working . . . great changes, in such an age as ours, the so-called statesman has far less influence than the many little men who, at various points, are silently maturing a regeneration of public opinion. This is a reading and thinking age, and great interests at stake quicken the general intellect. . . . Thanks to the Printing-Press, the people now do their own thinking, and statesmen, as they are styled,— men in office,—have ceased to be either the leaders or the clogs of society.

. . . . A newspaper paragraph, a county meeting, a gathering for conversation, a change in the character of a dozen individuals,—these are the several fountains and sources of public opinion. And, friends, when we gather, month after month, at such meetings as these [an antislavery convention], we should encourage ourselves with considerations of this kind:—that we live in an age of democratic equality; that, for a moment, a party may stand against the age, but in the end it goes by the board; that the man who launches a sound argument, who sets on two feet a startling fact, and bids it travel from Maine to Georgia, is just as certain that in the end he will change the government, as if, to destroy the Capitol, he had placed gunpowder under the Senate-chamber. . . .

Source: Wendell Phillips, "Public Opinion," in *Speeches, Lectures, and Letters* (Boston, 1902), pp. 37–38, 44–45, 48.

. . . .The moment we have the control of public opinion,—the women and the children, the school-houses, the school-books, the literature, and the newspapers,—that moment we have settled the question. . . .

DOCUMENT 9.3
Reform in a Democratic Society: A Foreign View

Alexis de Tocqueville, a young French aristocrat, visited the United States in 1831 with his friend, Gustave de Beaumont, ostensibly to report on American prisons but with a deeper interest in observing the workings of democracy. Like Phillips (who admired his work), he regarded private efforts as vitally important in the United States. He, however, saw reform organizations as one of many types of voluntary association by which Americans overcame the ill-effects of democratic individualism.

. . . . Americans of all ages, all conditions, and all dispositions constantly form associations. They have not only commercial and manufacturing companies, in which all take part, but associations of a thousand other kinds—religious, moral, serious, futile, extensive or restricted, enormous or diminutive. The Americans make associations to give entertainments, to found establishments for education, to build inns, to construct churches, to diffuse books, to send missionaries to the antipodes; and in this manner they found hospitals, prisons, and schools. If it be proposed to advance some truth, or to foster some feeling by the encouragement of a great example, they form a society. Wherever, at the head of some new undertaking, you see the government in France, or

a man of rank in England, in the United States you will be sure to find an association. . . .

Among democratic nations . . . all citizens are independent and feeble; they can do hardly anything by themselves, and none of them can oblige his fellow-men to lend him their assistance. They all, therefore fall into a state [of] incapacity, if they do not learn voluntarily to help each other. . . .

Feelings and opinions are recruited, the heart is enlarged, and the human mind is developed by no other means than by the reciprocal influence of men upon each other. I have shown that these influences are almost null in democratic countries; they must therefore be artificially created, and this can only be accomplished by associations. . . .

As soon as several of the inhabitants of the United States have taken up an opinion or a feeling which they wish to promote in the world, they look out for mutual assistance; and as soon as they have found each other out, they combine. From that moment they are no longer isolated men, but a power seen from afar, whose actions serve for an example, and whose language is listened to. . . .

Among the laws which rule human societies there is one which seems to be more precise and clear than all others. If men are to remain civilized, or to become so, the art of associating together must grow and improve, in the same ratio in which the equality of conditions is increased.

Source: Alexis de Tocqueville, *Democracy in America*, trans. Henry Reeve (New York: J. & H. G. Langley, 1843), vol. 2, pp. 114–18.

DOCUMENT 9.4
A Participant Assesses the Importance of Communitarianism

Notorious for the unorthodox sexual practices of his Oneida Community, John Humphrey

Source: John Humphrey Noyes, *History of American Socialisms* (Philadelphia, 1870), pp. 23–24, 26, 27.

Noyes was a careful student and somewhat a theoretician of communitarianism. A former minister, he was especially concerned to show the relationship between "socialisms"—by which he meant secular utopianism like Robert Owen and Charles Fourier—and revivalism like Charles G. Finney produced.

We must not think of the two great socialistic revivals [the Owenite and Fourierist] as altogether heterogeneous and separate. Their partizans maintained theoretical opposition to each other; but after all the main idea of both was *the enlargement of the home—the extension of family union beyond the little man-and-wife circle to large corporations.* In this idea the two movements were one; and this was the charming idea that caught the attention and stirred the enthusiasm of the American people. The two movements may, therefore, be regarded as one. . . .

As a man who has passed through a series of passional excitements, is never the same being afterward, so we insist that these socialistic paroxysms have changed the heart of the nation; and that a yearning toward social reconstruction has become a part of the continuous, permanent, inner experience of the American people. . . .

And these movements—Revivalism and Socialism—opposed to each other as they may seem, and as they have been in the creeds of their partizans, are closely related to their essential nature and objects, and manifestly belong together in the scheme of Providence, as they do in the history of this nation. They are to each other as inner to outer—soul to body— as life to its surroundings. The Revivalists had for their great idea the regeneration of the soul. The great idea of the Socialists was the regeneration of society, which is the soul's environment. These ideas belong together, and are the complements of each other. Neither can be successfully embodied by men whose minds are not wide enough to accept them both. . . .

Doubtless, the Revivalists and Socialists despise each other, and perhaps both will despise us for imagining that they can be reconciled. But we will say what we believe; and that is, that they have both failed in their attempts to bring heaven on earth, *because* they despised each other, and would not put their two great ideas together. The Revivalists failed for want of regeneration of society, and the Socialists failed for want of regeneration of the heart.

DOCUMENT 9.5
A Participant Recalls a Strike at Lowell

As a young girl, Harriet Hanson worked in the mills at Lowell and participated in early labor protest there. Later, she married a reform-minded journalist, joined in the antislavery movement, and, after the Civil War, became a leader of American feminism. As an older woman, she looked back on her time as a mill worker and at the experiences of other women in the factory and in labor agitation.

One of the first strikes of cotton-factory operatives that ever took place in this country was in Lowell, in October, 1836. When it was announced that the wages were to be cut down, great indignation was felt, and it was decided to strike, *en masse*. This was done. The mills were shut down, and the girls went in procession from their several corporations to the "grove" in Chapel Hill, and listened to "incendiary" speeches from early labor reformers. . . .

My own recollection of this first strike (or "turn out" as it was called) is very vivid. I worked in a lower room, where I had heard the proposed strike fully, if not vehemently,

Source: Harriet Robinson, *Loom and Spindle, or Life among the Early Mill Girls* (Boston, 1898), pp. 83–85.

discussed: I had been an ardent listener to what was said against this attempt at "oppression" on the part of the corporation, and naturally I took sides with the strikers. When the day came on which the girls were to turn out, those in the upper rooms started first, and so many of them left that our mill was at once shut down. Then, when the girls in my room stood irresolute, uncertain what to do, asking each other, "Would you?" or "Shall we turn out?" and not one of them having the courage to lead off, I, who began to think they would not go out, after all their talk, became impatient, and started on ahead, saying, with childish bravado, "I don't care what you do, *I* am going to turn out, whether any one else does or not"; and I marched out, and was followed by others.

As I looked back at the long line that followed me, I was more proud than I have ever been since at any success I may have achieved, and more proud than I shall ever be again until my own beloved states gives to its women citizens the right of suffrage.

DOCUMENT 9.6
Moral Suasion Gives Way to Coercion

The question of appropriate tactics vexed most antebellum reform movements. The essential issue, however, was the one confronted decisively in the following piece: whether to rely on persuading individual consciences— "moral suasion"—or to use institutions and coercion to achieve reformist goals.

. . . moral suasion is moral balderdash. "Words, my lord, words"—worse than words, they are a delusion. How long have they been sounded in the public ear and sounded in vain? The drunkard's mental and physical condition

Source: "The Maine Law vs. Moral Suasion," *American Temperance Magazine*, vol. 3, (1852), pp. 137–39.

pronounces them an absurdity. He is ever in one or other extreme condition—under the excitement of drink, or in a state of morbid collapse. Will it be said that words of suasion will commend themselves to a drunken man? Will he hear or heed them, or if he hear will there not be a prompting devil within, jeering at their blessedness? Reason with a man when all reason has fled, and it is doubtful whether he or you is the greater fool. But take him while in the other mood. Does he then need your counsel? Who can impart a bitterer poignancy to his memory? . . . self-reproach is his one unchanging feeling. . . . He is to himself a subject of abhorrence. He shudders to remember the actual debasement to which he reduced himself. . . .

Place the man we have been describing out of reach of temptation. He will have time to ponder. His mind and frame recover their native vigor. The public-house does not beset his path. Another and another day dawn upon him and find him clear and collected, confirming his purpose and imparting joy as well as firmness to his resolution. This is the true suasion. Thus, and thus only, will reformation and temperance be secured. And how is this accomplished? Never except through the instrumentality of the law. . . .

DOCUMENT 9.7
A Limit To Commitment

Not all foreign observers of antebellum America were as balanced in their judgments as Alexis de Tocqueville. Among the critics was Frances Trollope, an Englishwoman resident in the United States between 1827 and 1830. Her account of the Phrenological Society of Cincinnati stands as a reminder that sustaining commitment was often more difficult than stirring it.

Source: Frances Trollope, *Domestic Manners of Americans*, vol. 1, (New York, n.d.), pp. 94–95.

We had not long been at Cincinnati when Dr. Caldwell . . . arrived there, for the purpose of delivering lectures on phrenology. . . . His lectures . . . produced considerable effect. Between twenty and thirty of the most erudite citizens decided upon forming a phrenological society. A meeting was called, and fully attended; a respectable number of subscribers' names was registered, the payment of subscriptions being arranged for a future day. President, vice-president, treasurer, and secretary, were chosen, and the first meeting dissolved with every appearance of energetic perseverance in scientific research.

The second meeting brought together one-half of this learned body, and they enacted rules and laws, and passed resolutions, sufficient, it was said, to have filled three folios.

A third day of meeting arrived, which was an important one, as on this occasion the subscriptions were to be paid. The treasurer came punctually, but found himself alone. With patient hope, he waited two hours for the wise men of the west, but he waited in vain; and so expired the Phrenological Society of Cincinnati.

chapter

Female Dissent in Antebellum America

Linda K. Kerber
University of Iowa

What have I, as a woman, to do with politics? Even the government of our country, which is said to be the freest in the world, passes over women as if they were not.

> *Mrs. Carter, in Charles*
> *Brockden Brown, Alcuin*
> *(Philadelphia, 1798)*

The nation that was founded in revolutionary struggle defined itself in masculine terms. American colonists brought the European assumption that the relationship of women to the state was a distant and static one. The hope of gain, in the shape of political or military office, was thought to cement loyalties between king and subject. Because women, except for queens, did not hold political office, their connection to government was a subordinate one. They could express loyalties only second hand through husbands, fathers, and sons. They were not taken seriously as a potential source of power or resistance; for that reason, they were thought to have little to offer the state. Among the revolutionary theorists, only James Otis came close to asserting that the challenge to British rule, with all it implied by way of redefining political first principles, required the reformulation of the relationship of women to the Republic. But he was the exception, and he went mad. The more common position was that of John Adams, who whimsically shrugged off the injunction of his wife to "remember the ladies" in the new code of laws being drafted in Philadelphia in 1776.

The ambivalent relationship of women to the state was reflected in the legal system that Americans had inherited from England and adapted to their needs. As citizens, women were responsible for their criminal conduct; they might sue and be sued in court. The state would enforce contracts—including marriage settlements—made when they were unmarried; the state would protect their claim to dower (a life interest in one-third of their deceased husband's real estate).

But the old English fiction that man and woman become a single person upon their marriage—and that person, the man—was taken to imply that the state would not enforce contracts signed by a married woman unless her husband was also a signer; property that she brought to the marriage or earned during it

The quotation from Margaret Livingston on page 179 is from the Ridley Papers, Massachusetts Historical Society. The quotation from Elizabeth Drinker on page 180 is from her diary in the collections of the Historical Society of Pennsylvania.

became her husband's; to dispose of as he might. Divorce was difficult; except for Connecticut, Massachusetts, and Rhode Island— where the traditional Puritan view that marriage was a civil contract was used to authorize civil procedures by which marriage might be ended—divorce was available only through special legislative action. South Carolina took pride in never having authorized such a measure before 1817. Because most divorce petitions were tendered by women, the limited availability of divorce bore with particular weight on one sex. Although revolutionary rhetoric insisted on the right to be free of arbitrary masters, legal reformers were slow to address the implications of that right for married women.

The unusual woman whose husband was away at sea, or whose husband was mentally or physically incapacitated, and who wished to carry on a business in her own name and on her own responsibility, needed to apply for special permission from the court or legislature to carry it on as a *feme sole* trader. Although theoretically only married women were assumed to have no wills of their own, in practice, the assumption was extended to single women and widows. These women paid taxes, made wills, and were not subject to the obvious manipulation of wife by husband, but they still were not regarded as active participants in the political order.

Although the great political reformers of the revolutionary era—Adams, Madison, and Jefferson—rethought substantially the relationship of colonies to empire and of the responsibilities of the state to the adult males whom it governed, there were important relationships with which they did not deal. The most obvious relationships were slaves to masters and women to men. At least the revolutionaries were consistent in their conservatism. Believing that married women owed political obedience directly to their husbands, revolutionaries did not demand oaths of allegiance from women, and they were slow to penalize the wives of Tories

who left with their husbands. "A wife who left the country in the company of her husband," Judge Theodore Sedgwick maintained in 1805, "did not *withdraw* herself; but was . . . withdrawn by him. She did not deprive the government of the benefit of her personal services; she had none to render; none were exacted of her."

Women themselves often said they were not political beings. Ironically, these denials could serve as apologia for vigorous political analysis. Ann Gwinnett, sending political news to John Hancock during the revolutionary war, concluded, "these things (tho from a Woman, & it is not our sphere, yet I cannot help it) are all true." Margaret Livingston, after a long discussion of the propriety of demanding loyalty oaths in wartime concluded, "it is a very heart-hardening subject, too much so, for women to deal with."

There is no question, however, but that women experienced the trauma of the Revolution. In an era when the offices of quartermaster and commissary were run informally and inadequately, the army depended on hundreds of women who followed the troops, working as cooks, laundresses, nurses, and matrons. Women were a permanent—though rarely acknowledged—presence in the army; Washington repeatedly reminded his officers to be sure that the women marched in back with the baggage so they would not be noticed. But, this service was not translated into political influence, not even in so obvious a matter as pensions (which were not authorized by Congress for widows of enlisted men until fully fifty years after Yorktown).

"How many female minds, rich with native genius and noble sentiment," the *Royal American Magazine* asked in 1774, "have been lost to the world, and all their mental treasures buried in oblivion?" It seemed obvious that the postwar generation would have to be educated for self-reliance and independence. It was the limited nature of their education that inhibited women from taking a fully responsible role in the Republic—a conviction articulated by female columnists in the American press well before Mary Wollstonecraft's *Vindication of the Rights of Women* appeared in England.

> In education all the diff'rence lies;
> Women, if taught, wou'd be as learn'd and
>   wise
> As haughty man, improv'd by arts and rules;
> Where God makes one, neglect makes many
>   fools.

Theory was echoed by practice. All over the country, boarding schools and academies were founded. Some, like the Young Ladies Academy of Philadelphia, served a single sex; others, like the many town academies in Massachusetts, were coeducational. These schools needed teachers; as they grew, so did women's vocational opportunities. Maris Vinovskis has shown that women comprised more than 50 percent of the teachers in Massachusetts in 1834; by 1860, they filled nearly 78 percent of the positions. In the antebellum years, "approximately one out of five women in Massachusetts was a school teacher at some time in her life."

The literacy gap between men and women, which Kenneth Lockridge's studies of colonial New England wills show to have been substantial, slowly closed. By 1850, there was virtually none among northern whites. However, if girls learned to read, there remained much that they were not taught. Certain elements of the standard curriculum were considered unsuitable, and a frankly female curriculum was divised. Girls were not taught classical languages, required for entrance to the professions; the sciences were carefully simplified, and the natural philosophy in their books was geared to the kitchen.

This distinction between the proper spheres of men and women has often been explained, following the argument laid out by Barbara Welter, as "the Cult of True Womanhood,"

a false consciousness that insisted women were frail creatures fitted only for nurturant and dependent roles. One scholar has suggested that the urbanization and industrialization, which pulled men out of household employment and into the regimented workplaces of office and factory, was accompanied by a romanticization of the home as a place of retreat, a garden presided over by a lovely woman who soothed the anxieties of a competitive workday.

This argument has much that is persuasive. But, in emphasizing the shock of modernization, one can minimize the extent to which women's lives always had a domestic orientation. Domesticity does not necessarily mean ease and indulgence; it does not always imply a pedestal. "I stay much at home, and my business I mind," is the opening line of a poem by Elizabeth Drinker, a member of a prominent Philadelphia Quaker family, copied into her diary in 1795. In her youth, her business included substantial textile production of clothing for herself, her family, and her friends. When she grew older, her business included caring for a large family, nursing them through illness (and through the heroic treatments of physicians who complicated the illnesses—scarcely a month passed for thirty years in which she does not report in her diary that some friend or relative has been bled). Women sustained frequent pregnancies and lengthy childbirths in a preanesthetic age. Women who needed to labor to support themselves found few alternatives to a quasi-servitude that drained all their waking hours—whether it took the form of domestic service in someone else's home or piecework taken to their own home. The millions of enslaved black women had no choices. To read women's diaries in the years between the Revolution and the Civil War is to be impressed by the sheer amount of work they accomplished and the pain they endured.

It can, therefore, be more helpful to think of modernization as an expression of the industrial shift to new modes of production *and* of the cultural shift away from the values and habits of peasant communities and toward the habits and behaviors demanded by an industrial economy. In that context, perhaps we can conclude that middle-class women resisted inclusion in the modern world longer than did men.

Boys were educated for upward mobility, for access to roles and professions unavailable to their fathers. The glorification of progress so characteristic of Jacksonian ideology can be translated in part as encouragement to boys to be dissatisfied with the status into which they had been born. But girls were educated for horizontal stability; care was taken not to encourage dissatisfaction with domesticity and with tradition. Although girls were taught much that had been unavailable to their grandmothers, it was offered in a context that urged them to avoid individuality, upward social mobility, and self-fulfillment. John William Ward has identified the glorification of the will as central to the popular culture of the early Republic; women, who were not to glorify *their* wills, did not share in this ideology. The few women who sought to do so (Margaret Fuller is perhaps the most obvious example) were classified as anomalies by male observers, and even other women found them difficult to understand.

If this new competence and this growing political sensitivity could not be used for self-advancement, then for what could it be used? The women's ideology that most people found easiest to understand was a domestic feminism of the sort espoused by Sarah Josepha Hale, editor of *Godey's Lady's Book*. She maintained that because women were more pure and virtuous than men, they had special public responsibilities as teachers and as moralists. Religious rhetoric and religious institutions could also camouflage and justify behavior that would otherwise be scorned. Christian mission made political behavior acceptable. It is not surprising that much of the early collective behavior of women was framed as religious and charitable mission.

The tone was set by an anonymous 1797 pamphlet, *Women Invited to War,* in which a moral crusade against alcohol was the conflict women were urged to join. Instead of lobbying Congress for pension legislation, women organized Ladies Benevolent Societies for the assistance of widows and orphans. These voluntary associations usually had religious connections, their major fundraising effort being capped by an annual sermon delivered by some sympathetic minister. The net widened. The New York Female Moral Reform Society took prostitutes under its wing. From these moral reform societies, it was a short step into antislavery reform.

As Aileen Kraditor has shown, there was a distinctively female antislavery ideology. It repeated the standard issues of the general antislavery campaign, but it laid particular stress on certain themes: the moral squalor of the slave plantation where black women were vulnerable to sexual abuse by white masters, and the anguish of the enslaved mother who was separated by sale from husband and children. This ideology exploited the sanctification of domesticity to argue that a radical commitment to abolition must come naturally and normally out of a traditional commitment to the preservation of home and family. "Shall woman . . . rejoice in her home, her husband, her children," Sarah Grimké asked, "and forget her brethren and sisters in bondage, who know not what it is to call a spot of earth their own, whose husbands and wives are torn from them by relentless tyrants and whose children are snatched from their arms by their unfeeling task-masters?"

Women had been successful in preserving other benevolent issues as female issues; and so defined, male hostility was defused. But, they could not hope to retain sole custody of one issue: the plight of black women who were owned by white men. Female antislavery reformers were quickly perceived as speaking to a general public and sharply criticized for it. They learned that if they wanted to defend their right to speak for the enslaved woman, they first had to defend their own right to political speech. Public testimony seemed to be a direct intrusion into a politics that had as one of its most basic assumptions—though unexamined—the idea that women's relation to the state was distant, deferential, and subordinate. Even antislavery men found this assertive behavior disconcerting. When the American Anti-Slavery Society split in 1840—an event that had crucial and perhaps tragic implications for the future of the abolitionist movement—it did so over whether women would be allowed to speak in public and to hold office in the main organization (rather than in a female auxiliary).

The classic statement of how the female politics of antislavery triggered the more general female political resurgence of mid-century is Elizabeth Cady Stanton's. She and Lucretia Mott were sent as delegates to the World's Anti-Slavery Convention, which met in London in 1840. The great adventure and unusual opportunity turned into embarrassment and disappointment when their credentials were rejected because they were women. In a gesture of angry defiance, William Lloyd Garrison joined them in the ''Ladies Gallery.''

''As Mrs. Mott and I walked home, arm in arm, commenting on the incidents of the day,'' Stanton recalled years later, ''we resolved to hold a convention as soon as we returned home, and form a society to advocate the rights of women . . .The acquaintance of Lucretia Mott, who was a broad, liberal thinker on politics, religion, and all questions of reform, opened to me a new world of thought. . . . It was intensely gratifying to hear all that, through years of doubt, I had dimly thought, so freely discussed by other women.'' Despite their resolution, the project lapsed. By the time they encountered each other again, in 1848, they had learned that the woman question involved far more than the right to speak for the enslaved.

At stake were at least two other issues. The first was the legal position, and especially the property rights, of the married woman. Creditor desire for easy collection of debts from property owned by wives meant that male legislators developed an interest in simplifying the property rights of married women. At the same time, women reformers were anxious to certify the control of married women over the property they had brought to marriage or had earned after being married—without making use of the prenuptial contract, a complicated device long available to the politically sophisticated. The result was an odd political coalition; in New York, for example, it included the articulate refugee Ernestine Rose (whose motives included her memories of an arranged marriage she had escaped in Poland) and conservative legislators anxious to simplify commercial law, and conservative legislators anxious to preserve their daughters' inheritance from spendthrift sons-in-law. Married Women's Property Acts were passed in seventeen states by 1850. They were supported by those who wished to increase the efficiency of the market economy, and by women who were conscious of their economic self-interest.

The rights and working conditions of laboring women was a second issue. Perhaps the most dismaying feature of the ideology of ''true womanhood'' was the extent to which it masked the real situation of women who could not retreat from the industrial revolution into the sanctuary of their homes. From the earliest factories, like Samuel Slater's in Providence, Rhode Island, which opened in 1789, and which used engines for spinning and subsequently for weaving, it was traditional women's work that was first challenged by the new equipment. But, they went into Slater's mill, along with the children; and it was understood—as an index of the nation's prosperity—that men had better options and did not need, at least at first, to enter factories.

Along with industrialization came occupational segregation. Women's work was quickly perceived as unsuitable for men. "The disproportionate value set on the time and labor of men and of women," Sarah Grimke argued, was a measure of the "general opinion that women are inferior to men. . . . A woman who goes out to wash works as hard in proportion as a wood sawyer or a coal heaver but she is not generally able to make more than half as much by a day's work."

Middle-class women might look on with sympathy, but it was the mill women themselves who developed a sense of coherence and comradeship, and who resisted exploitation as effectively as they could. Their sense of union was reinforced by the fact that so many lived together in boardinghouses and therefore spent all their waking hours together. It resulted in scattered strikes in the 1820s and 1830s; and, in 1845, Sarah Bagley organized the mill women in Lowell, Massachusetts into the Female Labor Reform Association. It was quickly broken by employers, but not before it had articulated their sense that the Republic owed them some attention: "Shall we, operatives of America, the land where democracy claims to be the principle by which we live and by which we are governed, see the evil daily increasing which separates more widely and more effectively the favored few and the unfortunate many without one exertion to stay the progress?"

When Elizabeth Cady Stanton and Lucretia Mott finally made good on their promise to each other and formalized their criticism of the Republic, they did so on the broadest of grounds. The Declaration of Sentiments, drafted at Seneca Falls, New York in 1848, quickly became the manifesto of the women's movement. It drew its rhetoric from the Declaration of Independence. The conscious imitation was a way of emphasizing the extent to which the masculine pronouns of the Declaration of Independence were literal, not generic— a way of specifying the extent to which one

half of the population was in fact governed without their consent.

Like the rebellious colonist, woman was "compelled . . . to submit to laws, in the formation of which she had no voice." She was taxed without representation; she was denied the suffrage. To political criticism, the Declaration added scathing social and economic criticism. The male monopoly of "nearly all the profitable employments" doomed working women to drudgery and poverty. Denial of access to higher education and the professions thwarted the aspirations of competent women. Further criticism dealt with sensitive matters of psychology and self-image. It attacked the double sexual standard, and it accused men of endeavoring to destroy women's "confidence in her own powers, to lessen her self-respect, and to make her willing to lead a dependent and abject life." In its insistence that "the same transgressions should be visited with equal severity on both man and woman" and that "all laws which . . . place her in a position inferior to that of man, are . . . of no force or authority," the Declaration used standard republican precepts as a mode of fully including women in the Republic.

The agenda was in many ways simple, straightforward, and conservative, but the authors accurately predicted that "In entering upon the great work before us, we anticipate no small amount of misconception, misrepresentation and ridicule." Their task became substantially more difficult when, after the Civil War in 1869, the word *male* was introduced in the Constitution, in the second section of the Fourteenth Amendment. The agenda of 1848 remained a real one when the Centennial was celebrated in 1876; although many of its demands had been met, the Declaration had not lost its significance at the Centennial. Susan B. Anthony's great oration of July 4, 1876, retains its resonance: "And now, at the close of a hundred years . . .we declare our faith in the principles of self-government . . . that woman was made first for her own happiness, with the absolute right to herself, to all the opportunities and advantages life affords for her complete development . . . We ask . . . no special favors, no special privileges, no special legislation. We ask justice, we ask equality, we ask that all the civil and political rights that belong to citizens of the United States be guaranteed to us and our daughters forever.''

SUGGESTED READINGS

Basch, Norma. *In the Eyes of the Law: Women, Marriage and Property in Nineteenth Century New York*. Ithaca, N.Y.: Cornell University Press, 1982.

Cott, Nancy F. *In The Bonds of Womanhood: Woman's Sphere in New England*. New Haven, Conn.: Yale University Press, 1977.

Dublin, Thomas. *Women at Work: The Transformation of Work and Community in Lowell, Massachusetts, 1826–1860*. New York: Columbia University Press, 1979.

DuBois, Ellen. *Feminism and Suffrage: The Emergence of an Independent Women's Movement in America 1848–1869*. Ithaca, N.Y.: Cornell Univesity Press, 1978.

Flexner, Eleanor. *Century of Struggle: The Woman's Rights Movement in the United States*. Cambridge, Mass.: Harvard University Press, 1959.

Hewitt, Nancy. *Women's Activism and Social Change: Rochester, New York 1822–1872*. Ithaca, N.Y.: Cornell University Press, 1974.

Kerber, Linda K. *Women of the Republic: Intellect and Ideology in Revolutionary America*. New York: W. W. Norton, 1980, 1986.

Kessler-Harris, Alice. *Out to Work: A History of Wage-Earning Women*. New York: Oxford University Press, 1984.

Lerner, Gerda. *The Grimke Sisters from South Carolina: Pioneers for Women's Rights and Abolition*. Boston: Little, Brown, 1967.

Norton, Mary Beth. *Liberty's Daughters: The Revolutionary Experience of American Women*. Boston: Little, Brown 1980.

Sklar, Katherine Kish. *Catharine Beecher: A Study in American Domesticity*. New Haven, Conn.: Yale University Press, 1973.

Smith-Rosenberg, Carroll. *Disorderly Conduct: Visions of Gender in Victorian America*. New York: A. Knopf, 1985.

Stanton, Elizabeth Cady. *Eighty Years and More*. New York, 1898.

Sterling, Dorothy, ed. *We Are Your Sisters: Black Women in the Nineteenth Century*. New York: W. W. Norton, 1984.

Vinovskis, Maris, and Richard M. Bernard. ''The Female School Teacher in Ante-Bellum Massachusetts.'' *Journal of Social History*, 10 (1977) pp. 332–45.

Welter, Barbara. *Dimity Convictions: The American Woman in the Nineteenth Century*. Athens, Ohio: Ohio University Press, 1976.

DOCUMENT 10.1
Political Fund-Raising during the Revolution

The broadside printed below prefaced a campaign to raise contributions for American soldiers. A door-to-door collection, organized in Philadelphia by Esther deBerdt Reed and Sarah Franklin Bache in June, 1780, raised $300,000 in inflated continental currency. Refusing to agree to Washington's proposal that the money be deposited in the national treasury, and so merged with the funds of men, they insisted on using it to purchase materials for making shirts so that each soldier might know he had received an extraordinary contribution from the women of Philadelphia.

On the commencement of actual war, the Women of America manifested a firm resolution to contribute as much as could depend on them, to the deliverance of their country. Animated by the purest patriotism, they are sensible of sorrow at this day, in not offering

Source: ''The Sentiments of an American Woman,'' Broadside (June 1780). *Readex Microprint, Evans Number 16992.*

more than barren wishes for the success of so glorious a Revolution. They aspire to render themselves more really useful; and this sentiment is universal from the north to the south of the Thirteen United States. Our ambition is kindled by the fame of those heroines of antiquity, who have rendered their sex illustrious, and have proved to the universe, that, if the weakness of our Constitution, if opinion and manners did not forbid us to march to glory by the same paths as the Men, we should at least equal, and sometimes surpass them in our love for the public good. I glory in all that which my sex has done great and commendable. I call to mind with enthusiasm and with admiration, all those acts of courage, of constancy and patriotism, which history has transmitted to us: The people favoured by Heaven, preserved from destruction by the virtues, the zeal and the resolution of Deborah, of Judith, of Esther! The fortitude of the mother of the Macchabees, in giving up her sons to die before her eyes: Rome saved from the fury of a victorious enemy by the efforts of Volumnia, and other Roman Ladies: So many famous sieges where the Women have been seen forgetting the weakness of their sex, building new walls, digging trenches with their feeble hands, furnishing arms to their defenders, they themselves darting the missile weapons on the enemy, resigning the ornaments of their apparel, and their fortune, to fill the public treasury, and to hasten the deliverance of their country, burying themselves under its ruins; throwing themselves into the flames rather than submit to the disgrace of humiliation before a proud enemy.

Born for liberty, disdaining to bear the irons of a tyrannic Government, we associate ourselves to the grandeur of those Sovereigns, cherished and revered, who have held with so much splendour the scepter of the greatest States, the Matildas, the Elizabeths, the Maries, the Catharines, who have extended the empire of liberty, and contented to reign by sweetness and justice, have broken the chains of slavery,

forged by tyrants in times of ignorance and barbarity. . . .

We are at least certain, that he cannot be a good citizen who will not applaud our efforts for the relief of the armies which defend our lives, our possessions, our liberty. The situation of our soldiery has been represented to me; the evils inseparable from war, and the firm and generous spirit which has enabled them to support these. But it has been said, that they may apprehend, that, in the course of a long war, the view of their distresses may be lost, and their services be forgotten. Forgotten! never; I can answer in the name of all my sex. Brave Americans, your disinterestedness, your courage, and your constancy will always be dear to America, as long as she shall preserve her virtue.

We know that at a distance from the theatre of war, if we enjoy any tranquility, it is the fruit of your watchings, your labours, your dangers. If I live happy in the midst of my family; if my husband cultivates his field, and reaps his harvest in peace; if surrounded with my children I myself nourish the youngest, and press it to my bosom, without being afraid of seeing myself separated from it, by a ferocious enemy; if the house in which we dwell; if our barns, our orchards are safe at the present time from the hands of those incendiaries, it is to you that we owe it. And shall we hesitate to evidence to you our gratitude? Shall we hesitate to wear a cloathing more simple; hair dressed less elegant, while at the price of this small privation, we shall deserve your benedictions? Who, amongst us, will not renounce with the highest pleasure, those vain ornaments, when she shall consider that the valiant defenders of America will be able to draw some advantage from the money which she may have laid out in these . . . The time is arrived to display the same sentiments which animated us at the beginning of the Revolution, when we renounced the use of teas, however agreeable to our taste, rather than receive them from our persecutors; when we made it appear to them that we placed former necessaries in the rank of superfluities, when our liberty was interested; when our republican and laborious hands spun the flax, prepared the linen intended for the use of our soldiers; when as exiles and fugitives we supported with courage all the evils which are the concomitants of war. Let us not lose a moment; let us be engaged to offer the homage of our gratitude at the alter of military valour, and you, our brave deliverers, while mercenary slaves combat to cause you to share with them, the irons with which they are loaded, receive with a free hand our offering, the purest which can be presented to your virtue, By AN AMERICAN WOMAN.

DOCUMENT 10.2
Objections to Women in Politics

We do not know who signed his name "Philanthropos" in this letter to the editor, but he articulated many common objections to the inclusion of women in republican government.

TO THE PRINTERS . . .

The position, that "all mankind are born equal," may be taken in too extensive a sense, and may tend to destroy those degrees of subordination which nature seems to point out as indispensable for the regulation of society. The duty which a child owes to its parent, or a voluntary servant to his employer, cannot be affected by this principle of equality, which ought to be established only in opposition to the arbitrary encroachments of despotic power. The relative duties of women in private life may probably furnish a reason for their exclusion from political concerns. . . .

We are led to believe that woman was originally created in subordination to man; and, if

Source: *Virginia Gazette and Alexandria Advertiser,* April 22, 1790.

any reasons were necessary to convince us of this, there appear to be two that are obvious— That for the good government of any family or community there must be one person to rule, and that the most powerful will of course exercise that authority. It is likewise certain that nature (the surest guide) has pointed out for them a course of duties and employments totally inconsistent with a life of political bustle and anxiety—We, therefore, observe that men are more pleased with an exertion of feminine domestic qualifications, than with an awkward encroachment on the privileges of the other sex—And, however flattering the path of glory and ambition may be, a woman will have more commendation in being the mother of heroes, than in setting up, Amazon-like, for a heroine herself. The maternal duties, indeed, at the same time that they are themselves the most proper, in their consequences incapacitate the person from attending to the more arduous task of political employments. This, I think, is taken notice of by the *Spectator,* in his account of the Amazonian government—the operations of which were dangerously impeded by the *critical* situation of one of their Commanders. But there is another objection which probably has occasioned this exclusion, and which I hope (much as I love and esteem the sex) will be sufficient to continue it—It is the danger of *secret influence;* that bane of political integrity, which is already so generally complained of, and which, with bribery and corruption in its train, has so often destroyed the patriotic endeavours of honest Statemen[sic]—It is said that all men have their prices; and here would at once be a *price* for all men—A Female Orator, in haranguing an Assembly, might, like many crafty politicans, keep her *best argument* for the last, and would then be sure of victory—Men would be exposed to temptations too great for their strength, and those who could resist a bribe, offered in the common way, might reasonably yield to what it would be hardly possible for a *man* to refuse—A lady, then, instead of drawing crouds of attendants at a ball or a play, would make it her sport, or her ambition, to draw them from their political creeds; and it may easily be imagined which would be attended with the worst consequences—Many men prefer honesty and honour to riches; but, when assailed on this weak side, might adopt the sentiment of "All for love or the world well lost." A man who knew himself secure and invulnerable in every other respect, might yet fall (as many others have done) in such a cause; and we might fancy him exclaiming, with Macbeth,

"Approach thou like the rugged Russian bear,
"The arm'd Rhinoceros, or the Hircanian
  Tiger.
"Take any shape but *that,* and my firm nerves
"Shall never tremble."—

In short, the evils to be apprehended from such an innovation in politics appear so numerous and alarming that I flatter myself your correspondent, and other advocates as favourable as himself, will be induced to give it up, and that the dear creatures themselves will be contented with the share of influence which they already possess. The example of the Quakers cannot be considered a proper one, if we attend to the reasons on which it is founded—Professing, and believing, as they do, that their preachers hold forth at the moment in which they are moved by the spirit, it would be in vain for them to silence their female friends, unless the operations of the spirit were under their own controul—But I have never observed that the audience appeared much edified by this species of teachers. . . . [As for queens,] women govern well because they are ruled by men; as, on the other side, many Kings have been too much under the direction of female favourites. The instances that may be adduced from the histories of famous and learned women will not be of much importance, as they were generally deficient in those charms which it is the peculiar lot of the fair sex to excel in—

And, I hope, there are few that would not rather be the objects of love than admiration. However, although there exist these insuperable objections to their being *actually* represented, we can readily admit that the goodness and gentleness of their minds might have a happy effect in our public councils—Every virtuous sentiment would be cherished, and gratitude would not be forgot—*They* would not blush at a DISCRIMINATION in favour of those who had fought in their defence, and shielded them in the hour of danger—But they are not called by Providence to the important office of deciding on the rights of Speculators and Soldiers. They have, however, the power of being a solace and comfort under the pressure of every evil; and, in conferring their favours, they will, undoubtedly, where the pretensions are otherwise equal, make a *discrimination* in favour of those to whom their gratitude is due—And, while they have opportunities of exercising this heavenly virtue, and while, by their tenderness and irresistible powers of persuasion, they can mould our minds to a delicacy and purity of sentiment corresponding with their own, they will have little occasion to regret their exclusion from the perplexity and tumult of a political life.

PHILANTHROPOS
Maryland, April 3, 1790

DOCUMENT 10.3
Restructuring Women's Education

Emma Willard was an experienced teacher when, at the age of thirty two, she tried unsuccessfully to convince the New York legislature to fund state-supported schools for

Source: Emma Willard, *An Address to the Public, Particularly to the Members of the Legislature of New-York, Proposing a Plan for Improving Female Education,* (Middlebury, Conn.: 1819).

girls. The pamphlet she prepared combined shrewd criticism of established institutions with a demand for economically secure women's schools.

. . . Civilized nations have long since been convinced that education, as it respects males, will not, like trade, regulate itself; and hence, they have made it a prime object to provide that sex with everything requisite to facilitate their progress in learning: but female education has been left to the mercy of private adventurers; and the consequence has been to our sex, the same, as it would have been to the other, had legislatures left their accommodations, and means of instruction, to chance also.

Education cannot prosper in any community, unless, from the ordinary motives which actuate the human mind, the best and most cultivated talents of that community, can be brought into exercise in that way. Male education flourishes, because, from the guardian care of legislatures, the presidencies and professorships of our colleges are some of the highest objects to which the eye of ambition is directed. Not so with female institutions. Preceptresses of these, are dependent on their pupils for support, and are consequently liable to become the victims of their caprice. . . .

Institutions for young gentlemen are founded by public authority, and are permanent; they are endowed with funds, and their instructors and overseers, are invested with authority to make such laws, as they shall deem most salutary . . . With their funds they procure libraries, philosophical apparatus, and other advantages . . . Female schools present the reverse of this. Wanting permanency, and dependent on individual patronage, had they wisdom to make salutary regulations, they could neither enforce nor purchase compliance. The pupils are irregular in their times of entering and leaving school. . . .

. . . female education has not yet been systematized. Chance and confusion reign here.

Not even is youth considered in our sex, as in the other, a season which should be wholly devoted to improvement. Among families, so rich as to be entirely above labour, the daughters are hurried through the routine of boarding school instruction, and at an early period introduced into the gay world . . . Mark the different treatment, which the sons of these families receive. While their sisters are gliding through the mazes of the midnight dance, they employ the lamp, to treasure up for future use the riches of ancient wisdom; or to gather strength and expansion of mind, in exploring the wonderful paths of philosophy. When the youth of two sexes has been spent so differently, is it strange, or is nature in fault, if more mature age has brought such a difference of character, that our sex have been considered by the other, as the pampered, wayward babies of society, who must have some rattle put into our hands, to keep us from doing mischief to ourselves or others?

. . . It is the duty of a government, to do all in its power to promote the present and future prosperity of the nation, over which it is placed. This prosperity will depend on the character of its citizens. The characters of these will be formed by their mothers; and it is through the mothers, that the government can control the characters of its future citizens, to form them such as will ensure their country's prosperity. If this is the case, then it is the duty of our present legislators to begin now, to form the characters of the next generation, by controling that of the females, who are to be their mothers, while it is yet with them a season of improvement.

But should the conclusion be almost admitted, that our sex too are the legitimate children of the legislature; and that it is their duty to afford us a share of their paternal bounty; the phantom of a college-learned lady, would be ready to rise up, and destroy every good resolution . . . it is not a masculine education which is here recommended . . . a female institution might possess the respectability, permanency, and uniformity of operation of those appropriated to males, and yet differ from them, so as to be adapted to that difference of character and duties, to which the softer sex should be formed . . .

It is highly important, that females should be conversant with those studies, which will lead them to understand the operations of the human mind. The chief use to which the philosophy of the mind can be applied, is to regulate education by its rules . . . Natural philosophy has not often been taught to our sex. Yet why should we be kept in ignorance of the great machinery of nature, and left to the vulgar notion, that nothing is curious but what deviates from her common course? If mothers were acquainted with this science, they would communicate very many of its principles to their children in early youth. . . .

CONCLUSION

1. Females, by having their understandings cultivated, their reasoning powers developed and strengthened, may be expected to act more from the dictates of reason, and less from those of fashion and caprice.

2. With minds thus strengthened they would be taught systems of morality, enforced by the sanctions of religion; and they might be expected to acquire juster and more enlarged views of their duty, and stronger and higher motives to its performance.

3. This plan of education, offers all that can be done to preserve female youth from a contempt of useful labour. The pupils would become accustomed to it, in conjunction with the high objects of literature, and the elegant pursuits of the fine arts; and it is to be hoped that both from habit and association, they might in future life, regard it as respectable. . . . if housewifery could be raised to a regular art, and taught upon philosophical principles, it would become a higher and more interesting

occupation; and ladies of fortune, like wealthy agriculturalists, might find, that to regulate their business, was an agreeable employment.

4. The pupils might be expected to acquire a taste for moral and intellectual pleasures, which would buoy them above a passion for show and parade . . .

5. By being enlightened in moral philosophy, and in that, which teaches the operations of the mind, females would be enabled to perceive the nature and extent, of that influence, which they possess over their children. . . .

[Among females] . . . as among the other sex, will be found master spirits, who must have pre-eminence, at whatever price they acquire it. Domestic life cannot hold these, because they prefer to be infamous, rather than obscure. To leave such, without any virtuous road to eminence, is unsafe to community; for not unfrequently, are the secret springs of revolution, set in motion by their intrigues. Such aspiring minds, we will regulate, by education, we will remove obstructions to the course of literature, which has heretofore been their only honorable way to distinction; and we offer them a new object, worthy of their ambition; to govern, and improve the seminaries for their sex.

. . . Nations, calling themselves polite, have made us the fancied idols of a ridiculous worship, and we have repaid them in ruin for their folly. But where is that wise and heroic country, which has considered, that our rights are sacred, though we cannot defend them? that tho' a weaker, we are an essential part of the body politic, whose corruption or improvement must affect the whole? and which, having thus considered, has sought to give us by education, that rank in the scale of being, to which our importance entitles us? History shows not that country. It shows many, whose legislatures have sought to improve their various vegetable productions, and their breeds of useful brutes; but none, whose public councils have made it an object of their deliberations, to improve the character of their women . . .

DOCUMENT 10.4
This "Besetting Sin" of the Times

In a series of essays defending the voluntary benevolent societies of Philadelphia from the charge that they encouraged idleness, Mathew Carey offered vivid descriptions of the conditions of urban working women in the year of Jackson's election.

The case of the paltry, contemptible compensation for female labour, with its attendant suffering, wretchedness, and demoralization, presses so strongly on my mind, that I must resume it. Would to heaven I could do it justice—and that I had a portion of the eloquence of Curran or Burke, that I might enkindle such a spirit among the more favoured classes of the community, male and female, as would eradicate this "besetting sin" of the times, the disgrace and dishonour of our city; which places thousands of females . . . with no alternative but—"Starvation or Dishonour." What an odious state of society! I find on minute inquiries, that a skilful industrious seamstress, unencumbered by a family, cannot average more than about nine shirts, working early and late. Now let us examine the result of a year's close and painful labour, supposing sickness or want of employment to cut off only six weeks in the year—whereas I might with more propriety assume eight, ten, or twelve.

Forty-six weeks at $1.12½ per week	$51.75
Room rent, sometimes 62½, but say 50 cents per week	$23.00
Fuel, say 12½ cents per week	5.75
	28.75
Remains for raiment, meat, drink, and fuel, for self and children, if any, the sorry miserable pittance per annum of	23.00

Source: M. Carey, *Miscellaneous Essays* (Philadelphia, 1830), pp. 191–95.

To heighten the horror and abomination of this state of things, let us take into view the probable case of eight, ten, or twelve weeks' want of employment, or sickness. Suppose, instead of six weeks, there are ten, it reduces the pitiful remnant for food, raiment, and fuel, for a year's labour, to 18 dollars; 33 cents per week; or five cents per day! We are in the habit of commiserating the poorer classes in England; but it cannot be doubted that the case of many of the women in question is full as lamentable, and that they are as completely ground down to the earth.

Again. Suppose—a case of no uncommon occurrence—a woman with two or three small children to attend, with occasional sickness, and hence only making a shirt a day: she earns but 75 cents per week—little more than the amount of her rent and fuel—with twelve and a half cents for provisions or clothing! and yet we have eloquent orators declaiming against benevolent societies! Alas! for human nature!

* * * * *

I venture to propose a mode by which this evil may be brought before the community, and a reasonable chance be afforded of applying a remedy. Let a few ladies of high standing unite and ascertain, from personal inspection, what amount of wages can be earned by industrious women, at sewing, washing, spooling, shoe binding, folding sheets, &c. &c., and then recommend such an increase of wages in all these branches, as will enable such women to earn at least two dollars, or two dollars and a quarter per week. No measure so completely based on justice and humanity, if properly patronized, ever failed of success. I could name a dozen ladies, illustrious for their beneficence, who glide through life almost *"unseen, unknown,"* any one of whom would be proper to commence this laudable business, and would soon find aids in abundance. But I trust it is unnecessary to particularize—and that the plan only needs to be proposed, to be carried into operation.

The wages of female house servants, bear but a small proportion to those of males. They vary from 75 cents to a dollar and a half per week, with board and lodging—whereas those of men servants, who do not perform near so much labour, are from 8 to 12 dollars per month. However, the attire of male servants being much more costly than that of females, the disproportion, although too great, is not as striking as it appears at first glance.

The government employs about 400 seamstresses in this city to make shirts, pantaloons, &c. for the army. Their employment, as I understand from high authority, continues about eight months in the year—and expert seamstresses make from seven to nine articles per week, at 12½ cents each. I will suppose them to average nine, for which they receive the paltry sum of $1.12½ cents per week. The calculations already made apply to this case.

The government paid for this item in 1827, $23,200.

I have fondly hoped that a proper application to the secretary of war, respecting the effect of thus *"grinding the faces of the poor,"* could not fail of producing such a rise as would enable this ill fated, pitiable, and helpless class of society to earn $2.25 or $2.50 per week. The result has not been as anticipated; yet the difference would have been only about ten or fifteen thousand dollars per annum. What an immense mass of penury and wretchedness to be relieved, and of human happiness to be purchased, at so cheap a rate, by a country with a revenue of from 20 to $25,000,000 per annum, and which pays eight dollars a day to its representatives! Five days' salary of the Vice President, who is not employed by official duties more than about five or six months in the year, is more than one of the women working for the army can earn in a year.

The wages for spooling are, I understand, 15 to 20 cents per hundred hanks, and a woman cannot do more than from 600 to 700 in a week. Those who spin thread are, I believe, in as melancholy a situation—and cannot earn

more than a dollar or a dollar and a quarter per week. I ask, emphatically, is not this *"grinding the faces of the poor?"*

It gives me pleasure to be able to state, that there are certain classes of females, who are decently paid. Milliners and mantuamakers, and tayloresses, who work in private families, receive from 50 to 62½ cents per day, and their board. They are in great demand, particularly at certain seasons of the year, and are accordingly treated with considerable attention, frequently sitting at table with their employers. Colourists earn from two to three dollars a week—women employed in factories about the same. Seamstresses who are hired in families, receive but a quarter dollar a day and their board; and are thus reduced to a level with the higher order of female servants. Is it not unjust and partial to the highest degree, that a seamstress who works in her own room, and boards and lodges herself, cannot by any possibility, earn more than a dollar and an eighth, or a dollar and a quarter, while she who works in other people's houses, earns a dollar and a half, and her board?

DOCUMENT 10.5
Declaration of Sentiments

When, in the course of human events, it becomes necessary for one portion of the family of man to assume among the people of the earth a position different from that which they have hitherto occupied, but one to which the laws of nature and of nature's God entitle them, a decent respect to the opinions of mankind requires that they should declare the causes that impel them to such a course.

We hold these truths to be self-evident: that all men and women are created equal; that they are endowed by their Creator with certain inal-

Source: Susan B. Anthony, Elizabeth Cady Stanton, and Matilda Gage, *History of Woman Suffrage* (Rochester, N.Y., 1889), vol. 1, pp. 70–73.

ienable rights; that among these are life, liberty, and the pursuit of happiness; that to secure these rights governments are instituted, deriving their just powers from the consent of the governed. Whenever any form of government becomes destructive to these ends, it is the right of those who suffer from it to refuse allegiance to it, and to insist upon the institution of a new government, laying its foundation on such principles, and organizing its powers in such form, as to them shall seem most likely to effect their safety and happiness. Prudence, indeed, will dictate that governments long established should not be changed for light and transient causes; and accordingly all experience hath shown that mankind are more disposed to suffer, while evils are sufferable, than to right themselves by abolishing the forms to which they were accustomed. But when a long train of abuses and usurpations, pursuing invariably the same object evinces a design to reduce them under absolute despotism, it is their duty to throw off such government, and to provide new guards for their future security. Such has been the patient sufferance of the women under this government, and such is now the necessity which constrains them to demand the equal station to which they are entitled.

The history of mankind is a history of repeated injuries and usurpations on the part of man toward woman, having in direct object the establishment of an absolute tyranny over her. To prove this, let facts be submitted to a candid world.

He has never permitted her to exercise her inalienable right to the elective franchise.

He has compelled her to submit to laws, in the formation of which she had no voice.

He has withheld from her rights which are given to the most ignorant and degraded men—both natives and foreigners.

Having deprived her of this first right of a citizen, the elective franchise, thereby leaving her without representation in the halls of legislation, he has oppressed her on all sides.

He has made her, if married, in the eye of the law, civilly dead.

He has taken from her all right in property, even to the wages she earns.

He has made her, morally, an irresponsible being, as she can commit many crimes with impunity, provided they be done in the presence of her husband. In the covenant of marriage, she is compelled to promise obedience to her husband, he becoming, to all intents and purposes, her master—the law giving him power to deprive her of her liberty, and to administer chastisement.

He has so framed the laws of divorce, as to what shall be the proper causes, and in case of separation, to whom the guardianship of the children shall be given, as to be wholly regardless of the happiness of women—the law, in all cases, going upon a false supposition of the supremacy of man, and giving all power into his hands.

After depriving her of all rights as a married woman, if single, and the owner of property, he has taxed her to support a government which recognizes her only when her property can be made profitable to it.

He has monopolized nearly all the profitable employments, and from those she is permitted to follow, she receives but a scanty remuneration. He closes against her all the avenues to wealth and distinction which he considers most honorable to himself. As a teacher of theology, medicine, or law, she is not known.

He has denied her the facilities for obtaining a thorough education, all colleges being closed against her.

He allows her in Church, as well as State, but a subordinate position, claiming Apostolic authority for her exclusion from the ministry, and, with some exceptions, from any public participation in the affairs of the Church.

He has created a false public sentiment by giving to the world a different code of morals for men and women, by which moral delinquencies which exclude women from society, are not only tolerated, but deemed of little account in man.

He has usurped the prerogative of Jehovah himself, claiming it as his right to assign for her a sphere of action, when that belongs to her conscience and to her God.

He has endeavored, in every way that he could, to destroy her confidence in her own powers, to lessen her self-respect, and to make her willing to lead a dependent and abject life.

Now, in view of this entire disfranchisement of one-half the people of this country, their social and religious degradation—in view of the unjust laws above mentioned, and because women do feel themselves aggrieved, oppressed, and fraudulently deprived of their most sacred rights, we insist that they have immediate admission to all the rights and privileges which belong to them as citizens of the United States.

In entering upon the great work before us, we anticipate no small amount of misconception, misrepresentation, and ridicule; but we shall use every instrumentality within our power to effect our object. We shall employ agents, circulate tracts, petition the State and National legislatures, and endeavor to enlist the pulpit and the press in our behalf. We hope this Convention will be followed by a series of Conventions embracing every part of the country. . . .

Whereas, The great precept of nature is conceded to be, that "man shall pursue his own true and substantial happiness." Blackstone in his Commentaries remarks, that this law of Nature being coeval with mankind, and dictated by God himself, is of course superior in obligation to any other. It is binding over all the globe, in all countries and at all times; no human laws are of any validity if contrary to this, and such of them as are valid, derive all their force, and all their validity, and all their authority, mediately and immediately, from this original; therefore,

Resolved, That such laws as conflict, in any

way, with the true and substantial happiness of woman, are contrary to the great precept of nature and of no validity, for this is "superior in obligation to any other."

Resolved, That all laws which prevent woman from occupying such a station in society as her conscience shall dictate, or which place her in a position inferior to that of man, are contrary to the great precept of nature, and therefore of no force or authority.

Resolved, That woman is man's equal—was intended to be so by the Creator, and the highest good of the race demands that she should be recognized as such.

Resolved, That the women of this country ought to be enlightened in regard to the laws under which they live, that they may no longer publish their degradation by declaring themselves satisfied with their present position, nor their ignorance, by asserting that they have all the rights they want.

Resolved, That inasmuch as man, while claiming for himself intellectual superiority, does accord to woman moral superiority, it is pre-eminently his duty to encourage her to speak and teach, as she has an opportunity, in all religious assemblies.

Resolved, That the same amount of virtue, delicacy, and refinement of behavior that is required of woman in the social state, should also be required of man, and the same transgressions should be visited with equal severity on both man and woman.

Resolved, That the objection of indelicacy and impropriety, which is so often brought against woman when she addresses a public audience, comes with a very ill-grace from those who encourage, by their attendance, her appearance on the stage, in the concert, or in feats of the circus.

Resolved, That woman has too long rested satisfied in the circumscribed limits which corrupt customs and a perverted application of the Scriptures have marked out for her, and that it is time she should move in the enlarged sphere which her great Creator has assigned her.

Resolved, That it is the duty of the women of this country to secure to themselves their sacred right to the elective franchise.

Resolved, That the equality of human rights results necessarily from the fact of the identity of the race in capabilities and responsibilities.

Resolved, therefore, That, being invested by the Creator with the same capabilities, and the same consciousness of responsibility for their exercise, it is demonstrably the right and duty of woman, equally with man, to promote every righteous cause by every righteous means; and especially in regard to the great subjects of morals and religion, it is self-evidently her right to participate with her brother in teaching them, both in private and in public, by writing and by speaking, by any instrumentalities proper to be used, and in any assemblies proper to be held; and this being a self-evident truth growing out of the divinely implanted principles of human nature, any custom or authority adverse to it, whether modern or wearing the hoary sanction of antiquity, is to be regarded as a self-evident falsehood, and at war with mankind. . . .

Resolved, That the speedy success of our cause depends upon the zealous and untiring efforts of both men and women, for the overthrow of the monopoly of the pulpit, and for the securing to woman an equal participation with men in the various trades, professions, and commerce.

chapter

Manifest Destiny and the Mexican War

Ramon Eduardo Ruiz
University of California, San Diego

All nations have a sense of destiny. Spaniards braved the perils of unknown seas and the dangers of savage tribes to explore and conquer a New World for Catholicism. Napoleon's armies overran Europe on behalf of equality, liberty, and fraternity. Communism dictates the future of China and the Soviet Union. Arab expansionists speak of Islam. In the United States, Manifest Destiny in the nineteenth century was the equivalent of these ideologies or beliefs. Next-door neighbor Mexico first felt the brunt of its impact and suffered the most from it.

What was Manifest Destiny? The term was coined in December 1845 by John L. O'Sullivan, then editor and cofounder of the *New York Morning News*. Superpatriot, expansionist, war hawk, and propagandist, O'Sullivan lived his doctrine of Manifest Destiny, for that slogan embodied what he believed. O'Sullivan spoke of America's special mission, frequently warned Europe to keep hands off the Western Hemisphere, later joined a filibustering expedition to Cuba, and had an honored place among the followers of President James K. Polk, Manifest Destiny's spokesman in the Mexican War.

Manifest Destiny voiced the expansionist sentiment that had gripped Americans almost from the day their ancestors had landed on the shores of the New World in the seventeenth century. Englishmen and their American offspring had looked westward since Jamestown and Plymouth—confident that time and fate would open the vast West that stretched out before them. Manifest Destiny, then, was first territorial expansion—American pretensions to lands held by Spain, France, and later Mexico; some even spoke of a United States with boundaries from pole to pole. But Manifest Destiny was greater than mere land hunger; much more was involved. A spirit of nationalism was pervasive—the belief that what Americans upheld was right and good, and that providence had designated them the chosen people. In a political framework, Manifest Destiny stood for democracy as Americans conceived it; to spread democracy and freedom was the goal. Also included were ideals of regeneration: the conquest of virgin lands for the sake of their development, and concepts of Anglo-Saxon superiority. All these slogans and beliefs played a role in the Mexican question that culminated in hostilities in 1846.

Apostles of these slogans pointed out that Mexicans claimed lands from the Pacific to Texas but tilled only a fraction of them, and did so inefficiently. "No nation has the right to hold soil, virgin and rich, yet unproducing," stressed one U.S. representative. "No race but our own can either cultivate or rule the western hemisphere,'' acknowledged the *United States Magazine and Democratic Review*. The Indian, almost always a poor farmer in North America, was the initial victim of this concept of soil use; expansionists later included nearly everyone in the New World, and in particular, Mexicans. For, Caleb Cushing asked: ''Is not the occupation of any portion of the earth by those competent to hold and till it, a providential law of national life?''

Oregon and Texas, and the Democratic Party platform of 1844, kindled the flames of territorial expansion in the roaring forties. Millions of Americans came to believe that God had willed them all of North America. Expansion symbolized the fulfillment of ''America's providential mission or destiny''—a mission conceived in terms of the spread of democracy, which its exponents identified with freedom. Historian Albert K. Weinberg has written: ''It was because of the association of expansion and freedom in a means-end relationship, that expansion now came to seem most manifestly a destiny.''

Americans did not identify freedom with expansion until the forties. Then, fears of European designs on Texas, California, and Oregon, perhaps, prompted an identity of the two. Not only were strategic and economic interests at stake, but also democracy itself. The need to extend the area of freedom, therefore, rose partly from the necessity of keeping absolutistic European monarchs from limiting the area open to American democracy in the New World.

Other factors also impelled Americans to think expansion essential to their national life. Failure to expand imperiled the nation, for, as historian William E. Dodd stated, Westerners especially believed ''that the Union gained in stability as the number of states multiplied.'' Meanwhile, Southerners declared the annexation of Texas essential to their prosperity and to the survival of slavery, and for a congressional balance of power between North and South. Other persons insisted that expansion helped the individual states to preserve their liberties, for their numerical strength curtailed the authority of the central government—the enemy of local autonomy and especially autonomy of the South. Moreover, for Southerners extension of the area of freedom meant, by implication, expansion of the limits of slavery. Few planters found the two ideas incompatible. Religious doctrines and natural principles, in their opinion, had ruled the Negro ineligible for political equality. That expansion favored the liberties of the individual, both North and South agreed.

In the forties, the pioneer spirit received recognition as a fundamental tenet of American life. Individualism and expansion, the mark of the pioneer, were joined together in the spirit of Manifest Destiny. Expansion guaranteed not just the political liberty of the person, but the opportunity to improve himself economically as well, an article of faith for the democracy of the age. Furthermore, when antiexpansionists declared that the territorial limits of the United States in 1846 assured all Americans ample room for growth in the future, the expansionists-turned-ecologists replied that some 300 million Americans in 1946 would need more land, a prediction that overstated the case of the population-minded experts. And few Americans saw the extension of freedom in terms other than liberty for themselves—white, Anglo-Saxon, and Protestant. All these concepts, principles, and beliefs entered into the expansionist creed of Manifest Destiny.

None of these was a part of the Mexican heritage, the legacy of three centuries of Spanish rule and countless years of pre-Columbian civilization. Mexico and the United States could not have been more dissimilar in 1846. A comparison of colonial backgrounds helps to bring into focus the reasons that the two countries were destined to meet on the field of battle. One was weak and the other strong; Mexico had abolished slavery and the United

States had not; Americans had their Manifest Destiny, but few Mexicans believed in themselves.

Daughter of a Spain whose colonial policy embraced the Indian, Mexico was a mestizo republic, a half-breed nation. Except for a small group of aristocrats, most Mexicans were descendants of both Spaniards and Indians. For Mexico had a colonial master eager and willing to assimilate pre-Columbian man. Since the days of the conqueror Hernán Cortés, Spaniards had mated with Indians, producing a Mexican both European and American in culture and race. Offspring of the Indian as well as the Spaniard, Mexican leaders, and even the society of the time, had come to accept the Indian, if not always as an equal, at least as a member of the republic. To have rejected him would have been tantamount to the Mexican's self-denial of himself. Doctrines of racial supremacy were, if not impossible, highly unlikely, for few Mexicans could claim racial purity. To be Mexican implied a mongrel status that ruled out European views of race.

Spain bequeathed Mexico not merely a racial attitude but laws, religious beliefs, and practices that banned most forms of segregation and discrimination. For example, reservations for Indians were never a part of the Spanish heritage. Early in the 16th century, the Spaniards had formulated the celebrated Laws of the Indies—legislation that clearly spelled out the place of the Indian in colonial society. Nothing was left to chance, since the Spanish master included every aspect of life—labor, the family, religion, and even the personal relations between Spaniard and Indian. The ultimate aim was full citizenship for the Indian and his descendants. In the meantime, the Church ruled that the Indian possessed a soul; given Christian teachings, he was the equal of his European conqueror. "All of the people of the world are men," the Dominican Bartolomé de las Casas had announced in his justly famous 1550 debate with the scholar Sepúlveda.

Clearly, church and state and the individual Spaniard who arrived in America had more than charity in mind. Dreams of national and personal glory and wealth dominated their outlook. Yet, despite the worldly goals of most secular and clerical conquerors, they built a colonial empire on the principle that men of all colors were equal on earth. Of course, Spain required the labor of the Indian and therefore had to protect him from the avarice of many a conquistador. Spaniards, the English were wont to say, were notorious for their disdain of manual labor of any type. But Spain went beyond merely offering the Indian protection in order to insure his labor. It incorporated him into Hispanic-American society. The modern Mexican is proof that the Indian survived: all Mexicans are Indian to some extent. That the Indian suffered economic exploitation and frequently even social isolation is undoubtedly true, but such was the lot of the poor in the Indies—Indian, half-breed, and even Spaniard.

Spain's empire, as well as the Mexican republic that followed, embraced not just the land but the people who had tilled it for centuries before the European's arrival. From northern California to Central America, the boundaries of colonial New Spain, and later Mexico, the Spaniard had embraced the Indian or allowed him to live out his life. It was this half-breed population that in 1846 confronted and fell victim to the doctrine of Manifest Destiny.

America's historical past could not have been more dissimilar. The English master had no room for the Indian in his scheme of things. Nearly all Englishmen—Puritans, Quakers, or Anglicans—visualized the conquest and settlement of the New World in terms of the exclusive possession of the soil. All new lands conquered were for the immediate benefit of the new arrivals. From the days of the founding of Jamestown and Plymouth, the English had pushed the Indian westward, relentlessly driving him from his homeland. In this activity, the clergy clasped hands with lay authorities; neither offered the red man a haven. Except for a few hardy souls, invariably condemned by their peers, Englishmen of church and state gave little thought to the Indian. Heaven, hell, and the teachings of Christ were the exclusive domain of the conquerors.

Society in the thirteen colonies, and in the Union that followed, reflected English and European customs and ways of life. It was a transplanted society. Where the Indian survived, he found himself isolated from the currents of time. Unlike the Spaniards, whose ties with Africa and darker skinned peoples through seven centuries of Moorish domination had left an indelible imprint on them, most Englishmen had experienced only sporadic contact with people of dissimilar races and customs. Having lived a sheltered and essentially isolated existence, the English developed a fear and distrust of those whose ways were foreign to them. The Americans who walked in their footsteps retained this attitude.

Many American historians will reject this interpretation. They will probably allege that American willingness to accept millions of destitute immigrants in the nineteenth century obviously contradicts the view that the Anglo-Saxon conqueror and settler distrusted what was strange in others. Some truth is present here, but the weight of the evidence lies on the other side. What must be kept firmly in mind is that immigration to the English colonies and later to the United States—in particular, the tidal wave of humanity that engulfed the United States in the post-Civil War era—was European in origin. Whether Italians, Jews, or Greeks from the Mediterranean, Swedes, Scots, or Germans from the North, what they had in common far outweighed conflicting traits and cultural and physical differences. All were European, offspring of one body of traditions and beliefs. Whether Catholics, Protestants, or Jews, they professed adherence to Western religious practices and beliefs. The so-called melting pot was scarcely a melting pot at all; the ingredients were European in origin. All

spices that would have given the stew an entirely different flavor were carefully kept out— namely, the Black and the Indian.

It was logical that Manifest Destiny, that American belief in a Providence of special design, should have racial overtones. Having meticulously kept out the infidel, Americans could rightly claim a racial doctrine of purity and supremacy in the world of 1846. Had not the nation of Polk's era developed free of those races not a part of the European heritage? Had the nation not progressed rapidly? Most assuredly, the answer was yes. When American development was compared to that of the former Spanish-American colonies, the reply was even more emphatically in the affirmative. After all, the Latin republics to the south had little to boast about. All were backward, illiterate, and badly governed states. Americans had just cause for satisfaction with what they had accomplished.

Unfortunately for Latin America, and especially Mexico, American pride had dire implications for the future. Convinced of the innate racial supremacy which the slogan of Manifest Destiny proclaimed throughout the world, many Americans came to believe that the New World was theirs to develop. Only their industry, their ingenuity, and their intelligence could cope fully with the continental challenge. Why should half-breed Mexico—backward, politically a wasteland, and hopelessly split by nature and man's failures—hold Texas, New Mexico, and California? In Mexico's possession, all these lands would lie virgin, offering a home to a few thousand savage Indians, and here and there a Mexican pueblo of people scarcely different from their heathen neighbors. Manifest Destiny proclaimed what most Americans firmly believed—the right of Anglo-Saxons and others of similar racial origin to develop what Providence had promised them. Weak Mexico, prey of its own cupidity and mistakes, was the victim of this belief.

Manifest Destiny, writes Mexican historian Carlos Bosch García, also contradicts an old

American view that means are as important as ends. He stresses that the key to the history of the United States, as the doctrine of Manifest Destiny illustrates, lies in the willingness of Americans to accept as good the ultimate result of whatever they have undertaken. That the red man was driven from his homeland is accepted as inevitable and thus justifiable. American scholars might condemn the maltreatment of the Indian, but few question the final verdict.

Equally ambivalent, says Bosch García, is the American interpretation of the Mexican War. Though some American scholars of the post-Civil War period severely censured the South for what they called its responsibility for the Mexican War, their views reflected a criticism of the slavocracy rather than a heartfelt conviction that Mexico had been wronged. Obviously, there were exceptions. Hubert H. Bancroft, a California scholar and book collector, emphatically denounced Polk and his cohorts in his voluminous *History of Mexico* (1883–88). Among the politicians of the era, Abraham Lincoln won notoriety—and probably lost his seat in the House of Representatives—for his condemnation of Polk's declaration of war against Mexico. There were others, mostly members of the Whig Party, which officially opposed the war; but the majority, to repeat, was more involved with the problem of the South than with the question of war guilt.

Most Americans have discovered ways and means to justify Manifest Destiny's war on Mexico. That country's chronic political instability, its unwillingness to meet international obligations, its false pride in its military establishment—all, say scholars, led Mexican leaders to plunge their people into a hopeless war. Had Mexico been willing to sell California, one historian declares, no conflict would have occurred. To paraphrase Samuel F. Bemis, distinguished Yale University diplomatic scholar, no American today would undo the results of Polk's war. Put differently, to fall back on Bosch García, American writers have justified the means because of the ends. Manifest Des-

tiny has not only been explained but has been vindicated on the grounds of what has been accomplished in California and New Mexico since 1848. Or, to cite Hermann Eduard von Holst, a late nineteenth-century German scholar whose writings on American history won him a professorship at the University of Chicago, the conflict between Mexico and the United States was bound to arise. A virile and ambitious people whose cause advanced that of world civilization could not avoid battle with a decadent, puerile people. Moral judgments that applied to individuals might find Americans guilty of aggression, but the standards by which nations survive and prosper upheld the cause of the United States. Might makes right? Walt Whitman, then editor of the *Brooklyn Daily Eagle,* put down his answer succinctly:

> We love to indulge in thoughts of the future extent and power of this Republic—because with its increase is the increase in human happiness and liberty. . . . What has miserable Mexico—with her superstition, her burlesque upon freedom, her actual tyranny by the few over the many—what has she to do with the great mission of peopling the New World with a noble race? Be it ours, to achieve that mission! Be it ours to roll down all of the upstart leaven of the old despotism, that comes our way.

The conflict with Mexico was an offensive war without moral pretensions, according to Texas scholar Otis A. Singletary. It was no lofty crusade, no noble battle to right the wrongs of the past or to free a subjugated people, but a war of conquest waged by one neighbor against another. President Polk and his allies had to pay conscience money to justify a ''greedy land-grab from a neighbor too weak to defend herself.'' American indifference to the Mexican War, Singletary concludes, ''lies rooted in the guilt that we as a nation have come to feel about it.''

American racial attitudes, the product of a unique colonial background in the New World, may also have dictated the scope of territorial conquest in 1848 and, ironically, saved Mexico from total annexation. Until the clash with Mexico, the American experience had been limited to the conquest, occupation, and annexation of empty or sparsely settled territories, or lands already colonized by citizens of the United States, such as Oregon and Texas. American pioneers had been reincorporated into the Union with the annexation of Oregon and Texas and even with the purchase of Louisiana in 1803. The alien population proved small and of little importance in all three territories. White planters, farmers, and pioneers mastered the small Mexican population in Texas and easily disposed of the Indians and half-breeds in the Louisiana territory.

Expansionists and their foes had long considered both Indian and Black unfit for regeneration; both were looked on as inferior and doomed races. On this point, most Americans were in agreement. While not entirely in keeping with this view, American opinions of Latin Americans, and of Mexicans in particular, were hardly flattering. Purchase and annexation of Louisiana and Florida, and of Texas and Oregon, had been debated and postponed partly out of fear of what many believed would be the detrimental effect on American democracy resulting from the amalgamation of the half-breed and mongrel peoples of these lands. Driven by a sense of national aggrandizement, the expansionists preferred to conquer lands free of alien populations. Manifest Destiny had no place for the assimilation of strange and exotic peoples. Freedom for Americans—this was the cry, regardless of what befell the conquered natives. The location of sparsely held territory had dictated the course of empire.

James K. Polk's hunger for California reflected national opinion on races as well as desire for land. Both that territory and New Mexico, nearly to the same extent, were almost barren of native populations. Of sparsely settled California, in 1845, the *Hartford Times* eloquently declared that Americans could "redeem from unhallowed hands a land, above all others of heaven, and hold it for the use of a people who know how to obey heaven's behests." Thus, it was that the tide of conquest—the fruits of the conference table at Guadalupe Hidalgo—stopped on the border of Mexico's inhabited lands, where the villages of a people alien in race and culture confronted the invaders. American concepts of race, the belief in the regeneration of virgin lands—these logically ordered annexation of both California and New Mexico, but left Mexico's settled territory alone.

Many Americans, it is true, gave much thought to the conquest and regeneration of all Mexico, but the peace of 1848 came before a sufficiently large number of them had abandoned traditional thoughts on race and color to embrace the new gospel. Apparently, most Americans were not yet willing to accept dark-skinned people as the burden of the white man.

Manifest Destiny, that mid-nineteenth-century slogan, is now merely a historical question for most Americans. Despite the spectacular plums garnered from the conference table, the war is forgotten by political orators, seldom discussed in classrooms, and only infrequently recalled by historians and scholars.

But Mexicans, whether scholars or not, have not forgotten the war; their country suffered most from Manifest Destiny's claims to California. The war of 1846–48 represents one of the supreme tragedies of their history. Mexicans are intimately involved with it, unlike their late adversaries who have forgotten it. Fundamental reasons explain this paradox. The victorious United States went to a post-Civil War success story unequaled in the annals of Western civilization. Mexico emerged from the peace of Guadalupe Hidalgo bereft of half of its territory, a beaten, discouraged, and divided country. Mexico never completely recovered from the debacle.

Mexicans had known tragedy and defeat before, but their conquest by General Zachary Taylor and Winfield Scott represented not only a territorial loss of immense proportions, but also a cataclysmic blow to their morale as a nation and as a people. From the Mexican point of view, pride in what they believed they had mastered best—the science of warfare—was exposed as a myth. Mexicans could not even fight successfully, and they had little else to recall with pride, for their political development had enshrined bitter civil strife and callous betrayal of principle. Plagued by hordes of scheming politicians, hungry military men, and a backward and reactionary clergy, they had watched their economy stagnate. Guadalupe Hidalgo clearly outlined the scope of their defeat. There was no success story to write about, only tragedy. Mexicans of all classes are still engrossed in what might have been *if* General Antonio López de Santa Anna had repelled the invaders from the North.

Polk's war message to Congress and Lincoln's famous reply in the House cover some dimensions of the historical problem. Up for discussion are Polk's role in the affair, the responsibility of the United States and Mexico, and the question of war guilt—a question raised by the victorious Americans and their allies at Nuremberg after World War II. For if Polk felt "the blood of this war, like the blood of Abel, is crying to Heaven against him," as Lincoln charged, then both the war and Manifest Destiny stand condemned.

SUGGESTED READINGS

Bill, A. H. *Rehearsal for Conflict: The War with Mexico, 1846–1848.* New York: Alfred A. Knopf, 1947.

Billington, Ray A. *Westward Expansion: A History of the American Frontier.* New York: Macmillan, 1949.

Bulnes, Francisco. *Las Grandes Mentiras de Nuestra Historia.* Mexico: Editorial Nacional, 1969.

Castañeda, Carolos E., ed. *The Mexican Side of the Texas Revolution.* Dallas: P. L. Turner, 1928.

DeVoto, Bernard. *The Year of Decision, 1846.* Boston: Little, Brown, 1946.

Fuentes Mares, José. *Poinsett. La Historia de una Intriga.* Mexico: Editorial Jus, 1964.

Graebner, Norman A. *Empire on the Pacific.* New York: Ronald Press, 1955.

Merk, Frederick. *Manifest Destiny and Mission in American History: A Reinterpretation.* New York: Alfred A. Knopf, 1963.

Price, Glenn W. *Origins of the War with Mexico: the Polk-Stockton Intrigue.* Austin: University of Texas, 1967.

Ramirez, Jose Fernando. *Mexico during the War with the United States.* Columbia, Mo.: University of Missouri Press, 1950.

Roa Barcena, José María. *Recuerdos de la Invasión Norteamericana, 1846–1848.* 3 vols., Mexico: Editorial Porrúa, 1947.

Santa Anna, Antonio López de. *Mi Historia Militar y Política, 1810–1874.* Mexico: Editorial Nacional, 1958.

Singletary, Otis A. *The Mexican War.* Chicago: University of Chicago Press, 1960.

Smith, Justin H. *The War with Mexico.* 2 vols. New York: Macmillan, 1919.

Stephenson, Nathaniel W. *Texas and the Mexican War.* New Haven, Conn.: Yale University Press, 1921.

Valades, Jose C. *Santa Anna y la Guerra de Texas.* Mexico: Imprenta Mundial, 1935.

Vasconcelos, José. *Breve Historia de México.* Mexico: Editorial Continental, 1980.

Vázquez, Josefina. *Mexicanos y Norteamericanos Ante la Guerra Del 47.* Mexico: Secretaría de Educación Pública, 1972.

Weinberg, Albert K. *Manifest Destiny: A Study of Nationalist Expansion in American History.* Baltimore: Johns Hopkins Press, 1935.

DOCUMENT 11.1
Manifest Destiny

The Democratic lawyer and journalist John L. O'Sullivan was among the most prominent

Source: John L. O'Sullivan, "Annexation," *United States Magazine and Democratic Review* (July–August 1845), vol. 17, pp. 5–10.

spokesmen for expansion. As editor of the
United States Magazine and Democratic
Review, *he had ample opportunity to familarize
Americans with "Manifest Destiny" and
appeal to the powerful emotional impulse it
evoked.*

It is time now for opposition to the Annexation
of Texas to cease, all further agitation of the
waters of bitterness and strife, at least in connexion with this question,—even though it may
perhaps be required of us as a necessary condition of the freedom of our institutions, that
we must live on for ever in a state of unpausing
struggle and excitement upon some subject of
party division or other. But, in regard to Texas,
enough has now been given to Party. It is time
for the common duty of Patriotism to the Country to succeed;—or if this claim will not be
recognized, it is at least time for common sense
to acquiesce with decent grace in the inevitable
and the irrevocable.

Texas is now ours. Already, before these
words are written, her Convention has undoubtedly ratified the acceptance, by her
Congress, of our proffered invitation into the
Union; and made the requisite changes in her
already republican form of constitution to
adopt it to its future federal relations. Her
star and her stripe may already be said to have
taken their place in the glorious blazon of our
common nationality; and the sweep of our
eagle's wing already includes within its circuit
the wide extent of her fair and fertile land.
She is no longer to us a mere geographical
space—a certain combination of coast, plain,
mountain, valley, forest and stream. She is
no longer to us a mere country on the map.
She comes within the dear and sacred designa-
tion of Our Country. . . .

Why, were other reasoning wanting, in favor
of now elevating this question of the reception
of Texas into the Union, out of the lower region
of our past party dissensions, up to its proper
level of a high and broad nationality, it surely

is to be found, found abundantly, in the manner
in which other nations have undertaken to in-
trude themselves into it, between us and the
proper parties to the case, in a spirit of hostile
interference against us, for the avowed object
of thwarting our policy and hampering our
power, limiting our greatness and checking the
fulfilment of our manifest destiny to overspread
the continent allotted by Providence for the
free development of our yearly multiplying millions. . . .

It is wholly untrue, and unjust to ourselves,
the pretence that the Annexation has been a
measure of spoliation, unrightful and unrigh-
teous—of military conquest under forms of
peace and law—of territorial aggrandizement at
the expense of justice, and justice due by a double sanctity to the weak. This view of the question is wholly unfounded, and has been before
so amply refuted in these pages, as well as in a
thousand other modes, that we shall not again
dwell upon it. The independence of Texas was
complete and absolute. It was an independence,
not only in fact but of right. No obligation of
duty towards Mexico tended in the least degree
to restrain our right to effect the desired recov-
ery of the fair province once our own—whatever motives of policy might have prompted
a more deferential consideration of her feelings
and her pride, as involved in the question. If
Texas became peopled with an American population, it was by no contrivance of our government, but on the express invitation of that of
Mexico herself; accompanied with such guaranties of State independence, and the maintenance
of a federal system analogous to our own, as
constituted a compact fully justifying the
strongest measures of redress on the part of
those afterwards deceived in this guaranty, and
sought to be enslaved under the yoke imposed
by its violation. She was released, rightfully
and absolutely released, from all Mexican allegiance, or duty of cohesion to the Mexican
political body, by the acts and fault of Mexico
herself, and Mexico alone. There never was

a clearer case. It was not revolution; it was resistance to revolution; and resistance under such circumstances as left independence the necessary resulting state, caused by the abandonment of those with whom her former federal association had existed. What then can be more preposterous than all this clamor by Mexico and the Mexican interest, against Annexation, as a violation of any rights of hers, any duties of our? . . .

Nor is there any just foundation of the charge that Annexation is a great proslavery measure—calculated to increase and perpetuate that institution. Slavery had nothing to do with it. . . . The country which was the subject of Annexation in this case, from its geographical position and relations, happens to be—or rather the portion of it now actually settled, happens to be—a slave country. But a similar process might have taken place in proximity to a different section of our Union; and indeed there is a great deal of Annexation yet to take place, within the life of the present generation, along the whole line of our northern border. Texas has been absorbed into the Union in the inevitable fulfilment of the general law which is rolling our population westward; the connexion of which with that ratio of growth in population which is destined within a hundred years to swell our numbers to the enormous population of *two hundred and fifty millions* (if not more), is too evident to leave us in doubt of the manifest design of Providence in regard to the occupation of this continent. It was disintegrated from Mexico in the natural course of events, by a process perfectly legitimate on its own part, blameless on ours; and in which all the censures due to wrong, perfidy and folly, rest on Mexico alone. And possessed as it was by a population which was in truth but a colonial detachment from our own, and which was still bound by myriad ties of the very heartstrings to its old relations, domestic and political, their incorporation into the Union was not only inevitable, but the most natural, right and proper

thing in the world—and it is only astonishing that there should be any among ourselves to say it nay. . . .

California will, probably, next fall away from the loose adhesion which, in such a country as Mexico, holds a remote province in a slight equivocal kind of dependence on the metropolis. Imbecile and distracted, Mexico never can exert any real government authority over such a country. The impotence of the one and the distance of the other, must make the relation one of virtual independence; unless, by stunting the province of all natural growth, and forbidding that immigration which can alone develope its capabilities and fulfil the purposes of its creation, tyranny may retain a military dominion which is no government in the legitimate sense of the term. In the case of California this is now impossible. The Anglo-Saxon foot is already on its borders. Already the advance guard of the irresistible army of Anglo-Saxon emigration has begun to pour down upon it, armed with the plough and the rifle, and marking its trail with schools and colleges, courts and representative halls, mills and meeting-houses. A population will soon be in actual occupation of California, over which it will be idle for Mexico to dream of dominion. They will necessarily become independent. All this without agency of our government, without responsibility of our people—in the natural flow of events, the spontaneous working of principles, and the adaptation of the tendencies and wants of the human race to the elemental circumstances in the midst of which they find themselves placed. And they will have a right to independence—to self-government—to the possession of the homes conquered from the wilderness by their own labors and dangers, sufferings and sacrifices—a better and a truer right than the artificial title of sovereignty in Mexico a thousand miles distant, inheriting from Spain a title good only against those who have none better. Their right to independence will be the natural right of self-government belonging to any community strong enough to maintain it—distinct in position, origin and character, and free from any mutual obligations of membership of a common political body, binding it to others by the duty of loyalty and compact of public faith. This will be their title to independence; and by this title, there can be no doubt that the population now fast streaming down upon California will both assert and maintain the independence. Whether they will then attach themselves to our Union or not, is not to be predicted with any certainty. Unless the projected rail-road across the continent to the Pacific be carried into effect, perhaps they may not; though even in that case, the day is not distant when the Empires of the Atlantic and Pacific would again flow together into one, as soon as their inland border should approach each other. But that great work, colossal as appears the plan on its first suggestion, cannot remain long unbuilt. Its necessity for this very purpose of binding and holding together in its iron clasp our fast settling Pacific region with that of the Mississippi valley—the natural facility of the route—the ease with which any amount of labor for the construction can be drawn in from the overcrowded populations of Europe, to be paid in the lands made valuable by the progress of the work itself—and its immense utility to the commerce of the world with the whole eastern coast of Asia, alone almost sufficient for the support of such a road—these considerations give assurance that the day cannot be distant which shall witness the conveyance of the representatives from Oregon and California to Washington within less time than a few years ago was devoted to a similar journey by those from Ohio; while the magnetic telegraph will enable the editors of the "San Francisco Union," the "Astoria Evening Post," or the "Nootka Morning News" to set up in type the first half of the President's Inaugural, before the echoes of the latter half shall have died away beneath the lofty porch of the Capitol, as spoken from his lips.

Away, then, with all idle French talk of *balances of power* on the American Continent. There is no growth in Spanish America! Whatever progress of population there may be in the British Canadas, is only for their own early severance of their present colonial relation to the little island three thousand miles across the Atlantic; soon to be followed by Annexation, and destined to swell the still accumulating momentum of our progress. And whatsoever may hold the balance, though they should cast into the opposite scale all the bayonets and cannon, not only of France and England, but of Europe entire, how would it kick the beam against the simple solid weight of the two hundred and fifty or three hundred millions—and American millions—destined to gather beneath the flutter of the stripes and stars, in the fast hastening year of the Lord 1945?

DOCUMENT 11.2
The Superior Race and the Divine Command

Missouri Senator Thomas Hart Benton, possibly the most eloquent spokesman for Manifest Destiny in the 1840s, appealed for the annexation of Oregon. But he framed this plea in the broadest terms, thereby giving it meaning for expansionism generally. Reaffirming the dual themes of American glory and American destiny in this Senate speech of May 28, 1846, Benton contributed to a new aggressive nationalism that made no speculation too bold, no military or wilderness prospect too great. But he did more than give impulse and definition to a program of territorial conquest; he voiced a theme that would be viable for over a half century.

. . . Since the dispersion of man upon earth, I know of no human event, past or present,

Source: *Congressional Globe,* May 28, 1846.

which promises a greater, and more beneficent change upon earth than the arrival of the van of the Caucasian race (the Celtic-Anglo-Saxon division) upon the border of the sea which washes the shore of the eastern Asia. The Mongolian, or Yellow race, is there, four hundred millions in number, spreading almost to Europe; a race once the foremost of the human family in the arts of civilization, but torpid and stationary for thousands of years. It is a race far above the Ethiopian, or Black—above the Malay, or Brown (if we must admit five races)—and above the American Indian, or Red: it is a race far above all these, but still, far below the White; and, like all the rest, must receive an impression from the superior race whenever they come in contact. It would seem that the White race alone received the divine command, to subdue and replenish the earth! for it is the only race that has obeyed it—the only one that hunts out new and distant lands, and even a New World, to subdue and replenish. Starting from western Asia, taking Europe for their field, and the Sun for their guide, and leaving the Mongolians behind, they arrived, after many ages, on the shores of the Atlantic, which they lit up with the lights of science and religion, and adorned with the useful and elegant arts. Three and a half centuries ago, this race, in obedience to the great command, arrived in the New World, and found new lands to subdue and replenish. For a long time, it was confined to the border of the new field (I now mean the Celtic-Anglo-Saxon division); and even fourscore years ago the philosophic Burke was considered a rash man because he said the English colonists would top the Alleghanies, and descend into the valley of the Mississippi, and occupy without parchment if the Crown refused to make grants of land. What was considered a rash declaration eighty years ago, is old history, in our young country, at this day. Thirty years ago I said the same thing of the Rocky Mountains and the Columbia: it was ridiculed then: it is becom-

ing history to-day. The venerable Mr. Macon has often told me that he remembered a line low down in North Carolina, fixed by a royal governor as a boundary between the whites and the Indians: where is that boundary now? The van of the Caucasian race now top the Rocky Mountains, and spread down to the shores of the Pacific. In a few years a great population will grow up there, luminous with the accumulated lights of European and American civilization. Their presence in such a position cannot be without its influence upon eastern Asia. The sun of civilization must shine across the sea: socially and commercially, the van of the Caucasians, and the rear of the Mongolians, must intermix. They must talk together, and trade together, and marry together. Commerce is a great civilizer—social intercourse as great—and marriage greater. The White and Yellow races can marry together, as well as eat and trade together. Moral and intellectual superiority will do the rest: the White race will take the ascendant, elevating what is susceptible of improvement—wearing out what is not. The Red race has disappeared from the Atlantic coast: the tribes that resisted civilization, met extinction. This is a cause of lamentation with many. For my part, I cannot murmur at what seems to be the effect of divine law. I cannot repine that this Capitol has replaced the wigwam—this Christian people, replaced the savages—white matrons, the red squaws—and that such men as Washington, Franklin, and Jefferson, have taken the place of Powhattan, Opechonecanough, and other red men, howsoever respectable they may have been as savages. Civilization, or extinction, has been the fate of all people who have found themselves in the track of the advancing Whites, and civilization, always the preference of the Whites, has been pressed as an object, while extinction has followed as a consequence of its resistance. The Black and the Red races have often felt their ameliorating influence. The Yellow race, next to themselves in the scale of mental and moral excellence, and in the beauty of form, once their superiors in the useful and elegant arts, and in learning, and still respectable though stationary; this race cannot fail to receive a new impulse from the approach of the Whites, improved so much since so many ages ago they left the western borders of Asia. The apparition of the van of the Caucasian race, rising upon them in the east after having left them on the west, and after having completed the circumnavigation of the globe, must wake up and reanimate the torpid body of old Asia. Our position and policy will commend us to their hospitable reception: political considerations will aid the action of social and commercial influences. Pressed upon by the great Powers of Europe—the same that press upon us— they must in our approach see the advent of friends, not of foes—of benefactors, not of invaders. The moral and intellectual superiority of the White race will do the rest: and thus, the youngest people, and the newest land, will become the reviver and the regenerator of the oldest.

DOCUMENT 11.3
Texas Annexation and the Expansion of Slavery

In April 1844, Secretary of State John C. Calhoun signed a treaty of annexation with the Republic of Texas. Although the acquisition of Texas fitted the expansionist mood of the nation, the treaty was rejected by the Senate partly because Calhoun confided to the British minister, Richard Pakenham, that his primary motive was the protection of slavery. Texas was admitted by joint resolution after Polk's

Source: William R. Manning, ed., *The Diplomatic Correspondence of the United States: Inter-American Affairs, 1831–1860* (Washington, D.C.: Carnegie Endowment for International Peace, 1936), vol. 7, pp. 18–25.

election, but among Northerners there was a lingering suspicion that the ensuing war with Mexico was part of a southern effort to expand slave territory.

Washington, April 18, 1844

The Undersigned Secretary of State of the United States, has laid before the President the note of the Right Honorable Mr. Pakenham, Envoy Extraordinary and Minister Plenipotentiary of Her Britannic Majesty, addressed to this Department on the 26th of February last, together with the accompanying copy of a despatch of Her Majesty's Principal Secretary of State for Foreign Affairs to Mr. Pakenham.

* * * * *

So long as Great Britain confined her policy to the abolition of slavery in her own possessions and colonies, no other country had a right to complain. It belonged to her, exclusively, to determine according to her own views of policy whether it should be done or not. But when she goes beyond, and avows it as her settled policy, and the object of her constant exertions, to abolish it throughout the world, she makes it the duty of all other countries, whose safety or prosperity may be endangered by her policy, to adopt such measures as they may deem necessary for their protection.

It is with still deeper concern the President regards the avowal of Lord Aberdeen of the desire of Great Britain to see slavery abolished in Texas; and, as he infers, is endeavoring, through her diplomacy, to accomplish it, by making the abolition of slavery one of the conditions on which Mexico should acknowledge her independence. It has confirmed his previous impressions as to the policy of Great Britain in reference to Texas, and made it his duty to examine with much care the solicitude, what would be its effects on the prosperity and safety of the United States should she succeed in her endeavors. The investigation has resulted in the settled conviction that it would be difficult for Texas, in her actual condition, to resist what she desires, without supposing the influence and exertions of Great Britain would be extended beyond the limits assigned by Lord Aberdeen; and that, if Texas could not resist, the consummation of the object of her desire would endanger both the safety and prosperity of the Union. Under this conviction, it is felt to be the imperious duty of the Federal Government, the common representative and protector of the States of this Union, to adopt, in self-defence, the most effectual measures to defeat it.

This is not the proper occasion to state at large the grounds of this conviction. It is sufficient to say, that the consummation of the avowed object of her wishes in reference to Texas, would be followed by hostile feelings and relations between that country and the United States, which could not fail to place her under the influence and control of Great Britain. That, from the geographical position of Texas, would expose the weakest and most vulnerable portion of our frontier to inroads, and place, in the power of Great Britain, the most efficient means of effecting in the neighboring States of this Union, what she avows it to be her desire to do in all countries, where slavery exists. To hazard consequences which would be so dangerous to the prosperity and safety of this Union, without resorting to the most effective measures to prevent them, would be, on the part of the Federal Government, an abandonment of the most solemn obligation imposed by the guaranty, which the States, in adopting the constitution, entered into to protect each other against whatever might endanger their safety, whether from without or within. Acting in obedience to this obligation, on which our Federal System of Government rests, the President directs me to inform you that a treaty has been concluded between the United States and Texas, for the annexation of the latter to the former, as a part of its territory, which will be submitted without delay to the Senate for its approval. This step has been taken as the most effectual, if not the only, means of guarding against the threatened danger, and securing their permanent peace and welfare.

It is well known that Texas has long desired to be annexed to this Union; that her People, at the time of the adoption of her constitution, expressed by an almost unanimous vote, her desire to that effect; and that she has never ceased to desire it, as the most certain means of promoting her safety and prosperity. The United States have heretofore declined to meet her wishes; but the time has now arrived when they can no longer refuse consistently with their own security and peace, and the sacred obligation imposed by their constitutional compact, for mutual defence and protection. Nor are they any way responsible for the circumstances which have imposed this obligation on them. They had no agency in bringing about the state of things which has terminated in the separation of Texas from Mexico. . . . A large number of the States has decided, that it is neither wise nor humane to change the relation, which has existed from their first settlement, between the two races; while others, where the African is less numerous, have adopted the opposite policy.

It belongs not to this Government to question whether the former have decided wisely or not; and if it did, the Undersigned would not regard this as the proper occasion to discuss the subject. He does not, however, deem it irrelevant to state, that, if the experience of more than half a century is to decide, it would be neither humane nor wise in them to change their policy. The census and other authentic documents show that, in all instances in which the States have changed the former relation between the two races, the condition of the African, instead of being improved, has become worse. They have invariably sunk into vice and pauperism, accompanied by the bodily and mental inflictions [afflictions] incident thereto—deafness, blindness, insanity and idiocy, to a degree without example; while, in all other States which have retained the ancient relation between them, they have improved greatly in every respect—in number, comfort, intelligence, and morals, as the following facts, taken from such sources will serve to illustrate. . . .

DOCUMENT 11.4
The President's Call to Arms

James K. Polk, a Jacksonian Democrat and an ardent nationalist, spoke for American expansionists of the 1840s. Through diplomatic pressure, Polk hoped to persuade the Mexican government of the wisdom of: (1) accepting the Rio Grande as the border between the two nations, (2) satisfying American citizens' claims on Mexico through cession of territory in the Southwest, and (3) selling California to the United States. When such efforts proved unsuccessful and American troops were attacked in disputed territory between the Nueces River and the Rio Grande, Polk, whose patience with diplomatic negotiation had worn thin, did not hesitate to ask Congress for a declaration of war against Mexico.

The existing state of the relations between the United States and Mexico renders it proper that I should bring the subject to the consideration of Congress. In my message at the commencement of your present session, the state of these relations, the causes which led to the suspension of diplomatic intercourse between the two countries in March, 1845, and the long-continued and unredressed wrongs and injuries committed by the Mexican government on citizens of the United States, in their persons and property, were briefly set forth.

Source: James D. Richardson, ed., *A Compliation of the Messages and Papers of the Presidents, 1789–1897* (New York: Bureau of National Literature and Art, 1909), vol. 5, pp. 2287–93.

As the facts and opinions which were then laid before you were carefully considered, I cannot better express my present convictions of the condition of affairs up to that time, than by referring you to that communication.

The strong desire to establish peace with Mexico on liberal and honorable terms, and the readiness of this government to regulate and adjust our boundary, and other causes of difference with that power, on such fair and equitable principles as would lead to permanent relations of the most friendly nature, induced me in September last to seek the reopening of diplomatic relations between the two countries. Every measure adopted on our part had for its object the furtherance of these desired results. In communicating to Congress a succinct statement of the injuries which we had suffered from Mexico, and which have been accumulating during a period of more than twenty years, every expression that could tend to inflame the people of Mexico, or defeat or delay a pacific result, was carefully avoided. An envoy of the United States repaired to Mexico, with full powers to adjust every existing difference. But though present on the Mexican soil, by agreement between the two governments, invested with full powers, and bearing evidence of the most friendly dispositions, his mission has been unavailing. The Mexican government not only refused to receive him, or listen to his propositions, but, after a long continued series of menaces, have at last invaded our territory, and shed the blood of our fellow-citizens on our own soil.

It now becomes my duty to state more in detail the origin, progress, and failure of that mission. In pursuance of the instructions given in September last, an inquiry was made, on the thirteenth of October, 1845, in the most friendly terms, through our consul in Mexico, of the minister for foreign affairs, whether the Mexican government "would receive an envoy from the United States intrusted with full powers to adjust all the questions in dispute between the two governments''; with the assurance that ''should the answer be in the affirmative, such an envoy would be immediately despatched to Mexico.'' The Mexican minister, on the fifteenth of October, gave an affirmative answer to this inquiry, requesting, at the same time, that our naval force at Vera Cruz might be withdrawn, lest its continued presence might assume the appearance of menace and coercion pending the negotiations. This force was immediately withdrawn. On the 10th of November, 1845, Mr. John Slidell, of Louisiana, was commissioned by me as envoy extraordinary and minister plenipotentiary of the United States to Mexico, and was entrusted with full powers to adjust both the questions of the Texas boundary and of indemnification to our citizens. The redress of the wrongs of our citizens naturally and inseparably blended itself with the question of boundary. The settlement of the one question, in any correct view of the subject, involves that of the other. I could not, for a moment, entertain the idea that the claims of our much injured and long suffering citizens, many of which had existed for more than twenty years, should be postponed, or separated from the settlement of the boundary question.

Mr. Slidell arrived at Vera Cruz on the 30th of November, and was courteously received by the authorities of that city. But the government of General Herrera was then tottering to its fall. The revolutionary party had seized upon the Texas question to effect or hasten its overthrow. Its determination to restore friendly relations with the United States, and to receive our minister, to negotiate for the settlement of this question, was violently assailed, and was made the great theme of denunciation against it. The government of General Herrera, there is good reason to believe, was sincerely desirous to receive our minister; but it yielded to the storm raised by its enemies, and on the 21st of December refused to accredit Mr. Slidell upon the most frivolous pretexts. These are so fully and ably exposed in the note of Mr.

Slidell, of the 24th of December last, to the Mexican minister of foreign relations, herewith transmitted, that I deem it unnecessary to enter into further detail on this portion of the subject.

Five days after the date of Mr. Slidell's note, General Herrera yielded the government to General Paredes, without a struggle, and on the 30th of December resigned the presidency. This revolution was accomplished solely by the army, the people having taken little part in the contest, and thus the supreme power in Mexico passed into the hands of a military leader.

Determined to leave no effort untried to effect an amicable adjustment with Mexico, I directed Mr. Slidell to present his credentials to the government of General Paredes, and ask to be officially received by him. There would have been less ground for taking this step had General Paredes come into power by a regular constitutional succession. In that event his administration would have been considered but a mere constitutional continuance of the government of General Herrera, and the refusal of the latter to receive our minister would have been deemed conclusive, unless an intimation had been given by General Paredes of his desire to reverse the decision of his predecessor. But the government of General Paredes owes its existence to a military revolution, by which the subsisting constitutional authorities had been subverted. The form of government was entirely changed, as well as all the high functionaries by whom it was administered.

Under these circumstances, Mr. Slidell, in obedience to my direction, addressed a note to the Mexican minister of foreign relations, under date of the 1st of March last, asking to be received by that government in the diplomatic character to which he had been appointed. This minister, in his reply under date of the 12th of March, reiterated the arguments of his predecessor, and, in terms that may be considered as giving just grounds of offence to the government and people of the United States, denied the application of Mr. Slidell. Nothing, therefore, remained for our envoy but to demand his passports, and return to his own country.

Thus the government of Mexico, though solemnly pledged by official acts in October last to receive and accredit an American envoy, violated their plighted faith, and refused the offer of a peaceful adjustment of our difficulties. Not only was the offer rejected, but the indignity of its rejection was enhanced by the manifest breach of faith in refusing to admit the envoy, who came because they had bound themselves to receive him. Nor can it be said that the offer was fruitless from the want of opportunity of discussing it—our envoy was present on their own soil. Nor can it be ascribed to a want of sufficient powers—our envoy had full powers to adjust every question of difference. Nor was there room for complaint that our propositions for settlement were unreasonable—permission was not even given our envoy to make any proposition whatever. Nor can it be objected that we, on our part, would not listen to any reasonable terms of their suggestion—the Mexican government refused all negotiation, and have made no proposition of any kind.

In my message at the commencement of the present session, I informed you that, upon the earnest appeal both of the congress and convention of Texas, I had ordered an efficient military force to take a position "between the Nueces and the Del Norte." This had become necessary, to meet a threatened invasion of Texas by the Mexican forces, for which extensive military preparations had been made. The invasion was threatened solely because Texas had determined, in accordance with a solemn resolution of the Congress of the United States, to annex herself to our Union; and, under these circumstances, it was plainly our duty to extend our protection over her citizens and soil.

This force was concentrated at Corpus Christi, and remained there until after I had received such information from Mexico as rendered it probable, if not certain, that the Mexican government would refuse to receive our envoy.

Meantime Texas, by the final action of our Congress, had become an integral part of our Union. The Congress of Texas, by its act of December 19, 1836, had declared the Rio del Norte to be the boundary of that republic. Its jurisdiction had been extended and exercised beyond the Nueces. The country between that river and the Del Norte had been represented in the congress and in the convention of Texas; had thus taken part in the act of annexation itself; and is now included within one of our congressional districts. Our own Congress had, moreover, with great unanimity, by the act approved December 31, 1845, recognised the country beyond the Nueces as a part of our territory, by including it within our own revenue system; and a revenue officer, to reside within that district, has been appointed, by and with the advice and consent of the Senate. It became, therefore, of urgent necessity to provide for the defence of that portion of our country. Accordingly, on the 13th of January last, instructions were issued to the general in command of these troops to occupy the left bank of the Del Norte. This river, which is the southwestern boundary of the State of Texas, is an exposed frontier; from this quarter invasion was threatened; upon it, and in its immediate vicinity, in the judgment of high military experience, are the proper stations for the protecting forces of the government. In addition to this important consideration, several others occurred to induce this movement. Among these are the facilities afforded by the ports of Brazos Santiago and the mouth of the Del Norte, for the reception of supplies by sea; the stronger and more healthful military positions; the convenience for obtaining a ready and a more abundant supply of provisions, water, fuel, and forage; and the advantages which are afforded by the Del Norte in forwarding supplies to such posts as may be established in the interior and upon the Indian frontier.

The movement of the troops to the Del Norte was made by the commanding general, under positive instructions to abstain from all aggressive acts towards Mexico or Mexican citizens, and to regard the relations between that republic and the United States as peaceful, unless she would declare war, or commit acts of hostility indicative of a state of war. He was specially directed to protect private property, and rspect personal rights.

The army moved from Corpus Christi on the eleventh of March, and on the twenty-eighth of that month arrived on the left bank of the Del Norte, opposite to Matamoras, where it encamped on a commanding position, which has since been strengthened by the erection of field works. A depot has also been established at Point Isabel, near the Brazos Santiago, thirty miles in rear of the encampment. The selection of his position was necessarily confided to the judgment of the general in command.

The Mexican forces at Matamoras assumed a belligerent attitude, and, on the twelfth of April, General Ampudia, then in command, notified General Taylor to break up his camp within twenty-four hours, and to retire beyond the Nueces river, and, in the event of his failure to comply with these demands, announced that arms, and arms alone, must decide the question. But no open act of hostility was committed until the twenty-fourth of April. On that day, General Arista, who had succeeded to the command of the Mexican forces, communicated to General Taylor that ''he considered hostilities commenced, and should prosecute them.'' A party of dragoons, of sixty-three men and officers, were on the same day despatched from the American camp up the Rio del Norte, on its left bank, to ascertain whether the Mexican troops had crossed, or were preparing to cross, the river, ''became engaged with a large body of these troops, and, after a short affair, in

which some sixteen were killed and wounded, appear to have been surrounded and compelled to surrender.''

The grievous wrongs perpetrated by Mexico upon our citizens throughout a long period of years remain unredressed; and solemn treaties, pledging her public faith for this redress, have been disregarded. A government either unable or unwilling to enforce the execution of such treaties, fails to perform one of its plainest duties.

Our commerce with Mexico has been almost annihilated. It was formerly highly beneficial to both nations; but our merchants have been deterred from prosecuting it by the system of outrage and extortion which the Mexican authorities have pursued against them, whilst their appeals through their own government for indemnity have been made in vain. Our forbearance has gone to such an extreme as to be mistaken in its character. Had we acted with vigor in repelling the insults and redressing the injuries inflicted by Mexico at the commencement, we should doubtless have escaped all the difficulties in which we are now involved.

Instead of this, however, we have been exerting our best efforts to propitiate her goodwill. Upon the pretext that Texas, a nation as independent as herself, thought proper to unite its destinies with our own, she has affected to believe that we have severed her rightful territory, and in official proclamations and manifestoes has repeatedly threatened to make war upon us, for the purpose of reconquering Texas. In the meantime, we have tried every effort at reconciliation. The cup of forbearance had been exhausted, even before the recent information from the frontier of the Del Norte. But now, after reiterated menaces, Mexico has passed the boundary of the United States, has invaded our territory, and shed American blood upon the American soil. She has proclaimed that hostilities have commenced, and that the two nations are now at war.

As war exists, and, notwithstanding all our efforts to avoid it, exists by the act of Mexico herself, we are called upon by every consideration of duty and patriotism to vindicate with decision and honor, the rights, and the interests of our country.

Anticipating the possibility of a crisis like that which has arrived, instructions were given in August last, "as a precautionary measure" against invasion, or threatened invasion, authorizing General Taylor, if the emergency required, to accept volunteers, not from Texas only, but from the States of Louisiana, Alabama, Mississippi, Tennessee, and Kentucky; and corresponding letters were addressed to the respective governors of those States. These instructions were repeated; and, in January last, soon after the incorporation of "Texas into our union of States," General Taylor was further "authorized by the President to make a requisition upon the executive of that State for such of its militia force as may be needed to repel invasion, or to secure the country against apprehended invasion." On the second day of March he was again reminded, "in the event of the approach of any considerable Mexican force, promptly and efficiently to use the authority with which he was clothed to call to him such auxiliary force as he might need." War actually existing, and our territory having been invaded, General Taylor, pursuant to authority vested in him by my direction, has called on the governor of Texas for four regiments of State troops—two to be mounted, and two to serve on foot; and on the governor of Louisiana for four regiments of infantry, to be sent to him as soon as practicable.

In further vindication of our rights, and defence of our territory, I invoke the prompt action of Congress to recognise the existence of the war, and to place at the disposition of the Executive the means of prosecuting the war with vigor, and thus hastening the restoration of peace. To this end I recommend that authority should be given to call into the public service a large body of volunteers, to serve for not less than six or twelve months, unless sooner discharged. A volunteer force is beyond question more efficient than any other description of citizen soldiers; and it is not to be doubted that a number far beyond that required would readily rush to the field upon the call of their country. I further recommend that a liberal provision be made for sustaining our entire military force and furnishing it with supplies and munitions of war.

The most energetic and prompt measures, and the immediate appearance in arms of a large and overpowering force, are recommended to Congress as the most certain and efficient means of bringing the existing collision with Mexico to a speedy and successful termination.

In making these recommendations, I deem it proper to declare that it is my anxious desire not only to terminate hostilities speedily, but to bring all matters in dispute between this government and Mexico to an early and amicable adjustment; and, in this view, I shall be prepared to renew negotiations, whenever Mexico shall be ready to receive propositions, or to make propositions of her own.

I transmit herewith a copy of the correspondence between our envoy to Mexico and the Mexican minister for foreign affairs; and so much of the correspondence between that envoy and the Secretary of State, and between the Secretary of War and the general in command of the Del Norte, as is necessary to a full understanding of the subject.

DOCUMENT 11.5
The President is Arraigned

Abraham Lincoln did not have a particularly distinguished one-term career in the U.S.

Source: *Congressional Globe*, 30th Cong., 1st sess., New Series, No. 10, pp. 154–56.

House of Representatives, to which he was elected in 1846. His experience in Washington disappointed him and dissatisfied his Whig constituents in Illinois. Lincoln spoke rarely in the House and gave only two speeches of any real significance; one is the following arraignment of President Polk (January 12, 1848) for the war against Mexico.

. . . The President, in his first war message of May, 1846, declares that the soil was ours on which hostilities were commenced by Mexico, and he repeats that declaration almost in the same language in each successive annual message, thus showing that he deems that point a highly essential one. In the importance of that point I entirely agree with the President. To my judgment it is the very point upon which he should be justified, or condemned. In his message of December, 1846, it seems to have occurred to him, as is certainly true, that title—ownership—to soil or anything else is not a simple fact, but is a conclusion following on one or more simple facts; and that it was incumbent upon him to present the facts from which he concluded the soil was ours on which the first blood of the war was shed.

Accordingly, . . . in the message last referred to he enters upon that task; forming an issue and introducing testimony, extending the whole to a little below the middle of page fourteen. Now, I propose to try to show that the whole of this—issue and evidence—is from beginning to end the sheerest deception. The issue, as he presents it, is in these words: "But there are those who, conceding all this to be true, assume the ground that the true western boundary of Texas is the Nueces, instead of the Rio Grande; and that, therefore, in marching our army to the east bank of the latter river, we passed the Texas line and invaded the territory of Mexico." Now this issue is made up of two affirmatives and no negative. The main deception of it is that it assumes as true that one river or the other is necessarily the bound-

ary; and cheats the superficial thinker entirely out of the idea that possibly the boundary is somewhere between the two, and not actually at either. A further deception is that it will let in evidence which a true issue would exclude. A true issue made by the President would be about as follows: "I say the soil was ours, on which the first blood was shed; there are those who say it was not."

I now proceed to examine the President's evidence as applicable to such an issue. When that evidence is analyzed, it is all included in the following propositions:

1. That the Rio Grande was the western boundary of Louisiana as we purchased it of France in 1803.
2. That the Republic of Texas always claimed the Rio Grande as her western boundary.
3. That by various acts she had claimed it on paper.
4. That Santa Anna in his treaty with Texas recognized the Rio Grande as her boundary.
5. That Texas before, and the United States after, annexation had exercised jurisdiction beyond the Nueces—between the two rivers.
6. That our Congress understood the boundary of Texas to extend beyond the Nueces.

Now for each of these in its turn. His first item is that the Rio Grande was the western boundary of Louisiana, as we purchased it of France in 1803; and seeming to expect this to be disputed, he argues over the amount of nearly a page to prove it true; at the end of which he lets us know that by the treaty of 1819 we sold to Spain the whole country from the Rio Grande eastward to the Sabine. Now, admitting for the present that the Rio Grande was the boundary of Louisiana, what, under heaven, had that to do with the present boundary between us and Mexico? How, Mr. Chairman, the line that once divided your land from mine can still be the boundary between us after I have sold my land to you is to me beyond all comprehension. And how any man, with an honest purpose only by proving the truth, could ever have thought of introducing such a fact to prove such an issue is equally incomprehensible. His next piece of evidence is that "the Republic of Texas always claimed this river (Rio Grande) as her western boundary." That is not true, in fact. Texas has claimed it, but she has not always claimed it. There is at least one distinguished exception. Her State constitution—the republic's most solemn and well-considered act; that which may, without impropriety, be called her last will and testament, revoking all others—makes no such claim. But suppose she had always claimed it. Has not Mexico always claimed the contrary? So that there is but claim against claim, leaving nothing proved until we get back to the claims and find which has the better foundation. Though not in the order in which the President presents his evidence, I now consider that class of his statements which are in substance nothing more than that Texas has, by various acts of her Convention and Congress, claimed the Rio Grande as her boundary, on paper. I mean here what he says about the fixing of the Rio Grande's as her boundary in her old constitution (not her State constitution), about forming congressional districts, counties, etc. Now all of this is but naked claim; and what I have already said about claim is strictly applicable to this. If I should claim your land by word of mouth, that certainly would not make it mine; and if I were to claim it by a deed which I had made myself, and with which you had had nothing to do, the claim would be quite the same in substance—or rather, in utter nothingness. I next consider the President's statement that Santa Anna in his treaty with Texas recognized the Rio Grande as the western boundary of Texas. Besides the position so often taken, that Santa Anna while a

prisoner of war, a captive, could not bind Mexico by a treaty, which I deem conclusive—besides this, I wish to say something in relation to this treaty, so called by the President, with Santa Anna. If any man would like to be amused by a sight of that little thing which the President calls by that big name, he can have it by turning to "Nile's Register," Vol. L, p. 336. And if any one should suppose that "Nile's Register" is a curious repository of so mighty a document as a solemn treaty between nations, I can only say that I learned to a tolerable degree of certainty, by inquiry at the State Department, that the President himself never saw it anywhere else. By the way, I believe I should not err if I were to declare that during the first ten years of the existence of that document it was never by anybody called a treaty—that it was never so called till the President, in his extremity, attempted by so calling it to wring something from it in justification of himself in connection with the Mexican war. It has none of the distinguishing features of a treaty. It does not call itself a treaty. Santa Anna does not therein assume to bind Mexico; he assumes only to act as the President-Commander-in-Chief of the Mexican army and navy; stipulates that the then present hostilities should cease, and that he would not himself take up arms, nor influence the Mexican people to take up arms, against Texas during the existence of the war of independence. He did not recognize the independence of Texas; he did not assume to put an end to the war, but clearly indicated his expectation of its continuance; he did not say one word about boundary, and, most probably, never thought of it. It is stipulated therein that the Mexican forces should evacuate the territory of Texas, passing to the other side of the Rio Grande; and in another article it is stipulated that, to prevent collisions between the armies, the Texas army should not approach nearer than within five leagues—of what is not said, but clearly, from the object stated, it is of the Rio Grande. Now, if this is a treaty recognizing the Rio Grande as the boundary of Texas, it contains the singular features of stipulating that Texas shall not go within five leagues of her own boundry.

Next comes the evidence of Texas before annexation, and the United States afterward, exercising jurisdiction beyond the Nueces and between the two rivers. This actual exercise of jurisdiction is the very class or quality of evidence we want. It is excellent so far as it goes; but does it go far enough? He tells us it went beyond the Nueces, but he does not tell us it went to the Rio Grande. He tells us jurisdiction was exercised between the two rivers, but he does not tell us it was exercised over all the territory between them. Some simple-minded people think it is possible to cross one river and go beyond it without going all the way to the next, that jurisdiction may be exercised between two rivers without covering all the country between them. I know a man, not very unlike myself, who exercises jurisdiction over a piece of land between the Wabash and the Mississippi; and yet so far is this from being all there is between those rivers that it is just one hundred and fifty-two feet long by fifty feet wide, and not part of it much within a hundred miles of either. He has a neighbor between him and the Mississippi—that is, just across the street, in that direction—whom I am sure he could neither persuade nor force to give up his habitation; but which nevertheless he could certainly annex, if it were to be done by merely standing on his own side of the street and claiming it, or even setting down and writing a deed for it.

But next the President tells us the Congress of the United States understood the State of Texas they admitted into the Union to extend beyond the Nueces. Well, I suppose they did. I certainly so understood it. But how far beyond? That Congress did not understand it to extend clear to the Rio Grande is quite certain, by the fact of their joint resolutions for admission expressly leaving all questions of boundary to future adjustment. And it may be added that Texas herself is proved to have had the same understanding of it that our Congress had, by the fact of the exact conformity of her new constitution to those resolutions.

I am now through the whole of the President's evidence; and it is a singular fact that if any one should declare the President sent the army into the midst of a settlement of Mexican people who had never submitted, by consent or by force, to the authority of Texas or of the United States, and that there and thereby the first blood of the war was shed, there is not one word in all the President has said which would either admit or deny the declaration. This strange omission it does seem to me could not have occurred but by design. My way of living leads me to be about the courts of justice; and there I have sometimes seen a good lawyer, struggling for his client's neck in a desperate case, employing every artifice to work round, befog, and cover up with many words some point arising in the case which he dared not admit and yet could not deny. Party bias may help to make it appear so, but with all the allowance I can make for such bias, it still does appear to me that just such, and from just such necessity, is the President's struggle in this case. . . .

. . . Now, sir, for the purpose of obtaining the very best evidence as to whether Texas had actually carried her revolution to the place where the hostilities of the present war commenced, let the President answer the interrogatories I proposed, as before mentioned, or some other similar ones. Let him answer fully, fairly, and candidly. Let him answer with facts and not with arguments. Let him remember he sits where Washington sat, and so remembering, let him answer as Washington would answer. As a nation should not, and the Almighty will not, be evaded, so let him attempt no evasion—no equivocation. And, if, so answering, he can show that the soil was ours where the first blood of the war was shed,—that it was not within an inhabited country, or, if within such, that the inhabitants had submitted themselves to the civil authority of Texas or of the United States, and that the same is true of the site of Fort Brown,—then I am with him for his justification. In that case I shall be most happy to reverse the vote I gave the other day. I have a selfish motive for desiring that the President may do this—I expect to gain some votes, in connection with the war, which, without his so doing, will be of doubtful propriety in my own judgment, but which will be free from the doubt if he does so. But if he can not or will not do this,—if on any pretense or no pretense he shall refuse or omit it—then I shall be fully convinced of what I more than suspect already—that he is deeply conscious of being in the wrong; that he feels the blood of this war, like the blood of Abel, is crying to Heaven against him; that originally having some strong motive—what, I will not stop now to give my opinion concerning—to involve the two countries in a war, and trusting to escape scrutiny by fixing the public gaze upon the exceeding brightness of military glory—that attractive rainbow that rises in showers of blood—that serpent's eye that charms to destroy,—he plunged into it, and has swept on and on till, disappointed in his calculation of the ease with which Mexico might be subdued, he now finds himself he knows not where. How like the half-insane mumbling of a fever dream is the whole war part of his late message! At one time telling us that Mexico has nothing whatever that we can get but territory; at another showing us how we can support the war by levying contributions on Mexico. At one time urging the national honor, the security of the future, the prevention of foreign interference, and even the good of Mexico herself as among the objects of the war; at another telling us that "to reject indemnity, by refusing to accept a cession of territory, would be to abandon all our just demands, and to wage the war bearing all its expenses, without a purpose or

definite object." So then this national honor, security of the future, and everything but territorial indemnity may be considered the no-purposes and indefinite objects of the war! But, having it now settled that territorial indemnity is the only object, we are urged to seize, by legislation here, all that he was content to take a few months ago, and the whole province of Lower California to boot, and to still carry on the war—to take all we are fighting for, and still fight on. Again, the President is resolved under all circumstances to have full territorial indemnity for the expenses of the war; but he forgets to tell us how we are to get the excess after those expenses shall have surpassed the value of the whole of the Mexican territory. So again, he insists that the separate national existence of Mexico shall be maintained; but he does not tell us how this can be done, after we shall have taken all her territory. Lest the questions I have suggested be considered speculative merely, let me be indulged a moment in trying to show they are not. The war has gone on some twenty months; for the expenses of which, together with an inconsiderable old score, the President now claims about one half of the Mexican territory, and that by far the better half, so far as concerns our ability to make anything out of it. It is comparatively uninhabited; so that we could establish land offices in it, and raise some money in that way. But the other half is already inhabited, as I understand it, tolerably densely for the nature of the country, and all its lands, or all that are valuable, already appropriated as private property. How then are we to make anything out of these lands with this encumbrance on them? or how remove the encumbrance? I suppose no one would say we should kill the people, or drive them out, or make slaves of them; or confiscate their property. How, then, can we make much out of this part of the territory? If the prosecution of the war has in expenses already equaled the better half of the country, how long its future prosecution will be in equaling the less valuable half is not a speculative, but a practical, question, pressing closely upon us. And yet it is a question which the President seems never to have thought of. As to the mode of terminating the war and securing peace, the President is equally wandering and indefinite. First, it is to be done by a more vigorous prosecution of the war in the vital parts of the enemy's country; and after apparently talking himself tired on this point, the President drops down into a half-despairing tone, and tells us that "with a people distracted and divided by contending factions, and a government subject to constant changes by successive revolutions, the continued success of our arms may fail to secure a satisfactory peace." Then he suggests the propriety of wheedling the Mexican people to desert the counsels of their own leaders, and, trusting in our protestations, to set up a government from which we can secure a satisfactory peace; telling us that "this may become the only mode of obtaining such a peace." But soon he falls into doubt of this too; and then drops back onto the already half-abandoned ground of "more vigorous prosecution." All this shows that the President is in nowise satisfied with his own positions. First he takes up one, and in attempting to argue us into it he argues himself out of it, then seizes another and goes through the same process, and then, confused at being able to think of nothing new, he snatches up the old one again, which he has some time before cast off. His mind, taxed beyond its power, is running hither and thither, like some tortured creature on a burning surface, finding no position on which it can settle down to be at ease.

Again, it is a singular omission in this message that it nowhere intimates when the President expects the war to terminate. At its beginning, General Scott was by this same President driven into disfavor, if not disgrace, for intimating that peace could not be conquered in less than three or four months. But now, at the end of about twenty months, during which time

our arms have given us the most splendid successes, every department and every part, land and water, officers and privates, regulars and volunteers, doing all that men could do, and hundreds of things which it had ever before been thought men could not do—after all this, this same President gives a long message, without showing us that as to the end he himself has even an imaginary conception. As I have before said, he knows not where he is. He is a bewildered, confounded, and miserably perplexed man. God grant he may be able to show there is not something about his conscience more painful than all his mental perplexity.

DOCUMENT 11.6
Why Mexicans Did Not Fight

Mariano Otero (1817–1850), a native of the state of Jalisco, was a lawyer, orator, and writer during Mexico's chaotic years after the winning of independence. Although he enjoyed only a short life, dying of cholera at an early age, he left behind, among a legacy of rich works, a monumental essay: "Consideraciones Sobre la Situación Política y Social de la República Mexicana en el Año de 1847." A careful and thoughtful analysis of Mexico's ills on the eve of the War of 1846, it explains why Mexicans failed to defend their country against the Yankee aggressor.

That a foreign army of ten or twelve thousand men should have freely traveled from Vera Cruz to the very capital of the republic; that, with the exception of the bombarding of that port, the action at Cerrogordo, and minor skirmishes with Mexican troops in the suburbs of the capital; that this army has not found enemies with whom to fight—during its sweep across three of the key states of the Mexican Republic,

---

Source: Mariano Otero, *Obras*, ed. Jesús Reyes Heroles, 2 vols. (Mexico: Editorial Porrúa, 1967). Translation by Ramón Eduardo Ruiz.

states numbering more than two million inhabitants—these are facts that assume such importance that they cannot but give rise to the most
stark reflections.

Men of shallow minds who judge events
solely on the facts usually fall into grievous
errors. For this reason it is not strange that,
as we have already read in some foreign journals, the Mexican people have been characterized *as an effeminate people, as a degenerate
race that has not known how to govern or to
defend itself.*

But the thoughtful man, not willing to
merely accept the surface appearance of things,
looks for underlying causes, and readily finds
in Mexico the real reasons for why these people,
far from taking an active part in the campaign,
watched the conflict from afar. Once these reasons are acknowledged, only the blindly preju-
diced could argue that the situation is due to
defects in the Mexican race, and to the inevitable results of definite causes. What we propose
in this essay is to analyze with as much clarity
as possible those heterogeneous elements (and
their characteristic weakness) which make up
the society of the Mexican republic. Beyond
a doubt, this method is the best way to demonstrate the true and only causes that have led
to the decadence and prostration of the Mexican
republic. By undertaking such an examination,
we hope to correct the misinterpretations that
we hear from even literate people. We refer,
particularly, to those mistakes in judgement
which attribute defects to the Mexican people
which are, in fact, common to the entire human
race.

True the illiterate do not often think, nor
are they apt to forgive the defeated. Just as
certain, those who consider themselves above
this attitude and who value their own opinions
must then concede that, if they are to arrive
at a just conclusion, they must subject this
matter to thorough analysis and impartial
thought. Men of this type cannot reasonably
judge the Mexican republic in its current sad

situation as composed of a people who suffer
from defective origins because of effeminacy
or the degeneration of their race but rather as
a people who are the victims of a poor education
and a worse political organization. Given this
point of view, we believe that Mexico, far
from deserving the insults and mockery of other
nations, merits, in the name of universal justice,
if not the help which as a nation it might hope
for from other countries of the world, at least
the sympathy which any good soul should feel
toward a nation which defends a just cause
and which, after great sacrifices suffers defeat,
not so much because of the powerful forces
placed against it, but because of the inertia
which afflicts a society divided by the most
contrary and opposing interests.

We shall not exhaust ourselves in vain declamations. That, in the first place, is not our
style and, furthermore, such verbiage would
in no way vindicate the Mexican republic. Instead, let a simple analysis of the make up of
the nation suffice to explain its present situation.

In order to achieve our objectives with clarity, we have divided our exposition into two
parts: in the first, we treat the population as a
whole, with special attention to the productive
classes; in the second, we deal with the privileged classes.

PART ONE

POPULATION

The data that we have for the population of
the republic is not accurate. While some writers
calculate the population at only a bit more than
six million inhabitants, others maintain that
there are more than nine. We estimate the population as being seven million, of whom, according to the most reliable accounts, four million
are Indians and three million are Europeans;
these latter, for the most part, are mixed with
the indigenous race.

INDIANS

The Indians live throughout the entire territory of the republic, grouped in small communities and forming a family apart from the white and mixed races. The miserable way of life of the Indians today differs little, or not at all, from what it was when they were ruled by the emperor Montezuma. The only difference between the Indians of that time and those of today is the abolishment of idolatry with its barbarous sacrifices of human blood. Today's Indians have been taught to worship God *in their own manner,* and to hope for blessings in the life hereafter, something which, we might suppose, they believe, for they are completely convinced that nothing good awaits them in this vale of tears. Neither in the days of the viceroys nor since independence has there existed an adequate system of education for this race, which would, on the one hand, improve the condition of the individual, raising him from the brutalized state in which he lives and, on the other, make him useful to society. At no time have these people been taught anything but to fear God, the priest, and the mayor; and because of the ignorance in which they live, perhaps three-quarters of the Indians are still not aware of independence. That they remain in this state of ignorance is all the more credible in view of the fact that in many places they are still compelled to pay tribute to the king of Spain; this in the same spirit in which they are asked to donate money to ransome captives and for the holy places of Jerusalem.

The work that they are asked to do is to cultivate the earth for a small daily stipend. Since this pay is rarely enough to cover the costs of their sad existence, they ask the owner of the hacienda on which they work for advances on their wages, to be paid back by their labor, which compels them to stay on until they have paid their debt. Since the stipend the Indians earn hardly suffices to maintain life, the owner will lose the sum which he

has lent and the Indian will remain sold to the owner of the hacienda and in effect belong to him. The result of this situation is that—although contrary to law—there exists in many places in the republic Indian slavery.

Additionally, a nefarious system exists among the Mexican clergy. While the so-called higher clergy and bishops live opulently in the capital, the parish priests find that their very survival depends upon the income from their parish collections. So these representatives of the God of goodness and mercy make it a point not to allow any Indian to be born, to marry, or to die with impunity, that is, without paying the *established* duties. Thus the parish priests take their cut from the scant resources that the Indians count on for their livlihood.

Indians who live close to the great urban centers go there to sell vegetables, poultry, firewood, coal and other such goods which fetch them a small price, but even this paltry profit is reduced at the city gate by tax collectors who, in the name of the nation, impose on these people the most infamous and repugnant extortions.

To complete this canvas, which faithfully portrays the sadness of Indian life, we need but add that the only active part which the Indians take in the public life of the country is to serve as soldiers in the army, a role which is forced upon them. In this capacity, rather than serve their country, they act as instruments for the enrichment of their officers who, in times of peace, give them little bread but a hard time—*poco pan y mucho palo*—and in war often abandon them at the first sign of danger. For all these reasons, it is easy to understand why this important sector of the population has scant interest in keeping alive an order of things of which it is the victim. Hence the Indians watched the entrance of the North American army with the same indifference with which they earlier watched the Spanish armies taking over the country and, after the independence, they watched with the same indifference the comings and goings of troops engaged in our constant revolutions. Without needs beyond those demanded by their semi-savage level of existence, without ties or joys of any kind depended on society, with neither interests nor affections that link them to it, and with the confidence that their abject condition could not be worse, they look upon all that occurs with the most apathetic indifference.

THE WHITE AND MIXED RACES

We shall now examine the three million inhabitants of European or mixed descent who make up the population of the capitals and other cities and towns in the republic. Of this number, we can deduct 1,800,000 as being women, children, and old people. This leaves us over 1,200,000 useful men or, more precisely, men capable of being so, because in reality they are not, as we shall demonstrate.

With the exception of about 300,000 men, the maximum estimate for those employed in agriculture, industry, mining, business, and certain trades and offices, the 900,000 remaining account for the unproductive classes, such as the clergy with all of its subordinates and dependents, the military, the bureaucrats, lawyers, doctors and, finally, that horde of loafers and vagabonds that abounds in the cities of the republic.

From this not inflated estimate, we can judge the sad situation afflicting that quarter of the working population that must support the other three quarters. What an enormous disproportion! Here is the origin of the backwardness and discouragement that hampers the exploitation of the national wealth. Here is sufficient cause for the destruction of not merely the nascent Mexican republic. It would suffice to destroy the most flourishing nation on earth! . . .

In view of this, it is obvious why the property and working classes of Mexico have no material interests to defend in the current war. . . .

chapter 12

Slavery and Its Defense

Nathan I. Huggins
Harvard University

The problem of slavery in the United States grew out of contradictions between the system and its social and historical context. It was a permanent and arbitrary condition of unfreedom in a society which, as it developed historically, defined itself as free. It was an hereditary social status in a society that revolted against, among other things, heritable rank and class. In a society that proclaimed human rights were natural rights, it defined certain human beings as property, chattel, and, therefore, devoid of rights others needed to respect. Although believing themselves equal in the sight of God, Christians debased Christians as slaves for profit and power. Because American slavery was racial slavery, it created and sustained a population thought exotic and unable to be assimilated with the dominant race and culture.

Such contradictions have plagued the course of human bondage in the New World. They raise questions that need to be explored. What were the American origins of slavery? Why did slavery develop in a nation that continually gave expression to the goal of human freedom? What were some of the early antislavery expressions? Why did slavery continue to thrive? And what were the justifications invented by a moral people to affirm and defend it?

From 1619 (the date of the first reported slaves imported to a continental British colony) to the Civil War three and a half centuries later, these contradictions just noted plagued American society, both those sections having slaves and those that did not. From the beginning, there were persons who found the system repugnant, those who argued for abolition, as well as those who could tolerate it only at a distance. They all pointed to the conflict between deeply held values and the ownership and exploitation of other human beings. As one might expect, opposition and criticism of the institution brought forth rationalizations, apologies, and defenses, most often couched in terms of similar principles: the right to property, the defense of civilized culture against "savage" culture, and so on.

Given such conflict from the beginning, it is perplexing how slavery began and took hold in the British American colonies. Englishmen had said that English air was too free to abide slavery. Why in the colonies, if not in England? There were obvious reasons. Building new colonies required a large supply of cheap and controllable labor. The open and frontier conditions of seventeenth-century Virginia and Maryland gave English labor options not available to them at home. It was difficult to exploit the indigenous peoples. The well-established Atlantic slave trade made Africans available for purchase, and having neither place nor status, they

221

became especially vulnerable to the total control of a slave system.

Still, most historians write about the establishment of slave labor as an "unthinking decision" made by colonists. They simply started using more African labor and discovered themselves, in time, as masters of slaves. The generation of the Founding Fathers could hardly imagine their own forebears as responsible, and they tried to blame the slave system on the British Royal Africa Company and the mother country's need for a favorable trade balance. By the Revolution, few Americans were willing to admit that slavery was the deliberate choice of Americans.

In recent years, historians have conceived the origins of slavery in various ways. Oscar and Mary Handlin saw it as an outgrowth of the early seventeenth century labor shortage. If English and African labor had been equally available to the colonists, they argue, Africans would not have been used in large numbers and racial slavery would not have developed in Virginia, Maryland, and the Carolinas.

Furthermore, they pointed out, English servants and laborers, customarily tied as they were to their masters by indenture, long contracts, and custom, were not "free" men and women in our sense of the term. Thus, the argument goes, early in the century there was slight real difference between English and African servants. By mid-century, however, a sharp drop in the availability of English workers made Africans more attractive. Since Africans had no legal or customary rights within the English system, laws that formalized their "unfreedom," making it permanent and heritable, were possible and desirable. Such laws were enacted in the 1660s in Maryland and Virginia, and these laws became the model for slave codes and statutes elsewhere.

Never claiming the English colonists were without race prejudice, the Handlins argued that legal and institutional differentiation between English and African servants defined the one as free and the other as a permanently enslaved class. These distinctions of status in law and society became the basis of American racism.

Other scholars reverse cause and effect. Historians Carl Degler and Winthrop Jordan have stressed English antipathy toward nonwhites from virtually their first contacts. In other words, the English colonists brought with them such deep-seated racial fears and suspicions that the very presence of Africans in the colonies resulted in a special status outside normal community life.

For the one, slavery was a means of capturing an exotic and vulnerable population for a permanent labor force, generating in turn, racial attitudes to rationalize and support the institutions thus created. For the other, racial attitudes predetermined a special status for Africans. There is documentary evidence to support either emphasis. Records from the earliest time show that blacks suffered heavier penalties than whites for the same offenses, that blacks and not whites were likely to be considered "lifetime" indentures. On the other hand, the very laws that defined blacks as slaves complained that "diverse freeborn English women do . . . marry with" Africans, and often black and white servants stood accused as co-conspirators. This suggests that racial fears and hostilities may have reflected norms the governing classes wished to impose, but they did not pervade servant classes as much as has been imagined.

The historian, Edmund Morgan, has focused on this point in locating the origins of racial slavery in Virginia at the insurgency culminating in Bacon's Rebellion. The social disorders leading to this seventeenth-century uprising raised the specter of class conflict uniting black and white against the governing and propertied classes. Racial slavery, according to Morgan, served to divide permanently the classes most likely to rebel against established authority. Racial slavery defined all whites as free and gave them, in principle, a common status to defend regardless of class.

White men and women, regardless of socio-economic condition, knew they were free because they had the example of slavery conspicuously before them. American freedom thus was defined by American slavery.

Despite different emphases, all these scholars share one common insight: however one might explain its origins, racial slavery made the basic social divisions in America along race lines rather than class lines. Affluent and impoverished whites would concur in the enslavement and oppression of blacks, assuming an equality in race that could not exist in class. This concurrence formed the ground for the unlikely alliance of slave-owning and nonslave-owning whites in defending the institution against its critics.

Slavery existed in almost all the colonies. Only Georgia, a colony founded on philanthropic principles, prohibited slavery for a time; the prohibition was repealed in 1749. Under frontier conditions, the attraction of a totally controlled labor force in which one held capital value—being able to profit from price appreciation and natural increase through reproduction—was too compelling for settlers to resist. The number of slaves were few in New England colonies like Massachusetts; however, Rhode Island and Connecticut had a sizeable slave population. The Middle Colonies of New York, Pennsylvania, and New Jersey had significant slave forces. On none of these northern colonies, however, would slave labor have such a dominant economic and social effect as it would on the South.

Northerners were no more morally sensitive than Southerners. Differences in slave population and, therefore, differences in the influence slavery would have, economically and socially, had less to do with principle than with colonial circumstance. The early diversification of the economies in New England and the Middle Colonies made slave holding less necessary than in the South, where a virtually monolithic economic and social order developed around the slave system. Smaller, more diversified

holdings made slave labor only marginally efficient. With a substantial portion of the governing classes not slave owners, it was harder to fashion laws and social practice designed exclusively to protect and sustain slavery. Furthermore, New England life especially centered on community and social control. Puritans, who grew anxious about the threat to their social order from Quakers and other such interlopers, could hardly feel easy about the prospect of large numbers of Africans in their midst.

They were not uneasy, however, about slavery elsewhere. Few New Englanders had qualms about profiting from trade in slaves. Great merchant fortunes were built in Rhode Island and Massachusetts from the Atlantic slave trade.

Both New Englanders and Southerners held that slavery and the slave trade was justifiable since the Scriptures acknowledged it as proper to enslave "captives in just wars." Thus, the ongoing colonial conflict with Indians resulted in the enslavement of Indians, and the rationale was extended to assume that the African cargo in the Atlantic slave trade were such "captives."

In one of the earliest abolitionist tracts, Samuel Sewall attacked this reasoning as willful (and sinful) self-deception. Notably, however, Sewall's attack of slavery was only a partial condemnation of the oppression of innocent people for profit. It also rested on the belief that such an exotic people as the Africans could not be absorbed into the Christian community and would remain a source of social disorder. Sewall's argument, like much abolitionist writing to follow, was not so much pro-black or pro-African as it was antislavery. Sewall's ideal community had no blacks in it.

From the earliest time, we can see two broad approaches to the prospect of an African presence: (1) capture them into a cheap and controllable labor force, but remove them from the community through the institution of slavery; (2) Reject the advantages of African labor, but exclude blacks from the community, making them unwelcome. These basic patterns characterize the differences between South and North on matters of race and slavery throughout the antebellum period.

The American Revolution brought the contradictions of slavery in a free society sharply into focus. Most Americans of that generation found it difficult and embarrassing to both proclaim the ideals and principles of the Revolution embodied in the theory of the ''natural rights of man'' and defend the ownership of humans as slaves. Some slaveholders freed their slaves. George Washington was among them. We can trace most of the free black population of southern cities like Baltimore, Charleston, and Savannah to these manumissions.

Other slaveholders held their slaves. Thomas Jefferson was among them. For some, it was due to a belief in the system. For others, the cost of abrogating a large capital investment was the determinant. Most persons who continued to hold slaves shared Thomas Jefferson's views, as expressed in his *Notes on the State of Virginia,* that blacks and Indians were not quite *men* in the sense of the Declaration of Independence and that a republican community of equals could not survive if it was racially mixed. For three decades following the Revolution, Virginia and Maryland slaveholders complained about slavery as a burden rather than a boon, but felt trapped into continuing slavery because the alternatives were unthinkable.

One way out of this dilemma was to ''colonize'' free blacks (and slaves freed for that purpose) in Africa. As early as 1776, Jefferson proposed a plan for African colonization. Procolonization resolutions were passed by the Virginia Assembly in 1800, 1802, 1805, and 1816, and the American Colonization Society was established in 1817. Out of 143 emancipation societies in 1826, 103 of them were in the South, including four abolition newspapers.

Antislavery sentiment and the revolutionary ideals were able to prevail in New England and the middle states of New York, Pennsylvania, and New Jersey. Abolition was most easily accomplished in Massachusetts where, in a 1783 case involving a master's rights over his slave, the Supreme Judicial Court declared that by virtue of the Commonwealth's Declaration of Rights, ''slavery in this State is no more.'' So, by judicial decree, slavery was ended in Massachusetts.

Nowhere else was it so simple. Slave owners, asserting the principle of property rights, wanted just compensation to free their slaves. Nonslave owners did not want to be taxed to compensate owners, who had received labor from slaves throughout their lives. Moreover, nonslave owners wanted owners to guarantee the welfare of slave too young, too old, or too infirm to be self-supporting. Their fear was that masters would free slaves only to make them wards of the state and burdens on taxpayers.

The debate, particularly in New York, Pennsylvania, and New Jersey, was long and bitter. Each state, however, hit upon a form of gradual emancipation without compensating slave owners. New Jersey's last slave was freed in 1836.

However ambivalent about slavery the Founding Fathers were, they were not prepared to address the problem directly. Neither slavery nor Africans are mentioned in the Constitution, but compromises written into the text have much to do with them. Slaveholding states wanted slaves counted for purposes of representation although they would clearly have no voice in that representation. At the same time, Southerners did not want slaves counted for purposes of tax assessments. Nonslave states wanted the reverse. Article I, Section 2 words the compromise by the reckoning, ''three fifths of all other Persons'' for purposes of representation and direct taxes.

The Constitution provided for the ending of the importation of slaves in Section 9 of the same Article. Again, the language is revealing: ''The Migration or Importation of such Persons as any of the States now existing shall think proper to admit, shall not be prohibited by the Congress prior to the Year one thousand eight hundred and eight. . . .'' Yet, in Article

IV, Section 2, slave property is guaranteed: "No Person held to Service or Labour in one State, under the Laws thereof, escaping into another, shall, in Consequence of any Law or Regulation therein, be discharged from such Service or Labour, but shall be delivered up on Claim of the Party to whom such Service or Labour may be due." From 1793, there would be federal statutes obliging federal authorities to assist in the apprehension and return of fugitive slaves.

While the Constitution did not mention slavery, it supported the institution in several ways. By means of the three-fifths clause, it gave slaveholders added political power through added representatives. It placed the federal government against those slaves who managed to escape slave masters and cross state lines. By empowering the new government to call forth the militia to execute the laws and repel invasions, it also obliged the government to "suppress Insurrections." Thus, the whole power of the United States could be marshaled against slave uprisings.

While the Founding Fathers, in drafting the Constitution, seemed anxious not to attack slavery as it existed, there is reason to believe that they thought (or hoped) it would not extend far into the nation's future. The decision to end the foreign slave trade in 1808 indicates some expectation of a dying institution. Many of the same men who drafted the Constitution, while serving in Congress under the Articles of Confederation, designed a clearly nonslave future for the United States. The Northwest Ordinance of 1787 provided a blueprint for the future United States. It laid out the procedure by which the Old Northwest Territory (to become the states of Ohio, Indiana, Illinois, and Michigan) would come into the Union. Article six of the Ordinance prohibited both slavery and involuntary servitude in the territory. It, nevertheless, provided for the return of fugitives.

From the Revolution to the 1820s, there were few who could predict slavery would continue being economically viable. The severe economic depression following the Revolution and the loss of those advantages tobacco and rice growers gained from being part of the British mercantile system placed Virginia, Maryland, and the Carolinas in serious distress. The market price of slaves was low despite the end of the importation of Africans. Commodity prices were no longer subsidized by the British, and overused land was becoming less productive. Many southern spokesmen gloomily predicted a day when slave owners would run away from their slaves to avoid the cost of caring for them. Yet they could not be moved to convert to a free labor system. They feared the consequences of a racially mixed society (especially one based on republican principles). They could not discover a practical way to remove the black population, especially as there was no alternative labor force. Yet, at the same time, they feared slave insurrections such as the 1794 Haitian uprising. It's little wonder that some southerners were likely to express themselves tragically regarding slavery: they were victims of historical choices from which they could not escape.

Such tones changed in the 1830s. The English textile industry created a large and expanding market for cotton, and the cotton gin (invented in 1793 by Eli Whitney) made possible the profitable marketing of short-staple cotton. It was a crop suitable for cultivation throughout the South, and it could benefit from the economies of scale possible with mass slave labor. Furthermore, the Indian policy of Andrew Jackson succeeded by the mid-1830s in removing Indians from the Old Southwest to the trans-Mississippi West. The whole of the deep South was now open for settlement and exploitation. Like the original southern frontier on the Atlantic Ocean, this new land would be opened with slave labor.

These changes revitalized slavery. Even old South planters could shift into cotton production. Or they or their sons could move onto new lands in the Southwest, taking along some of their slaves. They could sell their slaves at a profit to the growing demand. Early in the 1830s, Southerners ceased their plaintive apologies for the "peculiar institution" and began to speak of it as a "positive good."

But never quite escaping the sense that slavery was morally corrupting, Southerners developed a rather elaborate intellectual defense of the peculiar institution. There was a racial and cultural ground; they argued that Africans and Afro-Americans were a savage people who were better off in American slavery than they would be in Africa. They were not ready to belong to normal, civilized society, and slavery was a kind of school that would, after a few generations, bring blacks up to European standards of civilization. Before then, blacks would either be enslaved or destroyed by white superiors.

Slavery's defenders also found support in the *Bible*. Both the Old and New Testaments acknowledged the existence of slavery and did not condemn it as such. They turned to *Genesis* and argued that blacks were Cannaanites, descendants of Ham, and thus cursed to hew wood and carry water. And they liked to quote Saint Paul's admonition: "slaves, obey your masters."

The most original defenses for slavery were the political and sociological arguments of John C. Calhoun and George Fitzhugh. Calhoun, the spokesman for slaveholders' interests, considered slavery as a political interest. By the 1840s, the South was a minority section of the country, and it had to defend itself against growing northern and western power. Calhoun wanted to design a defense of the South and of slavery through the Constitution and through guarantees of minority, that is, southern, rights. Furthermore, he hoped for an alliance of northern conservatives and southern planters to maintain political control over the nation's future. In his *Cannibals All, or Slaves without Masters,* and *Sociology for the South,* Fitzhugh

attacked the very basis of "free society" and *laissez-faire* capitalism, which left the working classes exploitable without institutional support or defense. Slaves, he claimed, were better off than free workers in the North or elsewhere in the world.

As slavery became more central to southern growth and development, and as the defense of slavery became more ardent, the South closed itself off from criticism. The southern abolitionist movement, which had been quite lively in the 1820s, was dead a decade later. Antislavery advocates and journalists either left the South, were forced out, or retreated into silence. Fearful of criticism, the South silenced its internal critics. Fearful of disorder through slave insurrection and uprisings, they tightened slave codes, enforcing them through citizen patrols, and made it illegal to manumit slaves in most of the South. By the 1850s, the South had become a totalitarian society—all in defense of slavery.

The revival and expansion of the southern slave economy shattered the hopes of those who imagined slavery would not expand, dying of its own weight. Militant abolitionism, thus, began in the 1830s just as Southerners were rediscovering value in their peculiar institution. Many southern voices that were critical of slavery found the only way to be heard was from northern cities. The abolitionist movement picked up the contradictory themes that had been felt from the beginning: slavery was an offense against Christian principles of human worth; it was an offense against democratic principles based on the natural rights of man; it corrupted the master, oppressed the slave, and sapped the moral character of the nation. The same mid-century reform spirit that fed movements for public education, care for the mentally ill, temperance, rehabilitation of criminals, women's rights, and so forth, fed the abolitionists, sharing as they did a common assumption of the divine nature of man and man's perfectibility. It was a powerful force for reform that passed by the South altogether due to slavery.

White and black abolitionists challenged in their papers and on the platform the moral basis of slavery and the moral character of slave owners. Blacks like Frederick Douglass, Sojourner Truth, and Harriet Tubman, all former slaves, were examples of the potential of all slaves. Douglass's newspaper, *The North Star,* along with others like the *Liberator* kept the moral issue before the public. Those, not opposed to political action, like James G. Birney, Gerrit Smith, and Salmon P. Chase, formed the Liberty Party in 1839 which, in the election of 1844, was responsible for the defeat of Henry Clay. Along with the Free Soil Party in 1848, it helped defeat Democratic candidate Lewis Cass.

Abolitionists, however, never accounted for large numbers of followers. William Lloyd Garrison's *Liberator* had a circulation of only 3,000 at its height. Their influence, however, reached far beyond their numbers. By the 1850s, they had succeeded in getting northerners, including persons uninterested in freeing slaves and even hostile to blacks, to characterize southern slaveholders as a corrupt planter aristocracy that was willing to oppress all labor for power and wealth. Many settlers in the West were themselves yeoman farmer refugees from what they considered an arrogant and tyrannical slaveocracy.

Northerners were no more ready to accept a racially mixed society than southerners. Even with their hostility toward slavery and slaveholders, they were seldom sympathetic with blacks, and many feared that general emancipation would free hoards of blacks to migrate north into free states. Each of the northwestern states, as they entered the Union, prohibited slavery but also placed major restrictions against black residents, requiring bonds of those who would settle permanently, denying them the right to vote, own property, or otherwise live as a citizen. Anxiety about black residence grew as the society became more democratic and extended the suffrage to all men. Generally speaking, universal suffrage meant white, manhood suffrage.

Northerners increasingly saw the future of the nation, particularly the future of the western territories, in light of the Northwest Ordinance's prohibition of slavery and involuntary servitude. The states of the Old Northwest had come into the Union as "free states." They fought over this principle in the territory west of the Mississippi that had been acquired in the Louisiana Purchase of 1803. That struggle seemed to be resolved in the Missouri Compromise of 1820—Maine was admitted as a free state and Missouri was admitted as a slave state, and the remainder of the Louisiana Purchase would be organized along the line forming the southern border of Missouri (36°–30″ latitude); south of that line would be slave territory, north of the line would be free states.

But the issue was not settled. Following the Mexican War, the territory ceded to the United States included land west to the Pacific Ocean. The issue of slavery in the territories was reopened. Southerners and slaveholders claimed that the West was as much a part of their patrimony as it was for Northerners and free farmers. Persons who called themselves "Free Soilers" wanted the West open for free white men—to establish free institutions without the unsettling presence of blacks and the dominating presence of a planter, slave-owning class.

The "free soil" position about slavery in the territories was incorporated into the Republican Party when it was formed, and Abraham Lincoln's views best represented that position. Speaking before the Illinois Republican State Convention in 1858, Lincoln declared, "A house divided against itself cannot stand." Neither Lincoln nor the Republican Party was prepared to attack slaveholders and slavery where it existed, but they stood against its extension into the territories and, thereby, its continued growth in the United States. It was this position, finally articulated in the Republican platform and the Lincoln candidacy of 1860, which the South found unacceptable and led to secession and civil war.

Lincoln wanted to maintain that the sanctity of the Union—not human rights—was the principle for which the war would be fought. He made attempts in the early war years to assure the South, particularly the border states, that slavery could continue within a Union under a Republican administration. Very reluctant to exploit the South's vulnerability, due to its dependency upon slave labor, Lincoln was willing to accept black volunteers into the Union army only after November 1862. By the end of the war, more than 250,000 blacks served in the military—greatly contributing to the Union victory.

North–South conflict brought into sharp focus the contradictions that slavery created in a free society. They could no longer be avoided or compromised as the politicians thought they had done in 1820 and 1850. Wartime exigencies forced Lincoln to issue his Emancipation Proclamation, freeing, as of January 1, 1863, all slaves in areas still in rebellion against the United States. Yet, the ambivalence about the consequences of a racially-mixed society remained. Along with others, Lincoln continued to seek a way to colonize blacks elsewhere, in Africa or in Central America, and he was reluctant to suggest extending the franchise to freed men.

These matters were settled in the law by the constitutional amendments that grew out of the war. The Thirteenth Amendment (1866) prohibited slavery and involuntary servitude. The Fourteenth Amendment (1868) defined citizenship so as to include blacks and extended federal protection of their rights. The Fifteenth Amendment (1870) denied to states the right to exclude persons from the vote on the ground of race, color, or previous condition of servitude. By these amendments, slavery was ended, freed men were defined as citizens with the rights of other citizens, and not to be denied the vote because of race or past slavery. The end of slavery was an expropriation of property. Four million slaves, the capital investment of their owners, were freed without compensating slaveholders for their loss. However, the slaves were also losers; their patrimony was expropriated in that they were set free without compensation. For over three centuries, their forebears had labored and produced wealth, compensated only by subsistence. Unlike other populations, slaves could accumulate nothing, build nothing, and pass nothing of material value to their heirs. When they were freed without compensation for the generations of labor and the creation of value, they were set loose with nothing. They had, as one historian has put it, nothing but freedom.

SUGGESTED READINGS

Blassingame, John. *The Slave Community*. New York: Oxford University Press, 1972.

Berlin, Ira. *Slaves Without Masters*. New York: Pantheon, 1974.

Degler, Carl. "Slavery and the Genesis of American Race Prejudice," *Comparative Studies in Society and History*, 2 (October 1959), pp. 49–66.

Foner, Eric. *Free Soil, Free Labor, Free Men*. New York: Oxford University Press, 1970.

Freehling, William W. *Prelude to Civil War, The Nullification Controversy in South Carolina*. New York: Harper & Row, 1966.

Genovese, Eugene. *Roll, Jordan, Roll*. New York: Pantheon, 1974.

Gutman, Herbert. *The Black Family in Slavery and Freedom*. New York: Pantheon, 1976.

Handlin, Oscar, and Mary Handlin. "Origins of the Southern Labor System," in *Race and Nationality in American Life*, chap. 1. Boston, Little, Brown, 1957.

Huggins, Nathan I. *Black Odyssey; the Afro-American's Ordeal in Slavery*. New York: Pantheon, 1978.

Stampp, Kenneth. *The Peculiar Institution*. New York: Alfred A. Knopf, 1957.

DOCUMENT 12.1
Slavery: Its Beginnings in Colonial America

The following three excerpts give examples of different legal treatments regarding slavery. This Maryland law that defined blacks as slaves is one of the earliest examples of colonial distinction between "negro and other slaves," and other forms of servitude and unfree labor. Reference is made to intermarriage between English women and blacks, it should be noted, and that the children of such unions followed the condition of the father. *In subsequent laws defining slave status, the white mates of slave men would be "captured" into slavery for the life of their husbands, and their children would be slaves for life. Otherwise, a slave woman's children would follow her status. The next example, from a Virginia law of 1667, removes any doubt that a master might have that a black who converted to Christianity could remain a slave. Finally, a case in colonial Virginia,* Re Negro John Punch, *McIlwaine 466, July 1640, illustrates the difference of treatment for black and white servants, suggesting the early imposition of slavery.*

A MARYLAND LAW[1]

"All negroes or other slaves within the province, and all negroes and other slaves to be hereafter imported into the province, shall serve *durante vita;* and all children born of any negro or other slave, shall be slaves as their *fathers* were for the term of their lives." Section 2. "And forasmuch as divers free-born *English* women, forgetful of their free condition and to the disgrace of our nation, do intermarry with negro slaves, by which also, divers suits may arise, touching the issue of such women,

and a great damage doth befall the master of such negroes, for preservation whereof, for deterring such free-born women from such shameful matches, *be it enacted, &.c.* That whatsoever free-born woman shall intermarry with any slave, from and after the last day of the present assembly, shall serve the master of such slave during the life of her husband, and that all the issue of such freeborn women, so married, shall be slaves as their FATHERS were."

A VIRGINIA LAW[2]

"Whereas some doubts have risen whether children that are slaves by birth, and by the charity and piety of their owners made pertakers of the blessed sacrament of baptisme, should by vertue of their baptisme be made free; It is enacted . . . that the conferring of baptisme doth not alter the condition of the person as to his bondage or freedome: that diverse masters, freed from this doubt, may more carefully endeavour the propagation of christianity by permitting children, though slaves, or those of greater growth if capable, to be admitted to that sacrament."

A VIRGINIA LEGAL CASE[3]

Re Negro John Punch, July 1640. "Whereas Hugh Gwyn hath . . . Brought back from Maryland three servants formerly run way . . . the court doth therefore order that the said three servants shall receive the punishment of whipping and to have thirty stripes apiece one called Victor, a dutchman, the other a Scotchman called James Gregory, shall first serve out their times with their master according to their Indentures, and one whole year apiece after the time

---

[1] Source: John C. Hurd, ed., *The Law of Freedom and Bondage in the United States* (Boston: Little, Brown, 1858), 1, p. 249.

[2] Source: William W. Heming, ed., *The Statutes at Large; Being a Collection of all The Laws of Virginia* (New York, 1823), 2, p. 260.

[3] Source: Helen T. Catterall, ed., *Judicial Cases Concerning American Slavery and the Negro* (Washington, D. C.: Carnegie Institute of Washington, 1926), 2, p. 77.

of their service is Expired. . . . and after that service . . . to serve the colony for three whole years apiece, and that the third being a negro named John Punch shall serve his said master or his assigns for the time of his natural Life here or elsewhere.''

DOCUMENT 12.2
An Early Massachusetts Protest Against Slavery

Reverend Samuel Sewall's 1700 tract, The Selling of Joseph, *argued against the continued importation of African slaves. His practical argument focused on problems of community coherence and social order.*

And seeing GOD hath said, *He that Stealeth a Man and Selleth him, or if he be found in his hand, he shall surely be put to Death.* Exod. 21.16. This Law being of Everlasting Equity, wherein Man Stealing is ranked amongst the most atrocious of Capital Crimes: What louder Cry can there be made of that Celebrated Warning, . . .

And all things considered, it would conduce more to the Welfare of the Province, to have White Servants for a Term of Years, than to have Slaves for Life. Few can endure to hear of a Negro's being made free; and indeed they can seldom use their freedom well; yet their continued aspiring after their forbidden Liberty, renders them Unwilling Servants. And there is such a disparity in their Conditions, Colour & Hair, that they can never embody with us, and grow up into orderly Families, to the Peopling of the Land: but still remain in our Body Politick as a kind of extravasat Blood. As many Negro men as there are among us, so many empty places there are in our Train Bands, and the places taken up of Men that might make Husbands for our Daughters. And the Sons and Daughters of *New England* would become more like *Jacob,* and *Rachel,* if this Slavery were thrust quite out of doors. Moreover it is too well know what Temptations Masters are under, to connive at the Fornication of their Slaves; lest they should be obliged to find them Wives, or pay their Fines. It seems to be practically pleaded that they might be Lawless; 'tis thought much of, that the Law should have Satisfaction for their Thefts, and other Immoralities; by which means, *Holiness to the Lord,* is more rarely engraven upon this sort of Servitude. It is likewise most lamentable to think, how in taking Negros out of *Africa,* and Selling of them here, That which GOD ha's joyned together men do boldly rend asunder; Men from their Country, Husbands from their Wives, Parents from their Children. How horrible is the Uncleanness, Mortality, if not Murder, that the Ships are guilty of that bring great Crouds of these miserable Men, and Women. Methinks, when we are bemoaning the barbarous Usage of our Friends and Kinsfolk in *Africa:* it might not be unseasonable to enquire whether we are not culpable in forcing the *Africans* to become Slaves amongst our selves. And it may be a question whether all the Benefit received by *Negro* Slaves, will balance the Accompt of Cash laid out upon them; and for the Redemption of our own enslaved Friends out of *Africa.* Besides all the Persons and Estates that have perished there.

DOCUMENT 12.3
A Landmark Antislavery Case

Commonwealth [Massachusetts] v. Jennison *(1781) is the court decision which, in effect, ended slavery in Massachusetts. Notably, Nathaniel Jennison, who claimed to own Quack Walker as a slave, received no compensation from this act of state.*

Source: Samuel Sewall, *The Selling of Joseph* (Boston, 1700).

Source: *Proceedings of the Massachusetts Historical Society. 1873–1875* (Boston, 1875), vol. 13, 293–94.

Commonwealth v. Jennison, Proc. Mass. Hist. Soc. 1873–75, 293. April 1783. "Indictment, found September, 1781, *vs.* Nathaniel Jennison of Barre, for an assault on Quack Walker, and beat with a stick 1st May, 1781, and imprisoned two hours. . . [Testimony for the Commonwealth] *Mr. Caldwell.* The Negro was at work in my field with a team . . . heard a screaming. . . Jennison and several others . . . had got the negro down, young fellow upon the negro, I took him off . . . and told Jennison his master had freed him—and Winslow let him go—wounds in his hands and arms. My brother said always he should be free at 25— . . . . *Quack.* I was harrowing. 10 years old when master Caldwell died. Mrs. lived a number of years before she married again. I lived with Dr. Jennison 7 years and ½ after I was 21. My old master said I should be free at 24 or 25. Mistress told me I should be free at 21—said so to Jennison, before and after marriage. Defence. From Zachariah Stone to Caldwell, deceased—Bill of Sale Mingo and Dinah, 1754, and Quaco, 9 months old . . . *Mr. Jones.* Quaco lived with Caldwell till he died—appraised at £40—set off to his Mrs. as part of her personal estate. She married Jennison about 1770, and died about 3 years after. *Joshua Winslow.* I was desired by defendant to help him reclaim Quaco." Charge of Cushing, C. J. [294] "Fact proved. Justification that Quack is a slave . . . that Mr. Jennison . . . was entitled to Quack as his property: and therefore he had a right to bring him home when he ran away; . . . And the defendant's counsel also rely on some former laws of the Province, which give countenance to slavery. . . As to the doctrine of slavery and the right of Christians to hold Africans in perpetual servitude . . . that (it is true) has been heretofore countenanced by the Province Laws. . . . . . but nowhere is it expressly enacted. . . . It has been a usage . . . But whatever sentiments have formerly prevailed in this particular or slid in upon us by the example of others, a different idea has taken place with

the people of America, more favorable to the natural rights of mankind, and to that natural, innate desire of Liberty, with which Heaven (without regard to color, complexion, or shape of noses, features) has inspired all the human race. And upon this ground our Constitution . . . by which the people of this Commonwealth have solemnly bound themselves, sets out with declaring that all men are born free and equal—and that every subject is entitled to liberty, . . . as well as life and property—and in short is totally repugnant to the idea of being born slaves. This being the case, I think the idea of slavery is inconsistent with our own conduct and Constitution; and there can be no such thing as perpetual servitude of a rational creature, unless his liberty is forfeited by some criminal conduct or given up by personal consent or contract." "Verdict guilty."

DOCUMENT 12.4
Thomas Jefferson's Views on Race

The following passage reveals Thomas Jefferson's notions about race and his profound doubts about the feasibility of a racially mixed society.

To emancipate all slaves born after passing the act. The bill reported by the revisors does not itself contain this proposition: but an amendment containing it was prepared, to be offered to the legislature whenever the bill should be taken up, and further directing, that they should continue with their parents to a certain age, then be brought up, at the public expence, to tillage, arts or sciences, according to their geniusses, till the females should be eighteen, and the males twenty-one years of

Source: Thomas Jefferson, "Notes on the State of Virginia" (1782), in Paul L. Ford (ed.), *The Writings of Thomas Jefferson* (New York, 1894) vol. 3, pp. 243–50.

age, when they should be colonized to such place as the circumstances of the time should render most proper, sending them out with arms, implements of household and of the handicraft arts, seeds, pairs of the useful domestic animals, &c. to declare them a free and independant people, and extend to them our alliance and protection, till they shall have acquired strength; and to send vessels at the same time to other parts of the world for an equal number of white inhabitants; to induce whom to migrate hither, proper encouragements were to be proposed. It will probably be asked, Why not retain and incorporate the blacks into the state, and thus save the expence of supplying, by importation of white settlers, the vacancies they will leave? Deep rooted prejudices entertained by the whites; ten thousand recollections, by the blacks, of the injuries they have sustained; new provocations; the real distinctions which nature has made; and many other circumstances, will divide us into parties, and produce convulsions which will probably never end but in the extermination of the one or the other race.—To these objections, which are political, may be added others, which are physical and moral. The first difference which strikes us is that of colour. Whether the black of the negro resides in the reticular membrane between the skin and scarf-skin, or in the scarf-skin itself; whether it proceeds from the colour of the blood, the colour of the bile, or from that of some other secretion, the difference is fixed in nature, and is as real as if its seat and cause were better known to us. And is this difference of no importance? Is it not the foundation of a greater or less share of beauty in the two races? Are not the fine mixtures of red and white, the expressions of every passion by greater or less suffusions of colour in the one, preferable to that eternal monotony, which reigns in the countenances, that immoveable veil of black which covers all the emotions of the other race? Add to these, flowing hair, a more elegant symmetry of form, their own

judgment in favour of the whites, declared by their preference of them, as uniformly as is the preference of the Oran ootan for the black women over those of his own species. The circumstance of superior beauty, is thought worthy attention in the propagation of our horses, dogs, and other domestic animals; why not in that of man? Besides those of colour, figure, and hair, there are other physical distinctions proving a difference of race. They have less hair on the face and body. They secrete less by the kidnies, and more by the glands of the skin, which gives them a very strong and disagreeable odour. This greater degree of transpiration renders them more tolerant of heat, and less so of cold, than the whites. Perhaps too a difference of structure in the pulmonary apparatus, which a late ingenious experimentalist has discovered to be the principal regulator of animal heat, may have disabled them from extricating, in the act of inspiration, so much of that fluid from the outer air, or obliged them in expiration, to part with more of it. They seem to require less sleep. A black, after hard labour through the day, will be induced by the slightest amusements to sit up till midnight, or later, though knowing he must be out with the first dawn of the morning. They are at least as brave, and more adventuresome. But this may perhaps proceed from a want of forethought, which prevents their seeing a danger till it be present. When present, they do not go through it with more coolness or steadiness than the whites. They are more ardent after their female: but love seems with them to be more an eager desire, than a tender delicate mixture of sentiment and sensation. Their griefs are transient. Those numberless afflictions, which render it doubtful whether heaven has given life to us in mercy or in wrath, are less felt, and sooner forgotten with them. In general, their existence appears to participate more of sensation than reflection. To this must be ascribed their disposition to sleep when abstracted from their diversions, and unemployed in labour. An animal whose body is at rest, and who does not reflect, must be disposed to sleep of course. Comparing them by their faculties of memory, reason, and imagination, it appears to me, that in memory they are equal to the whites; in reason much inferior, as I think one could scarcely be found capable of tracing and comprehending the investigations of Euclid; and that in imagination they are dull, tasteless, and anomalous. It would be unfair to follow them to Africa for this investigation. We will consider them here, on the same stage with the whites, and where the facts are not apocryphal on which a judgment is to be formed. It will be right to make great allowances for the difference of condition, of education, of conversation, of the sphere in which they move. Many millions of them have been brought to, and born in America. Most of them indeed have been confined to tillage, to their own homes, and their own society: yet many have been so situated, that they might have availed themselves of the conversation of their masters; many have been brought up to the handicraft arts, and from that circumstance have always been associated with the whites. Some have been liberally educated, and all have lived in countries where the arts and sciences are cultivated to a considerable degree, and have had before their eyes samples of the best works from abroad. The Indians, with no advantages of this kind, will often carve figures on their pipes not destitute of design and merit. They will crayon out an animal, a plant, or a country, so as to prove the existence of a germ in their minds which only wants cultivation. They astonish you with strokes of the most sublime oratory; such as prove their reason and sentiment strong, their imagination glowing and elevated. But never yet could I find that a black had uttered a thought above the level of plain narration; never see even an elementary trait of painting or sculpture. In music they are more generally gifted than the whites with accurate ears for tune and time, and they

have been found capable of imagining a small catch. Whether they will be equal to the composition of a more extensive run of melody, or of complicated harmony, is yet to be proved. Misery is often the parent of the most affecting touches in poetry.—Among the blacks is misery enough, God knows, but no poetry. Love is the peculiar oestrum of the poet. Their love is ardent, but it kindles the senses only, not the imagination. Religion indeed has produced a Phyllis Wheatly; but it could not produce a poet. The compositions published under her name are below the dignity of criticism. The heroes of the Dunciad are to her, as Hercules to the author of that poem. Ignatius Sancho has approached nearer to merit in composition; yet his letters do more honour to the heart than the head. They breathe the purest effusions of friendship and general philanthropy, and shew how great a degree of the latter may be compounded with strong religious zeal. He is often happy in the turn of his compliments, and his stile is easy and familiar, except when he affects a Shandean fabrication of words. But his imagination is wild and extravagant, escapes incessantly from every restraint of reason and taste, and, in the course of its vagaries, leaves a tract of thought as incoherent and eccentric, as is the course of a meteor through the sky. His subjects should often have led him to a process of sober reasoning: yet we find him always substituting sentiment for demonstration. Upon the whole, though we admit him to the first place among those of his own colour who have presented themselves to the public judgment, yet when we compare him with the writers of the race among whom he lived, and particularly with the epistolary class, in which he has taken his own stand, we are compelled to enroll him at the bottom of the column. This criticism supposes the letters published under his name to be genuine, and to have received amendment from no other hand; points which would not be of easy investigation. The improvement of the blacks in body and mind, in the first instance of their mixture with the whites, has been observed by every one, and proves that their inferiority is not the effect merely of their condition of life. We know that among the Romans, about the Augustan age especially, the condition of their slaves was much more deplorable than that of the blacks on the continent of America. The two sexes were confined in separate apartments, because to raise a child cost the master more than to buy one. Cato, for a very restricted indulgence to his slaves in this particular, took from them a certain price. But in this country the slaves multiply as fast as the free inhabitants. Their situation and manners place the commerce between the two sexes almost without restraint.—The same Cato, on a principle of economy, always sold his sick and superannuated slaves. He gives it as a standing precept to a master visiting his farm, to sell his old oxen, old waggons, old tools, old and diseased servants, and every thing else become useless. ''Vendat boves vetulos, plaustrum vetus, ferramenta, vetera, servum senem, servum morbosum, & si quid aliud supersit vendat.'' The American slaves cannot enumerate this among the injuries and insults they receive. It was the common practice to expose in the island of Æsculapius, in the Tyber, diseased slaves, whose cure was like to become tedious. The Emperor Claudius, by an edict, gave freedom to such of them as should recover, and first declared, that if any person chose to kill rather than to expose them, it should be deemed homicide. The exposing them is a crime of which no instance has existed with us; and were it to be followed by death, it would be punished capitally. We are told of a certain Vedius Pollio, who, in the presence of Augustus, would have given a slave as food to his fish, for having broken a glass. With the Romans, the regular method of taking the evidence of their slaves was under torture. Here it has been thought better never to resort to their evidence. When a master was murdered, all his slaves, in the same house, or within hearing, were con-

demned to death. Here punishment falls on the guilty only, and as precise proof is required against him as against a freeman. Yet notwithstanding these and other discouraging circumstances among the Romans, their slaves were often their rarest artists. They excelled too in science, insomuch as to be usually employed as tutors to their master's children. Epictetus, ⟨Diogenes, Phædon⟩, Terence, and Phædrus, were slaves. But they were of the race of whites. It is not their condition then, but nature, which has produced the distinction.—Whether further observation will or will not verify the conjecture, that nature has been less bountiful to them in the endowments of the head, I believe that in those of the heart she will be found to have done them justice. That disposition to theft with which they have been branded, must be ascribed to their situation, and not to any depravity of the moral sense. The man, in whose favour no laws of property exist, probably feels himself less bound to respect those made in favour of others. When arguing for ourselves, we lay it down as a fundamental, that laws, to be just, must give a reciprocation of right: that, without this, they are mere arbitrary rules of conduct, founded in force, and not in conscience: and it is a problem which I give to the master to solve, whether the religious precepts against the violation of property were not framed for him as well as his slave? And whether the slave may not as jusitfiably take a little from one, who has taken all from him, as he may slay one who would slay him? That a change in the relations in which a man is placed should change his ideas of moral right and wrong, is neither new, nor peculiar to the colour of the blacks. Homer tells us it was so 2600 years ago.

Ἥμισυ, γαξ τ᾽ ἀρετῆς ἀποαίννυἶαι εὐρύθπα Ζεὺς
Ἀνερος, ευτ᾽ ἄν μιν κατὰ δ8λιον ἦμαξ ἔλησιν.   *Od.* 17. 323.
Jove fix'd it certain, that whatever day
Makes man a slave, takes half his worth away.

But the slaves of which Homer speaks were whites. Notwithstanding these considerations which must weaken their respect for the laws of property, we find among them numerous instances of the most rigid integrity, and as many as among their better instructed masters, of benevolence, gratitude, and unshaken fidelity.—The opinion, that they are inferior in the faculties of reason and imagination, must be hazarded with great diffidence. To justify a general conclusion, requires many observations, even where the subject may be submitted to the Anatomical knife, to Optical glasses, to analysis by fire, or by solvents. How much more then where it is a faculty, not a substance, we are examining; where it eludes the research of all the senses; where the conditions of its existence are various and variously combined; where the effects of those which are present or absent bid defiance to calculation; let me add too, as a circumstance of great tenderness, where our conclusion would degrade a whole race of men from the rank in the scale of beings which their Creator may perhaps have given them. To our reproach it must be said, that though for a century and a half we have had under our eyes the races of black and of red men, they have never yet been viewed by us as subjects of natural history. I advance it therefore as a suspicion only, that the blacks, whether originally a distinct race, or made distinct by time and circumstances, are inferior to the whites in the endowments both of body and mind. It is not against experience to suppose, that different species of the same genus, or varieties of the same species, may possess different qualifications. Will not a lover of natural history then, one who views the gradations in all the races of animals with the eye of philosophy, excuse an effort to keep those in the department of man as distinct as nature has formed them? This unfortunate difference of colour, and perhaps of faculty, is a powerful obstacle to the emancipation of these people. Many of their advocates, while they wish to vindicate the liberty of human nature, are anx-ious also to preserve its dignity and beauty. Some of these, embarrassed by the question "What further is to be done with them?" join themselves in opposition with those who are actuated by sordid avarice only. Among the Romans emancipation required but one effort. The slave, when made free, might mix with, without staining the blood of his master. But with us a second is necessary, unknown to history. When freed, he is to be removed beyond the reach of mixture.

DOCUMENT 12.5
The Southern Reaction to Abolitionist Tracts

Southern defense of slavery intensified as the South became more isolated with its "peculiar" institution and its values. Strict regulations and restrictions of speech and press became common as slave societies became increasingly closed. On December 16, 1835, South Carolina's legislature passed the following resolutions regarding antislavery propaganda.

1. *Resolved,* That the formation of the abolition societies, and the acts and doings of certain fanatics, calling themselves abolitionists, in the non-slaveholding states of this confederacy, are in direct violation of the obligations of the compact of the union, dissocial, and incendiary in the extreme.

2. *Resolved,* That no state having a just regard for her own peace and security can acquiesce in a state of things by which such conspiracies are engendered within the limits of a friendly state, united to her by the bonds of a common league of political association, with-

Source: Thomas Cooper, ed., *Statutes at Large of South Carolina* (Columbia, S.C., 1837), vol. 2, pp. 153–54.

out either surrendering or compromising her most essential rights.

3. *Resolved,* That the Legislature of South Carolina, having every confidence in the justice and friendship of the non-slaveholding states, announces to her co-states her confident expectation, and she earnestly requests that the governments of these states will promptly and effectually suppress all those associations within their respective limits, purporting to be abolition societies, and that they will make it highly penal to print, publish, and distribute newspapers, pamphlets, tracts and pictorial representations calculated and having an obvious tendency to excite the slaves of the southern states to insurrection and revolt.

4. *Resolved,* That, regarding the domestic slavery of the southern states as a subject exclusively within the control of each of the said states, we shall consider every interference, by any other state of the general government, as a direct and unlawful interference, to be resisted at once, and under every possible circumstance.

5. *Resolved,* In order that a salutary negative may be put on the mischievous and unfounded assumption of some of the abolitionists—the non-slaveholding states are requested to disclaim by legislative declaration, all right, either on the part of themselves or the government of the United States, to interfere in any manner with domestic slavery, either in the states, or in the territories where it exists.

6. *Resolved,* That we should consider the abolition of slavery in the District of Columbia, as a violation of the rights of the citizens of that District, derived from the implied conditions on which that territory was ceded to the general government, and as an usurpation to be at once resisted as nothing more than the commencement of a scheme of much more extensive and flagrant injustice.

7. *Resolved,* That the legislature of South Carolina, regards with decided approbation, the measures of security adopted by the Post

Office Department of the United States, in relation to the transmission of incendiary tracts. But if this highly essential and protective policy, be counteracted by congress, and the United States mail becomes a vehicle for the transmission of the mischievous documents, with which it was recently freighted we, in this contingency, expect that the Chief Magistrate of our state, will forthwith call the legislature together, that timely measures may be taken to prevent its traversing our territory. (Resolutions of transmission.)

DOCUMENT 12.6
Some Typical Southern Arguments Justifying Slavery

De Bow's Review, *a journal of southern opinion, is a rich source of proslavery arguments. The following excerpt is an imagined conversation that makes a common argument for slavery.*

The White: My sable friends, we learn from those who have you in charge, that you are come from a far country, and it is now proposed that you become our servants. This we suppose was without your consent at first, and we know not whether you willingly yield to the arrangement as-yet. If you think by faithful service to rise to our level, to be admitted to our society as companions or fellow-citizens, either shortly or at any future time, we will tell you nay. Our races are different; so different that even good Christians are loth to believe that we are descended from the same pair. You may have been sent to us by the Great Being who rules and guides us all. But we say again: you come not here on terms of equality.

The African: Sons of Japhet and children of the white man, you know why we are here.

Source: *De Bow's Review,* vol. 20, (1856).

We came not willingly but we charge not our captivity to you. Yet we are here and we submit to our lot. It may have been for our sins or those of our fathers that we are torn from our native land. A long and fearful penance may be before us, but bitterer it cannot be than the oppression we have left behind. We never have been governed aright; we cannot govern ourselves. Take us, then, and mould us to your will. Fill our hands with proper tools; assign us some simple work not above our capacity; bear with our perverseness and correct us when needful, and we will serve you until the curse is removed from our race.

DOCUMENT 12.7
Southerners Defend Their Institutions

George Fitzhugh (1806–1881) was a southern intellectual who wrote extensively defending southern society and slavery. He argued that slavery was a better system for the laborer than free labor, and that the slaves were better off than northern free workers. The following excerpt is typical of his thinking.

Capital commands labour, as the master does the slave. Neither pays for labour; but the master permits the slave to retain a larger allowance from the proceeds of his own labour, and hence 'free labour is cheaper than slave labour.' You, with the command over labour which your capital gives you, are a slave owner—a master, without the obligations of a master. They who work for you, who create your income, are slaves, without the rights of slaves. Slaves without a master! The men without property, in free society, are theoretically in a worse condition than slaves. The capitalists, in free society,

Source: George Fitzhugh, *Cannibals All! or Slaves Without Masters* (Richmond, Va., 1857), pp. 353–56.

live in ten times the luxury and show that Southern masters do, because the slaves to capital work harder and cost less, than negro slaves. The negro slaves of the South are the happiest, and, in some sense, the freest people in the world. The children and the aged and infirm work not at all, and yet have all the comforts and necessaries of life provided for them. They enjoy liberty, because they are oppressed neither by care nor labour. The women do little hard work, and are protected from the despotism of their husbands by their masters. The free labourer must work or starve. He is more of a slave than the negro, because he works longer and harder for less allowance than the slave, and has no holiday, because the cares of life with him begin when its labours end. Free society, asserts the right of a few to the earth—slavery, maintains that it belongs, in different degrees, to all.

To treat free labourers badly and unfairly, is universally inculcated as a moral duty, and the selfishness of man's nature prompts him to the most rigorous performance of this cannibalish duty. Masters treat their sick, infant, helpless slaves well, not only from feeling and affection, but from motives of self-interest. Good treatment renders them more valuable. It is impossible to place labour and capital in harmonious or friendly relations, except by the means of slavery, which identifies their interests. What is called Free Society, is a very recent invention. It proposes to make the weak, ignorant and poor, free, by turning them loose in a world owned exclusively by the few, to get a living. In the fanciful state of nature, where property is unappropriated, the strong have no weapons but superior physical and mental power with which to oppress the weak. Their power of oppression is increased a thousand fold, when they become the exclusive owners of the earth and all the things thereon. They are masters without the obligations of masters, and the poor are slaves without the rights of slaves. . . .

We do not agree with the authors of the Declaration of Independence that governments 'derive their just powers from the consent of the governed.' The women, the children, the negroes, and but few of the non-property holders were consulted, or consented to the Revolution or the governments that ensued from its success. . . . Those governments originated in force, and have been continued by force. . . . In the South, the interest of the governing class is eminently conservative, and the South is fast becoming the most conservative of nations.

DOCUMENT 12.8

John C. Calhoun (1782–1850) found that racial slavery was the perfect arrangement for race relations. The following excerpt is from his speech to the U.S. Senate on February 6, 1837, "The Reception of Abolitionist Petitions."

We of the South will not, cannot surrender our institutions. To maintain the existing relations between the two races, inhabiting that section of the Union, is indispensable to the peace and happiness of both. . . . Be it good or bad, it has grown up with our society and institutions, and is so interwoven with them that to destroy it would be to destroy us as a people. But let me not be understood as admitting, even by implication, that the existing relations between the two races in the slaveholding States is an evil—far otherwise; I hold it to be a good. . . . Never before has the black race of Central Africa attained a condition so civilised and so improved, not only physically, but morally and intellectually. It came among us in a low, degraded, and savage condition,

and in the course of a few generations it has grown up under the fostering care of our institutions, reviled as they have been, to its present comparatively civilised condition. . . . I hold that in the present state of civilisation, where two races of different origin, and distinguished by colour, and other physical differences, as well 'as intellectual, are brought together, the relation now existing in the slaveholding States between the two, is, instead of an evil, a good— a positive good. . . .

I fearlessly assert that the existing relation between the two races in the South, against which blind fanatics are waging war, forms the most solid and durable foundation on which to rear free and stable political institutions. There is and always has been in an advanced stage of wealth and civilisation, a conflict between labour and capital. The condition of society in the South exempts us from the disorders and dangers resulting from this conflict; and which explains why it is that the political condition of the slaveholding States has been so much more stable and quiet than that of the North.

DOCUMENT 12.9
The Crime of Mrs. Margaret Douglas

The laws of all slave states prohibited teaching blacks to read. The following excerpt is the court verdict in a case of a Mrs. Douglas of Norfolk, Virginia (1853). Mrs. Douglas was accused and convicted of teaching black children.

Judge Baker. Upon an indictment found against you for assembling with negroes to instruct them to read and write, and for associating with them in an unlawful assembly, you were

Source: Richard K. Crallé, ed. *Speeches of John C. Calhoun* (New York: D. Appleton, 1860), vol. 2, pp. 630–32.

Source: John R. Lawson, ed., *American State Trials* (St. Louis, Missouri: F. H. Thomas, 1920), vol. 7, pp. 56–60.

found guilty, and a mere nominal fine imposed, on the last day of this court held in the month of November. . . . The Court is not called on to vindicate the policy of the law in question, for so long as it remains upon the statute book, and unrepealed, public and private justice and morality require that it should be respected and sustained. There are persons, I believe, in our community, opposed to the policy of the law in question. They profess to believe that universal intellectual culture is necessary to religious instruction and education, and that such culture is suitable to a state of slavery; and there can be no misapprehension as to your opinions on this subject, judging from the indiscreet freedom with which you spoke of your regard for the colored race in general. Such opinions in the present state of our society I regard as manifestly mischievous. It is not true that our slaves cannot be taught religious and moral duty, without being able to read the Bible and use the pen. . . .

A valuable report or document recently published in the city of New York by the Southern Aid Society sets forth many valuable and important truths upon the condition of the Southern slaves, and the utility of moral and religious instruction, apart from a knowledge of books. I recommend the careful perusal of it to all whose opinions concur with your own. It shows that a system of catechetical instruction, with a clear and simple exposition of Scripture, has been employed with gratifying success; that the slave population of the South are peculiarly susceptible of good religious influences. Their mere residence among a Christian people has brought a great and happy change in their condition. They have been raised from the night of heathanism to the light of Christianity, and thousands of them have been brought to a saving knowledge of the Gospel.

Of the one hundred millions of the negro race, there cannot be found another so large a body as the three millions of slaves in the United States at once so intelligent, so inclined to the Gospel, and so blessed by the elevating influence of civilization and Christianity. Occasional instances of cruelty and oppression, it is true, may sometimes occur, and probably will ever continue to take place under any system of laws; but this is not confined to wrongs committed upon the negro; wrongs are committed and cruelly practiced in a like degree by the lawless white man upon his own color; and while the negroes of our town and State are known to be surrounded by most of the substantial comforts of life, and invited both by precept and example to participate in proper, moral and religious duties, it argues, it seems to me, a sickly sensibility towards them to say their persons, and feelings, and interests are not sufficiently respected by our laws, which, in effect, tend to nullify the act of our Legislature passed for the security and protection of their masters.

. . . The first legislative provision upon this subject was introduced in the year 1831, immediately succeeding the bloody scenes of the memorable Southampton insurrection; and that law being found not sufficiently penal to check the wrongs complained of, was re-enacted with additional penalities in the year 1848, which last mentioned act, after several years' trial and experience, has been re-affirmed by adoption, and incorporated into our present code. After these several and repeated recognitions of the wisdom and propriety of the said act, it may well be said that bold and open opposition to it is a matter not to be slightly regarded, especially as we have reason to believe that every Southern slave state in our country, as a measure of self-preservation and protection, has deemed it wise and just to adopt laws with similar provisions.

There might have been no occasion for such enactments in Virginia, or elsewhere, on the subject of negro education, but as a matter of self-defense against the schemes of Northern incendiaries, and the outcry against holding our slaves in bondage. Many now living well remember how, and when, and why the anti-slavery fury began, and by what means its manifestations were made public. Our mails were clogged with abolition pamphlets and inflammatory documents, to be distributed among our Southern negroes to induce them to cut our throats. Sometimes, it may be, these libelous documents were distributed by Northern citizens professing Southern feelings, and at other times by Southern people professing Northern feelings. These, however, were not the only means resorted to by the Northern fanatics to stir up insubordination among our slaves. They scattered far and near pocket handkerchiefs, and other similar articles, with frightful engravings, and printed over with anti-slavery nonsense, with the view to work upon the feeling and ignorance of our negroes, who otherwise would have remained comfortable and happy. Under such circumstances there was but one measure of protection for the South, and that was adopted. . . .

In vindication of the policy and justness of our laws, which every individual should be taught to respect, the judgment of the Court is, in addition to the proper fine and costs, that you be imprisoned for the period of one month in the jail of this city. . . .

DOCUMENT 12.10
Lincoln Considers Slavery in 1858

Much of the debate between Abraham Lincoln and Stephen Douglas, in the 1858 campaign for senator from Illinois, centered on the extension of slavery into the western territories. In his "House Divided" speech before the Illinois Legislature of June 17, 1858, Lincoln made clear his discomfort with a nation "half slave and half free." In the following answer

Source: John G. Nicolay and John Hay, eds., *Abraham Lincoln: Complete Works* (New York, 1915), vol. 1, 508–509.

to Douglas at Alton, Illinois, on October 15, 1858, Lincoln firmly states that he sees the West (and the nation) as a country for whites.

MR. LINCOLN'S REPLY

. . . Now, irrespective of the moral aspect of this question as to whether there is a right or wrong in enslaving a negro, I am still in favor of our new Territories being in such a condition that white men may find a home,— may find some spot where they can better their condition; where they can settle upon new soil and better their condition in life. I am in favor of this, not merely (I must say it here as I have elsewhere) for our own people who are born amongst us, but as an outlet for *free white people everywhere*—the world over—in which Hans, and Baptiste, and Patrick, and all other men from all the world, may find new homes and better their conditions in life.

I have stated upon former occasions, and I may as well state again, what I understand to be the real issue in this controversy between Judge Douglas and myself. . . . The real issue in this controversy—the one pressing upon every mind—is the sentiment on the part of one class that looks upon the institution of slavery *as a wrong,* and of another class that *does not* look upon it as a wrong. The sentiment that contemplates the institution of slavery in this country as a wrong is the sentiment of the Republican party. It is the sentiment around which all their actions, all their arguments, circle, from which all their propositions radiate. They look upon it as being a moral, social, and political wrong; and while they contemplate it as such, they nevertheless have due regard for its actual existence among us, and the difficulties of getting rid of it in any satisfactory way, and to all the constitutional obligations thrown about it. Yet, having a due regard for these, they desire a policy in regard to it that looks to its not creating any more danger. They insist that it should, as far as may be, *be treated* as a wrong; and one of the methods of treating it as a wrong is to *make provision that it shall grow no larger*. They also desire a policy that looks to a peaceful end of slavery at some time, as being wrong. These are the views they entertain in regard to it as I understand them; and all their sentiments, all their arguments and propositions, are brought within this range. I have said, and I repeat it here, that if there be a man amongst us who does not think that the institution of slavery is wrong in any one of the aspects of which I have spoken, he is misplaced, and ought not to be with us. And if there be a man amongst us who is so impatient of it as a wrong as to disregard its actual presence among us and the difficulty of getting rid of it suddenly in a satisfactory way, and to disregard the constitutional obligations thrown about it, that man is misplaced if he is on our platform. We disclaim sympathy with him in practical action. He is not placed properly with us.

On this subject of treating it as a wrong, and limiting its spread, let me say a word. Has anything ever threatened the existence of this Union save and except this very institution of slavery? What is it that we hold most dear amongst us? Our own liberty and prosperity. What has ever threatened our liberty and prosperity, save and except this institution of slavery? If this is true, how do you propose to improve the condition of things by enlarging slavery,—by spreading it out and making it bigger? You may have a wen or cancer upon your person, and not be able to cut it out, lest you bleed to death; but surely it is no way to cure it, to engraft it and spread it over your whole body. That is no proper way of treating what you regard a wrong. You see this peaceful way of dealing with it as a wrong,—restricting the spread of it, and not allowing it to go into new countries where it has not already existed. That is the peaceful way, the old-fashioned way, the way in which the fathers themselves set us the example.

DOCUMENT 12.11
Lincoln Recommends Compensated Emancipation

Lincoln hoped throughout the Civil War that there could be a peaceful accommodation over slavery. In the following legislation aimed at border states, Lincoln held out the possibility of compensation to slave owners for the emancipation of their slaves. He also revealed his hopes for some plan to colonize blacks outside the United States. His plan found no takers.

1. MESSAGE TO CONGRESS

March 6, 1862

FELLOW-CITIZENS OF THE SENATE AND HOUSE OF REPRESENTATIVES:—I recommend the adoption of a joint resolution by your honorable bodies which shall be substantially as follows:

"*Resolved*, That the United States ought to co-operate with any State which may adopt gradual abolishment of slavery, giving to such State pecuniary aid, to be used by such State, in its discretion, to compensate for the inconveniences, public and private, produced by such change of system."

If the proposition contained in the resolution does not meet the approval of Congress and the country, there is the end; but if it does command such approval, I deem it of importance that the States and people immediately interested should be at once distinctly notified of the fact, so that they may begin to consider whether to accept or reject it. The Federal Government would find its highest interest in such a measure, as one of the most efficient means of self-preservation. The leaders of the existing insurrection entertain the hope that this govern-

Source: James G. Richardson, ed., *Messages and Papers of the Presidents* (New York, 1897), vol. 8, pp. 3269–70, 3337–43.

ment will ultimately be forced to acknowledge the independence of some part of the disaffected region, and that all the slave States north of such part will then say, "The Union for which we have struggled being already gone, we now choose to go with the Southern section." To deprive them of this hope substantially ends the rebellion, and the initiation of emancipation completely deprives them of it as to all the States initiating it. The point is not that *all* the States tolerating slavery would very soon, if at all, initiate emancipation; but that, while the offer is equally made to all, the more northern shall by such initiation make it certain to the more southern that in no event will the former ever join the latter in their proposed confederacy. I say "initiation" because, in my judgment, gradual and not sudden emancipation is better for all. In the mere financial or pecuniary view, any member of Congress with the census tables and treasury reports before him can readily see for himself how very soon the current expenditures of this war would purchase, at fair valuation, all the slaves in any named State. Such a proposition on the part of the General Government sets up no claim of a right by Federal authority to interfere with slavery within State limits, referring, as it does, the absolute control of the subject in each case to the State and its people immediately interested. It is proposed as a matter of perfectly free choice with them. . . .

The proposition now made (though an offer only). I hope it may be esteemed no offense to ask whether the pecuniary consideration tendered would not be of more value to the States and private persons concerned than are the institution and property in it in the present aspect of affairs.

While it is true that the adoption of the proposed resolution would be merely initiatory, and not within itself a practical measure, it is recommended in the hope that it would soon lead to important practical results. In full view of my great responsibility to my God and to my country, I earnestly beg the attention of Congress and the people to the subject.

Abraham Lincoln

2. MESSAGE TO CONGRESS
December 1, 1862

. . . Our strife pertains to ourselves—to the passing generations of men—and it can without convulsion be hushed forever with the passing of one generation.

In this view I recommend the adoption of the following resolution and articles amendatory to the Constitution of the United States:

Resolved by the Senate and House of Representatives of the United States of America, in Congress assembled, (two thirds of both Houses concurring). That the following articles be proposed to the Legislatures (or conventions) of the several States as amendments to the Constitution of the United States, all or any of which articles, when ratified by three fourths of the said Legislatures (or conventions), to be valid as part or parts of the said Constitution, viz:

ART.—Every State wherein slavery now exists which shall abolish the same therein at any time or times before the 1st day of January, A.D. 1900, shall receive compensation from the United States as follows, to wit:

The President of the United States shall deliver to every such State bonds of the United States bearing interest at the rate of—per cent, per annum to an amount equal to the aggregate sum of—for each slave shown to have been therein by the Eighth Census of the United States, said bonds to be delivered to such State by instalments or in one parcel at the completion of the abolishment, accordingly as the same shall have been gradual or at one time within such State: and interest shall begin to run upon any such bond only from the proper time of its delivery as aforesaid. Any State having received bonds as aforesaid and afterwards reintroducing or tolerating slavery therein shall refund to the United States the bonds so received, or the value thereof, and all interest paid thereon.

ART.——. All slaves who shall have enjoyed actual freedom by the chances of the war at any time before the end of the rebellion shall be forever free; but all owners of such who shall not have been disloyal shall be compensated for them at the same rates as is provided for States adopting abolishment of slavery, but in such way that no slave shall be twice accounted for.

ART.——. Congress may appropriate money and otherwise provide for colonizing free colored persons with their own consent at any place or places without the United States.

I beg indulgence to discuss these proposed articles at some length. Without slavery the rebellion could never have existed; without slavery it could not continue.

Among the friends of the Union there is great diversity of sentiment and of policy in regard to slavery and the African race amongst us. Some would perpetuate slavery; some would abolish it suddenly and without compensation: some would abolish it gradually and with compensation: some would remove the freed people from us, and some would retain them with us: and there are yet other minor diversities. Because of these diversities we waste much strength in struggles among ourselves. By mutual concession we should harmonize and act together. This would be compromise, but it would be compromise among the friends and not with the enemies of the Union. These articles are intended to embody a plan of such mutual concessions. If the plan shall be adopted, it is assumed that emancipation will follow, at least in several of the States.

As to the first article, the main points are, first, the emancipation; secondly, the length of time for consummating it (thirty-seven years); and, thirdly, the compensation.

The emancipation will be unsatisfactory to the advocates of perpetual slavery, but the length of time should greatly mitigate their dissatisfaction. The time spares both races from the evils of sudden derangement—in fact, from the necessity of any derangement—while most of those whose habitual course of thought will be disturbed by the measure will have passed away before its consummation. They will never see it. Another class will hail the prospect of emancipation, but will deprecate the length of time. They will feel that it gives too little to the now living slaves. But it really gives them much. It saves them from the vagrant destitution which must largely attend immediate emancipation in localities where their numbers are very great, and it gives the inspiring assurance that their posterity shall be free forever. The plan leaves to each State choosing to act under it to abolish slavery now or at the end of the century, or at any intermediate time, or by degrees extending over the whole or any part of the period, and it obliges no two States to proceed alike. It also provides for compensation, and generally the mode of making it. This, it would seem, must further mitigate the dissatisfaction of those who favor perpetual slavery, and especially of those who are to receive the compensation. Doubtless some of those who are to pay and not to receive will object. Yet the measure is both just and economical. In a certain sense the liberation of slaves is the destruction of property—property acquired by descent or by purchase, the same as any other property. It is no less true for having been often said that the people of the South are not more responsible for the original introduction of this property than are the people of the North, and when it is remembered how unhesitatingly we all use cotton and sugar and share the profits of dealing in them, it may not be quite safe to say that the South has been more responsible than the North for its continuance. If, then, for a common object this property is to be sacrificed, is it not just that it be done at a common charge?

And if with less money, or money more easily paid, we can preserve the benefits of the Union by this means than we can by the war alone, is it not also economical to do it? Let us consider it, then. Let us ascertain the sum we have expended in the war since compensated emancipation was proposed last March, and consider whether if that measure had been promptly accepted by even some of the slave States the same sum would not have done more to close the war than has been otherwise done. If so, the measure would save money, and in that view would be a prudent and economical measure. . . . The aggregate sum necessary for compensated emancipation of course would be large. But it would require no ready cash, nor the bonds even any faster than the emancipation progresses. This might not, and probably would not, close before the end of the thirty-seven years. At that time we shall probably have a hundred millions of people to share the burden, instead of thirty-one millions as now. . . .

The proposed emancipation would shorten the war, perpetuate peace, insure this increase of population, and proportionately the wealth of the country. With these we should pay all the emancipation would cost, together with our other debt, easier than we should pay our other debt without it. . . .

This fact would be no excuse for delaying payment of what is justly due, but it shows the great importance of time in this connection—the great advantage of a policy by which we shall not have to pay until we number 100,000,000 what by a different policy we would have to pay now, when we number but 31,000,000. In a word, it shows that a dollar will be much harder to pay for the war than will be a dollar for emancipation on the proposed plan. And then the latter will cost no blood, no precious life. It will be a saving of both. . . .

The third article relates to the future of the freed people. It does not oblige, but merely authorizes Congress to aid in colonizing such as may consent. This ought not to be regarded as objectionable on the one hand or on the other, insomuch as it comes to nothing unless by the mutual consent of the people to be deported and the American voters through their representatives in Congress. . . .

The plan consisting of these articles is recommended, not but that a restoration of the national authority would be accepted without its adoption.

Nor will the war nor proceedings under the proclamation of September 22, 1862, be stayed because of the *recommendation* of this plan. Its timely *adoption,* I doubt not, would bring restoration, and thereby stay both.

And notwithstanding this plan, the recommendation that Congress provide by law for compensating any State which may adopt emancipation before this plan shall have been acted upon is hereby earnestly renewed. Such would be only an advance part of the plan, and the same arguments apply to both.

This plan is recommended as a means, not in exclusion of, but additional to, all others for restoring and preserving the national authority throughout the Union. The subject is presented exclusively in its economical aspect. The plan would, I am confident, secure peace more speedily and maintain it more permanently than can be done by force alone, while all it would cost, considering amounts and manner of payment and times of payment, would be easier paid than will be the additional cost of the war if we rely solely upon force. It is much, very much, that it would cost no blood at all.

The plan is proposed as permanent constitutional law. It cannot become such without the concurrence of, first, two thirds of Congress, and afterwards three fourths of the States. The requisite three fourths of the States will necessarily include seven of the slave States. Their concurrence, if obtained, will give assurance of their severally adopting emancipation at no very distant day upon the new constitutional terms. This assurance would end the struggle now and save the Union forever. . . .

Fellow-citizens, *we* can not escape history. We of this Congress and this administration will be remembered in spite of ourselves. No personal significance or insignificance can spare one or another of us. The fiery trial through which we pass will light us down in honor or dishonor to the latest generation. We *say* we are for the Union. The world will not forget that we say this. We know how to save the Union. The world knows we do know how to save it. We, even *we here,* hold the power and bear the responsibility. In *giving* freedom to the *slave* we *assure* freedom to the *free*— honorable alike in what we give and what we preserve. We shall nobly save or meanly lose the last, best hope of earth. Other means may succeed; this could not fail. The way is plain, peaceful, generous, just—a way which if followed the world will forever applaud and God must forever bless.

Abraham Lincoln.

Chapter 13

Slavery Is Essential Guilt: The Case for Abolitionism

Bertram Wyatt-Brown
University of Florida

"I am aware that many object to the severity of my language; but is there not cause for severity? I *will be* as harsh as truth, and as uncompromising as justice. . . I am in earnest—I will not equivocate—I will not excuse—I will not retreat a single inch—AND I WILL BE HEARD.'' With these ringing words in *The Liberator,* published in Boston on January 1, 1831, William Lloyd Garrison fired the opening gun in the polemical war against slavery.

His message was as clear and blunt as his rhetoric. According to Garrison, as the first document reveals, slaveholding was a sin. Its continuation threatened God's wrath on all persons complicit in ''men-stealing'' no matter how distantly or indirectly involved. Protecting slavery in the Constitution made the nation an abomination in God's eyes. The remedy, Garrison insisted, was the mandate of immediatism—repentance of both northern and southern Christians and the elimination of bondage by manumission and statute, without compensation to owners, without removal of freedmen from native soil and, above all, without delay.

This radical plan of emancipation set abolitionists apart. Other critics of slavery—and

their numbers grew throughout the era—merely adopted the position that masters were not individually guilty, yet slave ownership was detrimental to American interests and values. They acknowledged the constitutional validity of slavery where it already existed, but they opposed its wanton expansion. These were the opinions, for instance, of Abraham Lincoln. As slaveholders and southern politicians became ever more aggressive in their demands upon the free states, antisouthern suspicions, quite apart from any strong disapproval of slavery per se, added another dimension to the sectional dispute. The consolidation of these sentiments, not abolitionism by itself, made the North a formidable opponent of secession. Yet, the voice of radical antislavery forces was a key factor in the complex events leading to the Civil War and emancipation. What about this voice? Did it speak in one or many tongues? What factors shaped the extreme (''ultra'') position? What were the roots of abolitionism? Who was drawn to the antislavery movement? What was its appeal for them? These are some questions that need to be addressed.

To place the abolitionists in the context of their times, three issues are worth exploring: (1) the early history of the movement; (2) the identity of its membership; and (3) its impact on the coming of the Civil War.

With regard to the first issue, abolitionism was an outgrowth of the general humanitarian impulse that began in the eighteenth century and gathered greater force in the nineteenth century. The rise of a new economic order from the ashes of feudalism was a major factor in the changing attitude toward the value of human life and individual moral growth. Modern capitalism was based on two interdependent values: the personal ambitions and conscientiousness of the entrepreneur and the necessity for reliability and cooperation of others in conducting business. Like all human institutions, free-labor capitalism—with its industrial proletariat—did not match these ideals, but its success encouraged the perception that man could control his social and natural environment. Abolitionists firmly believed that free labor in a capitalistic society rested upon the God-given principles of self-reliance, hard work, and property acquisition. In strenuous opposition, southern apologists for slavery, like John C. Calhoun of South Carolina, argued that "wage slavery," as practiced in northern and British factories, was infinitely worse than black servitude. They reasoned that burdened with long hours, uncertain employment, and low wages, industrial workers toiled under greedy bosses. Slaves, on the other hand, served benevolent overlords who provided a leisurely work pace, shelter, clothing, food, and Christian advice in good and bad times. The abolitionist response to such views is illustrated in Document 13.2.

Second, the enlightened ideas of republicanism contributed to the abolition cause. American Revolutionaries resisted monarchy and imperialism on the rhetorical grounds that the British sought to enslave them—a disgrace not to be endured by proud freemen. Such a view found expression in the Declaration of Independence even though southern thinkers, including Thomas Jefferson, seldom wondered if "all men" might mean blacks as ones to share the benefits of equality and inalienable rights. Nonetheless, republican principle, carried out in the prohibition against slavery in Thomas Jefferson's Northwest Ordinance of 1787 and in its gradual elimination in the northern states, set the stage for the sterner program of the abolitionists.

The third revolution was equally significant: a vigorous revival of evangelical Protestantism, particularly in the northern states during the first quarter of the nineteenth century. The mid-eighteenth century Great Awakening, which preceded it, had quickened Quaker opposition to slaveholding, but the second religious upsurge provided a broad denominational basis for important reform and evangelistic efforts. Presbyterians, Congregationalists, Baptists, and Methodists, inspired by such zealous preachers as Charles G. Finney, founded societies to spread the Gospel, improve American habits and morality, and aid the worthy poor and helpless.

Amid the array of such organizations as the Temperance Union and American Tract Society, there arose the American Anti-Slavery Society, founded two years after Garrison had begun *The Liberator.* Dedicated to immediatism, the new agency "for doing good," was at first devoted largely to the conversion of other evangelical Christians rather than the mass of Americans. Wealthy Manhattan businessmen Arthur and Lewis Tappan soon enlisted a core of such young, often clerical idealists as Theodore Dwight Weld, Elizur Wright, and the Rev. Joshua Leavitt to champion immediatism by special mailings, newspaper production, and lecture tours—mostly to Protestant church congregations. Such activity, along with Garrison's severe denunciations, undermined the influence of the rival American Colonization Society, with its Liberian experiment for the expatriation of freed blacks and the Christianization of Africa.

In 1835, the New York headquarters launched a widespread publicity campaign, posting antislavery pamphlets and papers to leading pious citizens throughout the nation, North and South. Infuriated, southern mobs broke into post offices, destroyed the ''incendiary'' literature, and burned the Tappans and Garrison in effigy. In the North, Whig and Democratic politicians organized rallies against ''firebrands,'' the ultras, who trampled on the Stars and Stripes, they claimed, and raised the banner of race ''amalgamation.'' In Boston, the mayor placed Garrison in the custody of the city jailer to protect him from a howling mob. It was led, Garrison mocked, by ''Gentlemen of Property and Standing.'' Even in the rural hinterlands, so masterful a speaker as Theodore Weld faced angry throngs. On an antislavery tour in Ohio, the Rev. James Thome looked ''like a stoned gander,'' remarked an amused friend afterwards, when stinking eggs ''stream'd in ropy masses through the house.'' During an antiabolitionist riot, Elijah P. Lovejoy, a fiery editor, was killed in 1837 at Alton, Illinois, while defending his printing press. Yet, despite abolitionist unpopularity, northern reaction was less repressive than one might expect, a fastidiousness that Southerners quickly noted. Partly because Northerners recognized the dangers to free speech and free press that rowdyism entailed, demonstrations subsided in the late 1830s. Abolitionism had obtained a foothold in the northern conscience. Nevertheless, during the first decade of agitation, the abolition ranks never exceeded one in twenty northern voters.

Turning to the second issue, the abolitionists' identity and psychology, one is impressed with their hopefulness and persistence in the face of difficulties. In closely fraternal camaraderie they found the means to overcome adversity. In fact, a number of studies have recently shown that a common cultural and moral heritage made possible the abolitionists' resilience and dedication to the cause.

By and large, reformers of this kind belonged neither to the very wealthy nor the very poor ranks of society. In the upper North and Northwest, they were chiefly drawn from Congregational, Quaker, or Separate Baptist families. Reformers from Pennsylvania and New Jersey ordinarily grew up in evangelical (Hicksite) Quaker and Presbyterian households. By and large, antislavery leaders reached higher than average levels of education and therefore often constituted the intellectual elite of small localities—the professional class of teachers, ministers, physicians, and, occasionally, merchants. Rank and file abolitionists often plied a skilled craft or worked their own small farms. But where manufacturing existed, abolitionists tended to be more associated with new technology, as owners or workers, than with handicraft production. In other words, these reformers participated in the building of the new economic order—as document 13.2 suggests.

Nearly all the major abolitionists were raised as strict believers in Christian principle—violations of which aroused pangs of guilt and deep fears of lost faith. The leaders of the crusade tended to be highly intelligent, sensitive youngsters whose mothers gave them a strong sense of personal destiny—particularly in working for Christian ideals. Some abolitionists remembered an early and touching encounter with a black American that portended the future interest. Contradictory impulses of empathy toward others and self-determination, humility and pride, righteousness and doubt seemed part of the abolitionist temperament. The early history of Samuel J. May illustrates these matters with unusual poignancy in Document 13.4. Some black abolitionists also fit this characterization. For instance, Frederick Douglass, the greatest of them all, born a slave on the Maryland Eastern Shore, never learned who was his father, a white man, and he barely knew his mother, who died early in his life. Yet, a succession of strong-minded and caring white and black women nurtured him and admired his natural charm and alertness. Though spared the full rigors of bondage, he understood the common slave's misery, as Document 13.5 illuminates.

The psychology of black abolitionists differed little from that of white reformers. Most of them, whether slave or free, remembered appreciatively a dominant maternal figure who encouraged the virtues of piety, self-discipline, and educational advance. Almost a third of the leadership was drawn from clerical ranks—partly because it was one of the few professions open to gifted blacks. Often burdened with covert racism even within antislavery circles, northern black community leaders were concerned not only with slavery but with the evils of racism in northern society, as document 13.3 explains. Also, contrary to legend, they, rather than white friends, operated most "stations" on the "Underground Railroad." A few, like Harriet Tubman, even dared to reenter slave country to rescue particular victims.

The participation of white women in the cause arose from the same wellsprings as those of the men, white or black. A high proportion of female immediatists were the wives of reforming husbands. Seldom in those days did women have the economic capacity or the emotional strength to defy fathers or husbands on political or social issues. Most antislavery women were conventional in religious and domestic ways. They perceived abolitionism as a cause similar to the popular foreign mission and antidrink movements. Much like the men, they divided according to class and background. In the Rochester, N.Y. Female Anti-Slavery Society, for instance, upper-class women were poorly represented; the majority belonged to the shopkeeping and artisan class, the most dynamic part of the local economy.

Although custom dictated modest demeanor, women were highly visible in the reform. They were responsible for much of the political work of the cause—securing signatures on petitions, mailing Liberty Party materials, and organizing fairs. Despite disfranchisement, antislavery women exercised a hidden political influence. Yet, a few intellectually gifted women went much further. Lydia Maria Child, a popular

novelist, risked (and lost) her wide readership when she published a major attack on slavery in 1833; also in that year, Prudence Crandall, a Connecticut schoolteacher, endangered her life and livelihood by continuing to teach a school of white and black children regardless of mob actions and state regulation. In 1837, Angelina and Sarah Grimké spoke before audiences of men and women, a defiance of custom when such behavior was considered "promiscuous." Out of the controversy that they unwittingly raised sprang the feminist movement, as document 13.6 describes and illuminates. Despite the ideological and motivational differences of these three groups—the white men, the women, and the blacks—they all shared similarities of background, values, and faith in divine inspiration.

With regard to the political effect of the abolitionist movement, the leaders found themselves unable to move the great mass of voters and their representatives, especially at the start. In the 1830s, large-scale petition campaigns were mounted against slavery and the interstate slave trade insofar as they were subject to Congressional authority. Despite the protests of such moderate antislavery Representatives as John Quincy Adams and Joshua Giddings from Ohio, "gag" rules prevented the petitions from reaching the floor for debate.

Equally damaging was abolitionist disarray. By 1840, the American Anti-Slavery Society, debt-ridden and demoralized from internal strains, split into three antagonistic factions. The first of these was the highly intellectual group of Bostonians under Garrison's leadership. As a moral perfectionist, Garrison proclaimed the sinfulness of war, the subjection of women, religious orthodoxy, and even the institutional organization of society. Neither church nor government, he claimed, were needed to cleanse humanity of sin. No less shocking was Garrison's declaration of "No Union with Slaveholders," a call for free-state withdrawal that he proclaimed from the 1840s until the eve of Southern secession.

At the annual American Anti-Slavery Society convention in New York in May 1840, the dispute reached a climax. On a question of seating a woman as a society officer, the Garrisonians' oversized delegation took control. Their outraged evangelical opponents, under Lewis Tappan, stormed out leaving Garrison triumphant. The dissidents formed the largest group of immediatists, bound as they were by ties of antifeminism, mistrust of politics as a vehicle for godly reform, and strong evangelical convictions. Their activities within the various denominations had much to do with the splintering of the national churches, North and South, in the 1840s. Although conservative and narrow-spirited about women's participation in public affairs, the evangelical abolitionists remained the backbone of the cause.

The third group to wheel off in the 1840 split entered the political arena as the Liberty Party, a partisan effort that both the Garrisonians and the evangelical circle thought was corrupting because zeal for officeholding inevitably meant betrayal of principle; i.e., participation in a government that sanctioned slavery was immoral. In the elections of 1840 and 1844, Gerrit Smith, a wealthy and radical reformer, Joshua Leavitt, and others ran James J. Birney for President. He had been a slaveholder and colonizationist leader whom Theodore Weld had converted to abolitionism. The party fared poorly at the polls and gradually relinquished principle—just as abolitionist critics had feared. In 1848, the Liberty men coalesced with main-party dissenters to form the Free Soil Party, which in turn developed into the Republican Party (1854–55). Yet, while abolitionists dutifully voted for candidates who best reflected their views, seldom were the politicians, with an instinct for survival, committed to immediate emancipation itself. Abolitionists could boast of little harmony and no common political policy. What was accomplished, however, was a constant flow of petitions, polemics, and protest about each sectional question,

from the Nullification crisis of the early 1830s to the opening gunfire at Fort Sumter.

In some respects, abolitionism appeared to be making great strides forward. The movement was no longer confined to church activities and the sporadic antiblack or antiabolitionist riot. From 1840 to 1860, abolitionist speakers like Wendell Phillips and Theodore Parker could move great masses to indignation over a fugitive slave case without a reference to narrow religious matters. In fact, many of the abolitionists had turned from strictly evangelical trinitarianism to what was called "free religion" or a form of secularized moral absolutism—Christian ethics with God's existence left out.

These changes meant that abolitionism was reaching different audiences in different styles, acting as a prod to move the indifferent toward moderate antislavery, and the moderates toward greater commitment. Yet in the calculus of events leading to war, abolitionism was less a factor in its own right than it was an element whose effectiveness depended upon other forces. This circumstance was partly a matter of deliberate policy. Serving as prophets and witnesses of wrongdoing, the abolitionists rejected coercive means, including incitement of slaves to rebel. As Nathaniel P. Rogers, a New Hampshire abolitionist editor, declared, "We have nothing to say, in this enterprise, to the slave," a policy that the Rev. Henry Highland Garnet and other black abolitionists vainly protested. As a result, abolitionists were less likely to create events than to react to them with verbal and written clamor.

In the meantime, northern opinion was gradually coalescing in opposition to the "Great Slave Power," an alleged conspiracy of arrogant slaveholders to gain full sway over the territorial spoils of the Mexican War. Even for persons seldom sympathetic to abolitionism, the enactment of the harsh Fugitive Slave Law, as part of the Compromise of 1850, was an abject surrender of sectional interest. Northern mobs were more likely to rough up a slave-catcher pursuing a victim like runaway Anthony Burns in Boston (1854) than they were to assault an abolitionist. In the free states, outcries against the passage of the proslavery Kansas-Nebraska Act (1854), the bludgeoning of antislavery Senator Charles Sumner of Massachusetts by a Carolinian Congressman (1856), the pro-southern rampages in Kansas, and the slaveholders' victory in the Supreme Court's *Dred Scott* decision (1857) grew ever more shrill. Abolitionists helped to stir reactions to these crises, but clearly their movement was fully entangled in a much broader transformation of northern opinion. At the same time, the political events of the 1850s helped to make abolitionism seem less obnoxious and extremist than the southern politicians demanding more concessions and threatening secession if they were not forthcoming.

In one dramatic particular, though, the abolitionist cause seized the initiative—and the headlines—only this time it was in defiance of longstanding pacifist policy: John Brown's Raid at Harpers Ferry in October 1859. The grizzled Calvinist warrior of "Bloody Kansas" had never followed Tappan, Garrison, or the political activists. Yet, although he was a loner, Brown knew exactly how to play upon abolitionist—and Northern—sentiments of Christian love and upon passions for virile retribution—as document 13.7 discloses. Wendell Phillips hailed him as "the impersonator of God's law" and "a regular Cromwellian dug up from two centuries."

Even so, John Brown's raid, a military failure but political success, would have accomplished nothing without an infuriated southern white reaction. Southerners might have ignored abolitionist criticism and awaited a subsiding of Republican fortunes. Instead, southern "hotheads" argued that submission to majority antislavery rule was as unthinkable in 1859 and 1860 as surrender to monarchy had been in 1775 and 1776. Brown's raid—and northern sympathy for it—seemed to prove the "fire-eaters'" right. Secession appeared the only manly response to Yankee insult. The significance of Harpers Ferry, however, was magnified in Abraham Lincoln's victory. In the South, it was deemed a virtual invitation to a duel.

In the North, the Republican triumph represented a convergence of antislavery and anti-southern feelings, which the abolitionists had done so much to engender. Yet, as Document 13.8 divulges, dedicated reformers like Wendell Phillips were skeptical of Lincoln and his party. At the same time, they perceived that the Republican victory signified the final struggle between freedom and slavery was about to begin.

In this sequence of thrust and counterthrust, the abolitionists could scarcely claim to be marching toward their goals by the peaceful, spiritual means that they had so long proclaimed. But Union victories and the prospect of slavery becoming a casualty of war, gave them, they assumed, welcome assurance of God's approval. The abolitionists prepared the free states with a moral imperative for crushing bondage. Yet, if race equality was the primary abolitionist goal, the movement—indeed the nation—failed to seize the prize. Nonetheless, the reformers remained optimistic—trusting others to complete the task. Frederick Douglass summed up their outlook some years later: "I remember that God reigns in eternity, and that, whatever delays, disappointments and discouragements may come, truth, justice, liberty, and humanity will prevail." No abolitionist ever doubted it.

SUGGESTED READINGS

Abzug, Robert H. *Passionate Liberator: Theodore Dwight Weld and the Dilemma of Reform.* New York: Oxford University Press, 1980.

Bolt, Christine, and Seymour Drescher. eds. *Anti-Slavery, Religion and Reform: Essays in Memory of Roger Anstey.* New York: Archon Press, 1980.

Davis, David Brion. *Slavery and Human Progress.* New York: Oxford University Press, 1984.

Duberman, Martin, ed. *The Antislavery Vanguard: New Essays on the Abolitionists.* Princeton: Princeton University Press, 1965.

Friedman, Lawrence F. *Gregarious Saints: Self and Community in American Abolitionism, 1830–1870.* New York: Cambridge University Press, 1982.

Haskell, Thomas. "Capitalism and the Origins of the Humanitarian Sensibility, Part I." *American Historical Review* 90 (April 1985), pp. 339–61 and "Part II," Ibid., (June 1985), pp. 547–66.

Kraut, Alan M., ed. *Crusaders and Compromisers: Essays on the Relationship of the Antislavery Struggle to the Antebellum Party System.* Westport, Conn.: Greenwood Press, 1983.

Lerner, Gerda. *The Grimké Sisters from South Carolina: Rebels against Slavery.* Boston: Houghton Mifflin, 1967.

McPherson, James M. *The Struggle against Equality: Abolitionists and the Negro in the Civil War and Reconstruction.* Princeton: Princeton University Press, 1964.

Martin, Waldo E., Jr. *The Mind of Frederick Douglass.* Chapel Hill: University of North Carolina Press, 1985.

Oates, Stephen B. *To Purge This Land with Blood: A Biography of John Brown.* New York: Harper & Row, 1970.

Pease, Jane H. and William H. Pease. *They Who Would Be Free: Blacks' Search for Freedom, 1830–1861.* New York: Atheneum, 1974.

Perry, Lewis and Michael Fellman. eds. *Antislavery Reconsidered: New Perspectives on the Abolitionists.* Baton Rouge: Louisiana State University Press, 1979.

Preston, Dickson J. *Young Frederick Douglass: The Maryland Years.* Baltimore: Johns Hopkins University Press, 1980.

Stewart, James Brewer. *Wendell Phillips: Liberty's Hero.* Baton Rouge: Louisiana State University Press, 1986.

_____. *Holy Warriors: The Abolitionists and American Slavery.* New York: Hill and Wang, 1976.

Walters, Ronald G. *The Antislavery Appeal: American Abolitionism after 1830.* Baltimore: Johns Hopkins University Press, 1976.

Wyatt-Brown, Bertram. *Yankee Saints and Southern Sinners.* Baton Rouge: Louisiana State University, 1985.

_____. *Lewis Tappan and the Evangelical War against Slavery.* New York: Atheneum, 1971.

DOCUMENT 13.1
The Garrisonian Message

William Lloyd Garrison's truculent language and opinions are clear from this selection, published in the Liberator *in 1832. His purpose was to shock a complacent public into recognizing the enormity of the national sin as he saw it. A dozen years later, he offered the platform:* No union with slaveholders, *because, he declared, "in withdrawing from the American Union, we have the God of justice with us." Such convictions were indeed provocative at a time when the young nation had not established a firm sense of national identity or purpose. It was Garrison's aim to provide both ideals in accordance with his views.*

THE GREAT CRISIS!

There is much declamation about the sacredness of the compact which was formed between the free and slave states, on the adoption of the Constitution. A sacred compact, forsooth! We pronounce it the most bloody and heaven-daring arrangement . . . ever exhibited on earth. Yes—we recognize the compact, but with feelings of shame and indignation; and it will be held in everlasting infamy by the friends of justice and humanity throughout the world. It was a compact formed at the sacrifice of the

Source: *The Liberator* (Boston), December 29, 1832.

bodies and souls of millions of our race, for the sake of achieving a political object—an unblushing and monstrous coalition to do evil that good might come. Such a compact was, in the nature of things and according to the law of God, null and void from the beginning. No body of men ever had the right to guarantee the holding of human beings in bondage. Who or what were the framers of our government, that they should dare confirm and authorise such high-handed villany [sic]—such flagrant robbery of the inalienable rights of man—such a glaring violation of all the precepts and injunctions of the gospel—such a savage war upon a sixth part of our population?—They were men like ourselves—as falliable, as sinful, as weak, as ourselves. By the infamous bargain which they made themselves, they virtually dethroned, the Most High God, and trampled beneath their feet their own solemn and heaven-attested Declaration, that all men are created equal, and endowed by their Creator with certain inalienable rights—among which are life, liberty, and the pursuit of happiness. They had no lawful power to bind themselves, or their posterity, for one hour—for one moment—by such an unholy alliance. It was not valid then—it is not valid now. Still they persisted in maintaining it. A sacred compact! a sacred compact! What, then, is wicked and ignominious?

DOCUMENT 13.2
Slave Labor and Free-Labor Poverty

Abolitionist polemics focused on the physical tortures, degradations, and tragic family separations that slavery and slave trading entailed. But, often the reformers offered cerebral and abstract rationales for

Source: Octavius Brooks Frothingham, "Pauperism and Slavery," *Liberty Bell* (1853), pp. 164–70.

emancipation. One of the more successful arguments was this selection written by Octavius Brooks Frothingham (1822–1895), a liberal-minded Boston minister and prolific writer. With disarming simplicity, Frothingham explained why pauperism was not comparable with slavery, why free-labor arrangements were preferable to slave-labor arrangements, thus showing the interconnections of abolitionism and industrial capitalism. The Liberty Bell, *in which this essay appeared, was a handsome, bound magazine published by Maria Weston Chapman, the redoubtable Boston "bluestocking," as women intellectuals were then called.*

We are perpetually told even at this day, that there is nothing peculiar in the miseries of Slavery: that all its woes, in every shape, are found elsewhere, are common to every state of poverty. The poor always suffer—suffer from want, from hunger and thirst and the elements, from physical deprivation of every kind. They suffer from ignorance, mental and moral. They have no advantage of culture. They work under compulsion, beneath the stinging lash of necessity, which cuts deeper into the flesh and into the spirit than the overseer's whip. The poor man . . . groans under the tyranny of the capitalist or the manufacturer's agent. He must go where he can get employment. He must remain in the service tha gives him bread. He is chained by circumstances to a place or a master. Providence binds men to a servitude that is in every way as abject and terrible as the Slavery of America. Why have so much to say about the black Slaves? Are there not white Slaves in greater numbers and worse off? Are there not Slaves of Labor, and Slaves of Capital, and Slaves of Machinery? Why single out the African for our peculiar commiseration? Such is the argument. . .

In support of our cause we do not plead the awful miseries of Slavery, nor are we in the least indisposed to allow for misery else-where, or to contribute our utmost endeavor towards its alleviation and removal. We war against Slavery because it is a *crime:* because as an evil in society, it is wholly dependent upon man's will, upon *individual* man's will, and is therefore entirely of the nature of human *guilt.* Let this be clearly understood. For in this one respect Slavery is perfectly distinguished from every kind of Poverty. Other evils are *providential,* as we call them; that is to say they grow out of the inevitable condition of things: nobody in particular causes them, or is answerable for them. But Slavery is a voluntary sin. Pauperism, in all its dismal shapes, with all its terrible sorrows, is an old fact resulting from man's ignorance, error, and general imperfection, and will be outgrown as man becomes more wise and powerful, as he better understands himself and the world, and acquires more extensive command over the materials furnished for his well-being. This process must be long and painful; all such development necessarily is. Slavery, on the other hand, is an institution which the conscious will of man has built up, and which the same will, faithfully exerted, might, for anything outside of itself to interfere, abolish in a year, a month, a week, a day, in the brief moment that suffices to make a moral resolution. To remove Pauperism, the very elements of society must be transmuted; the ingredients of human nature must be newly mingled; the fields of mortal passion must be sown with other seed; the race must attain to a nobler stature. To remove Slavery, one deep moral conviction, such as motives of humanity and religion might impart, is alone necessary. Slavery is an excrescence, an accident, a monstrous exception to the providential tenor of society. It is not implicated in the very progress, woven into the very texture of civilization as Pauperism is; all civilization is against it, is impatient of it; the lowest form of civilization cries out at it. Pauperism, from its nature, involves no direct Guilt. Slavery is essential Guilt.

DOCUMENT 13.3
American Racism and the Black Abolitionist Response

Pauperism, as Frothingham noted in the previous selection, was woven into the fabric of civilization. That scourge outlasted slavery, as he guessed it would, but so did race prejudice, the third affliction that has scarred black American history. In this selection, published in 1837, Hosea Easton, a black religious leader in Boston, described in passionate, biting terms how deeply race prejudice was entrenched in white language and behavior, North and South, as deep, perhaps, as the condition of penury in the whole culture.

I have no language wherewith to give slavery, and its auxiliaries, an adequate description, as an efficient cause of the miseries it is capable of producing. It seems to possess a kind of omnipresence. It follows its victims in every avenue of life. . . Negro or nigger, is an opprobrious term, employed to impose contempt upon them as an inferior race, and also to express their deformity of person. Nigger lips, nigger shins, and nigger heels, are phrases universally common among the juvenile class of society. . . Children in infancy receive oral instruction from the nurse. The first lessons given are, Johnny, Billy, Mary, Sally . . . go to sleep, if you don't the old *nigger* will carry you off; don't cry—Hark, the old *nigger's* coming—how ugly you are, you are worse than a little *nigger*. . . See nigger's thick lips—see his flat nose—nigger eye shine—that slick looking nigger—nigger, where you get so much coat?—that's a nigger priest—are sounds emanating from little urchins of Christian villages. . . .

Source: Hosea Easton, *A Treatise on the Intellectual Character, and Civil and Political Condition of the Colored People of the United States; and the Prejudice Exercised Toward Them* (Boston, 1837).

If he [a black man] should chance to be found in any other sphere of action than that of a slave, he magnifies to a monster of wonderful dimensions, so large that they cannot be made to believe it would be safe to admit him into stages, steam-boat cabins, and tavern dining-rooms. . . . If he be a slave, his corporeality becomes so diminished as to admit him into ladies' parlors, and into small private carriages, and elsewhere, without being disgustful on account of his deformity. . . This prejudice seems to possess a magical power, by which it makes a being appear most odious one moment, and the next, beautiful—at one moment too large to be on board a steam-boat, the next, so small as to be convenient most any where. . .

Mind acts on matter. Contemplate the numerous free people of color under the despotic reign of predjuce—contemplate his first early hopes blasted by the frost of prejudice. . . Witness the ardor of youth aspiring him to a second and third trial, and as often repelled by this monster foe. . . . The effect of these discouragements are every where manifest among the colored people. . . O prejudice, I cannot let thee pass without telling thee and thy possessors, that thou art a compound of all evil—of all the corrupt passions of the heart. Yea, thou art a participant in all the purposes of the wicked one—thou art the very essence of hell.

DOCUMENT 13.4
Growing Up Northern, White, and Antislavery

This selection concerns the ways in which abolitionists were raised so that there was an early predisposition to the claims of conscience, especially in so personally dangerous a cause. Like so many other abolitionist leaders, Samuel Joseph May

Source: *Memoir of Samuel Joseph May* (Boston: Roberts Brothers, 1874), pp. 5–12.

(1797–1871) belonged to an old and distinguished Puritan family from Roxbury, Massachusetts. A lifelong friend of Garrison, May was one of the few Unitarian ministers intimately involved in abolitionism. He was unexceptional in tracing his abolitionism to a specific childhood encounter with a black. May's relatives were not particularly mordant. Death, in those times, was a common reality. But, May's feelings of guilt were unusually intense: serving the cause of black freedom was perhaps an unconscious means to repay his dead brother for his own survival.

I had a brother, Edward, two years older than myself. He was a fair-haired boy, with blue eyes, bright, playful, affectionate, and particularly fond of me. . . One day, when he was six years and eight months old, he . . . climbed the fence against the barn, pretending to sweep the chimney; and, when the imaginary work was done, he attempted to get down by resting his weight upon the slender post of a chair, the top of which was broken off. The post gave way, and its splintered point penetrated his body, several inches, under his arm. Screams from the servants, who were near by, brought our fond mother to the spot. . . . But the dear, beautiful boy was dead. The agony of my parents, the crying of my elder brother and sisters, assured me that something dreadful had happened; and there my beloved Edward was, eyes shut, body cold, giving no replies to the tender things that were said to him, taking no notice of all that was being done to him or about him.

. . . [At bedtime] I . . . asked that I might be permitted to go back to the chamber and lie by the side of Edward. My request was granted; and there I lay, until my grief was forgotten in sleep, when I must have been removed, for I found myself next morning in the bed where I had usually slept with my brother, in my mother's chamber. But I hurried back to the corpse of Edward and kept with it almost all the time until I was taken from it forever . . . [After the funeral] my uncle, Samuel May, took me in his arms, descended with me into the family vault. . . . He pointed out the little coffins in which were the remains of several of my brothers and sisters, who had lived and died before I was born. . . . He opened one of the coffins and let me see how decayed the body had become, told me that Edward's body was going to decay in like manner, and at last become like the dust of the earth. But he again [like the other family members] most tenderly assured me that Edward. . . had gone to live in heaven with God and Christ and the angels. Then he lifted once more the lid of Edward's coffin, and let me kiss again and for the last time his cheek, his lips, his forehead. . . . When night came, I was put to bed in the room where I had so often lain and slept with Edward. Sleep soon came to relieve my young spirit wearied with grief and strange excitement. And I dreamt. . . . The ceiling of the room opened, over where I was lying: a bright, glorious light burst in, and from the midst of it came down my lost brother, attended by a troop of little angels. . . He lay by me as he used to do, his head on my arm or my head on his. He told me how happy he was, what a beautiful place heaven was. . . There he lay until morning, when the ceiling above opened again, and the troop of angels came to bear him back to heaven. . . The next night, and for several nights afterwards, I enjoyed the felt presence of my brother. . . [until gradually] my grief abated. . . .

[Some years later, when] six or seven years of age. . . I fell, struck my temple upon a stone, and lay senseless. On recovering my consciousness, I found myself in the arms of a large black woman. As soon as I opened my eyes, she said very soothingly, 'Don't be afraid, little boy. I know who you are. I'll carry you to your mamma.' On reaching home,—my face, bosom, and hand smeared with the blood . . . [made my mother greatly fear] that, like Edward, I had met with some fatal accident. . . [Finding no deep injury],

she then thought of the kind woman who had picked me up, and looked around gratefully to thank and to offer her some reward. But my benefactress had disappeared. . . Nor could we find out . . . who she was, though my mother made much inquiry, wishing to make some return for the good deed she had done.

DOCUMENT 13.5
Growing up Southern, Black, and Slave

In his autobiography, a nineteenth-century literary classic, Frederick Douglass (1818–1895), the foremost black abolitionist spokesman of his day, tried to capture the essence of slavery. He was raised on a plantation belonging to Colonel Edward Lloyd, Maryland's largest slaveholder, but he had the good fortune to leave for Baltimore to serve a kind mistress, the daughter of his owner. When his master died, young Douglass was returned for the settlement of the estate, a circumstance that separated slave families as commonly as outright sales for debt or cruel calculation.

We were all ranked together at the valuation. Men and women, old and young, married and single, were ranked with horses, sheep, and swine. There were horses and men, cattle and women, pigs and children, all holding the same rank in the scale of being, and were all subjected to the same narrow examination. Silvery-headed age and sprightly youth, maids and matrons, had to undergo the same indelicate inspection. At this moment I saw more clearly than ever the brutalizing effects of slavery upon both slave and slaveholder.

After the valuation, then came the division. I have no language to express the high excite-

Source: *Narrative of Frederick Douglass, An American Slave, Written by Himself* (Boston: American Anti-Slavery Society, 1845), pp. 47–49.

ment and deep anxiety which were felt among us poor slaves during this time. Our fate was now to be decided. We had no more voice in that decision than the brutes among whom we were ranked. A single word from the white men was enough—against all our wishes, prayers, and entreaties—to sunder forever the dearest friends, dearest kindred, and strongest ties known to human beings. In addition to the pain of separation, there was the horrid dread of falling into the hands of Master Andrew. He was known to us all as being a most cruel wretch,—a common drunkard, who had, by his reckless mismanagement and profligate dissipation, already wasted a large portion of his father's property. We all felt that we might as well be sold at once to the Georgia traders, as to pass into his hands . . . I suffered more anxiety than most of my fellow-slaves. I had known what it was to be kindly treated; they had known nothing of the kind. They had seen little or nothing of the world. They were in very deed men and women of sorrow, and acquainted with grief. Their backs had been made familiar with the bloody lash, so that they had become callous; mine was yet tender. . . . Thanks to a kind Providence, I fell to the portion of Mrs. Lucretia, and was sent immediately back to Baltimore, to live again in the family of Master Hugh . . . I had escaped a worse than lion's jaws. I was absent from Baltimore, for the purpose of the valuation and division just about one month, but it seemed to have been six.

DOCUMENT 13.6
Women in the Cause

Angelina and Sarah Grimké were among the most remarkable abolitionists of their day.

Sarah Grimké and Angelina Grimké to Henry C. Wright, August 27, 1837, in *Letters of Theodore Dwight Weld, Angelina Grimké Weld, and Sarah Grimké 1822–1844*, Gilbert H. Barnes and Dwight L. Dumond, eds., Gloucester, Mass.: Peter Smith Publisher, Inc., 1965, 1, pp. 436–41.

Raised in an aristocratic and accomplished South Carolina family, they left their plantation home for the North, converted to Quakerism and then to abolitionism. A year after publishing An Appeal to the Christian Women of the South, *Angelina, accompanied by her sister Sarah, lectured in over sixty churches and halls to overflowing crowds throughout New England. Local clergy—some of them veteran abolitionists—denounced their public appearances as indecent and ungodly, a charge scarcely credible, many thought, in light of their obvious piety, Quaker plainness, and respectability. The following letter from Sarah Grimké to the sympathetic Henry C. Wright, a leading Garrisonian, along with a postscript from Angelina, shows the Grimkés' quiet, firm determination, the ambivalent response to abolitionists John Greenleaf Whittier and Theodore Dwight Weld, Angelina's future husband, and the beginnings of the Women's Rights movement—of which William Lloyd Garrison heartily approved.*

Brookline [Mass.] 8/27/37.

Dear brother Wright. . . .

My very soul is sick of the narrow minded policy of Christians, of abolitionists, trying to keep asunder the different parts of Christianity as if it were not a beautiful and harmonious system which could not be divided . . . Dear Angelina is quite troubled; she is more downcast than I have yet seen her, because our coming forth in the A[nti] S[lavery] cause seems really to be at the bottom of this clerical defection; but the Lord knows that we did not come to forward our own interests but in simple obedience to his commands and I do not believe we are responsible for the consequences of doing the will of God . . . Brothers Whittier [the antislavery Quaker poet] and Weld are anxious we should say nothing on the woman question, but I do not feel as if I could surrender my right to discuss any great moral subject . . . How much is comprehended in thy desire that we may be entirely emancipated from *all servitude to man.* I reciprocate it. . . . Dear Brother Garrison has been passing the day with us . . . and it has cheered my spirit to find that he unites fully with us on the subject of the rights of woman . . . [Sarah Grimké] MY DEAR BROTHER . . . What would you think of the Liberator abandoning Abolitionism as a *primary* object and becoming the vehicle of all these grand principles? Is not the time rapidly coming for such a change[?] . . . I trust brother G[arrison] may be divinely directed . . . O how lamentably superficial we are, to suppose that one truth can hurt another; as well might we suppose that to teach one branch of science is to undermine another . . . A[ngelina] E. Grimké

DOCUMENT 13.7
Violent Abolitionism: John Brown and Harpers Ferry

When John Brown (1800–1859) and company stormed the federal arsenal at Harpers Ferry in October 1859, he, more than any other abolitionist, affected the course of American history. His act represented an early use of terrorism as a means of sowing political mistrust and channeling events toward war for ideological ends. Unaccountably delaying his escape, he invited capture in hope, perhaps, of earning a martyr's crown. To Yankees, he seemed a personification of free-labor spirit, secular manhood, and Christian conscience. The following selection, Brown's reply to a Quaker pacifist correspondent, demonstrates his uncanny ability to reconcile military failure with polemical success, Christian kindliness

Source: John Brown to "E.B.," November 1, 1860, in *The Life and Letters of John Brown, Liberator of Kansas and Martyr of Virginia*, Franklin B. Sanborn, ed., (New York: New American Library, 1969, pp. 582–83.

with fiery vengeance and personal responsibility with divine determinism.

Charlestown, Jefferson County, Va. Nov. 1, 1859

My Dear Friend E.B. of R.I. . . . [M]ay the Lord reward you a thousandfold for the kind feeling you express toward me; but more especially for your fidelity to the 'poor that cry, and those that have no help.' For this I am a prisoner in bonds. It is solely my own fault, in a military point of view, that we met with our disaster. I mean that I mingled with our prisoners and so far sympathized with them and their families that I neglected my duty in other respects. But God's will, not mine, be done.

You know that Christ once armed Peter. So also in my case I think he put a sword into my hand, and there continued so long as he saw best, and then kindly took it from me. I mean when I first went to Kansas. I wish you could now with what cheerfulness I am now wielding the 'sword of the Spirit' on the right hand and on the left. I bless God that it proves 'mighty to the pulling down of strongholds.' I always loved my Quaker friends, and I commend to their kind regard my poor bereaved widowed wife and my daughters-in-law, whose husbands fell at my side . . . I do not feel conscious of guilt in taking up arms; and had it been in behalf of the rich and powerful, the intelligent, the great (as men count greatness), or those who form enactments to suit themselves and corrupt others, or some of their friends, that I interfered, suffered, sacrificed, and fell, it would have been doing very well. But enough of this. These light afflictions, which endure but a moment, shall but work for me 'a far more exceeding and eternal weight of glory.' . . . Farewell. God will surely attend to his own cause in the best possible way and time, and he will not forget the work of his own hands. Your friend, JOHN BROWN.

DOCUMENT 13.8
Lincoln's Election and the Abolitionist Cause

For most abolitionists, Abraham Lincoln was by no means an ideal choice for the Republican candidacy in 1860. At the time of the party's Chicago convention, Wendell Phillips (1811–1884), Garrison's loyal colleague and eloquent spokesman for radicalism, tagged the former Illinois Congressman with the soubriquet, "Slave-Hound of Illinois": Lincoln had once upheld the Fugitive Slave Law of 1793. Like many other Americans of that era, Phillips underestimated Lincoln's potential. Yet, in this speech delivered two days after the election, he linked Brown's abolitionist assault, Northern antislavery conviction, and Lincoln's election.

Ladies and Gentlemen: If the telegraph speaks the truth, for the first time in our history, the *slave* has chosen a President of the United States. (Cheers.) We have passed the Rubicon, for Mr. Lincoln rules to-day as much as he will after the 4th of March. It is the moral effect of this victory, not anything which his administration can or will probably do, that gives value to this success. Not an Abolitionist, hardly an anti-slavery man, Mr. Lincoln consents to represent an anti-slavery idea. A pawn on the political chessboard, his value is in his position; with fair effort, we may soon change him for Knight, Bishop or Queen, and sweep the board. (Applause.) This position he owes to no merit of his own, but to lives that have roused the nation's conscience, and deeds that have ploughed deep into its heart. Our childish eyes gazed with wonder at Maelzel's chess player, [a famous automaton of the day] and the pulse almost stopped when, with the pulling of wires and creaking of wheels, he moved a pawn and 'Check!' Our wise fathers saw a man in the box. There was a great noise at Chicago, much pulling of wires and creaking of wheels, then forth steps Abraham Lincoln. But John Brown was behind the curtain, and the cannon of March 4th will only echo the rifles at Harpers Ferry. Last year, we stood looking sadly at that gibbet against the Virginia sky. One turn of the kaleidoscope—it is Lincoln in the balcony of the Capitol, and a million of hearts beating welcome below. (Cheers.)

Source: *The Liberator* (Boston), November 16, 1860.

chapter

The Causes of the Civil War

John G. Sproat
University of South Carolina

Early on the morning of April 12, 1861, a battery of Confederate mortars opened fire on the federal military installation at Fort Sumter. Three days later, President Lincoln issued a proclamation, calling on the state militias to suppress "combinations too powerful to be suppressed by the ordinary course of judicial proceedings." Thus began the Civil War, the tragic conflict that racked America for four years. Thus began, too, a war of words among historians as to the causes of the conflict. No event in American history has received more painstaking attention from historians than the Civil War, and over the years we have enlarged our knowledge and deepened our understanding of this great national crisis. Yet, the unending debate on the fundamental question of why war came serves as a stubborn reminder of the historian's inability to relate history "as it actually happened."

Interpretations range from the simple to the complex. Perhaps the most obvious explanation of the war is that it came in 1861 because the South was determined to confirm and defend the sovereign independence of the new Confederacy, while the North was just as determined to maintain the integrity of the old federal Union. As it relates to the immediate crisis that produced the fighting, this simple interpretation has merit. After all, Jefferson Davis and

his colleagues went in earnest about the difficult work of establishing the Confederacy and providing for its defense. And there was no sophistry in Lincoln's assertion that the North fought to preserve the Union. But this unadorned interpretation does not explain the division into two warring parties of a people who had so much in common—language, revolutionary heritage, representative government, respect for the Constitution, and faith in America's future. Why did Southerners elect to deny this communion in favor of creating a nation of their own? Why did Northerners refuse to respect their choice and, instead, treat secession as a rebellion to be crushed by force? Why did the fatal separation come in 1861, when it might have come in 1850, 1833, 1820, or, for that matter, 1787? The student who seeks to learn the causes of the war is plunged into the labyrinth of the sectional conflict and its causes. For without the sectional conflict, there would have been no secession and no Civil War.

Rivalry between the North and the South was as old as the Union. It had embroiled the Constitutional Convention, made a mockery of George Washington's resolve to preclude factionalism in the new government, flared angrily during the clouded era of the Napoleonic Wars, precipitated a soul-searching national debate when Missouri applied for statehood, and provoked Andrew Jackson's wrath against the abortive nullifiers of 1833. Although Americans in both sections had given impetus to the expansionist thrust westward during the 1840s, regional prejudices had spawned deep differences of opinion on the purpose of Manifest Destiny. If no single eruption of sectional fever had succeeded in crippling the nation, taken together, these recurrent seizures had, by the middle of the nineteenth century, gravely weakened the organic structure of the federal Union.

In 1850, the state of the Union appeared wretched to many thoughtful Americans. For almost three years, an angry debate had raged over the question of slavery in California and the Mexican cession. Almost daily, threats of personal violence, secession, and civil conflict embittered the deliberations of Congress. Taking their cue from the Wilmot Proviso, antislavery men insisted that the federal government guarantee the principles of ''Free Soil, Free Speech, Free Labor, and Free Men,'' not alone in the lands recently conquered from Mexico, but in all present and future territorial holdings as well. At the Nashville convention, southern leaders argued among themselves what action to take should Congress block the further expansion of slavery. Counseling a policy of cautious vigilance, moderate men maintained control of the convention from the start; but a minority of extremists, led by Robert Barnwell Rhett, seared the proceedings with a demand that the South secede from the Union immediately, unconditionally, and for good. If secession meant war, they argued, let it come then rather than later.

Serious as the crisis was, it did not result in secession or in war. Statesmen, in the past, had relied on the remedy of compromise to relieve sectional fever, and statesmen in 1850 reached naturally for the same specific. Ministering to the most obvious symptoms of the present disorder, their Compromise of 1850 checked the immediate threat of disunion and bolstered the forces of moderation in both sec-

tions. But did it penetrate to the primary infection? Did it provide relief from the corrosive antagonism engendered by issues more fundamental than fugitive slave laws, slavery, and the slave trade in the District of Columbia and adjustment of the Texas-New Mexico boundary? Was it not the responsibility of statesmen in 1850 to deal directly and forcefully with such difficult questions as the future of slavery as an institution, the rights of political minorities in a representative government, and the reconciliation of agrarian and industrial interests? Their compromise did nothing to tranquilize the diehard secessionists in the South, and it only temporarily slowed the spread of antislavery sentiment in the North. However robust the patient appeared in 1851, relapses were inevitable due to the circumstances. They came in quick succession during the following years, and ultimately the old remedy of compromise, overworked and drained of relevancy, proved useless even as a palliative. Had it ever been more than a nostrum?

What fundamental differences between North and South account for this mordant sectional enmity? Where they so insuperable that not even such political giants as Jefferson, Madison, the two Adamses, Jackson, Benton, Clay, Webster, Calhoun, Seward, Davis, Douglas, and Lincoln could find a formula for permitting the two sections to live harmoniously as parts of the same nation? Were the differences amenable to settlement only by the ultimate instrument of civil war? Issues dividing the sections can readily be identified—rivalry for control of the central government, the rights of states, the disposition of western lands, the future of slavery, the competition between agrarian capitalism and rising industrial capitalism—and the student can venture to rank them in some order of importance as causes of the sectional conflict. But a consideration of such intriguing questions as why sectional conflict became a civil war and whether or not war was inevitable will yield only hypothetical answers, owing much to the student's estimate of the relative influence in human affairs exerted by emotions and rational factors. As in all great historical situations, both sets factors are evident in the sectional conflict.

One assessment of the issues leads to an explanation of the conflict almost exclusively in terms of opposing theories of government. Thus, it is argued that antebellum Northerners, reading into the Constitution prerogatives never contemplated by the Founding Fathers, sought to elevate the federal government to a position of omnipotence over the states. Southerners, contending that the states antedated the Union, viewed the Constitution as a compact entered into voluntarily by the states as separate, independent entities. Each state retained certain sovereign rights—inviolable and transcending even the Constitution.

Sectional conflict resulted from an incompatability of the two theories, evidenced most clearly in the persistent refusal of Northerners to restrain the federal government from interference in the domestic affairs of the southern states. To counter this subversion of the Constitution, Southerners evoked the doctrines of interposition, nullification, and concurrent majorities. They had no choice, once these defenses collapsed, save to repudiate the compact and take their states out of the Union. War ensued only because Republican politicians in Washington, with a sovereign contempt for the sovereign rights of independent states, undertook to impose forcibly their own spurious theory of government on Americans who were defending the Constitution as it was written. From this interpretation, essentially southern in origin, was derived the postwar liturgy of "the lost cause."

Because such able men as John C. Calhoun and Alexander H. Stephens labored long at shaping a particularist theory of the Constitution based on the rights of the states, it might be assumed that the controversy about the nature of the Union was, indeed, the essence of the conflict. In fact, as Arthur M. Schlesinger observes, it was more a "storm cellar," in which antebellum Southerners took shelter from the tempest raging around them. They were not the only Americans before the war to champion the rights of states, nor did they adhere to their theory of government with orthodox fidelity. Quick to denounce the personal liberty laws, which were manifestations of a northern states' rightism in the 1850s, they labeled all such attempts to nullify the federal Fugitive Slave Law as nothing less than sedition. And when antislavery leaders called, in effect, for willful disobedience to the *Dred Scott* decision, Southerners dashed from their shelter long enough to praise the Supreme Court and remind federal officers of their solemn duty to enforce the ruling. Like other erstwhile champions of states' rights, antebellum Southerners kept a sharp eye on the political barometer and took refuge whenever the glass read foul weather. If they seemed to take up permanent residence in the cellar during the late 1850s, it was less because they enjoyed the surroundings than because the storm outside raged almost incessantly in those years.

But to conclude that states' rights as an issue between the sections was not the essence of the conflict is not to dismiss the doctrine as a cause of the war. Indeed, as carried by Southerners to the extreme of secession and disunion, it begot the condition that Lincoln and other northern nationalists found intolerable. Moreover, the vexing question of just how far a state could go in asserting its rights was one of the few issues definitively settled by the war.

In declaiming against the power of the federal government, southern spokesmen were actually protesting their own section's loss, real and prospective, of control over that power. Rivalry for political control of a government can lead to war. In antebellum America, political rivalry embittered session after session of Congress; the passions it excited sometimes pushed people into a mood of belligerence. More importantly, its cumulative effect on many Southerners was to imbue them gradually with a grim sense of desperation, which, in turn, lured them toward secession.

Especially after the Mexican War, secessionists learned that their most telling argument for disunion was that the South soon would be completely at the mercy of northern politicians. The birth and rapid rise of the Republican Party strengthened their argument, while the election of a Republican President in 1860 seemed to validate it beyond much question. In speeches and correspondence during the late 1850s, southerners evinced a growing fear— an irrational, allusive fear—that northerners were preparing some unknown but surely awful fate for the South. Every headline event, whether an implausible raid at Harpers Ferry by a handful of fanatics or a routine national election, fed this misgiving.

As a matter of practical, everyday politics, the southern fear of northern politicians in general and of Republicans in particular made little sense. At no time during the sectional conflict were Southerners lacking strong political allies in the North, nor were they ever in immediate danger of losing their powerful voice in national affairs. Even after Lincoln's election, they retained a strong grip on the federal bureaucracy and an outright domination of the Supreme Court. In the Senate, they had more than enough votes to harass, even to hamstring, an unfriendly President. Certainly, they retained the power to prevent any Republican tampering with either the institution of slavery in the cotton states or the federal Constitution.

But the matter went beyond everyday politics. The Republican triumph in 1860 meant that a northern party had at last succeeded in uniting the many political factions that for a variety of reasons opposed southern domination of the national government. No matter that some Republicans were free traders and sound-money men, while others were protectionists and inflationists; some form of Whiggish economic program would take shape under a Republican administration. No matter that the party leaders disclaimed sympathy with abolitionism; the party already had provided a rallying point for antislavery men of all hues. And what of slavery in the territories, the very issue that brought the party into being? Republicans would fight every southern attempt to extend the "peculiar institution," while at the same time they would open the gates to a flood of new free-soil western states, solidly Republican in politics and hostile to the South's interests. Once in power, Republican leaders would obey the law of politics, and would move heaven and earth to increase their power. It was only a matter of time until the South's voice in Washington would be muted to a whisper. So ran the argument for secession, and by 1860, southern moderates saw enough truth in it that they gave ground to the extremists.

Did the Republican victory pose a stark threat to the South? After the election, Lincoln went out of his way to assure the nation that it did not. He insisted that he and his party felt no animosity toward Americans of any section, and he promised to respect the Constitution and to refrain from interfering in the purely domestic affairs of the states. But Lincoln was committed, both by conviction and by his party's platform, to blocking any further expansion of slavery and to promoting economic legislation of a kind that southern leaders detested. Moreover, the Republican party contained a small but effective faction of radicals—men dedicated to the destruction of slavery wherever it existed. How long would Lincoln be able to resist their constant agitation for some positive action against the institution? Given the general Republican attitude toward interests that southern leaders deemed vital to their section's welfare, the party's triumph in 1860 signaled new troubles for the South—if not immediately then surely within the near future.

Events in the West during the 1850s dramatized both northern intentions and southern fears. Some historians agree with Stephen A. Douglas in contending that the whole question of slavery in the territories was a meaningless abstraction. They argue that geography, if not popular sovereignty, would have decided against the expansion of slavery, since even with forced labor the cultivation of cotton could never have become a profitable undertaking in the arid regions of the West. The fact that some western states, in recent years, have become major producers of cotton undercuts this argument. Moreover, we know today that slave labor can be used in a wide variety of enterprises wholly unconnected with staple crop agriculture.

In any case, this struggle in the West was hardly an abstraction to the politicans, North and South, who were competing for control of the national government. Southerners demanded the extension of slavery, not so much because they hoped the institution would flourish in the West, but because they wanted to establish new state governments that would be sympathetic to their own interests. In alliance, the South and the West could effectively block any national legislation detrimental either to slavery or to agrarian capitalism. Where South Carolina's nullifiers had failed in 1833 to bring down the forces of protectionism, southern expansionists in the 1850s saw a chance to thwart indefinitely any northern attempts to enact high tariffs. They favored expansion and slavery in the West, not as conspirators, as some northerners charged, but simply as men seeking political and economic advantages over their rivals. Northern politicians sought the same advantages. When they spoke of free labor, they meant labor free from foreign as well as slave competition. When they spoke of free soil, they meant land open to exploitation by northern bondholders as well as closed to debasement by southern slaveholders.

Yet, in addition to its political and economic significance, the struggle for the West also had great symbolic significance; and in this sense, perhaps, the question of slavery in the territories was an abstraction, although hardly a meaningless one. During the winter of 1860–61, as moderate men in both sections worked desperately to find a last-minute formula for averting catastrophe, Lincoln handed down an injunction to the northern negotiators. "Let there be no compromise on the question of *extending* slavery," he told them privately. "Have none of it. Stand firm." Why did the President-elect take such an uncompromising stand? Were his motives only those of a politician seeking material advantage for his party and section? Did he underestimate the seriousness of the crisis and recklessly choose to face down the South on a trifling, essentially unreal issue? Or did he act on principle? Had he come to believe the question of slavery in the territories could be compromised only if he and the North surrendered a moral position? We know that Lincoln, like most Northerners, was no abolitionist, that he was quite willing to leave slavery untouched where it already existed. Why, then, did he refuse to permit the extension of the institution, especially into an area where it would have difficulty in surviving?

If Lincoln was not an active antislavery advocate, he was the leader of a party that had been born out of the controversy over slavery in territories. In 1856, the Republican platform included two unequivocal demands—respect for the principles of the Declaration of Independence and unswerving opposition to the expansion of slavery. In the presidential election of that year, the party won well over a million votes; four years later, with a platform only slightly less explicit, it captured the presidency, albeit with less than an absolute majority of the votes. Consequently, Lincoln and at least a sizable minority of northern voters were pledged to a defense of freedom and a denial of southern expansionist aims, and they considered the two commitments wholly interrelated. A victory for southern expansionism, however slight, they would interpret as a defeat for freedom. A triumph of northern expansionism they could justify as an extension of principles embodied in the Declaration of Independence.

Judged in relation to the spirit of nationalism then sweeping through much of Western civilization, the whole struggle for the American West was an unequal contest. On the one hand, the northern nationalists championed the expansion not only of a dynamic, modern, industrially oriented society based on free labor, but also of the liberal idealism that was so congenial to prevailing concepts of how civilized nations should develop. To accompany the spread of their relatively static agrarian way of life, on the other hand, southern expansionists could offer only an extension of human slavery—an institution that most of the Western world by then considered altogether anachronistic. Southern leaders attempted to evoke a nationalism of their own, but they succeeded only in producing a narrow sectionalism, based on economic self-interest and a unique social system, and lacking the leaven of either a commitment to purposes higher than self-interest or a viable rationalization of the social system.

Both the self-interest and the social system were anchored to the institution of chattel slavery. Was slavery the central irritant in the sectional conflict? Or would the South, even without slavery, have clashed with the North over such issues as the tariff, internal improvements, states' rights, and westward expansion? One recalls South Carolina's attempt to nullify the tariffs of 1828 and 1832, at a time when slavery was for most people an issue of no particular moment. Given the long history of antagonism between agrarian and commercial-industrial interests in America, extending well back into the colonial era, it seems likely that the two sections would have found themselves in frequent disagreement—that is, as long as the South remained primarily an agricultural society. But, without slavery would this disagreement have burgeoned into a rasping conflict

and ultimately into war? Were the economic and political differences between the sections amenable to compromise, leaving slavery as the one uncompromisable issue? Or was slavery, too, a problem that responsible politicians, seriously applying themselves to the task, could have eliminated as a divisive factor?

The precise effect of the "peculiar institution" on southern society and political behavior is beyond the scope of this essay. It may be noted, however, that Southerners displayed hostility to any discussion of slavery's future as early as 1787, at the Constitutional Convention. To be sure, by 1831, strong antislavery sentiment in Virginia almost succeeded in committing the Old Dominion to a policy of gradual emancipation and colonization, but after a bitter debate in the legislature the effort failed. Slavery had always been an effective device for controlling race relations in the interests of white men. In the early 1830s, it began to expand significantly as a labor system, becoming within a few years the largest single investment of southern capital and the cornerstone of the cotton economy. As a labor system, as an investment, as a social regimen, slavery thus became for Southerners the determining consideration in all political and economic matters that affected their section and its future. Defense of the institution as a necessary evil was not enough; it had to be projected as a positive good, championed as a system worthy of adoption in other societies, defended everywhere in the name of the Constitution.

Granted, by 1850 many northerners were resolved to prevent the further expansion of slavery, does it follow that they opposed slavery and threatened its existence where it was already established? Did they consider it an evil to be eradicated or an inconvenience to be contained? Radical abolitionists such as William Lloyd Garrison and Theodore Parker waged uncompromising war against slavery. Less fervent idealists such as James S. Pike called for its overthrow but also proposed that Negroes be ''penned up'' in one or two specially designated southern states. Colonizers sought funds and ships for sending all Blacks back to Africa, and they had a strong sympathizer in Abraham Lincoln. Free-Soil men wanted only to keep slavery out of the territories. Thousands of Northerners, touched by moral or religious qualms, doubtless felt uncomfortable about the persistence of a forced labor system in a supposedly free republic. And again, nationalist sentiment in the North, while its emphasis on freedom and equality of opportunity as well as its regard for territorial aggrandizement, probably insinuated vague antislavery notions in the minds of men who never spoke out on the subject. Only a small minority of Northerners gave serious thought to the actual plight of the bondsmen, but many others disliked the effects slavery had on free institutions in the country as a whole.

For Southerners and Northerners alike, the question of slavery gradually began to take on moral and emotional connotations, especially as crisis followed crisis during the late 1850s. North of the Mason-Dixon Line, Harriet Beecher Stowe's picture of slavery in *Uncle Tom's Cabin* became the popular view of the institution. In the cotton states, John Brown became the epitome of relentless northern aggression against slaveholders. Once the question entered the realm of emotions, was any reconciliation of the sections possible? Here, the student encounters the clash between rational and irrational factors.

If there had been no slavery in the United States, would there have been a Civil War? From the outset of the hostilities, southern leaders seemed to believe that a final decision on the future of slavery was among the war's highest stakes. The soldiers in gray might fight fiercely for independence and the right to be let alone, but few doubted that if they lost the war they would also lose the ''peculiar

institution.'' Northerners were less conscious of these high stakes; certainly, the boys in blue did not march off in 1861 to free the slaves. If Yankees had won a quick, decisive victory, very likely the institution of slavery in the South would have survived substantially intact. But they won no such victory, and the war dragged on through four years of terrible fighting. By 1865, people who earlier had shown little or no interest in the cause of the black slave had convinced themselves that all along the struggle had been one of freedom against oppression, democracy against tyranny, good against evil. Were they the victims of self-deception, or had they at last come to understand the compelling logic of the conflict?

SUGGESTED READINGS

Davis, David B. *The Slave Power Conspiracy and the Paranoid Style.* Baton Rouge: Louisiana State University Press, 1982.

Donald, David. *Lincoln Reconsidered: Essays on the Civil War Era.* 2nd ed. New York: Vintage Books, 1961.

Foner, Eric. *Politics and Ideology in the Age of the Civil War.* New York: Oxford University Press, 1980.

Holt, Michael F. *The Political Crisis of the 1850s.* New York: Wiley, 1978.

McCardell, John. *The Idea of a Southern Nation.* New York: W. W. Norton, 1978.

Potter, David. *The Impending Crisis, 1848–1861.* New York: Harper & Row, 1976.

Pressly, Thomas J. *Americans Interpret Their Civil War.* New York: Free Press, 1965.

Rozwenc, Edwin C., ed. *The Causes of the Civil War.* 2nd ed., Boston: D. C. Heath, 1972.

Stampp, Kenneth M. *And the War Came: The North and the Secession Crisis, 1860–1861.* Baton Rouge: Louisiana State University Press, 1950.

————. *The Imperiled Union: Essays on the Background of the Civil War.* New York: Oxford University Press, 1980.

DOCUMENT 14.1
Extremes Beget Extremes

In the sectional conflict's vocabulary of opprobrium, the word "doughface" denoted a northern man with southern sympathies. Perhaps Franklin Pierce, President of the United States, 1853–57, best epitomized the term. A Yankee by birth, he permitted proslavery men to dominate his administration and split the Democratic Party over the Kansas question. Aggrieved that the issue of slavery in the territories should excite so many of his countrymen, he pleaded in his fourth annual message on December 2, 1856, for an end to "agitation" and "extremism."

Perfect liberty of association for political objects and the widest scope of discussion are the received and ordinary conditions of government in our country. Our institutions, framed in the spirit of confidence in the intelligence and integrity of the people, do not forbid citizens, either individually or associated together, to attack by writing, speech, or any other methods short of physical force that Constitution and the very existence of the Union. Under the shelter of this great liberty, and protected by the laws and usages of the Government they assail, associations have been formed in some of the States of individuals who, pretending to seek only to prevent the spread of the institution of slavery into the present or future inchoate States of the Union, are really inflamed with desire to change the domestic institutions of existing States. To accomplish their objects they dedicate themselves to the odious task of depreciating the government organization which stands in their way and of calumniating

Source: James D. Richardson, ed., *A Compilation of the Messages and Papers of the Presidents, 1789–1897* (New York: Bureau of National Literature and Art, 1909), vol. 4. pp. 2931–32.

with indiscriminate invective not only the citizens of particular States with those laws they find fault, but all others of their fellow-citizens throughout the country who do not participate with them in their assaults upon the Constitution, framed and adopted by our fathers, and claiming for the privileges it has secured and the blessings it has conferred the steady support and grateful reverence of their children. They seek an object which they well know to be a revolutionary one. They are perfectly aware that the change in the relative condition of the white and black races in the slave-holding States which they would promote is beyond their lawful authority; that to them it is a foreign object; that it can not be effected by any peaceful instrumentality of theirs; that for them and the States of which they are citizens the only path to its accomplishment is through burning cities, and ravaged fields, and slaughtered populations, and all there is most terrible in foreign complicated with civil and servile war; and that the first step in the attempt is the forcible disruption of a country embracing in its broad bosom a degree of liberty and an amount of individual and public prosperity to which there is no parallel in history, and substituting in its place hostile governments, driven at once and inevitably into mutual devastation and fratricidal carnage, transforming the now peaceful and felicitous brotherhood into a vast permanent camp of armed men like the rival monarchies of Europe and Asia. Well knowing that such, and such only, are the means and the consequences of their plans and purposes, they endeavor to prepare the people of the United States for civil war. . . .

. . . Extremes beget extremes. Violent attack from the North finds its inevitable consequence in the growth of a spirit of angry defiance at the South. Thus in the progress of events we had reached that consummation, which the voice of the people has now so pointedly rebuked, of the attempt of a portion of the States, by a sectional organization and movement, to usurp the control of the Government of the United States.

I confidently believe that the great body of those who inconsiderately took this fatal step are sincerely attached to the Constitution and the Union. They would upon deliberation shrink with unaffected horror from any conscious act of disunion or civil war. But they have entered into a path which leads nowhere unless it be to civil war and disunion, and which has no other possible outlet. . . .

DOCUMENT 14.2
An Irrepressible Conflict

Few men in the 1850s did more than William H. Seward to establish the new Republican party's position on slavery. A former Whig governor of New York and longtime opponent of slavery, Seward argued that the "peculiar institution" was subject to a "higher law" than the Constitution. In 1858, he spoke of an "irrepressible conflict" between two radically different systems, and the phrase caught on among extremists in both sections. Seward's reputation as a radical—not entirely deserved—cost him the presidential nomination in 1860, but he remained a powerful force within his party during the Lincoln and Johnson administrations.

Our country is a theatre, which exhibits, in full operation, two radically different political systems; the one resting on the basis of servile or slave labor, the other on the basis of voluntary labor of freemen.

The laborers who are enslaved are all negroes, or persons more or less purely of African derivation. But this is only accidental. The principle of the system is, that labor in every society, by whomsoever performed, is neces-

---

Source: George E. Baker, ed., *Recent Speeches and Writings of William H. Seward, 1854–1861* (New York: Redfield, 1861), pp. 289–302.

sarily unintellectual, groveling and base; and that the laborer, equally for his own good and for the welfare of the state, ought to be enslaved. The white laboring man, whether native or foreigner, is not enslaved, only because he cannot, as yet, be reduced to bondage.

You need not be told now that the slave system is the older of the two, and that once it was universal.

The emancipation of our own ancestors, Caucasians and Europeans as they were, hardly dates beyond a period of five hundred years. The great melioration of human society which modern times exhibit, is mainly due to the incomplete substitution of the system of voluntary labor for the old one of servile labor, which has already taken place. This African slave system is one which, in its origin and in its growth, has been altogether foreign from the habits of the races which colonized these states, and established civilization here. It was introduced on this new continent as an engine of conquest, and for the establishment of monarchical power, by the Portuguese and the Spaniards, and was rapidly extended by them all over South America, Central America, Louisiana and Mexico. Its legitimate fruits are seen in the poverty, imbecility, and anarchy, which now pervade all Portuguese and Spanish America. The free-labor system is of German extraction, and it was established in our country by emigrants from Sweden, Holland, Germany, Great Britain and Ireland.

We justly ascribe to its influences the strength, wealth, greatness, intelligence, and freedom, which the whole American people now enjoy. One of the chief elements of the value of human life is freedom in the pursuit of happiness. The slave system is not only intolerable, unjust, and inhuman, towards the laborer, whom, only because he is a laborer, it loads down with chains and converts into merchandise, but is scarcely less severe upon the freeman, to whom, only because he is a laborer from necessity, it denies facilities for employment, and whom it expels from the community because it cannot enslave and convert him into merchandise also. It is necessarily improvident and ruinous, because, as a general truth, communities prosper and flourish or droop and decline in just the degree that they practise or neglect to practise the primary duties of justice and humanity. . . .

The slave system is one of constant danger, distrust, suspicion, and watchfulness. It debases those whose toil alone can produce wealth and resources for defense, to the lowest degree of which human nature is capable, to guard against mutiny and insurrection, and thus wastes energies which otherwise might be employed in national development and aggrandizement.

The free-labor system educates all alike, and by opening all the fields of industrial employment, and all the departments of authority, to the unchecked and equal rivalry of all classes of men, at once secures universal contentment, and brings into the highest possible activity all the physical, moral and social energies of the whole state. In states where the slave system prevails, the masters, directly or indirectly, secure all political power, and constitute a ruling aristocracy. In states where the free-labor system prevails, universal suffrage necessarily obtains, and the state inevitably becomes, sooner or later, a republic of democracy.

*   *   *   *   *

Hitherto, the two systems have existed in different states, but side by side within the American Union. This has happened because the Union is a confederation of states. But in another aspect the United States constitute only one nation. Increase of population, which is filling the states out to their very borders, together with a new and extended net-work of railroads and other avenues, and an internal commerce which daily becomes more intimate, is rapidly bringing the states into a higher and more perfect social unity or consolidation. Thus, these antagonistic systems are continually coming into closer contact, and collision results.

Shall I tell you what this collision means? They who think that it is accidental, unnecessary, the work of interested or fanatical agitators, and therefore ephemeral, mistake the case altogether. It is an irrepressible conflict between opposing and enduring forces, and it means that the United States must and will, sooner or later, become either entirely a slaveholding nation, or entirely a freelabor nation. Either the cotton and ricefields of South Carolina and the sugar plantations of Louisiana will ultimately be tilled by free labor, and Charleston and New Orleans become marts for legitimate merchandise alone, or else the rye-fields and wheat-fields of Massachusetts and New York must again be surrendered by their farmers to slave culture and to the production of slaves, and Boston and New York become once more markets for trade in the bodies and souls of men. It is the failure to apprehend this great truth that induces so many unsuccessful attempts at final compromise between the slave and free states, and it is the existence of this great fact that renders all such pretended compromises, when made, vain and ephemeral. Startling as this saying may appear to you, fellow citizens, it is by no means an original or even a moderate one. Our forefathers knew it to be true, and unanimously acted upon it when they framed the constitution of the United States. They regarded the existence of the servile system in so many of the states with sorrow and shame, which they openly confessed, and they looked upon the collision between them, which was then just revealing itself, and which we are now accustomed to deplore, with favor and hope. They know that either the one or the other system must exclusively prevail.

*   *   *   *   *

The very constitution of the democratic party commits it to execute all the designs of the slaveholders, whatever they may be. It is not a party of the whole Union, of all the free states and of all the slave states; nor yet is it a party of the free states in the north and in the northwest; but it is a sectional and local party, having practically its seat within the slave states, and counting its constituency chiefly and almost exclusively there. . . .

A party is in one sense a joint stock association, in which those who contribute most direct the action and management of the concern. The slaveholders contributing in an overwhelming proportion to the capital strength of the democratic party, they necessarily dictate and prescribe its policy. . . .

To expect the democratic party to resist slavery and favor freedom, is as unreasonable as to look for protestant missionaries to the catholic propaganda of Rome.

*   *   *   *   *

I think, fellow citizens, that I have shown you that it is high time for the friends of freedom to rush to the rescue of the constitution, and that their very first duty is to dismiss the democratic party from the administration of the government.

Why shall it not be done? All agree that it ought to be done. What, then, shall prevent its being done? Nothing but timidity or division of the opponents of the democratic party.

Some of the opponents start one objection, and some another. Let us notice these objections briefly. One class say that they cannot trust the republican party; that it has not avowed its hostility to slavery boldly enough, or its affection for freedom earnestly enough.

I ask, in reply, is there any other party which can be more safely trusted? Every one knows that it is the republican party, or none, that shall displace the democratic party. But I answer, further, that the character and fidelity of any party are determined, necessarily, not by its pledges, programmes, and platforms, but by the public exigencies, and the temper of the people when they call it into activity. Subserviency to slavery is a law written not only on the forehead of the democratic party, but also in its very soul—so resistance to slavery, and devotion of freedom, the popular ele-

ments now actively working for the republican party among the people, must and will be the resources for its ever-renewing strength and constant invigoration.

*   *   *   *   *

Others will not venture an effort, because they fear that the Union would not endure the change. Will such objectors tell me how long a constitution can bear a strain directly along the fibres of which it is composed? This is a constitution of freedom. It is being converted into a constitution of slavery. It is a republican constitution. It is being made an aristocratic one. Others wish to wait until some collateral questions concerning temperance, or the exercise of the elective franchise are properly settled. Let me ask all such persons, whether time enough has not been wasted on these points already, without gaining any other than this single advantage, namely, the discovery that only one thing can be effectually done at one time, and that the one thing which must and will be done at any one time is just that thing which is most urgent, and will no longer admit of postponement or delay. Finally, we are told by fainthearted men that they despond; the democratic party, they say is unconquerable, and the dominion of slavery is consequently inevitable. I reply that the complete and universal dominion of slavery would be intolerable enough, when it should have come, after the last possible effort to escape should have been made. There would then be left to us the consoling reflection of fidelity to duty.

But I reply further, that I know—few, I think, know better than I—the resources and energies of the democratic party, which is identical with the slave power. I do ample prestige to its traditional popularity. I know, further—few, I think, know better than I—the difficulties and disadvantages of organizing a new political force, like the republican party, and the obstacles it must encounter in laboring without prestige and without patronage. But, understanding all this, I know that the democratic party must go down, and that the republican party must rise into its place. The democratic party derived its strengh, originally, from its adoption of the principles of equal and exact justice to all men. So long as it practised this principle faithfully, it was invulnerable. It became vulnerable when it renounced the principle, and since that time it has maintained itself, not by virtue of its own strength, or even of its traditional merits, but because there as yet had appeared in the political field no other party that had the conscience and the courage to take up, and avow, and practice the life-inspiring principle which the democratic party had surrendered. At last, the republican party has appeared. It avows, now, as the republican party of 1800 did, in one word, its faith and its works, "Equal and exact justice to all men." Even when it first entered the field, only half organized, it struck a blow which only just failed to secure complete and triumphant victory. In this, its second campaign, it has already won advantages which render that triumph now both easy and certain.

The secret of its assured success lies in that very characteristic which, in the mouth of scoffers, constitutes its great and lasting imbecility and reproach. It lies in the fact that it is a party of one idea; but that idea is a noble one— an idea that fills and expends all generous souls; the idea of equality—the equality of all men before human tribunals and human laws, as they all are equal before the Divine tribunal and Divine laws.

I know, and you know, that a revolution has begun. I know, and all the world knows, that revolutions never go backward. Twenty senators and a hundred representatives proclaim boldly in congress to-day sentiments and opinions and principles of freedom which hardly so many men, even in this free state, dared to utter in their own homes twenty years ago. While the government of the United States, under the conduct of the democratic party, has been all that time surrendering one plain and castle after another to slavery, the people of the United States have been no less steadily

and perserveringly gathering together the forces with which to recover back again all the fields and all the castles which have been lost, and to confound and overthrow, by one decisive blow, the betrayers of the constitution and freedom forever.

DOCUMENT 14.3
A Matter of Life and Death

In the cause of freedom for Blacks, no man had a greater stake than Frederick Douglass. Born in slavery, he escaped its bonds in 1838, educated himself, and became a central figure in the abolition movement. For Douglass, there could be no true Union until slavery was overthrown.

Now, what disturbs, divides and threatens to bring on civil war, and to break up and ruin this country, but slavery. Who but one morally blind can fail to see it; and who but a moral coward can hesitate to declare it.—Fifteen States are bent upon the ascendency, and endless perpetuation of this system of immeasurable wickedness and numberless crimes, and are determined either to make it the law of the whole country, or destroy the Government. Against this inhuman and monstrous purpose are arraigned the enlightenment of the age, checking and overthrowing tyranny, liberating the bondman from his chains in all quarters of the globe, and extending constitutional liberty to long oppressed nationalities; against it are the instinctive sentiments of humanity, shuddering at the thought of chattelized humanity; against it are the eternal laws of liberty, goodness, justice and progress, dispelling the darkness of barbarism, exposing the hollowness of a corrupt priesthood, under the sanction of

Source: *Douglass' Monthly*, February 1861, quoted in Philip S. Foner, *The Life and Writings of Frederick Douglass* (New York: International Publishers Co., Inc., 1952), vol. 3, pp. 62–63.

whose dark mummeries all the hell-black crimes of human bondage have found, in this country, their greatest security; against it are the ever-increasing triumphs in the arts of civilization, reducing the importance of mere brute force to nothing in comparison with intellectual power; against it are all the promptings, aspirations, convictions and sympathies of unperverted human nature, and the God in history everywhere pronouncing the doom of those nations which frame mischief by law, and revel in selfishness and blood. It is the concussion of these natural elements against slavery which now rock the land, and sends us staggering about as if shaken by an earthquake. Here is the cause of the trouble. It is slavery, the sum of all villainies, on the one hand, and all the silent but mighty forces of nature on the other. Here is and must ever remain the irrepressible conflict, until slavery is abolished or human nature, with all its divine attributes, is changed and made to reflect the image of hell instead of heaven.

Slavery is the disease, and its abolition in every part of the land is essential to the future quiet and security of the country. Any union which can possibly be patched up while slavery exists, must either completely demoralize the whole nation, or remain a heartless form, disguising, under the smiles of friendship, a vital, active and ever-increasing hate, sure to explode in violence. It is a matter of life and death. Slavery must be all in the Union, or it can be nothing.

DOCUMENT 14.4
The Wolf and Its Victim

William Gilmore Simms wrote poetry and novels to please the slaveowning oligarchs of his beloved South Carolina. In return, they

Source: Mary C. Simms Oliphant et al., eds., *The Letters of William Gilmore Simms* (Columbia: University of South Carolina Press, 1952–56), vol. 4, pp. 287–306.

ignored his work and snubbed him as a person. Although his real admirers were men of the North, he became an ardent champion of the South's leaders and their "peculiar institution." When a northern friend, John J. Bockee, pleaded with him to honor and respect the "blessed Union," Simms replied in the impassioned rhetoric of a typical fire-eater or ardent secessionist. His letter is dated September 12, 1860.

Why, my dear deluded friend, do you still desire to save the Union? Of what sort of value, to a Christian man, is that sort of union which persists in keeping men in the same household, who hate and blaspheme each other? And can you be really a friend to the South—a wise one you certainly are not—when you desire us, the *minority* States, to submit to the uncontrolled legislation of a majority, which has not only proved faithless to all its pledges, but which has declared its determined purpose to subdue, rule and destroy the minority, and abrogate all its rights and securities?

Suffer me, my dear friend, to hint to you a few other matters. How is it that, in all the trespasses and exactions of the North, upon and from the South, you never wrote such a letter to the aggressors and the trespassers, in behalf of the South, as you now write to me in behalf of the Union? I never got from you a letter of indignation, when the North was taxing the sweat and labor of the South, even to its ruin, by protective tariffs, for the benefit and greed of the manufacturing monopolists of New England and Pennsylvania. I never heard from you—addressed either to me or to the enemies of my people—in anger, at the abrogation of the Fugitive Slave law by some twelve or fifteen of your States, your own among them! You never cried out your griefs, or your wrath, when our slaves were hurried from us by underground railroads—by wretches, exulting doubly when, robbing the master of his slaves, they succeeded in persuading them to murder him also; and, when the fugitives from justice were withheld, and the pursuing owners or officers were seized and mobbed, and maltreated, and doomed to the penitenitary—why was your voice silent? Nor do I know, or believe, when, violating the Missouri Compromise, the hostile and abolition North refused to the South their recognized rights south of the line of 36° 30', that you ever made your clamors heard in defence of Southern rights and privileges, and in the maintenance of a sacred stipulation. And yet, in that very conquest of Mexico and California, the South sent 46,000 volunteers into the field; the North but 22,000; and with a handsome proportion of the New England troops refusing to fight when they got to Vera Cruz, alleging, in the hour of battle, their conscientious scruples about the morals of war in general, and this war in particular! The battle fought, the victory won, the territory gained, their moral scruples all gave way, at the gathering of the spoils! They grasped the whole territory with the eagerness of a half starved parish boy, blessed with the unexpected sight of a sudden plum pudding within his reach! By a majority vote in Congress, they took it all—some 700 miles on the Pacific coast; and drove out the Southern slaveholders, who had fought the battle! As Edward said to Bruce, "Have I nothing to do but to win kingdoms for you?" And where were you, and other friends of the South, while this royal robbery went on? Not a voice was heard in opposition; and I do not find in any of the frequent friendly letters which I have had from you, that you even once allude to *our* wrongs at all, or in the language of indignation. You never seem to have foreseen that a fatal blow was given to the Union *then*—in that very hour—in that stroke of a policy so very cunning as to—cut its own throat!

I look in vain, my excellent friend, among all your excellent letters to me, to find one single expression of your horror at the John Brown raid in Virginia! Your indignation, I

suppose, was so intense as to keep you dumb! I cannot, of course, suppose that you were indifferent! Oh! no; your expressions of love forbid that idea! So, too, I see not a word of your wrath and indignation, in any of these letters, at the burnings of our towns, and the poisoning of our fountains, in Texas, by creatures of the same kidney with the vulture Brown! And when Brown is made a martyr of in the North, and his day made a sacred record in the Northern calendar, I do not perceive that you covered your head with sackcloth and ashes, and wrote to me lamenting!

And, when your people *did* rise, after a fashion, and at a very late hour—you among them—to oppose Abolitionism, you had neither the virtue, nor the wisdom, to take issue with the enemy by a manly justification of the South! You only moved *to save the Union*—in other words, *not to lose the keeping of that excellent milch cow,* whose dugs have yielded, for sixty years, so large a proportion of the milk and butter which have fattened your hungry people. You claimed nothing for the South—asserted nothing; asked nothing; had no purpose beyond the preservation of the Confederacy, *as it was;* the South being the victim still—the North wolf.

DOCUMENT 14.5
The Union Is Perpetual

Expressions of nationalism abound in the speeches and writings of antebellum Northerners. They range from trumpet flourishes announcing the expansionist destiny of the United States to modest reminders of the unique democratic polity enjoyed by Americans. No one presented the nationalist case with greater calm, reason, and force than did Abraham Lincoln. Doubtless, his first

Source: James D. Richardson, ed., *A Compilation of the Messages and Papers of the Presidents, 1789–1897* (New York: Bureau of National Literature and Art, 1909), vol. 5, pp. 3206–13.

inaugural address, March 4, 1861, expressed
perfectly the sense of most people in the North,
and of many Unionists in the South as well.

Physically speaking, we can not separate. We
can not remove our respective sections from
each other nor build an impassable wall between them. A husband and wife may be di-
vorced and go out of the presence and beyond
the reach of each other, but the different parts
of our country can not do this. They can not
but remain face to face, and intercourse, either
amicable or hostile, must continue between
them. Is it possible, then, to make that intercourse more advantageous or more satisfactory
after separation than *before?* Can aliens make
treaties easier than friends can make laws? Can
treaties be more faithfully enforced between
aliens than laws can among friends? Suppose
you go to war, you can not fight always; and
when, after much loss on both sides and no
gain on either, you cease fighting, the identical
old questions, as to terms of intercourse, are
again upon you. . . .

The Chief Magistrate derives all his authority from the people, and they have conferred
none upon him to fix terms for the separation
of the States. The people themselves can do
this also if they choose, but the Executive as
such has nothing to do with it. His duty is to
administer the present Government as it came
to his hands and to transmit it unimpaired by
him to his successor.

Why should there not be a patient confidence
in the ultimate justice of the people? Is there
any better or equal hope in the world? In our
present differences, is either party without faith
of being in the right? If the Almighty Ruler
of Nations, with His eternal truth and justice,
be on your side of the North, or on yours of
the South, that truth and that justice will surely
prevail by the judgment of this great tribunal
of the American people. . .

My countrymen, one and all, think calmly
and *well* upon this whole subject. Nothing valuable can be lost by taking time. If there be

an object to *hurry* any of you in hot haste to
a step which you would never take *deliberately,*
that object will be frustrated by taking time;
but no good object can be frustrated by it.
Such of you as are now dissatisfied still have
the old Constitution unimpaired, and, on the
sensitive point, the laws of your own framing
under it; while the new Administration will
have no immediate power, if it would, to
change either. If it were admitted that you who
are dissatisfied hold the right side in the dispute,
there still is no single good reason for precipitate action. Intelligence, patriotism, Christianity, and a firm reliance on Him who has never
yet forsaken this favored land are still competent to adjust in the best way all our present
difficulty.

In *your* hands, may dissatisfied fellow-coun-
trymen, and not in *mine,* is the momentous
issue of civil war. The Government will not
assail *you.* You can have no conflict without
being yourselves the aggressors. *You* have no
oath registered in heaven to destroy the Government, while I shall have the most solemn one
to "preserve, protect, and defend it."

I am loath to close. We are not enemies,
but friends. We must not be enemies. Though
passion may have strained it must not break
our bonds of affection. The mystic chords of
memory, stretching from every battlefield and
patriot grave to every living heart and hearth-
stone all over this broad land, will yet swell
the chorus of the Union, when again touched,
as surely they will be, by the better angels of
our nature.

DOCUMENT 14.6
Slavery: The Cornerstone

After the war, Alexander H. Stephens of
Georgia defended the principle of secession
and argued that the Civil War had been fought
over constitutional issues. However, in March

Source: Frank Moore, ed., *The Rebellion Record* (New
York, 1861–64), vol. 1, pp. 44–49.

1861, shortly after he had been inauguarated as vice president of the Confederate States of America, he spoke of an issue more immediate than the argument over the nature of the Union. In one of his best-known speeches, Stephens insisted that slavery was the cornerstone of the new Southern republic.

. . . [The] new Constitution [Confederate] has put at rest *forever* all the agitating questions relating to our peculiar institution—African slavery as it exists among us—the proper *status* of the negro in our form of civilization. *This was the immediate cause of the late rupture and present revolution.* JEFFERSON, in his forecast, had anticipated this, as the "rock upon which the old Union would split." He was right. What was conjecture with him, in now a realized fact. But whether he fully comprehended the great truth upon which that rock *stood* and *stands,* may be doubted. *The prevailing ideas entertained by him and most of the leading statesmen at the time of the formation of the old Constitution were, that the enslavement of the African was in violation of the laws of nature; that it was wrong in principle, socially, morally and politically.* It was an evil they knew not well how to deal with; but the general opinion of the men of that day was, that, somehow or other, in the order of Providence, the institution would be evanescent and pass away. This idea, though not incorporated in the Constitution, was the prevailing idea at the time. The Constitution, it is true, secured every essential guarantee to the institution while it should last, and hence no argument can be justly used against the constitutional guarantees thus secured, because of the common sentiment of the day. *Those ideas, however, were fundamentally wrong. They rested upon the assumption of the equality of races. This was an error.* It was a sandy foundation, and the idea of a Government built upon it—when the "storm came and the wind blew, it *fell.*"

Our new Government is founded upon exactly the opposite ideas; its foundations are laid, its cornerstone rests, upon the great truth that the negro is not equal to the white man; that slavery, subordination to the superior race, is his natural and moral condition. [Applause.] *This, our new Government, is the first, in the history of the world, based upon this great physical, philosophical, and moral truth.* . . .Many Governments have been founded upon the principles of certain classes; but the classes thus enslaved, were of the same race, and in violation of the laws of nature. Our system commits no such violation of nature's laws. The negro by nature, or by the curse against Canaan, is fitted for that condition which he occupies in our system. The architect, in the construction of buildings, lays the foundation with the proper material—the granite—then comes the brick or the marble. The substratum of our society is made of the material fitted by nature for it, and by experience we know that it is the best, not only for the superior but for the inferior race, that it should be so. It is, indeed, in conformity with the Creator. *It is not for us to inquire into the wisdom of His ordinances or to question them.* For His own purposes He has made one race to differ from another, as He has made "one star to differ from another in glory."

The great objects of humanity are best attained, when conformed to his laws and degrees, in the formation of Governments as well as in all things else. Our Confederacy is founded upon principles in strict conformity with these laws. This stone which was rejected by the first builders *"is become the chief stone of the corner"* in our new edifice. [Applause.]

DOCUMENT 14.7
Slavery: A Pretext

In 1861, the poet-critic Edmund Clarence Stedman served as a war correspondent for

Source: Laura Stedman and George M. Gould, *Life and Letters of Edmund Clarence Stedman* (New York: Moffat Yard, 1910), pp. 240–47.

the New York World. A somewhat pedantic, often bombastic young man, he saw the war as a thorough justification of the North's claim to superiority over the South in all things. In a letter to his mother, early in the war, he explained why the conflict had come.

September 26, 1861

The War is a duty on the part of the North. It is not waged by abolitionists, is *not* the result of abolitionism. We are not sure but that slavery is a very good thing in the Cotton states. In other latitudes I see for myself that it is good enough for the negroes, but ruinous to the whites. There is a theory, that the Virginia and Kentucky gentry own slaves; this is false; I have seen for myself that the *niggars own the gentry.* Now I wish to make you . . . understand that, although we see that this War will probably settle the slavery question, and possibly forever limit slavery to the Cotton states, *yet we are not fighting the negro's cause.* Slavery has been the cause of the War in no sense other than that it has added another distinctness to the line betwixt North and South which climate and race had already drawn. The real cause of the War is a bitter and criminal hatred, entertained by the South against the North, and based on other than slave interests. For fifty years the *character* of Southerners has become daily more domineering, insolent, irrational, haughty, scornful of justice. They have so long cracked their whips over negroes that they now assume a certain inherent right to crack them over *white men;* assume the positive rights of a superior race; and have taken advantage of the North's desire for quiet and peace to impose upon us without stint. For years the tone of their actions and speeches, in Congress and society has expressed this sen-

timent and determination. Even Southern students at College, when I was a Yale, adopted the same tactics. One hundred of them—poor scholars, but blustering with rum and bowie-knives—lorded it over four hundred studious New Englanders, simply because the latter *were* studious and desired to attain the objects aimed at in a collegiate course. At length the thing became degrading, and we arose one day and kicked them all out. For fifty years the same plan has been practised on a larger scale in our national affairs. The South, assisted by Northern merchants whom it has governed, has been true enough to the Union, so long as every election gave *it* the power, and as foreign missions, army and navy commissions, presidencies, etc., were held in its own hands. But the census of 1850 showed that the enterprising and industrious North was getting the balance of power. Then the South began to rebel and would have seceded had not the Clay compromise taken away *its sole pretext.* Now the census of 1860, and the Lincoln election have revived *both the desire and the pretext,* and *it has seceded.* To give you an illustration of my meaning: The South and the North have been like a large and small boy at school— the former thrashing the latter without mercy for years, and the latter constitutionally submitting to the joke; now the North has grown big enough to lick the South and has done it for the first time—whereupon the irrational South gets angry and secedes. Slavery furnishes a plausible pretext. That's all. If the slaves should now rebel, as they probably will, and commit atrocities, we should probably *unite with the South* to save our white brothers and sisters—but should then insist on the cause of such horrors being forever removed, *for the sake of the white man.*

chapter 15

The Civil War as a Crisis in American Political Theory

William W. Freehling

Johns Hopkins University

W hy in the world, most late-twentieth-century Americans instinctively wonder, did so many mid-nineteenth-century Northerners wrestle with guilty consciences about supporting the Civil War? As armed combats go, after all, the campaign of northern armies seems, in retrospect, a relatively legitimate enterprise. No one likes the thought that the democratic method failed to work peacefully in 1861, or the related thought that 620,000 young men paid for the failure with their lives, Still, once the minority South had seceded from the Union rather than accept Lincoln's election, the North, as most Americans continue to see it, had to march to war rather than accept the downfall of majority rule.

The combat results appear to vindicate that ethical conclusion. When Lee surrendered to Grant at Appomatox, majority rule was saved, the nation was preserved, and Black slavery was destroyed. Never again has an American minority used secession; and whatever the tribulations of twentieth-century Blacks, never again have Americans been enslaved. How many wars have solved such difficult problems so long and so well?

The difficulty with this simplistic conclusion is that it obscures subtle problems that the Civil War raises. The collapse of a democracy demonstrates not only the practical difficulties with a republic but also tensions and ambiguities in the theory underlying the system. Nowhere was the Civil War more a profound American crisis than in the questions it raised about national democratic dogma.

According to classical American democratic dogma, at least three conditions must be met before a republic becomes legitimate. The majority must rule, the governed must consent to be ruled, and the government must not impinge on natural rights. When democracy works, the three principles do not clash. Everyone consents to be governed by the election winners; and the winners restrain from violating the losers' natural rights.

In a civil war, however, the three American tenets clash so seriously that a theorist is tempted to pick one and damn the others. What ought to be done, for example, when a substantial minority withdraws its consent to be ruled and contracts to establish its own democratic government? Furthermore, what ought to happen when the minority defends its right to withdraw consent by invoking a cherished American principle—the natural right of revolution against oppression? Permitting the withdrawal will destroy majority rule and may create anarchy. Yet can a government that calls itself democratic coerce people to consent?

For many Americans who lived through the Civil War, these abstract questions were made more acute by disturbing analogies with the American Revolution. If the American Revolution was right, could the southern rebellion be wrong? If England was wrong in 1776 to seek to repress American rebels, could the North be right in 1861 to war against southern seceders? The right of revolution and the right to consent to be governed did not terminate when the American Revolution triumphed. On the contrary, patriots of 1776 sought to establish universal principles applicable to all men at all times. The men of Concord and Lexington claimed that governments "derive their just powers from the consent of the governed;" they claimed "the right of the people to alter or abolish" an old government and to institute a new one. The men who fired on Fort Sumter were seeking no less. The distressing conclusion to not a few Northerners was that Lincoln's crusade was as illegitimate as that of King George.

For intellectuals in the North, the problem of coercively forcing southern consent was compounded by another difficulty—the problem of arbitrarily jailing northern dissenters. The North might lose the war if Lincoln protected everyone's natural right to a speedy jury trial. A rebellion by its nature involves disloyalty; and in the American Civil War disloyalty was not limited to the rebellious region. Southern sympathizers in northern states sometimes sought to sabotage the war effort by blowing up railroads and encouraging troop desertions. If Lincoln employed only customary means of justice, these so-called Copperheads might undermine the Army. Using the writ of habeas corpus, they could be temporarily free to sabotage while awaiting trial. Using their influence over other traitors in the community, they might

win permanent freedom from friendly judges or juries. The government might be able to indict no one—or to win any convictions.

Thus, under abnormal Civil War conditions, Lincoln believed that normal processes of justice must sometimes be suspended. By suspending the writ of habeas corpus, northern generals could lock up suspected traitors without substantial evidence; by employing military courts, the government could try alleged rebel sympathizers without risking trial by jury. Such denials of civil liberties were a temporary price worth paying to preserve the Republic and to return to the halcyon days when government by consent, government by majority rule, and government by natural law did not come in mortal conflict.

Many contemporary critics wondered if the prize was worth the price. If preserving the Republic required revoking the right of revolution and repressing trial by jury, then democracy seemed to them but despotism. For centuries, political theorists had questioned whether a republic based on consent could coercively put down disorder. Now, as Lincoln massed the power of the state under the press of civil war, men wondered whether a coercive government could be called democratic at all. As Lincoln once summed it up in one penetrating question: Must a democracy be either too strong for popular liberties or too weak to preserve itself?

One characteristic of the secession crisis made these problems a little less distressing. The South did not usually defend secession by invoking natural law. Southern orators reiterated that secession was a legal rather than a natural right—a right under the Constitution rather than a right of revolution.

Indeed the South had spent the previous three decades denying that natural rights existed. When immediate abolitionism emerged on the American scene in the early 1830s, Southerners had turned against natural law and proclaimed

Jefferson a fanatic. Natural rights to liberty and natural rights of revolution were no doctrines for men defending slavery. Proslavery theorists insisted that no abstract rights exist, that one cannot postulate how societies ought to be but rather must examine them as they are, that southern chattel slavery was a superior institution to northern wage slavery.

This passion to destroy airy abstractions and to deal with concrete practicalities led Southerners to concentrate on the concrete federal Constitution rather than on the airy Declaration of Independence. Since the days of Calhoun's nullification theory and Hayne's debate with Webster, southern extremists had emphasized that individual states, rather than the common government, were now and had always been the ultimate constitutional sovereign. The colonies had revolted from England as separate entities rather than in a single group: individual states had been all-powerful under the Articles of Confederation; the states had each ratified the Constitution, reserving all powers except authority explicitly delegated to the federal government. Among the powers states had never explicitly delegated and therefore retained was the sovereign authority to withdraw from the Union. As mere agent, the federal government could hardly say nay to the superior sovereign state. Secession was a constitutional right.

This legalistic argument set the contours of debate. The northern task was to answer the South; and since the South wanted to talk about the Constitution, the North spun out endless constitutional doctrine. Indeed, for men like Lincoln, the ability to answer southern legal grounds meant that disturbing questions of extralegal natural law could be avoided.

Following in Daniel Webster's tradition, Northerners claimed that the nation had preceded the states; that the colonies had jointly, rather than separately, adopted the Declaration of Independence; that the people of the United States, rather than each state, had ratified the

Constitution; that once the federal government was established and given *supreme* power, no inferior state could negate superior federal laws. Repressing secession meant merely enforcing supreme law.

Whoever got the better of this constitutional argument (and the case can still be argued either way), the terms of debate never completely satisfied northern intellectuals. If Southerners eschewed natural rights, northern thinkers could not forget the Jeffersonian heritage. They knew that a political act had to be morally and legally right, that it had to conform to higher law and be in accord with the Constitution. Moreover, often enough to disturb intellectuals, southern orators talked about natural rights of revolution. For example, no less a man than Jefferson Davis, on no less an occasion than his inauguration as president of the Confederacy, sounded like Thomas Jefferson as he defended secession. Establishment of the Confederate States of America, Davis claimed, "illustrates the American idea that government rests upon the consent of the governed, and that it is the right of the people to alter and abolish governments whenever they become destructive to the ends for which they were established." Southerners, he continued, had "merely asserted the right which the Declaration of Independence of 1776 defined to be inalienable." All the constitutional doctrine in the world could not answer *this* Davis argument.

To combat nagging doubts about war legitimacy, northern intellectuals had to deny the parallel with 1776 and destroy southern claims to a right of revolution. The keys to their case were the various qualifications written into the Declaration of Independence. The Founding Fathers, well aware of the dangers of anarchy, did not sanction whimsical revolution. They insisted that grievances be deep and long-lasting, not "light and transient;" they proclaimed that peaceful modes of redress must first be attempted. The colonies had revolted after ten years of appeals to England. Their grievances included numerous violations of natural rights, especially the imposition of standing armies and the passage of taxation without representation. The heritage of the Revolution offered a tradition of revolutionary action only after endless oppression.

Most Northerners, in 1861, believed that the South had suffered no such oppression. Southerners were represented in Congress, and they had controlled many federal decisions throughout the 1850s. The major southern complaint did not concern what had been done in the past but rather what Republicans might do in the future. Where were outrageous oppressions comparable to the Stamp Act and the Intolerable Acts?

Nor could Northerners see that the South had used up peaceful modes of redress. Southerners had lost only the election of 1860. The South had not attempted to use the traditional minority right, the right to try to win next time. Southerners had not appealed to Congress for redress—indeed, had not waited for Congress to pass hostile legislation. Finally, slaveholders had not appealed to a national constitutional convention. Where was the record of continual appeals to the oppressor that matched the efforts of the men of 1776?

Northerners considered this supposed lack of grievances the more serious because the South had participated in the election of 1860. The act of stepping in the polling place, according to their argument, implies the act of abiding by the results. In a broader sense, northern intellectuals wondered whether men had a right of revolution as long as free elections continued. It was one thing to revolt against an arbitrary government that denied representation. It was quite another to vent one's spleen against a liberal democracy that had passed to the control of one's opponents.

Finally, and most importantly, the chief southern objective—the preservation of slavery—seemed itself a violation of natural law. Could some men use a natural right of revolution to keep other men unnaturally enslaved? After all, Blacks, a substantial southern minority, had not been allowed to vote in the supposed decision of the southern people to change their government. Moreover, if the Confederate states were allowed to depart, Blacks would never vote, much less be free. On the other hand, in the course of the Civil War, northern victories might vindicate the Declaration of Independence by securing emancipation.

Thus, Northerners developed a powerful argument against a southern right of revolution. Instead of ten years of oppression, the South had lost one election; instead of being taxed without representation, Southerners often controlled the government; instead of seeking natural law, slaveholders sought to protect human bondage; instead of seeking redress for past grievances, the South wanted to avoid future possibilities. A right of revolution to deny the results of a legitimate election and to preserve a despotic institution: It was enough to make Mr. Jefferson turn over in his grave!

A handful of northern political theorists, however, did not believe the case was quite so pat. They doubted that American Revolutionaries had suffered such horrid oppressions. The British standing army of the 1760s, they pointed out, was largely a frontier police force seeking to ward off Indian marauders. The Stamp Act was passed to finance a part of the French-Indian War, which benefited all Americans by sweeping France from the New World. As for "no taxation without representation," England, perhaps with tongue in cheek, had offered the colonies representation in Parliament. Colonial leaders had scorned the proposal because colonial representatives could not control an English parliament and would only make parliamentary taxation appear legitimate. What "no taxation without representation'' really meant was no taxation except by local colonial legislatures that Americans could control. How different was the South's claim that since Southerners could never again control Congress, continued southern representation would only make oppression seem legitimate? How different was the South's desire to give their own local legislatures control over their own institutions?

Other Northerners urged that southern grievances were indeed comparable to those of the colonists. They thought, for example, that slaveholders were right to be horrified by John Brown's raid, and were right to be shocked at the way Northern leaders like Ralph Waldo Emerson proclaimed Brown a hero. Then, too, Southerners were legitimately angry that Northerners virtually nullified federal fugitive slave laws by helping runaway slaves. What English deeds compared with these ''chilling'' attempts to make Blacks restless in their chains?

On the issue of participating in an election and then failing to abide by its results, a few northern intellectuals again believed that the South had a case. The election of 1860, they believed, was no ordinary election. It showed that the South was in a permanent minority and could never again control the government. Why should Southerners suffer more lost elections when their minority position was already clear? Why should they appeal to a constitutional convention that would turn them down? In a broader sense, when could a minority withdraw its consent? If a minority seceded before an election, the majority would shout about failure to seek legal redress. If seceders acted after an election, the majority would shout about breaking the rules. In this perspective, the northern case seemed a circular argument that *always* denied a right of revolution. And the point, as a few Northerners continued to see it, was that American theory proclaimed that men *could* withdraw their consent to be governed.

Finally, some Northerners scoffed at the notion that southern slavery made Yankee armies right. The sad truth, they pointed out, was that neither many Northerners nor Southerners favored emancipation at the beginning of the Civil War. During the secession winter, the national Congress, with Lincoln's blessing, passed by a two-thirds vote and sent on to the states an unamendable constitutional amendment forever guaranteeing slavery in the South. While the war halted the ratification process, emancipation did not become a Union war aim until two years after hostilities began. As late as August 1862, Lincoln was writing to Horace Greeley that his only object was to save the Union. ''If I could save the Union without freeing *any* slave,'' declared the President, ''I would do it.'' Even Lincoln's Emancipation Proclamation of January 1, 1863 was a paper edict that did not free a slave. No wonder, then, that in 1861, at the moment the decision for armed combat was made, the war was a white man's fight with both armies determined to keep Blacks in their place.

Furthermore, to argue that secession was illegitimate because Blacks lacked civil rights was to argue that every American political decision was null and void. If slaveholders could not use a right of revolution, then Jefferson himself was an illegitimate revolutionist. If slaves had to vote to make revolutions legitimate, then the American Revolution was an immoral enterprise. And if Blacks had to vote in any popular decision, then Lincoln's election in the North, where few Blacks could vote, was also null and void. Indeed, if revolutionists had to be snowy pure, guiltless of violation of natural rights, then every revolution had been immoral and the right of revolution was academic.

Thus, those who continued to believe in the South's right to secede devised an intriguing answer to the dominant northern position. Instead of suffering no grievances, the South had endured John Brown's raid; instead of ignoring peaceful redress, the South had waited until its permanent minority status was sealed; instead of wanting only to preserve slavery, Southerners were also seeking the same sort of local government American colonists had desired. Most importantly, a substantial portion of American society had decided it had sufficient reasons to withdraw its consent to be governed. Who was to say they were wrong? To go to war to make them consent was to leave the issue in the hands of the strongest army. Did democracy in the end then mean might makes right? It was enough to make thoughtful men ponder as Grant hacked through the wilderness and Sherman turned toward the sea.

The proposition that the South had a right to secede was the concern of relatively few Northerners. On the other hand, the position that Lincoln had the right to hail citizens before military tribunes became a major Civil War issue. Northern Democrats continually denounced Lincoln as a despot who had forgotten that America was a land of law.

The alleged despot himself never doubted that arbitrary justice was sometimes necessary. Lincoln cold not abide the thought that northern soldiers were dying because Confederate spies ran loose. Nor could he swallow the notion that a President should save jury trials for the moment at the risk of losing the Republic forever. As Lincoln saw it, hundreds of thousands of Confederate sympathizers, organized in secret Knights of the Golden Circle, were rank saboteurs who counted on using natural rights to cut down democracy. Trying these Copperheads in civil courts was both impossible and inexpedient. It was impossible because courts moved too slowly and evidence was too hard to procure. It was inexpedient because executing traitors would create martyrs. Lincoln wanted to prevent treason rather than slay traitors; he preferred to let suspected spies cool their heels in prison until danger had passed.

Arresting men *before* they acted and before overwhelming evidence could be procured required suspending the writ of habeas corpus and subjecting citizens to military tribunals. Thus, Lincoln proclaimed in unlimited terms the President's power to impose martial law whenever and wherever he deemed it militarily necessary.

Lincoln's extralegal authority, if sweeping in theory, was restrained in practice. Nothing in the Civil War compares with the English Star Chamber, the French Revolutionary Tribunal, or American detention camps for the Japanese in World War II. No one was executed for treason in this horrendous Civil War; no sedition laws were passed despite dangers of disloyal opposition. Robert E. Lee was said to read northern newspapers at breakfast to check on the whereabouts of the Union Army, and the story may have been true. At least by twentieth-century standards, Abraham Lincoln was a paltry dictator.

Still, enough arbitrary arrests occurred to make the issue significant. When the Maryland legislature showed signs of voting to secede, the Lincoln administration jailed some of its members; after Clement L. Vallandigham, a leading opponent of Lincoln, criticized the President, he was temporarily imprisoned; during the war, over 15,000 citizens were arbitrarily arrested. We know now that the supposedly disloyal Knights of the Golden Circle was largely a patriotic wing of the Democratic Party, and that amidst the passion of war, Lincoln somewhat overestimated the extent of disloyalty. Does the Civil War experience suggest that civil justice must *always* be protected against presidential overraction and repression?

This was the question raised in the well-known *Milligan* decision, handed down by the U. S. Supreme Court a year after the war ended. Justice David Davis, who, ironically, had been Lincoln's campaign manager in 1860, spoke for a unanimous Court in declaring that the

President had violated the Constitution. Four judges urged that the President could never subject citizens to military courts without congressional concurrence. Davis and, presumably, the rest of the Court, believed that even Congress had no such authority except in special circumstances. Davis asserted that if either the President or Congress could override civil courts whenever they deemed it necessary, civil liberties were in danger. Trial by jury must rest on a firmer basis than the conscience of a President or a Congress; and a wartime situation, when citizens are most tempted to forget the Constitution, is exactly the time when constitutional safeguards are most needed. Military justice, Davis concluded, could be meted out to civilians only when the fortunes of war left no choice. Martial law could be imposed only when successful invasion had closed civil courts in a combat area.

The Davis decision has been hailed as a landmark in American constitutional law. Lincoln would have regarded it as a dubious landmark and a dangerous decision. Lincoln had often declared that saboteurs can do as much damage behind the lines as in the combat arena. Stopping troop recruitment or blowing up factories can wreck a war effort as fast as anything done on the battlefield. To Lincoln, the crucial question was always whether a republican government had the power to put down domestic insurrection and thus preserve democracy for future generations. Davis' opinion, Lincoln would have concluded, by forcing the President to twiddle his thumbs while traitors created chaos on the home front, was merely another way of placing temporary salvation of civil justice above permanent preservation of the republic.

Did Davis's severe restraints leave the President with enough power to save a democracy? On the other hand, could not Lincoln's notion of suspending civil courts go far to reduce democracy to shambles? Here was another subtle problem in political theory, perhaps even more difficult than the questions raised by a southern right of revolution.

The purpose of this essay and of the documents that follow is not to proclaim the judgments that the northern war effort was illegitimate or that Lincoln was a despot. The point is that before judgments can be made, one must see Civil War issues in all their complexity. Few other American crises pose so insistently the problems of what Americans really mean by concepts of majority rule, consent of the governed, right of revolution, and trial by jury. Few other crises enable one to see so clearly the ambiguities in the concepts and the priorities among them. Thus, few other crises bring one so close to the central meaning of American democracy.

SUGGESTED READINGS

Belz, Herman. *Reconstructing the Union: Theory and Policy during the Civil War*. Ithaca. N. Y.: Cornell University Press, 1969.

Frederickson, George M. *The Inner Civil War: Northern Intellectuals and the Crisis of the Union*. New York: Harper & Row, 1965.

Gray, Wood. *The Hidden Civil War: The Story of the Copperheads*. New York: Viking Press, 1942.

Hyman, Harold M. *Northern Loyalty Tests during the Civil War and Reconstruction*. Philadelphia: University of Pennsylvania Press, 1954.

Klement, Frank L. *The Copperheads in the Middle West*, Chicago: University of Chicago Press, 1960.

————. *The Limits of Dissent: Clement L. Vallandigham and the Civil War*. Lexington: University of Kentucky Press, 1970.

Milton, George Fort. *Abraham Lincoln and the Fifth Column*. New York: Vanguard Press, 1942.

Randall, James G. *Constitutional Problems under Lincoln*. Urbana: University of Illinois Press, 1951.

Randall, James G., and David Donald. *The Civil War and Reconstruction*. 2nd ed. Boston: D. C. Heath, 1973.

Silver, David M. *Lincoln's Supreme Court.* Urbana: University of Illinois Press, 1956.

Thomas, Benjamin P. *Abraham Lincoln.* New York: Alfred A. Knopf, 1952.

DOCUMENT 15.1
A New Declaration of Independence

While most Southerners based the right of secession on legalist-constitutional grounds, some slaveholders wandered into the forbidden area of Jeffersonian natural rights to find grounds for separation. For example, in the following editorial, "The Constitution—The Union—The Laws," the secessionist New Orleans Daily Crescent echoed with precision the arguments and tone of the Declaration of Independence.

. . . The Declaration of Independence itself says: "Whenever any form of government becomes destructive of these ends, (life, liberty and the pursuit of happiness) it is the right of the people to alter or to abolish it, and to institute a new government, laying its foundation on such principles, and organizing its powers in such form, as to them shall seem most likely to effect their safety and happiness." Higher authority than the above is not to be found in the history of the United States. The principle it enunciates constitutes the very corner stone of the temple of American liberty—of liberty everywhere. Wherever the principle is unrecognized, sheer and unadulterated despotism prevails. . . .

The history of the Abolition or Black Republican party of the North is a history of repeated injuries and usurpations, all having in direct object the establishment of absolute tyranny. . . . From the beginning, we have asked to be let alone in the enjoyment of our plain, inalienable rights, as explicitly guaranteed in our common organic law. We have never aggressed upon the North, nor sought to aggress upon the North. Yet every appeal and expostulation has only brought upon us renewed insults and augmented injuries. They have robbed us of our property, they have murdered our citizens while endeavoring to reclaim that property by lawful means, they have set at naught the decrees of the Supreme Court, they have invaded our States and killed our citizens, they have declared their unalterable determination to exclude us altogether from the Territories, they have nullified the laws of Congress, and finally they have capped the mighty pyramid of unfraternal enormities by electing Abraham Lincoln to the Chief Magistracy, on a platform and by a system which indicates nothing but the subjugation of the South and the complete ruin of her social, political and industrial institutions. . . .

We submit and appeal to a candid and honorable world, whether the Southern people have not been astonishingly patient under gross provocation—whether they have not exhibited remarkable forbearance—whether they have not been long suffering, slow to anger and magnanimous, on numerous occasions where indignation was natural, and severe measures of retaliation justifiable? There can be no doubt on this point. For the sake of peace, for the sake of harmony, the South has compromised until she can compromise no farther, without she is willing to compromise away character, political equality, social and individual interest, and every right and franchise which freemen hold dear. . . .

Source: *New Orleans Daily Crescent*, November 13, 1860.

DOCUMENT 15.2
Let the Erring Brothers Go

The notion that the Declaration of Independence authorized southern separation

Source: *New York Herald Tribune*, December 17, 1860.

found northern adherents, especially during the four months between the secession of South Carolina and the firing on Fort Sumter. For example, in the following well-known editorial, "The Right of Secession," Horace Greeley, a prominent New York Republican, urged that the erring brothers be allowed to go in peace.

. . . We have repeatedly asked those who dissent from our view of this matter to tell us frankly whether they do or do not assent to Mr. Jefferson's statement in the Declaration of Independence that governments "derive their *just* powers from *the consent of the governed;* and that, whenever any form of government becomes destructive of these ends, *it is the right of the people to alter or abolish it.*"
. . . *We do* heartily accept this doctrine, . . . and if it justified the secession from the British Empire of Three Millions of colonists in 1776, we do not see why it would not justify the secession of Five Millions of Southrons from the Federal Union in 1861. . . . We cannot see how Twenty Millions of people can rightfully hold Ten or even Five in a detested union with them, by military force.

Of course, we understand that the principle of Jefferson, like any other broad generalization, may be pushed to extreme and baleful consequences. We can see why Governor's Island should not be at liberty to secede from the State and Nation and allow herself to be covered with French or British batteries commanding and threatening our City. There is hardly a great principle which may not be thus "run into the ground." But if seven or eight contiguous States shall present themselves authentically at Washington, saying, "We hate the Federal Union; we have withdrawn from it; we give you the choice between acquiescing in our secession and arranging amicably all incidental questions on the one hand, and attempting to subdue us on the other"—we could not stand up for coercion, for subjugation, for we do not think it would be just. We hold the right of Self-Government sacred, even when

invoked in behalf of those who deny it to others. . . . And we do not see how we could take the other side without coming in direct conflict with those Rights of Man which we hold paramount to all political arrangements, however convenient and advantageous.

DOCUMENT 15.3
The Rights of Blacks

For a time during the secession winter of 1860–61, many prominent abolitionsts, including William Lloyd Garrison and Wendell Phillips, opposed the drift toward war. But when armed combat began, most antislavery veterans supported the military effort. A crucial reason for the shift was the Declaration of Independence. As Wendell Phillips asks in the following speech, could the South use its so-called natural right of revolution to protect human bondage, especially when northern victory might liberate four million slaves?

. . . I know the whole argument for secession. Very briefly let me state the points. No government provides for its own death; therefore there can be no constitutional right to secede. But there is a revolutionary right. The Declaration of Independence establishes, what the heart of every American acknowledges, that the people—mark you, THE PEOPLE!—have always an inherent, paramount, inalienable right to change their governments, whenever they think—whenever *they* think—that it will minister to their happiness. That is a revolutionary right. . . . South Carolina alleges that she has gone out by convention. So far, right. She says that when the *people* take the State rightfully out of the Union, the right to forts and national property goes with it. . . .

THE PEOPLE,—mark you! . . . I recognize the right of THE PEOPLE of South Caro-

---

Source: Wendell Phillips, *Speeches, Lectures, and Letters* (Boston, 1864), pp. 396–99, 402–405, 407–408, 412.

lina to model their government. Yes, I recognize the right of the three hundred and eighty-four thousand white men, *and* four hundred and eighty-four thousand black men to model their Constitution. Show me one that *they* have adopted, and I will recognize the revolution. But the moment you tread outside of the Constitution, the black man is not three fifths of a man,—he is a whole one.'' Yes, the South has the right of revolution; the South has a right to model her government; and the moment she shows us four million of black votes thrown even against it, and balanced by five million of other votes, I will acknowledge the Declaration of Independence is complied with,—that the PEOPLE south of Mason and Dixon's line have remodelled their government to suit themselves; and our function is only to recognize it.

Further than this, we should have the right to . . . remind them that no faction, in what has been recognized as one nation, can claim, by any law, the right of revolution to set up or to preserve a system which the common conscience of mankind stamps as wicked and infamous. . . . The right of revolution means the right of the people to protect themselves, not the privilege of tyrants to tread under foot good laws, and claim the world's sympathy in riveting weakened chains. . . .

I hear a good deal about Constitutional liberty. The mouths of Concord and Lexington guns have room only for one word, and that is LIBERTY. . . . The noise and dust of the conflict may hide the real question at issue. Europe may think, some of us may, that we are fighting for forms and parchments, for sovereignty and a flag. But really the war is one of opinions: it is Civilization against Barbarism: it is Freedom against Slavery. The cannonshot against Fort Sumter was the yell of pirates against the DECLARATION OF INDEPENDENCE; the war-cry of the North is the echo of that sublime pledge. The South, defying Christianity, clutches its victim. The North of-

fers its wealth and blood in glad atonement for the selfishness of seventy years. The result is as sure as the throne of God. . . .

DOCUMENT 15.4
The Responsibilities of an Electorate

Another reason why most Northerners lined up to fight was that the pretext of southern secession was Lincoln's election. When a group participates in an election, as the South had participated in the 1860 election, can it repudiate the results of the ballot box? As the Wheeling Daily Intelligencer *inquires in the following editorial, "The Test of Self-Government," can popular institutions endure if an elected majority lacks the natural right to govern?*

. . . What has happened has taken place under the forms of the Constitution. . . . Under that Constitution—under its several specifications—the people of every State in this Union of States went into an election. As a matter of course, all the parties to the canvass could not be successful. One candidate had to be chosen, either by the people or their representatives, and three candidates had to be beaten. This necessary result was just as apparent at the commencement as at the end of the canvass. The party that was successful, had the same candidate, the same platform, the same record, the same everything at the starting in that they had at the coming out. The other parties knew all this—saw it all just as plain and fully and satisfactorily at the first as at the last, and seeing and knowing and understanding it all, they entered the lists, and took their chances of success. They tried hard to succeed, made every possible combination, used every strategy of

Source: *Wheeling Daily Intelligencer*, December 24, 1860.

war, used money, used government patronage, used everything available, but to no effect.— They were beaten,—fairly, honorably, constitutionally, overwhelmingly beaten.—What is the sequel? They submit, of course? No; they do not. Two parties, for the most part, do. The third does not. It was not their intention to submit from the first. . . . They have repudiated.—They have raised a foreign flag—the flag of treason—and have shouted and hooted from their housetops and shipping the flag of their country, the glorious Stars and Stripes.

This is our position before the eyes of the English people and before the world. Seeing this position, is it wonderful that they distrust the issue of popular government? They can say with perfect legitimacy, your position has proved our conclusions. It makes no odds for the legitimacy of those conclusions, who of you is right or wrong. The fact that you each accepted the issue tendered by the other, and upon it went to the country, and a portion of you were beaten, and afterwards repudiated the popular voice constitutionally expressed, proves all we say. . . . It remains with you now to make the grand test, and show that your government is proof against the anarchical element. Failure now is demoralization forever. Will we be able to pass through the ordeal? Will we, in the face and against the hopes of anxious millions in the old world, turn the hands back on the dial plate of progress, and prove that popular institutions are impossible in practice? . . .

DOCUMENT 15.5
The Dangers of Anarchy

Still another reason most Northerners deplored secession was that the southern action could

Source: James Russell Lowell, *Political Essays* (Boston, 1892), pp. 45–48, 52–59, 66, 71–72, 84–85, 89–90.

contagiously destroy all legitimate authority. If the South could secede from the Union, couldn't any county or any city secede from any state? In the following essay, written in 1861, abolitionist and poet James Russell Lowell emphasizes that if pushed to extremes, the consent of the government might turn democracy into anarchy.

. . . If the public spirit of the whole country be awakened in time by the common peril, . . . we shall have learned what is meant by a government of laws, and that allegiance to the sober will of the majority, concentrated in established forms and distributed by legitimate channels, is all that renders democracy possible, is its only conservative principle, the only thing that has made and can keep us a powerful nation instead of a brawling mob. . . . Either we have no government at all, or else the very word implies the right, and therefore the duty, in the governing power, of protecting itself from destruction and its property from pillage. . . . The doctrine of the right of secession . . . is simply mob-law under a plausible name. . . . Rebellion smells no sweeter because it is called Secession, nor does Order lose its divine precedence in human affairs because a knave may nickname it Coercion. Secession means chaos, and Coercion the exercise of legitimate authority. . . .

Suppose, on the eve of a war with England, Michigan should vote herself out of the Union and declare herself annexed to Canada, what kind of a reception would her commissioners be likely to meet in Washington, and what scruples should we feel about coercion? . . . Is the only result of our admitting a Territory on Monday to be the giving it a right to steal itself and go out again on Tuesday? Or do only the original thirteen States possess this precious privilege of suicide? We shall need something like a Fugitive Slave Law for runaway republics! . . .

It is all very fine signing Declarations of Independence, . . . [but] the first and greatest benefit of government is that it keeps the peace, that it insures every man his rights. . . . In order to do this, its first requisite is stability. . . . The matter now in hand is the reëstablishment of order, the reaffirmation of national unity, and the settling once for all whether there can be such a thing as a government without the right to use its power in self-defence. . . . There can be no permanent settlement except in the definite establishment of the principle, that this Government, like all others, rests upon the everlasting foundations of just Authority,—that that authority, once delegated by the people, becomes a common stock of Power to be wielded for the common protection, and from which no minority or majority of partners can withdraw its contribution under any conditions. . . .

Instead of keeping closely to the real point, and the only point, at issue, namely, the claim of a minority to a right of rebellion when displeased with the result of an election, . . . the secret friends of the secession treason in the Free States have done their best to bewilder the public mind . . . by talking about the *right* of revolution, as if it were some acknowledged principle of the Law of Nations. There is a right and sometimes a duty of rebellion, as there is also a right and sometimes a duty of hanging men for it! . . . There is no question here of dynasties, races, religions, but simply whether we will consent to include in our Bill of Rights—not merely as of equal validity with all other rights, whether natural or acquired, but by its very nature transcending and abrogating them all—the Right of Anarchy. We must convince men that treason against the ballot-box is as dangerous as treason against a throne, and that, if they play so desperate a game, they must stake their lives on the hazard. . . .

DOCUMENT 15.6
The Immorality of Coercion

Some northern intellectuals did not find their qualms altogether assuaged by the above arguments. For example, James Freeman Clarke, a leading minister and abolitionist, remained unable to square the Declaration of Independence with the coercion of the South. At the end of his important pamphlet on the subject (in a brief statement omitted here), Clarke claimed that the southern rebellion might still legitimately be put down, because Southerners had exercised their right of revolution in a revolutionary rather than orderly way. This curious argument aside, Clarke's essay remains a superb example of how some Northern radicals agonized over the consent of the governed at the moment rebellion turned into war.

. . . To us it seems clear, that, according to the fundamental principles of our Government, the secessionists are right in their main principle. If a state considers itself oppressed in the Union, it has a right to leave the Union peaceably. This is only affirming the priniciples of self-government, which are asserted in the Declaration of Independence, and in almost every State Constitution. . . .

Acting on this principle, which is the foundation of all republics, that sovereign power resides in the people, and that they have a right to change, abolish, or renew their form of government at pleasure, we have seen this year several States in Europe vote themselves out of one union and into another. The people of Savoy and Nice have voted to secede from Sardinia, and join themselves to France. . . . We have also seen Parma, Modena, Tuscany, Naples and Sicily, and most of the provinces

Source: James Freeman Clarke, *Secession, Concession, or Self Possession: Which?* (Boston, 1861), pp. 13–14, 17–21.

of the Pontifical States, annex themselves by popular vote to the Kingdom of Sardinia. . . . Even the despotic governments of Europe acquiesce in the exercise of this right of secession. We also approve of it when it is exercised by an Italian State, Shall we deny the right only to the people of our own States? . . .

It is idle to hope to keep States in the Union against their will. . . . Suppose that, by using the whole military and naval power of the United States, we should conquer South Carolina. What should we do with it after it is conquered? How hold it as a conquered State? How guarantee to it republican institutions, when we are occupying it with a military force? Such questions show how impossible it is to attempt to prevent secession by exercising the force of the Government. . . .

DOCUMENT 15.7
Lincoln the Dictator

Once war began, the Lincoln administration's arbitrary arrests raised another critical theoretical problem. The issue was dramatized in 1863 by the military arrest of Clement L. Vallandigham, the leading Ohio Peace Democrat, who had allegedly encouraged troop desertions by attacking the legitimacy of the war. Although the Lincoln administration soon freed Vallandigham and permitted him to run for governor of Ohio, the question remained: Could a Civil War President arbitrarily jail individuals on grounds of military necessity?

On May 16, 1863, shortly after Vallandigham's arrest, a group of Democrats met in Albany, New York to protest against

Source: Resolutions adopted by a meeting in Albany, New York, May 16, 1863, reprinted in Frank Moore, ed., *The Rebellion Record: A Diary of American Events* (New York, 1864), vol. 7, pp. 298–99.

Lincoln's arbitrary arrests. Three days later, the meeting, chaired by Erastus Corning, sent the President the following resolutions.

Resolved, That the Democrats of New York point to their uniform course of action during the two years of civil war through which we have passed, to the alacrity which they have evinced in filling the ranks of the army, to their contributions and sacrifices, as the evidence of their patriotism and devotion to the cause of our imperilled country. . . .

Resolved, That as Democrats we are determined to maintain this patriotic attitude, and, despite of adverse and disheartening circumstances, to devote all our energies to sustain the cause of the Union. . . .

Resolved, That while we will not consent to be misapprehended upon these points, we are determined not to be misunderstood in regard to others not less essential. We demand that the Administration shall be true to the Constitution; shall recognize and maintain the rights of the States and the liberties of the citizen; shall everywhere, outside of the lines of necessary military occupation and the scenes of insurrection, exert all its powers to maintain the supremacy of the civil over military law. . . .

Resolved, That in view of these principles we denounce the recent assumption of a military commander to seize and try a citizen of Ohio, Clement L. Vallandigham. . . .

Resolved, That this assumption of power by a military tribunal, if successfully asserted, not only abrogates the right of the people to assemble and discuss the affairs of government, the liberty of speech and of the press, the right of trial by jury, the law of evidence, and the privilege of habeas corpus, but it strikes a fatal blow at the supremacy of law, and the authority of the State and federal constitutions. . . .

Resolved, That these safeguards of the rights of the citizen against the pretensions of arbitrary power were intended more especially for his protection in times of civil commotion. . . . They have stood the test of seventy-six years of trial, under our republican system, under circumstances which show that, while they constitute the foundation of all free government, they are the elements of the enduring stability of the republic. . . .

DOCUMENT 15.8
In Defense of Martial Law

Lincoln answered the Democrats with his Corning Letter of June 12, 1863. Lincoln's letter sweepingly defended a President's right to use military arrests whenever necessary to put down rebellion.

Gentlemen Your . . . resolutions assert and argue, that certain military arrests and proceedings following them for which I am ultimately responsible, are unconstitutional. I think they are not. . . .

Prior to my instalation here it had been inculcated that any State had a lawful right to secede from the national Union; and that it would be expedient to exercise the right, whenever the devotees of the doctrine should fail to elect a President to their own liking. I was elected contrary to their liking; and accordingly, . . . they had taken seven states out of the Union, had seized many of the United States Forts, and had fired upon the United States' Flag, all before I was inaugurated. . . . It undoubtedly was a well pondered reliance with them that in their own unrestricted effort to destroy Union, constitution, and law, all together, the government would, in great degree, be restrained by the same constitution, and law, from arresting their progress. Their sympathiz-

ers pervaded all departments of the government, and nearly all communities of the people. From this material, under cover of "Liberty of speech" "Liberty of the press" and *"Habeas corpus"* they hoped to keep on foot amongst us a most efficient corps of spies, informers, supplyers, and aiders and abettors of their cause in a thousand ways. . . .

Nothing is better known to history than that courts of justice are utterly incompetent to such cases. . . . Even in times of peace, bands of horsethieves and robbers frequently grow too numerous and powerful for the ordinary courts of justice. But what comparison, in numbers, have such bands ever borne to the insurgent sympathizers even in many of the loyal states? Again, a jury too frequently have at least one member, more ready to hang the panel than to hang the traitor. And yet again, he who dissuades one man from volunteering, or induces one soldier to desert, weakens the Union cause as much as he who kills a union soldier in battle. . . .

The provision of the constitution that "the privilege of the writ Habeas Corpus shall not be suspended, unless when in cases of Rebellion or Invasion, the public Safety may require it" . . . plainly attests the understanding of those who made the constitution that ordinary courts of justice are inadequate to "cases of Rebellion"—attests their purpose that in such cases, men may be held in custody whom the courts acting on ordinary rules, would discharge. . . . Indeed, arrests by process of courts, and arrests in cases of rebellion, do not proceed altogether upon the same basis. . . . In the latter case, arrests are made, not so much for what has been done, as for what probably would be done. The latter is more for the preventive, and less for the vindictive, than the former. In such cases the purposes of men are much more easily understood, than in cases of ordinary crime. The man who stands by and says nothing, when the peril of his government is discussed, can not be misunder-

Source: Roy P. Basler, ed., *The Collected Works of Abraham Lincoln* (New Brunswick, N. J.: Rutgers University Press, 1953), vol. 6, pp. 260–67.

stood. If not hindered, he is sure to help the enemy. Much more, if he talks ambiguously—talks for his country with "buts" and "ifs" and "ands." Of how little value the constitutional provision I have quoted will be rendered, if arrests shall never be made until defined crimes shall have been committed, may be illustrated by a few notable examples. Gen. John C. Breckinridge, Gen. Robert E. Lee, Gen. Joseph E. Johnston, Gen. John B. Magruder, Gen. William B. Preston, Gen. Simon B. Buckner, and Comodore [Franklin] Buchanan, now occupying the very highest places in the rebel war service, were all within the power of the government since the rebellion began, and were nearly as well known to be traitors then as now. Unquestionably if we had seized and held them, the insurgent cause would be much weaker. But no one of them had then committed any crime defined in the law. Every one of them if arrested would have been discharged on Habeas Corpus, were the writ allowed to operate. In view of these and similar cases, I think the time not unlikely to come when I shall be blamed for having made too few arrests rather than too many.

By the third resolution the meeting indicate their opinion that military arrests may be constitutional in localities where rebellion actually exists; but that such arrests are unconstitutional in localities where rebellion, or insurrection, does not actually exist. They insist that such arrests shall not be made "outside of the lines of necessary military occupation, and the scenes of insurrection" . . . I insist that in such cases, they are constitutional *wherever* the public safety does require them—as well in places to which they may prevent the rebellion extending, as in those where it may be already prevailing—as well where they may restrain mischievous interference with the raising and supplying of armies, to suppress the rebellion, as where the rebellion may actually be—as well where they may restrain the enticing men out of the army, as where they would

prevent mutiny in the army—equally constitutional at all places where they will conduce to the public Safety, as against the dangers of Rebellion or Invasion. . . .

Must I shoot a simple-minded soldier boy who deserts, while I must not touch a hair of a wiley agitator who induces him to desert? This is none the less injurious when effected by getting a father, or brother, or friend, into a public meeting, and there working upon his feelings, till he is persuaded to write the soldier boy, that he is fighting in a bad cause, for a wicked administration of contemptible government, too weak to arrest and punish him if he shall desert. I think that in such a case, to silence the agitator, and save the boy, is not only constitutional, but, withal, a great mercy.

If I be wrong on this question of constitutional power, my error lies in believing that certain proceedings are constitutional when, in cases of rebellion or Invasion, the public Safety requires them, which would not be constitutional when, in absence of rebellion or invasion, the public Safety does not require them. . . . I can no more be persuaded that the government can constitutionally take no strong measure in time of rebellion, because it can be shown that the same could not be lawfully taken in time of peace, than I can be persuaded that a particular drug is not good medicine for a sick man, because it can be shown to not be good food for a well one. Nor am I able to appreciate the danger, apprehended by the meeting, that the American people will, by means of military arrests during the rebellion, lose the right of public discussion, the liberty of speech and the press, the law of evidence, trial by jury, and Habeas corpus, throughout the indefinite peaceful future which I trust lies before them, and more than I am able to believe that a man could contract so strong an appetite for emetics during temporary illness, as to persist in feeding upon them through the remainder of his healthful life. . . .

DOCUMENT 15.9
The Right to Trial by Jury

*In 1864, another well-known Peace Democrat,
Lambdin P. Milligan, was convicted in military
court for allegedly sabotaging the war effort.
Milligan's conviction was appealed to the
U. S. Supreme Court. In December 1866,
Judge David Davis, speaking for the Court,
freed the prisoner. In the following opinion,
Davis denounced the Lincolnian dictum that
a Civil War President can impose whatever
martial law he deems necessary. The President
does indeed have constitutional authority to
delay trial by suspending the writ of habeas
corpus, Davis urged. Such suspension is
sufficient to maintain order in a noncombat
zone. But once the government brings a man
to trial, it cannot use military courts unless
armed invasion has closed civil courts in a
combat zone.*

*Lincoln would have answered that when
suspension of the writ of habeas corpus is not
sufficient, a President must not observe other
legal niceties while rebels tear up the
noncombat areas and destroy the Republic.
The question remains: Does Lincoln or Davis
get the best of this debate about civil rights
in a democracy?*

. . . The Constitution of the United States is
a law for rulers and people, equally in war
and in peace, and covers with the shield of
its protection all classes of men, at all times,
and under all circumstances. No doctrine, involving more pernicious consequences, was
ever invented by the wit of man than that any
of its provisions can be suspended during any
of the great exigencies of government. Such
a doctrine leads directly to anarchy or despotism. . . .

From what source did the military commis-

sion that tried Milligan derive their authority?
Certainly no part of the judicial power of the
country was conferred on them; because the
Constitution expressly vests it "in one supreme
court and such inferior courts as the Congress
may from time to time ordain and establish,"
and it is not pretended that the commission
was a court ordained and established by Congress. . . . Congress could grant no such
power; and to the honor of our national legislature be it said, it has never been provoked by
the state of the country even to attempt its
exercise. One of the plainest constitutional
provisions was, therefore, infringed when Milligan was tried by a court not ordained and
established by Congress, and not composed
of judges appointed during good behavior. . . .

If it was dangerous, in the distracted conditions of affairs, to leave Milligan unrestrained
of his liberty, because he "conspired against
the government, afforded aid and comfort to
rebels, and incited the people to insurrection,"
the *law* said arrest him, confine him closely,
render him powerless to do further mischief;
and then present his case to the grand jury of
the district, with proofs of his guilt, and, if
indicted, try him according to the course of
the common law. If this had been done, the
Constitution would have been vindicated, the
law of 1863 enforced, and the securities for
personal liberty preserved and defended. . . .

This nation, as experience has proved, cannot always remain at peace, and has no right
to expect that it will always have wise and
humane rulers, sincerely attached to the principles of the Constitution. Wicked men, ambitious of power, with hatred of liberty and contempt of law, may fill the place once occupied
by Washington and Lincoln; and if this right
is conceded, and the calamities of war again
befall us, the dangers to human liberty are
frightful to contemplate. If our fathers had
failed to provide for just such a contingency,
they would have been false to the trust reposed

Source: David Davis' majority opinion, in *4 Wallace
2*, 1866.

in them. . . . For this, and other equally weighty reasons, they secured the inheritance they had fought to maintain, by incorporating in a written constitution the safeguards which *time* had proved were essential to its preservation. Not one of these safeguards can the President, or Congress, or the Judiciary disturb, except the one concerning the writ of habeas corpus.

It is essential to the safety of every government that, in a great crisis, like the one we have just passed through, there should be a power somewhere of suspending the writ of habeas corpus. In every war, there are men of previously good character, wicked enough to counsel their fellow-citizens to resist the measures deemed necessary by a good government. . . . In the emergency of the times, an immediate public investigation according to law may not be possible; and yet, the peril to the country may be too imminent to suffer such persons to go at large. Unquestionably, there is then an exigency which demands that the government . . . shall not be required to produce the persons arrested in answer to a writ of habeas corpus. The Constitution goes no further. It does not say after a writ of habeas corpus is denied a citizen, that he shall be tried otherwise than by the course of the common law; if it had intended this result, it was easy by the use of direct words to have accomplished it. The illustrious men who framed that instrument . . . [knew] that a trial by an established court, assisted by an impartial jury, was the only sure way of protecting the citizen against oppression and wrong. Knowing this,

they limited the suspension to one great right, and left the rest to remain forever inviolable. . . .

This is not a question of the power to proclaim martial law, when war exists in a community and the courts and civil authorities are overthrown. . . . [Our point is that] martial law cannot arise from a *threatened* invasion. The necessity must be actual and present; the invasion real, such as effectually closes the courts and deposes the civil administration. . . .

There are occasions when martial rule can be properly applied. If, in foreign invasion or civil war, the courts are actually closed, and it is impossible to administer criminal justice according to law, *then*, on the theatre of active military operations, where war really prevails, there is a necessity to furnish a substitute for the civil authority, thus overthrown, to preserve the safety of the army and society; and as no power is left but the military, it is allowed to govern by martial rule until the laws can have their free course. As necessity creates the rule, so it limits its duration; for, if this government is continued *after* the courts are reinstated, it is a gross usurpation of power. Martial rule can never exist where the courts are open. . . . It is also confined to the locality of actual war. Because, during the late Rebellion it could have been enforced in Virginia, where the national authority was overturned and the courts driven out, it does not follow that it should obtain in Indiana, where that authority was never disputed, and justice was always administered. . . .

chapter 16

Reconstruction: The Nation's Unfinished Business

Henry F. Bedford
Albuquerque Academy

Reconstruction, Abraham Lincoln remarked, as he received the news of Appomattox, "is fraught with great difficulty." The President soberly emphasized the uncertain future, rather than the Union's triumph, for he did not expect military victory alone to restore sectional peace. He knew that the nation had no agreed terms for reunion to offer the defeated states, and no formula for new racial relationships to replace slavery.

Statesmen of the time discussed these issues in legal and constitutional terms. Were southern states entitled to constitutional rights as if they had never rebelled? Or were they, as Thaddeus Stevens claimed, "conquered provinces," subject to the unlimited power of Congress over federal territories? Was Reconstruction the President's prerogative, for his power to pardon was certainly relevant; or was it, instead, the responsibility of Congress, which must consent before the South would again be represented in the national legislature? Could Congress demand the ratification of a constitutional amendment as a condition for readmission? Could a state that was unqualified to participate in Congress legally ratify any amendment?

The Constitution held no final answers to these questions, as those who posed them knew.

The legalistic debate simply masked a basic disagreement over policy. Defenders of the South claimed the protection of continuous statehood in order to preserve what remained of the old way of life. Advocates of racial justice, by contrast, argued that the seceded states had abandoned the protection of the Constitution when they abandoned the Union.

Lincoln dismissed the prolonged argument about the legality of secession as "a merely pernicious abstraction." He believed Reconstruction could be accomplished "without deciding or even considering" whether the Confederacy had been outside the Union. Lincoln stressed agreement, not dispute: "We all agree that the seceded States, so called, are out of their proper practical relation with the Union; and that the sole object of the government . . . is to again get them into that proper practical relation."

Some Republicans thought the President's political conception of Reconstruction was too narrow. These critics, imprecisely called Radicals, did not at first agree on the severity of punishment the South must endure or on the measure of equality that Blacks must be conceded. Some Radicals—both in Washington and elsewhere—unquestionably used Reconstruction to serve their own careers and purses. Others meant to safeguard the civil rights of Blacks, their citizenship, and equality before the law. Still others advocated Negro suffrage, often on the condition that prospective voters satisfied a property qualification or passed a literacy test. And a few—very few—Radicals hoped that Reconstruction might ultimately result in real racial equality.

Thaddeus Stevens, the Pennsylvania congressman who was the sternest Radical of all, proposed to confiscate all southern land except individual holdings of less than 200 acres. He suggested that some of this land be granted to Negroes to assure their economic independence. The rest, Stevens said, should be sold to reduce the national debt, to establish a fund for Union soldiers or their widows and children, and to replace northern property destroyed during the war. For if the South paid no reparation, northern taxpayers would, in effect, subsidize the defeated enemy by bearing the war's indirect costs. That situation, Stevens charged, was absurd.

Tough, unyielding Thaddeus Stevens may have been right. Without economic security, Black freedom was not firmly based; peonage and slavery have much in common. Yet for all Stevens' egalitarian conviction, even his motives were probably mixed. His interest in compensating northern propertyholders for wartime losses surely derived in part from the fact that Confederate forces had destroyed his iron mines. And he admitted forthrightly his concern that emancipation might endanger Republican political supremacy and the program of economic nationalism the party had enacted. The fortuitous secession of the South had permitted passage of protective tariffs (which, like other ironmasters, Stevens believed were essential), the national banking system, the Homestead Act, and federal aid to transcontinental railroads. When Stevens and other Republicans protested that the Republic could not be entrusted to ''whitewashed rebels,'' they had this

program, as well as the freedmen, in mind.

They had reason for concern. The Thirteenth Amendment, as Stevens pointed out, abolished the former practice of counting a slave as three-fifths of a person; as a result, the South once readmitted would be entitled to more Congressmen than had represented the section before the war. More Congressmen meant more electoral votes, thus endangering Republican control of the White House, for Democrats could fuse their northern minority with the South to create a national majority. Besides endangering economic legislation already adopted, such a coalition might accept the notion that national bonds should be redeemed in the inflated greenbacks with which they had often been purchased—instead of in gold as the bond promised. Northern businessmen, whose opinions weighed heavily with Republican politicians, preferred fiscal orthodoxy. The North glimpsed the promise of industrial plenty; it seemed no time for economic experimentation.

The South was equally unready for social and political experimentation in the form of Radical Reconstruction, and perhaps Abraham Lincoln agreed. A deadlock between Congress and the President seemed possible when Lincoln pocket vetoed the Wade-Davis bill, the first Radical attempt to punish and reshape the South. Once a staunch Whig, Lincoln may have hoped to gain support for gradual change from the same coalition of moderates in both sections that had sustained his old party. Some Radicals so mistrusted the President that they welcomed Johnson's succession. For Andrew Johnson seemed to have nothing in common with those substantial Southerners whom Lincoln hoped might become the pillars of a southern Republican Party. But to the surprised dismay of the Radicals, the self-made man from Tennessee, who had never acted like a Southerner during the war, appeared ready to join the Confederacy after Appomattox.

For in 1865, Johnson used his power to pardon almost without limit. While Radicals fumed because Congress was in impotent recess, Johnson encouraged amnestied Southerners to establish new constitutions, hold elections, and complete Reconstruction before Congress resumed in December. He insisted that the South ratify the Thirteenth Amendment, repudiate the Confederate debt, and repeal ordinances of secession. White Southerners hastened to adopt Johnson's terms, which were surely among the most generous ever imposed on a defeated foe. Although the President withheld political rights from a few prominent former Confederates, voters all over the South chose many of the men who had led them out of the Union to lead them back in. Mississippi and South Carolina elected Confederate generals as governors; Georgia chose the Confederacy's vice president, Alexander Stephens, for the Senate of the United States. Southern whites demonstrably did not understand that defeat had changed the rules and that, for the moment, their elections had to satisfy a northern constituency as well as record the verdict of local voters.

Returns in 1865 heightened northern suspicion that a costly victory was given away cheaply. Negroes and others who had added equality to such war aims as abolition and union, denounced Johnson's program. For example, a group of Black Virginians pointed out that Johnson's plan permitted former Confederates, who were organizing and dominating the state government, to suppress both black and white supporters of the Union. The President had left them, these freedmen complained, "entirely at the mercy of . . . unconverted rebels," and they appealed for "an *equal chance* with the white *traitors*" whom the President had pardoned. Without the protection of the ballot and federal arms to enforce equal rights, the Blacks expected that their former masters would make freedom "more intolerable" than slavery.

Those whom Johnson pardoned did indeed try to preserve as much of the prewar social order as possible. Most white Southerners believed slavery was essential to the region's civilization; they still believed that legal freedom could never make their former slaves the equal of any white man. So the black codes that southern legislatures adopted to replace slave codes fell well short of racial equality.

The black codes allowed freedmen to form families. They permitted one black to marry another and made black parents legally responsible for their children. Most statutes also defined the legal rights of freedmen, and they often made blacks the legal equals of whites in the courtroom, although in some states blacks could not testify against whites.

Equality ceased with these provisions. Apprenticeship regulations bounded the economic and social freedom of young blacks; courts ordered the apprenticeship of unemployed young freedmen and gave preference to their former masters, an arrangement that often differed little from slavery. Vagrancy regulations and laws forbidding disorderly conduct gave enforcement officers wide discretion and similarly restricted the social and economic life of Black adults. Any Mississippi Negro who could not pay the poll tax or who lacked regular employment was guilty of vagrancy. Those convicted could be leased to employers who would pay fines and costs; former masters again had preference, and again the result might be only technically distinguishable from bondage. Even if a freedman avoided these statutes, other laws kept him out of the white community. For instance, the only black passengers permitted in first-class railroad cars in Mississippi were maids, who were allowed to wait on their white mistresses.

But the South's version of Reconstruction was incomplete without the approval of Congress, where reaction to the black codes was prompt and hostile. Even Republican moderates were unconvinced that the governments Johnson had approved represented loyal, reformed, and contrite Southerners. Radicals denounced Johnson's work as a sham and urged Congress to undertake genuine Reconstruction.

Rebels had proudly reestablished " 'the white man's Government,' " Thaddeus Stevens reported, and Congress ought to prove resolutely that such governments were entirely unacceptable components of the federal Republic. Demagogues, including "some high in authority," he continued with a barbed reference to the President, had appealed to the "lowest prejudices of the ignorant" to maintain the dominance of southern whites. Stevens held that the white race had "no exclusive right forever to rule this nation," nor did he shrink from the conclusion: This nation, he said, must not be " 'the white man's Government,' " but rather "the Government of all men alike. . . ."

Stevens was still ahead of his party. Most northern states did not yet permit blacks to vote, and most Republicans were not yet ready to demand equal political rights for the freedmen. But northern Republicans did insist on more change than Johnson had secured. Congress sent the southern legislators home in December 1865 and established congressional terms for reunion in two bills and a proposed constitutional amendment. The President vetoed both bills and joined those who opposed the amendment. His intransigence blighted any hope for a compromise program. For moderate Republicans, forced to choose between Stevens' radicalism and the unreconstructed governments Johnson had endorsed, chose radicalism. Andrew Johnson's political ineptitude and the adamant refusal of white Southerners to concede blacks more than technical emancipation drove the Republican Party to Thaddeus Stevens and military reconstruction.

Moderates began with a bill to prolong the life of the Freedmen's Bureau and to give it a quasi-judicial authority over disputes arising from discrimination or denial of civil rights. The bill deprived state courts of jurisdiction in such cases and specifically contradicted southern black codes by making punishable the discrimination that they permitted. Though the bill's sponsors thought they had secured

the President's approval, Johnson vetoed the measure. The bureau, he held, had grown out of the war's emergency and was based on the constitutional grant of power for war, which Congress could not legitimately invoke in peace. Once ordinary institutions, including civil courts, were reestablished, the bureau should disband.

Congress could not immediately override Johnson's veto, and moderates again tried to resolve the impasse with the Civil Rights bill of 1866. This measure specifically made blacks American citizens, thus overturning the *Dred Scott* decision, and guaranteed "the full and equal benefit of all laws . . . for the security of person or property" to all citizens. Federal courts had jurisdiction in cases where citizens were deprived of equal rights. The bill received the support of every House Republican and all but three Republican senators. And Andrew Johnson vetoed it because it infringed on the reserved powers of the states.

Congress overrode that veto, and, for good measure, salvaged the Freedmen's Bureau bill, which also passed over Johnson's veto. To preserve its handiwork, Congress then framed what became the fourteenth amendment. Johnson could not prevent the submission of the amendment to the states, but his hostility encouraged southern states to block ratification temporarily. Tennessee, the President's own state, ratified the amendment and was rewarded by full restoration to the Union. Other Southerners rejected the amendment and waited.

They waited too long, for the price of readmission went up. Andrew Johnson took his cause to the country in the congressional election of 1866. His performance on the stump struck the public as undignified, and his tour was as inept as his performance in the White House. Voters sent to Washington a new Congress with enough Radical votes to overwhelm the President.

Radicals lost no time. Congress took the initiative on Reconstruction and asserted its control over the rest of the government as well.

The presidential authority to command the army was abridged by a requirement that all orders be issued through the Army Chief of Staff, Ulysses S. Grant, who could not be removed or reassigned without the Senate's consent. The Tenure of Office Act required the Senate's approval for removal of any official for whom senatorial confirmation was necessary; Radicals hoped thereby to protect members of Johnson's Cabinet, particularly Secretary of War Edwin Stanton, who opposed the President's program. Control of the Army was crucial to the Radicals because they expected to develop a plan of military reconstruction. Congress took steps to eliminate involuntary congressional recesses and limited the power of the Supreme Court to decide cases that might invalidate congressional programs.

Andrew Johnson was not intimidated. He vetoed the Reconstruction Act and those supplemental measures Congress later added to make the program comprehensive. Since Congress promptly overrode them, his vetoes were futile. By these acts, Congress combined ten states into five military districts and subordinated state governments to military commanders. The governments and constitutions Johnson had approved in 1865 were discarded, and new constitutions granting Negro suffrage and guaranteeing racial equality were required. This legislation unquestionably mocked the traditional rights of states, as both Johnson and the South claimed. Radicals, however, had minimal interest in the constitutional pretenses of the defeated section and counted the doctrine of states' rights an unmourned casualty of the Civil War.

They set out to make the Presidency an unmourned casualty of Reconstruction. Although the resolution of the House impeached Andrew Johnson, the target at which many Radicals aimed was the office itself. The charge against Johnson specified eleven offenses, most of which arose from the President's attempt to remove Stanton from the Cabinet. But, Thad-deus Stevens confessed, he, for one, did not impeach the President for any particular offense, or even for all of them together. Stevens wanted to remove Johnson for his political mistakes, not for his moral or legal lapses. Impeachment, Stevens believed, was simply the only available method of ridding the nation of the President's wretched judgment.

The House debated all of Andrew Johnson's alleged crimes: his partiality toward the South, his public disrespect of Congress and its leadership, his undignified inauguration as Vice President, his baselessly rumored complicity in Lincoln's assassination, and his deliberate violations of the Tenure of Office Act. The President was acquitted partly because the Senate found the bill of particulars too flimsy a basis for so unprecedented a step. He was also acquitted because a few senators chose to support the independence of the executive branch rather than establish a precedent that might lead to a ministry responsible to the legislature, as is a parliamentary cabinet. The margin of the Senate was slim; Johnson survived by one vote. Thirty-five Republicans voted to convict; twelve Democrats and seven Republicans found for the President. With the roll calls in the Senate, Washington ceased to be the main forum for debate over Reconstruction. The President was isolated; Congress had done its part. At last, Reconstruction was to occur in the South.

Americans since the 1870s have harshly judged the process. Black Reconstruction was an undignified, corrupt, expensive, and regrettable social experiment from which enlightened white conservatives freed the South in 1877. The freedmen, their often venal northern allies the carpetbaggers, and a few unprincipled southern white scalawags looted southern treasuries, discredited themselves, and demonstrated the political incapacity of the black population. Return to white control, according to this view, preserved the section from bankruptcy and barbarism.

The belief, like most stereotypes, had a factual basis. Reconstruction did bring unprecedented taxes to the southern states; not all the money was honestly spent. Negroes did not universally resist financial temptation, nor were they always dignified and wise in their legislative deliberations. Illustrative statistics abound. Florida spent more for printing in 1869 than the entire state government had cost in 1860. Sometimes, bookkeeping was so casual that even a state legislature could not calculate the state debt. According to one estimate, the South Carolina debt tripled in three years, while another figure indicated that it had increased nearly six times. South Carolina also maintained at public expense a luxurious restaurant and bar that impartially dispensed imported delicacies to legislators of both races.

But the term Black Reconstruction is misleading, and the usual view of the process that the phrase describes is inaccurate. Only in South Carolina did blacks ever control the legislature—and only in one house at that. They held high office elsewhere in the South—Mississippi sent two blacks to the Senate of the United States—but they were by no means so dominant as the term Black Reconstruction implied. White politicians, to be sure, had to have black support to succeed, but the simplistic picture of black rule is incorrect.

Nor is the image of corrupt extravagance entirely justified. Rebuilding after a war is always expensive, and taxpayers always resent the bill. Further, Reconstruction governments not only had to restore public buildings and services; they also had to furnish new facilities and services that had been inadequate in most of the South. In many southern states, for example, public education for either race dates from these legislatures. Often, for the first time, states also accepted limited responsibility for the welfare of the indigent and the sick.

The notorious corruption of Reconstruction frequently came from ambitious schemes to bring new life to the southern economy and to break the region's dependence on agriculture by introducing railroads and industry. Only the state commanded enough credit to entice the railroads that seemed to be the indispensable foundation of prosperity. Southern states issued bonds to finance railroad construction, but the proceeds sometimes vanished before the track was laid. Fraud in the development of the American rail network, however, was not peculiar to the South; as had happened elsewhere, public funds were converted to private use, and politicians pocketed fees that might more candidly have been called bribes. Nor were corrupted legislatures confined to the South in the post-Civil War era. The peculation of southern legislators was trifling by comparison with the simultaneous scandals of the Grant administration.

And not all corrupt southerners were black. Some blacks were bribed and some misused public funds, though no individual stole so much as the white treasurer of Mississippi embezzled immediately after the state was supposedly saved from irresponsible blacks. And for every purchased politician, there must have been a buyer. The fast-buck promoters of railroads and industry were whites, not blacks, few of whom were enriched by the plunder they were said to have secured from public treasuries.

Few blacks, indeed, were able to find even a legitimate source of wealth. Their lack of property reinforced provisions in the black codes that limited mobility. Any freedman who could not prove steady employment had to have a license authorizing some other arrangement. The contract that proved employment often specified annual wage payments, a practice that forced employees into debt for what was consumed while earning the first year's wage. And if a black left his employer before the contract expired, he forfeited wages earned earlier in the year.

Wages were ordinarily paid with a portion of the crop, for the war-shattered southern economy lacked local capital to renew agricultural production. Forced to rebuild their farms on credit, impoverished landowners hired impoverished farmers to work the land, and both looked to a big harvest to pay bills and interest already charged at the local store. If a profit resulted, it was probably too small to carry either owner or laborer through the subsequent season, and so the cycle continued.

When the laborer was black, as he often was, contract and credit effectively replaced the restrictions of slavery. For without economic independence, blacks lacked the means to sustain constitutional equality. Usually, a threat to turn him off the land or stop his credit at the store was enough to make a sharecropper docile. Often, an unfulfilled contract or an unpaid debt legally required him to remain on a plot of land that had already proved unprofitable. When he resisted economic leverage and legal restraint, the Ku Klux Klan and its imitators perfected direct and brutal means of reminding him of his inferiority. So credit, statute, and terror evolved as new ways to return the freed black as nearly as possible to his old bondage. Constitutional amendments were unenforced in some areas, even before federal troops retired. As blacks were intimidated, whites passed laws to keep their former slaves from the polls and from the company of their former masters. Formal segregation and constitutional disfranchisement were natural sequels in another generation.

Black Reconstruction depended on a benevolent national administration that would keep troops in the South until whites could be won to toleration or blacks could secure their own equality. Bayonets are perhaps an unlikely method of securing equality; in any case, the northern voter and, hence, the national government, tired of the task too soon. The use of military means for democratic ends is only one of the ambiguities that plague those who would understand and evaluate Reconstruction, for the period is replete with dilemmas of ends

and means. White Southerners wanted to preserve what they could of their customary way of life: in the process, some were deceitful; some were cruel; most were unyielding on the central issue of white supremacy. Blacks wanted to become free Americans, and in the attempt, some were foolish and some were corrupt, but most were humbly patient. Radicals wanted to reconstruct the South: most of them expected to assure continued Republican hegemony; some expected to get rich; others intended to secure racial justice.

The tragedy of Reconstruction is that so little was permanently accomplished. White Southerners took refuge in a sentimentalized past. Blacks displayed more patience and more humility and in the end were the principal victims of the tragedy. Radicals died, and their party found laissez faire a more congenial ideology than racial equality.

SUGGESTED READINGS

Benedict, Michael L. *A Compromise of Principle.* New York: W. W. Norton, 1975.

———. *The Impeachment and Trial of Andrew Johnson.* New York: W. W. Norton, 1973.

Berlin, Ira, et al. *Freedom: A Documentary History of Emancipation.* Cambridge: Cambridge University Press, 1985.

Brodie, Fawn M. *Thaddeus Stevens: Scourge of the South.* New York: W. W. Norton, 1959.

Carter, Dan T. *When the War Was Over.* Baton Rouge: Louisiana State University Press, 1985.

Donald, David. *Charles Sumner and the Rights of Man.* New York: Alfred A. Knopf, 1970.

———. *The Politics of Reconstruction, 1863–1867.* Baton Rouge: Louisiana State University Press, 1965.

DuBois, W. E. Burghardt. *Black Reconstruction.* New York: Russell & Russell, 1935.

Fleming, Walter L., ed., *Documentary History of Reconstruction.* Gloucester, Mass.: Peter Smith, 1960.

Franklin, John Hope. *Reconstruction.* Chicago: University of Chicago Press, 1962.

Gutman, Herbert G. *The Black Family in Slavery and Freedom.* New York: Pantheon, 1976.

Hyman, Harold M. *A More Perfect Union.* New York: Alfred A. Knopf, 1973.

Litwack, Leon F. *Been in the Storm So Long.* New York: Alfred A. Knopf, 1979.

McKitrick, Eric. *Andrew Johnson and Reconstruction.* Chicago: University of Chicago Press, 1960.

McPherson, James M. *The Struggle for Equality.* Princeton: Princeton University Press, 1964.

Painter, Nell I. *The Exodusters.* Lawrence, Kansas: University Press of Kansas, 1977.

Richardson, Joe M. *Christian Reconstruction.* Athens: University of Georgia Press, 1986.

Rose, Willie Lee. *Rehearsal for Reconstruction.* Indianapolis: Bobbs-Merrill, 1964.

Stampp, Kenneth M. *The Era of Reconstruction, 1865–1877.* New York: Alfred A. Knopf, 1965.

Williamson, Joel. *After Slavery: The Negro in South Carolina during Reconstruction.* Chapel Hill: University of North Carolina Press, 1965.

Woodward, C. Vann. *Reunion and Reaction.* Boston: Little, Brown, 1951.

DOCUMENT 16.1
The Constitutional Basis for Reconstruction

THE AMENDMENTS

The Thirteenth [proposed 1 Feb. 1865; declared ratified 18 Dec. 1865]:

Section 1. Neither slavery nor involuntary servitude, except as a punishment for crime whereof the party shall have been duly convicted, shall exist within the United States, or any place subject to their jurisdiction.

The Fourteenth (proposed 16 June 1866; declared ratified 28 July 1868]:

Section 1. All persons born or naturalized in the United States, and subject to the jurisdiction thereof, are citizens of the United States and of the State wherein they reside. No State shall make or enforce any law which shall abridge the privileges or immunities of citizens of the United States; nor shall any State deprive any person of life, liberty, or property, without due process of law; nor deny to any person within its jurisdiction the equal protection of the laws.

Section 2. Representatives shall be apportioned among the several States according to their respective numbers, counting the whole number of persons in each State, excluding Indians not taxed. But when the right to vote at any election for the choice of electors for President and Vice President of the United States, Representatives in Congress, the Executive and Judicial officers of a State, or the members of the Legislature thereof, is denied to any of the male inhabitants of such State, being twenty-one years of age, and citizens of the United States, or in any way abridged, except for participation in rebellion, or other crime, the basis of representation therein shall be reduced in the proportion which the number of such male citizens shall bear to the whole number of male citizens twenty-one years of age in such States.

Section 3. No person shall be a Senator or Representative in Congress, or elector of President and Vice President, or hold any office, civil or military, under the United States, or under any State, who, having previously taken an oath, as a member of Congress, or as an officer of the United States, or as a member of any State legislature, or as an executive or judicial officer of any State, to support the Constitution of the United States, shall have engaged in insurrection or rebellion against the same, or given aid and comfort to the enemies thereof. But Congress may by a vote of two-thirds of each House, remove such disability.

Section 4. The validity of the public debt of the United States authorized by law, including debts incurred for payment of pensions and bounties for services in suppressing insurrection or rebellion, shall not be questioned. But neither the United States nor any state shall assume or pay any debt or obligation incurred in aid of insurrection or rebellion against the United States, or any claim for the loss or emancipation of any slave; but all such debts, obligations, and claims shall be held illegal and void.

Section 5. The Congress shall have power to enforce, by appropriate legislation, the provisions of this article.

The Fifteenth [proposed 27 Feb. 1869; declared ratified 30 Mar. 1870]:

Section 1. The right of citizens of the United States to vote shall not be denied or abridged by the United States or by any State on account of race, color, or previous condition of servitude.

Section 2. The Congress shall have power to enforce this article by appropriate legislation.

DOCUMENT 16.2
Black Codes

After Appomattox, the southern states conceded military defeat and acknowledged legal emancipation. But the black codes that were enacted throughout much of the Confederacy in the year following Lee's surrender derived from the statutes and customs of slavery—as the police regulations of a Louisiana parish demonstrate.

Whereas it was formerly made the duty of the police jury to make suitable regulations for the police of slaves within the limits of the parish; and whereas slaves have become emancipated by the action of the ruling powers; and whereas it is necessary for public order, as well as for the comfort and correct deportment of said freedmen, that suitable regulations should be established for their government in their changed condition, the following ordi-

Source: W. L. Fleming, ed., *Documentary History of Reconstruction* (Cleveland: Arthur H. Clark, 1906), vol. 1, pp. 279–81.

nances are adopted with the approval of the United States military authorities commanding in said parish, viz:

Sec. 1. *Be it ordained by the police jury of the parish of St. Landry,* That no negro shall be allowed to pass within the limits of said parish without special permit in writing from his employer. Whoever shall violate this provision shall pay a fine of two dollars and fifty cents, or in default thereof shall be forced to work four days on the public road, or suffer corporeal punishment as provided hereinafter.

Sec. 2. . . . Every negro who shall be found absent from the residence of his employer after ten o'clock at night, without a written permit from his employer, shall pay a fine of five dollars, or in default thereof, shall be compelled to work five days on the public road, or suffer corporeal punishment as hereinafter provided.

Sec. 3. . . . No negro shall be permitted to rent or keep a house within said parish. Any negro violating this provision shall be immediately ejected and compelled to find an employer; and any person who shall rent, or give the use of any house to any negro, in violation of this section, shall pay a fine of five dollars for each offence.

Sec. 4. . . . Every negro is required to be in the regular service of some white person, or former owner, who shall be held responsible for the conduct of said negro. But said employer or former owner may permit said negro to hire his own time by special permission in writing, which permission shall not extend over seven days at any one time. . . .

Sec. 5. . . . No public meetings or congregations of negroes shall be allowed within said parish after sunset, but such public meetings and congregations may be held between the hours of sunrise and sunset, by the special permission in writing of the captain of patrol, within whose beat such meetings shall take place. This prohibition, however, is not to prevent negroes from attending the usual church services, conducted by white ministers and priests. . . .

Sec. 6. . . . No negro shall be permitted to preach, exhort, or otherwise declaim to congregations of colored people, without a special permission in writing from the president of the police jury. . . .

Sec. 7. . . . No negro who is not in the military service shall be allowed to carry firearms, or any kind of weapons, within the parish, without the special written permission of his employers, approved and indorsed by the nearest and most convenient chief of patrol. Any one violating the provisions of this section shall forfeit his weapons and pay a fine of five dollars, or in default of the payment of said fine, shall be forced to work five days on the public road, or suffer corporeal punishment as hereinafter provided.

Sec. 8. . . . No negro shall sell, barter, or exchange any articles of merchandise or traffic within said parish without the special written permission of his employer, specifying the article of sale, barter or traffic. . . .

Sec. 9. . . . Any negro found drunk, within the said parish shall pay a fine of five dollars, or in default thereof work five days on the public road, or suffer corporeal punishment as hereinafter provided. . . .

Sec. 14. . . . The corporeal punishment provided for in the foregoing sections shall consist in confining the body of the offender within a barrel placed over his or her shoulders, in the manner practiced in the army, such confinement not to continue longer than twelve hours, and for such time within the aforesaid limit as shall be fixed by the captain or chief of patrol who inflicts the penalty.

DOCUMENT 16.3
The Vision of One Radical

Whatever his motives, and regardless of Presidents and lesser obstacles, Thaddeus Stevens meant to punish the South for its war and to force white society to begin immediate restitution for the ancient wrong of bondage.

THE SOUTH MUST BE PUNISHED (1865)[1]

Unless the rebel States, before admission, should be made republican in spirit, and placed under the guardianship of loyal men, all our blood and treasure will have been spent in vain. I waive now the question of punishment which, if we are wise, will still be inflicted by moderate confiscations. . . . Impartial suffrage, both in electing the delegates and ratifying their proceedings, is now the fixed rule. There is more reason why colored voters should be admitted in the rebel States than in the Territories. In the States they form the great mass of the loyal men. Possibly with their aid loyal governments may be established in most of those States. Without it all are sure to be ruled by traitors; and loyal men, black and white, will be oppressed, exiled, or murdered. There are several good reasons for the passage of this bill. In the first place, it is just. I am now confining my argument to negro suffrage in the rebel States. Have not loyal blacks quite as good a right to choose rulers and make laws as rebel whites? In the second place, it is a necessity in order to protect the loyal white men in the seceded States. The white Union men are in a great minority in each of those States. With them the blacks would act in a body; and it is believed that in each of said States, except one, the two united would form a majority, control the States, and protect themselves. Now they are the victims of daily murder. . . .

Another good reason is, it would insure the ascendency of the Union party. . . . I believe . . . that on the continued ascendency of that party depends the safety of this great nation. If impartial suffrage is excluded in the rebel States, then every one of them is sure to send a solid rebel representative delegation to Congress, and cast a solid rebel electoral vote.

---

[1] Source: *Congressional Globe,* January 3, 1867, p. 252.

They, with their kindred Copperheads of the North, would always elect the President and control Congress. While slavery sat upon her defiant throne, and insulted and intimidated the trembling North, the South frequently divided on questions of policy between Whigs and Democrats, and gave victory alternately to the sections. Now, you must divide them between loyalists, without regard to color, and disloyalists, or you will be the perpetual vassals of the free-trade, irritated, revengeful South. . . . I am for negro suffrage in every rebel State. If it be just, it should not be denied; if it be necessary, it should be adopted; if it be a punishment to traitors, they deserve it.

THE SOUTH MUST PAY (1867)

Whereas it is due to justice, as an example to future times, that some proper punishment should be inflicted on the people who constituted the "confederate States of America," both because they, declaring an unjust war against the United States for the purpose of destroying republican liberty and permanently establishing slavery, as well as for the cruel and barbarous manner in which they conducted said war, in violation of all the laws of civilized warfare, and also to compel them to make some compensation for the damages and expenditures caused by said war: Therefore,

Be it enacted . . . That all the public lands belonging to the ten States that formed the government of the so-called "confederate States of America" shall be forfeited by said States and become forthwith vested in the United States.

Sec. 2. . . . The President shall forthwith proceed to cause the seizure of such of the property belonging to the belligerent enemy as is deemed forfeited by the act of July 17, A. D. 1862, and hold and appropriate the same as enemy's property, and to proceed to condemnation with that already seized. . . .

Sec. 4. . . . Out of the lands thus seized and confiscated the slaves who have been liberated by the operations of the war and the amendment to the Constitution or otherwise, who resided in said "confederate States" on the 4th day of March, A. D. 1861, or since, shall have distributed to them as follows, namely: to each male person who is the head of a family, forty acres; to each adult male, whether the head of a family or not, forty acres; to each widow who is the head of a family, forty acres—to be held by them in fee simple, but to be inalienable for the next ten years after they become seized thereof. . . . At the end of ten years the absolute title to said homesteads shall be conveyed to said owners or to the heirs of such as are then dead.

Sec. 5. . . . Out of the balance of the property thus seized and confiscated there shall be raised, in the manner hereinafter provided, a sum equal to fifty dollars, for each homestead, to be applied by the trustees hereinafter mentioned toward the erection of buildings on the said homesteads for the use of said slaves; and the further sum of $500,000,000, which shall be appropriated as follows, to-wit: $200,-000,000 shall be invested in United States six per cent, securities; and the interest thereof shall be semi-annually added to the pensions allowed by law to the pensioners who have become so by reason of the late war; $300,-000,000, or so much thereof as may be needed, shall be appropriated to pay damages done to loyal citizens by the civil or military operations of the government lately called the "confederate States of America."

Sec. 6. . . . In order that just discrimination may be made, the property of no one shall be seized whose whole estate on the 4th day of March, A. D. 1865, was not worth more than $5,000, to be valued by the said commission, unless he shall have voluntarily become an officer or employee in the military or civil service of "the Confederate States of America," or in the civil or military service of some one of said States, and in enforcing all confiscations the sum or value of $5,000 in real or personal property shall be left or assigned to the delinquent. . . .

DOCUMENT 16.4
Terror

The Ku Klux Klan and its imitators intimidated blacks to keep them from demanding the rights allowed by law. The narrative below is that of Elias Hill, a crippled black preacher from South Carolina.

On the night of the 5th of last May, after I had heard a great deal of what they had done in that neighborhood, they came. It was between 12 and 1 o'clock at night when I was awakened and heard the dogs barking, and something walking, very much like horses. As I had often laid awake listening for such persons, for they had been all through the neighborhood, and disturbed all men and many women, I supposed that it was them. They came in a very rapid manner, and I could hardly tell whether it was the sound of horses or men. At last they came to my brother's door, which is in the same yard, and broke open the door and attacked his wife, and I heard her screaming and mourning. I could not understand what they said, for they were talking in an outlandish and unnatural tone, which I had heard they generally used at a negro's house. I heard them knocking around in her house. I was lying in my little cabin in the yard. At last I heard them have her in the yard. She was crying, and the Ku-Klux were whipping her to make her tell where I lived. I heard her say, "Yon is his house." She has told me since that they first asked who had taken me out of her house. They said, "Where's Elias?" She said, "He doesn't stay here; yon is his house." They

Source: *Report of the Joint Select Committee to Inquire into the Condition of Affairs in the Late Insurrectionary States* (Washington, D. C., 1872), vol. 1, pp. 44–46.

were then in the yard, and I had heard them strike her five or six licks when I heard her say this. Some one then hit my door. It flew open. One ran in the house, and stopping about the middle of the house, which is a small cabin, he turned around, as it seemed to me as I lay there awake, and said, "Who's here?" Then I knew they would take me, and I answered, "I am here." He shouted for joy, as it seemed, "Here he is! Here he is! We have found him!" and he threw the bed-clothes off of me and caught me by one arm, while another man took me by the other and they carried me into the yard between the houses, my brother's and mine, and put me on the ground beside a boy. The first thing they asked me was, "Who did that burning? Who burned our houses?"—ginhouses, dwelling-houses and such. Some had been burned in the neighborhood. I told them it was not me; I could not burn houses; it was unreasonable to ask me. Then they hit me with their fists, and said I did it, I ordered it. They went on asking me didn't I tell the black men to ravish all the white women. No, I answered them. They struck me again with their fists on my breast. . . . Two of them went into the house. My sister says that as quick as they went into the house they struck the clock at the foot of the bed. I heard it shatter. One of the four around me called out, "Don't break any private property, gentlemen, if you please; we have got him we came for, and that's all we want." I did not hear them break anything else. They staid in there a good while hunting about and then came out and asked me for a lamp. I told them there was a lamp somewhere. They said "Where?" I was so confused I said I could not tell exactly. They caught my leg— you see what it is—and pulled me over the yard, and then left me there knowing I could not walk nor crawl, and all six went into the house. I was chilled with the cold lying in the yard at that time of night, for it was near 1 o'clock, and they had talked and beat me and so on until half an hour had passed since they first approached. After they had staid in the house for a considerable time, they came back to where I lay and asked if I wasn't afraid at all. They pointed pistols at me all around my head once or twice, as if they were going to shoot me, telling me they were going to kill me; wasn't I ready to die, and willing to die? Didn't I preach? That they came to kill me—all the time pointing pistols at me. This second time they came out of the house, after plundering the house, searching for letters, they came at me with these pistols, and asked if I was ready to die. I told them that I was not exactly ready; that I would rather live; that I hoped they would not kill me that time. They said they would; I had better prepare. One caught me by the leg and hurt me, for my leg for forty years has been drawn each year, more and more year by year, and I made moan when it hurt so. One said "G—d d—n it, hush!" He had a horsewhip, and he told me to pull up my shirt, and he hit me. He told me at every lick, "Hold up your shirt." I made a moan every time he cut with the horsewhip. I reckon he struck me eight cuts right on the hip bone; it was almost the only place he could hit my body, my legs are so short—all my limbs drawn up and withered away with pain. I saw one of them standing over me or by me motion to them to quit. They all had disguises on. I then thought they would not kill me. One of them then took a strap, and buckled it around my neck and said, "Let's take him to the river and drown him." "What course is the river?" they asked me. I told them east. Then one of them went feeling about, as if he was looking for something, and said, "I don't see no east! Where is the d—d thing?" as if he did not understand what I meant. After pulling the strap around my neck, he took it off and gave me a lick on my hip where he had struck me with the horsewhip. . . . He said I would now have to die. I was somewhat afraid, but one said not to kill me. They said, "Look here! Will you put a card in the paper next week like June Moore and Sol Hill?" They had been prevailed on to put a card in the paper to renounce all republicanism and never vote. I said, "If I had the money to pay the expense, I could." They said I could borrow, and gave me another lick. They asked me, "Will you quit preaching?" I told them I did not know. I said that to save my life. They said I must stop that republican paper that was coming to Clay Hill. It has been only a few weeks since it stopped. The republican weekly paper was then coming to me from Charleston. It came to my name. They said I must stop it, quit preaching, and put a card in the newspaper renouncing republicanism, and they would not kill me; but if I did not they would come back the next week and kill me. With that one of them went into the house where my brother and my sister-in-law lived, and brought her to pick me up. As she stooped down to pick me up one of them struck her, and as she was carrying me into the house another struck her with a strap. She carried me into the house and laid me on the bed. Then they gathered around and told me to pray for them. I tried to pray. They said, "Don't you pray against Ku-Klux, but pray that God may forgive Ku-Klux. Don't pray against us. Pray that God may bless and save us." I was so chilled with cold lying out of doors so long and in such pain I could not speak to pray, but I tried to, and they said that would do very well, and all went out of the house. . . .

DOCUMENT 16.5
The Return of White Supremacy

Even before federal troops left the region, southern whites began to substitute political organization for overt terror in their attempt

Source: W. L. Fleming, ed., *Documentary History of Reconstruction* (Cleveland: Arthur H. Clark, 1906), vol. 2, pp. 387–88; 394–95.

to end Reconstruction. The excerpts from newspapers below come from Mississippi and Georgia; the political resolutions were adopted by most county Democratic organizations in Alabama. Together the readings reflect the region's determination to maintain white supremacy.

A MISSISSIPPI EDITORIAL (1875)

The republican journals of the North made a great mistake in regarding the present campaign in Mississippi in the light of a political contest. It is something more earnest and holy than that—it is, so far as the white people and land-owners are concerned, a battle for the control of their own domestic affairs; a struggle to regain a mastery that has been ruthlessly torn from them by selfish white schemers and adventurers, through the instrumentality of an ignorant horde of another race which has been as putty in their hands, molded to our detriment and ruin.

The present contest is rather a revolution than a political campaign—it is the rebellion, if you see fit to apply that term, of a downtrodden people against an absolutism imposed by their own hirelings, and by the grace of God we will cast it off next November, or cast off the willfully and maliciously ignorant tools who eat our bread, live in our houses, attend the schools that we support, come to us for aid and succor in their hour of need, and yet are deaf to our appeals when we entreat them to assist us in throwing off a galling yoke that has been borne until further endurance is but the basest of cowardice. . . .

We favor a continuance of the canvass upon the broad and liberal basis that has heretofore characterized it, that is, we favor appealing to the negro by everything good and holy to forsake his idols and unite with us in ridding the State of a way that we despise; but at the same time that we extend the olive-branch and plead for alliance and amity, we should not hesitate

to use the great and all-powerful weapon that is in our control; we should not falter in the pledge to ourselves and our neighbors to discharge from our employ and our friendship forever, every laborer who persists in the diabolical war that has been waged against the white man and his interests ever since the negro has been a voter.

A GEORGIA EDITOR ASKS FOR "BRUTE FORCE" (1874)

Let there be White Leagues formed in every town, village and hamlet of the South, and let us organize for the great struggle which seems inevitable. The radicalism of the republican party must be met by the radicalism of white men. We have no war to make against the United States Government, but against the republican party our hate must be unquenchable, our war interminable and merciless. Fast fleeting away is the day of wordy protests and idle appeals to the magnanimity of the republican party. By brute force they are endeavoring to force us into acquiescence to their hideous programme. We have submitted long enough to indignities, and it is time to meet brute-force with brute-force. . . . It will not do to wait till radicalism has fettered us to the car of social equality before we make an effort to resist it. The signing of the [Civil Rights] bill will be a declaration of war against the southern whites. It is our duty to ourselves, it is our duty to our children, it is our duty to the white race whose prowess subdued the wilderness of this continent, whose civilization filled it with cities and towns and villages, whose mind gave it power and grandeur, and whose labor imparted to it prosperity, and whose love made peace and happiness dwell within its homes, to take the gage of battle the moment it is thrown down. If the white democrats of the North are men, they will not stand idly by and see us borne down by northern radicals and half-barbarous negroes. But no matter what they may do, it is time for us to organize. We have been temporizing long enough. Let northern radicals understand that military supervision of southern elections and the civil-rights bill mean war, that war means bloodshed, and that we are terribly in earnest, and even they, fanatical as they are, may retrace their steps before it is too late.

RESOLUTION OF ALABAMA DEMOCRATS (1874)

Resolved, That we, the people. . . . for the protection of our dearest and most sacred interests, our homes, our honor, the purity and integrity of our race, and to conserve the peace and tranquility of the country, accept the issue of race thus defiantly tendered and forced upon us, notwithstanding our determination and repeated efforts to avoid it; and further

Resolved, That nothing is left to the white man's party but social ostracism of all those who act, sympathize or side with the negro party, or who support or advocate the odious, unjust, and unreasonable measure known as the civil rights bill; and that from henceforth we will hold all such persons as enemies of our race, and we will not in the future have intercourse with them in any of the social relations of life.

Index